SATHER

For Cliff,
with best regards,
Greg
1. May. 02

OXFORD STUDIES IN
SOCIAL AND CULTURAL ANTHROPOLOGY

Editorial Board

DUALISM AND HIERARCHY

OXFORD STUDIES IN SOCIAL AND CULTURAL ANTHROPOLOGY

Oxford Studies in Social and Cultural Anthropology represents the work of authors, new and established, that will set the criteria of excellence in ethnographic description and innovation in analysis. The series serves as an essential source of information about the world and the discipline.

DUALISM AND HIERARCHY

PROCESSES OF BINARY COMBINATION IN KEO SOCIETY

GREGORY FORTH

OXFORD
UNIVERSITY PRESS

OXFORD

UNIVERSITY PRESS

Great Clarendon Street, Oxford OX2 6DP

Oxford University Press is a department of the University of Oxford.
It furthers the University's objective of excellence in research, scholarship,
and education by publishing worldwide in

Oxford New York

Athens Auckland Bangkok Bogotá Buenos Aires Cape Town
Chennai Dar es Salaam Delhi Florence Hong Kong Istanbul Karachi
Kolkata Kuala Lumpur Madrid Melbourne Mexico City Mumbai Nairobi
Paris São Paulo Shanghai Singapore Taipei Tokyo Toronto Warsaw
and associated companies in Berlin Ibadan

Oxford is a registered trade mark of Oxford University Press
in the UK and in certain other countries

Published in the United States
by Oxford University Press Inc., New York

British Library Cataloguing in Publication Data

Data available

Library of Congress Cataloging in Publication Data

Data applied for

ISBN 0–19–823424–4

1 3 5 7 9 10 8 6 4 2

Typeset in Ehrhardt by
Cambrian Typesetters, Frimley, Surrey
Printed in Great Britain
on acid-free paper by
T.J. International Ltd.
Padstow, Cornwall

for
Aidan and Joel

PREFACE

This study is the result of field research conducted in the western Keo region of Flores island, Indonesia. The research was initiated in 1984–85 and continued during six subsequent visits, most recently in 1999. In total, these amounted to well over a year in the field. The period is difficult to specify precisely since I regularly combined fieldwork in Keo with ethnographic investigations conducted in the neighbouring Nage region (see Forth 1998). Enquiries were carried out both in Bahasa Indonesia (the Indonesian national language), in which the great majority of Keo are now fluent, and in the local language. Working conditions were on the whole excellent, due mainly to the generosity, hospitality, and co-operation of my many hosts. As I travelled alone to Flores, I lodged in Keo houses mainly in the villages of Pajo Mala and Pau Lundu and in the modern residential complex called Wolo Sambi, near the main road between Pau Lundu and Guyu Wolo (see Map 2). For shorter periods, I stayed in several other villages.

In view of the diverse kinds of support and assistance given by many men and women, one is reluctant to mention individuals by name. I therefore address my gratitude first of all to the residents of all Keo villages described in this study, for tolerating what must sometimes have seemed an intrusive, demanding, and rather curious presence. At the same time, it is only fitting to acknowledge the help provided by particular individuals, including regular hosts and informants. Foremost among these were G. Jago Uko and his wife K. Béka, in whose house in Upper Pajo Mala I frequently lodged. Other regular hosts included F. Gélu and his wife B. Wae, resident in Wolo Sambi, and the family of Mohd. Jago Kunda (alias Kepala Hema) in Lower Pau Lundu. G. Jago Uko also served as a constant source of information on numerous aspects of western Keo culture and history. A similarly valuable and regular resource was M. Dhae Menge, of the village of Pajo Réja. In addition to the names just mentioned, others who generously provided assistance included B. Babo (in the village of Sawu), D. Dutu (Kuyu Wulu), J. Gale and M. Tenga (Guyu Wolo), M. Goa and G. Noko (Pau/Lower Pau Lundu), C. Gore (Keo Bélo), F. Jata (Pau Leka), L. Lengi, P. Teri, and R. Jago (Lundu), J. Kutu (Suga Bhoja), P. Meno and G. Céme (Muka), J. Moa and G. Sawi (Keo Ondo), A. Ndona (Munde), J. Sile (Wulu/Déna), and P. Suta (Wulu Wayu/Bo'a Ora). I am also grateful to present and former administrative personnel in the sub-district of Mauponggo for providing geographical, statistical, and other information on the region.

Special thanks are due to Nikolaus Nua, a man about my age from the village of Wulu who, with his wife and children, now lives in Wolo Sambi where he operates a farmers' credit union. By his own admission, 'Pak Niko' (as he is usually known) has a limited knowledge of local social forms and traditions, yet his contribution to this study can hardly be exaggerated. Despite other demands on his time, Niko enthusiastically served as my constant guide and companion, transporting me safely over sometimes difficult terrain on his motorbike, introducing me and helping explain my intentions to numerous local people, and thus 'oiling and greasing' other wheels as well.

Finally, I wish to mention the late E. Waso Ea and his family in Bo'a Wae, the centre of the neighbouring Nage region, who provided initial introductions to ritual partners, relatives, and others with whom they are connected in Keo.

If I have any regrets regarding my work in Keo they concern the fact that I can never truly repay the people for all they have given me. I can only hope that this study, whose aims they appeared thoroughly to endorse, will in some small and perhaps unforeseen way contribute to their lives and those of their children and descendants.

Research in Keo was initially sponsored by the Indonesian Institute of Sciences (LIPI), the former Lembaga Riset Kebudayaan Nasional, and Nusa Cendana University in Kupang. Subsequent visits were facilitated by Artha Wacana University in Kupang. Funding was provided at various times by the British Academy's Institute in Southeast Asia, the Social Sciences and Humanities Research Council of Canada, and the Central Research Fund of the University of Alberta. I am naturally grateful to all of these bodies for their support.

CONTENTS

LIST OF MAPS

LIST OF FIGURES

LIST OF PLATES

NOTE ON ORTHOGRAPHY

Transcription of Keo words is based largely on standard Indonesian (Bahasa Indonesia; hereafter abbreviated as BI), and except for the acute accent on the /é/, the spelling employed here corresponds to that used by modern Keo themselves when writing their own language. Letters of the Roman alphabet, in four instances in combination with another, distinguish the following sounds.

Vowels: a, e, é, i, o, u

Consonants: b, bh, c, d/nd, dh, f, g, gh, j, k, l, m, n, p, r, s, t, w, y

An /h/ occurs in some villages, in place of the /y/.

/'/ marks the glottal stop. This occurs initially as well as between vowels, but never in a final position.

The /e/ represents the schwa in initial and medial positions, while /é/ is long, resembling a pure form of the /a/ in English 'bay'. (A third /e/, like the sound in English 'bet', is also heard, but does not possess a separate phonemic value.) Where /e/ occurs in a final position (as in *se*, *bale*, *nage*), it is always long; hence for reasons of economy it is left unmarked.

/C/ is pronounced as in English 'church'. In some villages closer to the coast it is replaced by /s/; hence *co'o* ('small'), for example, becomes *so'o*.

/Nd/ represents a nasalized variant of /d/ encountered in most parts of the present study area, except for several villages near the northern and western limits. It does not differ phonemically from /d/. /Bh/ and /dh/ are implosives, contrasting respectively with /b/ and /nd/ (or /d/). /Gh/ is a voiced pharyngal fricative. /W/ denotes a sound somewhere between English /w/ and /v/, but is closer to the latter in initial positions.

With few exceptions, Keo words are either monosyllabic or dissyllabic. The relative pronoun *ta'a* ('that, which', 'that which, what') is commonly shortened to *ta*. I employ the short form throughout.

NOTE ON CROSS-REFERENCING
AND ABBREVIATIONS

This book is divided into two parts, with the chapters of each part numbered separately. In order to facilitate extensive cross-referencing throughout, upper case roman numerals are used for the two parts, Arabic numerals for the chapters, and lower case roman for sections of chapters. For example, I: 3: ii means Part 1, Chapter 3, Section 2, whereas II: 1: iii means Part 2, Chapter 1, Section 3.

KINSHIP NOTATION

The following standard abbreviations are used for genealogical relatives in both the text and Appendix 1.

F	father
M	mother
P	parent
B	brother
Z	sister
S	son
D	daughter
C	child
H	husband
W	wife
e	elder
y	younger
m.s.	man speaking
w.s.	woman speaking

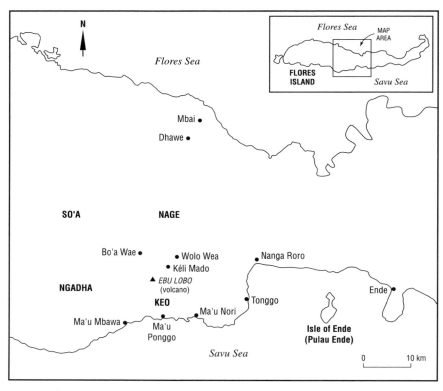

MAP 1. Central Flores

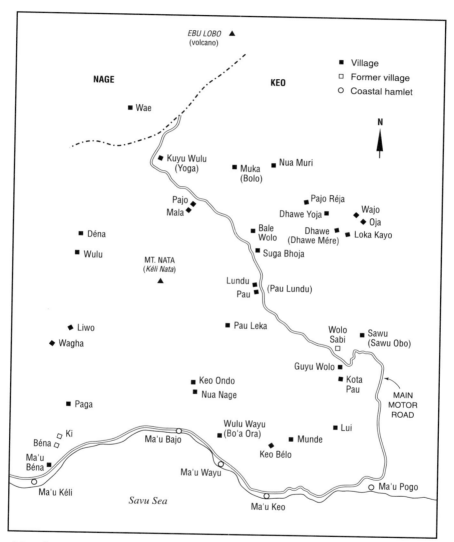

MAP 2. Western Keo

Introduction

This study introduces a people called Keo who reside in the south-central part of the Indonesian island of Flores. To an even greater extent than their Nage neighbours immediately to the north (Forth 1989*a*, 1998), inhabitants of the Keo region are among the least described populations, not only of Flores but of the whole of eastern Indonesia. The present monograph more particularly concerns a part of this population I specify as western Keo. In describing western Keo society, I focus on its most pervasive feature: dualism. In Keo, dualism is revealed not only in instances of 'dual symbolic classification'—a common enough feature of eastern Indonesian societies—but, more importantly, in manifold forms of social dualism. While the 'social' itself necessarily incorporates a 'symbolic' dimension (and vice versa), by 'social dualism' I refer in the first instance to local arrangements whereby social groups of a relatively fixed composition (clans, villages, and clan or village segments) are paired, typically in spatially defined ways.

Of special interest for the analysis that follows, and constituting a special problem, are what I call 'double settlements'. Composing the most inclusive form of Keo social dualism, the settlements comprise two formally identical villages conjoined without a regular basis in any specific or exclusive social relationship or ideological rationale. The discovery of these manifestly dualistic residential forms in fact provided much of my original ethnographic interest in western Keo. In 1984, during my first field trip to central Flores, I was struck by the appearance of villages I encountered while travelling along the main road that leads from the Nage centre of Bo'a Wae to Ma'u Ponggo (see Map 1). Despite their apparent possession of single names, two settlements in particular, Pau Lundu and Pajo Mala, appeared both to comprise two separate villages, each with a full complement of ritual structures. As I was later to confirm, such structures figure as indexes of unity and ceremonial independence and do, indeed, distinguish separate villages. Brief enquiries provided little insight into this arrangement, though local remarks suggested it might be common in the region. As my visit to Indonesia was nearing its end, and since my attention at the time was focused on the neighbouring Nage, I decided to reserve further investigation for future trips to Flores.

I am not quite the first Western investigator of Flores culture to write about Keo. Not long after my 1984 visit, I came across a brief comparative note in a long work by the missionary ethnographer, Paul Arndt, on the Ngadha region to the west. Here, Arndt describes Keo villages as comprising 'two moieties divided by a stone wall' and adds that 'the young men of one half take wives from the other half and vice versa' (1954: 19). As I later discovered, Arndt was quite wrong about localized exogamous moieties directly exchanging women.

Like other eastern Indonesians, Keo in fact marry in accordance with rules that are explicitly asymmetric, and no grouping in this society which might be designated with the term 'moiety' functions as a unit of marriage alliance. In time, therefore, my investigations of Keo became focused on a problem raised long ago by van Wouden (1968 [1935]) and Lévi-Strauss (1956; 1963: 154), namely, the occurrence in Indonesia of dualistic social forms in combination with asymmetric marriage. Arndt's characterization of single villages divided in half was also inexact in so far as stone walls frequently mark what Keo consider to be the bounds of separate, though adjacent 'villages' (*nua*)—or the components of what, in a later publication (1963), Arndt himself described as 'double villages'. Lacking a distinct generic name in the Keo lexicon, these are the dualistic aggregates I prefer to call double settlements.

As remarkable as the extent of Keo social dualism is the variety of morphological pairings encountered within a narrow geographical compass, dualistic order in one village being manifest in specific arrangements that differ from what is found in neighbouring villages. Accordingly, the present study describes western Keo society as a collection of small communities formed of dual components internally articulated in partly divergent ways. It moreover explores these particular dualities both synchronically and through time. Implicit here is a conviction that Keo social structure can be fully comprehended only with reference to a diachronic process, discernible in the structure of local historical knowledge, which informs variable patterns observable at present. In addition to spatial organization, therefore, social dualism among Keo consists in the way people regularly represent the past in narrative traditions specific to clans and villages.

1. Keo Society and the Anthropological Study of Dualism

Apart from introducing a society that has remained virtually unknown until the end of the twentieth century, the present investigation has an obvious bearing on a widespread pattern of culture and social order that has occupied anthropological attention for over one hundred years. Forming one of a select series of theoretical topics that marked the origin of social anthropology as a distinct discipline, social dualism—conceived as 'the dual organization'—attracted evolutionist theorists who considered it an especially 'primitive', and primordial, form of social order (see, for example, Frazer 1910 i, 258). Within this theoretical frame, a particular relevance for Keo ethnography is found in generalizations advanced by Rivers and Hocart. In his earlier work, Rivers characterized an original dual organization as consisting of exogamous matrilineal moieties effecting a division of a pre-existing social whole. Deriving from this bifurcate organization were classificatory kin terminology (or more specifically a symmetric form thereof) and bilateral cross-cousin marriage, usages which in a typically evolutionist perspective he conceived as survivals of a more widespread dual organization (1914, 1924). Later, Rivers revised his theory, arguing instead that fusion—a combination of indigenous groups and superior immigrants—produced the original social dualism (1914 ii, 557). These contrasting possibilities resonate in Keo local dualism, which predominantly involves a conjunction of two groups distinguished as temporally precedent and subsequent. Combination is thus by far the more prevalent process among Keo, even though division, typically expressed in an agnatic distinction of elder and younger defining locally paired clans, is not entirely absent.

Rivers's revision is further pertinent in so far as it links fusion, as the *modus* of morphological dualism, with social and historical inequality. Contrary to his earlier association of dual division with reciprocal exchanges of spouses entailed by exogamous moieties and bilateral cross-cousin marriage, dualism founded on asymmetry confronts principles of reciprocity and equality which, even to the present, many analysts have regarded as essential attributes of dualistic social organization. While Rivers seems not to have questioned the operation of reciprocity between unequally ranked exogamous moieties, Keo ethnography sheds special light on these long-standing issues. For what is most striking in this case is the absence, between consistently unequal components of local dualistic combinations, of definitive reciprocal relations, which is to say, exchange relationships exclusive or essential to particular forms of social dualism. In contrast to Rivers's model of Melanesian history moreover, in Keo society it is older groups that are superior to more recently arrived junior partners. With remarkable regularity, the superordinate position of older elements finds expression in an identification, manifested quite variously in different instances, with a local unity, or whole. This, however, is not a pre-existing unity that has become divided, but one formed in a process of combination. An older member of a pair, longer established in a given territory, subsumes a younger, which, by virtue of this subsumption, forfeits whatever wholeness it might previously have possessed. By the same token, the older component not only retains its wholeness but, subsequent to combination, becomes the superior member of a pair by virtue of its identification with the emergent whole. In this, one can glimpse a recurrent motivation for dualistic combination. Social superiority in Keo turns on established groups inviting others to join them, a regularly expressed theme in local history. Later arrivals then become part of an established domain—but not to the extent of transcending the dualism of older and younger, which is the source of the original component's superordination.

A rejection of division, or 'bisection' (Frazer 1910), as the essence of social dualism is also discernible in the work of Hocart. Hocart (1970[1936]: 289) was perhaps the first to recognize that division cannot explain dual organization since what he calls 'dichotomy', a process of successive division, can result in any total. Of course, the observation similarly applies to combination, inasmuch as any number of groups can join together to form a social aggregate.

With the accumulation of evidence for the existence of moieties that were neither exogamous nor in any other way implicated in marital reciprocity, Hocart advanced 'mutual ministration' as the persistent feature of dual organization. Communities comprising two exhaustive halves were thus to be understood by reference to the 'interaction' of their components, exhibited in a provision of reciprocal services and the performance of complementary tasks essential to the operation of the entire social system. Keo social organization, however, challenges this interpretation as well, again by virtue of an absence of any special reciprocity defining the relation between parts of dualistic groupings.

In later, structuralist, writing, the enduring spell of reciprocity found further expression in Lévi-Strauss's kinship opus, where reciprocity is identified as the basis of dual organization everywhere, even in spite of the author's acknowledgement that moieties need not be exogamous, nor fulfil any particular institutional role (1969[1949]: 70). By contrast, in his famous essay of 1956 (English transl. 1963), Lévi-Strauss characterized dual organization in a rather different way, as a surface feature disguising an underlying tripartition and a concomitant inequality of dualistic components. In addition, the possible existence of structurally significant binary opposition unconnected with manifest reciprocity—or any sort of social function—is accommodated by a notion of 'zero value' (1963: 159).

Although the empirical inadequacies of this essay are well known, the approach appears relevant to Keo morphological dualism, particularly as, in a number of instances, formal pairing turns out to articulate three or more groups. Yet various sources of evidence indicate that, rather than being an epiphenomenon, dualistic structuring must be understood as a fundamental feature of Keo society, especially when viewed beyond a strictly synchronic frame. In a work briefly cited by Lévi-Strauss (1963: 140), van Wouden (1969[1935]) similarly considered instances of Indonesian social dualism in relation to hypothetically tripartite schemes. His purpose, however, was to document the coexistence of moieties and other dualistic forms with the implicitly tripartite model of asymmetric marriage alliance (or 'exclusive cross-cousin marriage') and to demonstrate their independence. This independence is fully confirmed by Keo ethnography; what is not borne out is van Wouden's interpretation of social dualism as a function of implicit or explicit rules of descent, a matter I return to presently.

The long-standing assumption that some special exchange relationship, affinal or otherwise, necessarily underlies dualistic social form evidently stems from the status of the pair as the minimum condition of reciprocal relationships. From this derives the expectation that the most basic forms of social reciprocity are discoverable in inclusive social dualities (such as moieties). Yet binary contrast can equally be conceived as the minimum of social differentiation, and thus, prospectively at least, of disunity and inequality. How far, and in what manner, components of dualistic communities actually achieve unity or equality is thus a matter of major importance for students of human society, and another reason for a continuing interest, both theoretical and practical, in social dualism. Functionalist writers, especially, have tended to assume that social pairs exist as a unity founded on interdependence. But while unity articulated by reciprocity might involve an undifferentiated equality of the two parts (as in the case of exogamous moieties), what each part provides to its opposite may on the contrary be different, and hence differently valued, so that exchange reinforces rather than reduces or transcends asymmetry.[1]

Where asymmetry is pronounced (as it generally is in eastern Indonesia) anthropologists have often proposed complementarity as essential to dualistic social relations and—since complementarity pertains as much to ideology—to binary cosmology as well. A conspicuous illustration of this approach is found in Maybury-Lewis's editorial introduction to a recent collection of papers, all concerned with 'thought and society in the dualistic mode'. Here, dualistic schemes in general are characterized as emphasizing a 'necessary complementarity of opposites' (1989a: 6) aimed at the realization of a 'harmonious balance' and 'cosmic harmony'.[2] In this connection, it is worth recalling that complementarity, considered as a logical relation, involves terms that mutually define one another (as in the case of wife-giver and wife-taker, or older and younger). At the same time, social units (groups, statuses, individuals) can be complementary in a functional sense, when they contribute, and contribute differently, to a single enterprise which they jointly render complete. In contrast to logical complementarity, functional complementarity is not restricted to binary relationships since it may involve any number of units. Even so, the pair represents the minimum condition of functional complementarity, just as it does of reciprocity; and, of course, reciprocity is a common expression, or concomitant, of complementary social relations.

The relevance of these observations to the present investigation lies in the circumstance that, in western Keo, functional complementarity, like reciprocity, is not in fact an obvious or crucial entailment of a range of dualistically ordered social groupings. To be sure, components of individual pairings (such as two clans composing a single village) may be related, for example, as 'wife-giver' and 'wife-taker'. Yet internal comparison reveals that this relationship is by no means universal among, or limited to, morphological pairs. In western

[1] Relevant here is Wagner's seminal suggestion that reciprocity always involves an exchange of unequal values since, in order to make exchange worthwhile, what is exchanged is necessarily valued differently by the parties to the exchange (1975: 154).

[2] Maybury-Lewis later argues that dualistic societies can accommodate 'asymmetry', which he equates with 'hierarchy' (1989b: 112; 1989a: 10) and identifies with 'imbalance' and 'disequilibrium' (1989b: 112, 113). Yet it is apparently by virtue of the symmetric aspects or tendencies of 'dual organization' that these societies are able to 'control' (ibid.: 110) asymmetry, in order to realize the balance that Maybury-Lewis considers fundamental. It seems, therefore, that for this author asymmetry, while present in dualistic systems, is subordinated to symmetry. The notion of 'balance', moreover implies an equality which he nevertheless wishes to deny as an essential feature of dualism (1989b: 110, 112).

Keo, social dualism is not consistently associated even with widespread, culturally specific category pairs, such as that of 'land mother' and 'defender' (see I:
1), terms which themselves are frequently, but not invariably, associated with
affinal connection. As these illustrative references may suggest, a primary
interest of the present analysis lies in the way Keo social dualities (paired
villages, clans, and houses) cannot be reduced to relationships defined by
universal binary categories. Accordingly, a major aim is to demonstrate how
dualistic social forms may subsist independently of a culture-wide dual classification.

   This is not, however, to suggest that binary categories (whether primarily
'social' or 'symbolic') are structurally dissimilar to Keo morphological pairs.
Indeed, another finding of the study is their formal similarity; for completely
general category pairs, like 'wife-giver' and 'wife-taker', are identically
conceived as entailing the subsumption of a subordinate by a superordinate
term. The point is exemplified by the botanic contrast of 'trunk' and 'tip (the
uppermost part of a plant or tree)', a widespread Austronesian metaphorical
pair which in Keo articulates affinal alliance while quite separately defining a
fundamental ritual dualism internal to villages (I: 2: vi). Whereas the pair
might be interpreted as a simple logical complementarity, the Keo term for
'trunk' simultaneously designates an entire tree, a whole which subsumes a
'tip', and so can denote an entity conceived independently of the opposite
term. As the metaphor of botanical growth may itself suggest, this sort of
binary contrast, and the social relations with which it is inextricably linked,
pertain to an ongoing process in which one term is only relatively, or contextually, distinguished from a superior term that is logically prior. As a plant
grows, what was the 'tip' becomes part of the trunk, while at the same time new
tips are constantly emerging from existing trunks. It is arguably consistent with
this relation that, contrary to what might be expected in an eastern Indonesian
context, Keo leaders distinguished as 'trunk' and 'tip' do not divide religious
and worldly authority. As accords with their lack of functional complementarity, this instance of the botanical pair thus does not define a diarchy, nor any
manifestation of the 'mutual ministration' that Hocart attributed to social
dualities. Rather, what appears basic is not functional interdependence or
mutuality but, simply, the duality itself, which tends toward unity by way of
the subsumption of one part by the other, representing the whole.

   Taken together with the inequality inherent in Keo social dualism, the foregoing allusions to part–whole relations evoke a more radical approach to binary
order. While not explicitly addressed either to the sort of social morphology
manifested in Keo dualities or to societies composed of exogamous moieties,
dualism is nevertheless implicit in Dumont's conception of hierarchy, or 'hierarchical opposition', defined as a relation between two terms, one of which
'encompasses' the other. In his most detailed exposition of the principle,
Dumont (1979, 1986) moreover formulates hierarchical opposition as a

counter-thesis to Needham's explication of dual symbolic classification as articulated by a general principle of complementary opposition (Needham 1973: xix). Similarly, it is in the analysis of an African system of binary symbolism that a follower of Dumont, Serge Tcherkézoff (1987), attempts a comprehensive demonstration of Dumontian hierarchy while elaborating the former's critique of Needham's approach to similar ethnographic materials.

Of particular relevance for the present study is Dumont's charge that complementary opposition, construed as an instance of 'distinctive opposition', implies a view of the inequality, or asymmetry, of component terms as something 'superadded unto' (Dumont 1986: 228) a prior symmetry or equality. With hierarchical opposition, by contrast, asymmetry inheres in the very constitution of dualistic relations. For in this model, one term of a pair is superior to the other by virtue of a pre-existing identity with a whole that encompasses both. Dumont's theory finds exemplars in Keo society in so far as encompassment occurs as an organizing principle in a plurality of dualistic contexts. At the same time, it is less obviously a property of the most inclusive form of Keo morphological dualism, those territorial pairings I designate as 'double settlements', where identification of one part with a whole, and hence subsumption of one part by the other, is not always unambiguously attested.

Also questionable in the Keo case is whether encompassment articulates a single value opposition, as Dumont's thesis, developed in the context of the Indian caste system and the ideological contrast of 'pure' and 'impure', would seem to require (see Fox 1989, 1994; Mosko 1994). Such an opposition is possibly found in a pervasive category pair which contextually operates as a single and self-reciprocal (and in this sense 'holistic') category, albeit one that is manifestly dualistic. Designated as *ka'e ari* ('older/elder–younger'; I: 4: i), and discernible in all instances of Keo social dualism, this relation, however, implies a temporal contrast whereby two parties (villages, clans, persons) are distinguishable, if not always in practice then at least in principle, as senior (or 'original') and junior.

Elaborating a notion of encompassment in the explication of Keo dualities, therefore, requires re-evaluation of Dumont's original paradigm, the import of which is entirely synchronic. By the same token, the temporal aspect of Keo social dualism signals a connection with an emerging approach centred on the notion of 'precedence'. A product of detailed ethnographic studies of a series of Indonesian societies, precedence has been developed by James Fox and his students in an exploration of 'origin structures'—complexes of asymmetric status differentials articulated by a binary contrast of 'origin (or source)' and 'derivative' (see, for example, Fox 1988, 1994; Lewis 1988).

How this applies to Keo dualities is already suggested by the above-mentioned opposition of 'trunk' and 'tip'. Indeed, describing Keo society without some recourse to 'precedence' would hardly be possible. Yet, contrary to what criticisms by some advocates of the analytical concept might suggest, precedence does not exclude—nor can it fully substitute for—hierarchical encompassment as a fundament of Keo dualistic relations. Among Keo, the single most important public expression of asymmetric order is a display of sacrificial precedence initiated by two leaders dualistically distinguished by reference to their associations with the 'trunk' and 'tip' of a common sacrificial instrument (*peo*). In this context, members of groups longer established in a given territory slaughter animals before more recent arrivals. Yet in sacrificing, as in other articulations of local social order, precedence involves more than higher standing based on mere chronological priority. Inasmuch as the senior-most pair, those identified as 'trunk' and 'tip', are identified with an entire sacrificial series, they constitute a sort of dual metonymy, representing a social whole and subsuming junior co-residents in a way corresponding to Dumont's sense of hierarchy. In addition, by virtue of his closer association with the instrument of sacrifice—most often a living tree—the party identified as the 'trunk' encompasses the 'tip'. In Keo, therefore, precedence and encompassment must be seen as inseparable aspects of a single structure.

In marked contrast to Dumont's approach, yet equally testifying to the 'fascination' that Terence Turner (1991) attributes to an abiding anthropological interest in dualism, is the recent collection of essays edited by Maybury-Lewis and Uri Almagor (1989). The merit of this volume, however, lies mostly in its original ethnographic content, for it largely fails to provide new insight into dualistic social or cultural forms, relying instead on older conceptualizations of reciprocity and complementarity. Symptomatic in this respect is Maybury-Lewis's editorial introduction where, in addition to identifying harmony and balance as generic features of binary organization, he characterizes 'dualistic thinking' as serving to prevent 'antitheses' from becoming 'antipathies' (1989*a*: 13), and as valuing 'state and stability' over 'process and change' (ibid.: 15). Recalling Lévi-Strauss's contrast of 'cold' and 'hot' societies, the approach thus de-emphasizes the importance of diachronic process, just as it posits a mode of thought—also described as dualistic 'theory' and cosmology—as a determinant of binary social form.

As indicated, Keo social organization argues against social dualism as a direct reflection of symbolic dualism. Contrary to the attribution of harmony, moreover, the facts of Keo social pairing, including local historical commentary, reveal contestation, even conflict, as being a concomitant of, rather than anathema to, dualistic social order. Recalling the 'condition of hostility' attributed by Rivers to Melanesian moieties deriving from a fusion of originally separate groups (1914 ii: 557–8), the local contestability of asymmetric order defining particular social combinations among Keo (whereby the two parties disagree on which is superordinate or has 'precedence') might appear also to challenge Dumont's representation of hierarchical opposition as determined by value contrasts universal within a given society. How far it actually does so, and to what extent contestation can eventuate in a reversal of established orders of precedence, may be judged from specific inversions I discuss below (II: 1, 2, 3). As will be seen, whatever its extent, a reversal of this sort does not result in symmetry, since it merely perpetuates a basic asymmetry. Nor, by the same token, does it promote social harmony.

Surprisingly, most contributors to Maybury-Lewis and Almagor (1989) ignore Dumont's theory of hierarchy, as do the editors themselves (cf. Turner 1991: 217). Three, however, do not, and it may be significant that all of these deal with eastern Indonesian dualism (see Fox 1989; Traube 1989; and Valeri 1989). The essays by Valeri and Traube have a particular comparative relevance for the present investigation. Not only do both make effective use of a notion of 'encompassment', but Traube, writing on the Mambai of Timor, sets out to show how hierarchical encompassment 'demands a diachronic perspective' (1989: 324), a point fully borne out by my analysis of Keo. With regard to contestation as a potential feature of Keo asymmetries, one interest of Valeri's article is his argument that Moluccan moieties express 'two opposite hierarchical evaluations', with each viewing itself as 'the centre of the other' (1989: 137, 138). Although explicitly critical of Dumont, James Fox, in a comparative review of eastern Indonesian dual classification, nevertheless interprets applications of category pairs as exhibiting a formal principle of 'recursive complementarity', whereby X, being one term of an opposition X/Y, admits a further contrast (x/y) that replicates the initial opposition (Fox 1989: 44; cf. Sperber 1975, who describes the same principle as 'reduction'). How the relation X = x/y corresponds with 'hierarchical opposition' should be obvious. Its relevance for the present investigation concerns the operation of such recursion in a variety of Keo representations and practices (see for example I: 2: v). As I have shown elsewhere (Forth 1998), the principle is similarly pervasive among the neighbouring Nage.

Exemplified by Fox's essay, as by many other recent analyses of individual eastern Indonesian societies, the most general development in anthropological studies of dualism during the twentieth century has been a shift of focus from institutional arrangements to symbolic categories and metaphors (see also Fox 1980*c*: 330–2; Schefold 1994: 809). With increasing attention to classification and conceptual organization by opposition, dualism in both social and symbolic forms has further come to be considered as reflecting an innate property of human cognition, albeit one notably more developed in some societies than in others (see Needham 1973: xxxi–xxxv; 1987: 12). Expressions of this idea have been various. In regard to dual social organization, Terence Turner thus alludes to a 'powerful, nonarbitrary motivation' that seems to underlie, and perhaps contradict, the 'apparent formal arbitrariness of moiety systems' (1991: 216). In a rather different—but perhaps ultimately related—vein, Willis (1990:12), drawing on recent work in cognitive psychology, describes the irreducible unit of all human societies as 'the dyad of self and other'. On the other hand, some cognitive anthropologists (for example, Boyer 1993: 16–17) have rejected claims, most closely associated with the structuralism of Lévi-Strauss, that binary opposition is fundamental to cultural thought (or 'the mental representation of concepts and categories') and, as one may infer, to behaviour as well. Similarly, Hallpike suggests that dualism reflects not a mental predisposition so much as a predominance of binary phenomena in the world (1979: 170, 228, 235).[3]

This sort of disagreement has undoubtedly contributed to a waning of anthropological enthusiasm for constructing a new and comprehensive theory of dualism (see Almagor 1989*a*: 22). So, too, has an increasing awareness of the cross-cultural variety of dualistic forms. Thus, whatever their connection with universal structures of cognition, different instances of dualistic social morphology—for example, Austronesian and South American moieties—still appear explicable as contingent outcomes of quite various social and historical processes (see Maybury-Lewis 1989*b*: 113). If the comparative study of dualism has produced one clear conclusion, it is that dual symbolism and classification are more widely encountered than morphological dualism. In itself, this differential incidence signals the latent independence of the two forms. It might also suggest quite distinct cognitive sources for dualistic categories and binary social morphology respectively. However that may be, the present study demonstrates their variable conjunction (or possible disjunction) precisely where one might least expect to find it: within an eastern Indonesian society with a commitment to dual classification and binary symbolism, a system of asymmetric marriage, and an extensively dualistic ordering of social groups.

Further testifying to a continuing anthropological engagement with dualism (including its cognitive implications) are Rodney Needham's most recent pronouncements on the topic (1987). In the present context, the relevance of Needham's work lies mainly in his elaborate critique of Dumont's theory of hierarchy, conducted largely with reference to issues of formal consistency and the linguistic status of its guiding concepts. Being devoted to a defence of the author's well-known views on complementary opposition and analogical classification (see, for example, Needham 1973), the book does not significantly advance an empirical understanding of dualistic social forms. Indeed, like Tcherkézoff (1987), whose Dumontian analysis of East African dual classification is his major target, Needham is primarily concerned with the analysis of binary categories rather than with social morphology. Nevertheless, a distinct interest of Needham's deconstruction of 'hierarchical opposition' is his accusation that Dumont's theory relies excessively on spatial idioms bound up with the status of 'opposition' itself as a spatial metaphor (1987: 144–5).

In the present ethnographic context, such an idiomatic tendency, far from constituting a weakness, may be counted as fortuitously advantageous. For Keo

---

[3] The position of Maybury-Lewis and Almagor is equivocal in this connection. Noting that a predilection for dualism is 'widespread but not universal', they conclude that the phenomenon cannot therefore 'simply be attributed to binary tendencies in human thought' (1989: vii). The key word here is of course 'simply'.

social dualisms are most immediately attested in diametric spatial arrangements, which is to say, physical combinations or conjunctions. By the same token, encompassment obtains most clearly where one member of a morphological pair is associated with a larger territory which, quite literally, subsumes an area occupied by the other.

Within western Keo settlements, the most salient forms of social combination are more particularly associated with a pervasive directional contrast, widely attested in Austronesia (see Senft 1997), of 'landward' and 'seaward'. In Keo and elsewhere, this spatial opposition regularly coincides with the further contrast of 'above' and 'below'. With reference to another Austronesian-speaking society, that of Fiji, Toren (1990: 246), employing evidence from child development, has latterly construed this spatial distinction as of primary importance for 'the cognitive construction of a hierarchy-scheme', by which she refers to the reproduction of social inequality. The present investigation does not extend to the developmental aspects of Keo dualism in individual psychology. Nevertheless, it should be remarked how, in this society, neither landward and seaward, nor above and below consistently define social superordination and subordination, so that 'landward', for example, is not invariably associated with social superiority. This applies even though the spatial oppositions regularly articulate the relative physical locations of members of social pairs distinguished as older and younger, and thus as superior and inferior.

Among Keo, social dualism is further defined with reference to another spatial opposition, that of centre and periphery—a contrast that Almagor (1989*b*: 144) lists as one of six common components of dual organization.[4] As I demonstrate, a distinction of centre and periphery, like that of above and below, is also discernible in social relationships that Keo articulate in another spatial idiom, that of 'descent'. From Rivers to van Wouden to more recent writers, dual organization has regularly been linked with descent as an explicit or implicit principle of social order. In this respect as well, Keo ethnography casts new light on social dualism. For with very few exceptions, the components of Keo morphological pairs are not, according to any strict definition, 'descent groups', even where they can be described as 'clans' or 'moieties'.[5] More specifically, dualistic components are not groups defined by a segmentary order of lineal descent effecting divisions within a social whole; nor are they consistently exogamous groups. Relevant here is an indigenous conception of 'descent' (*poro*; I: 5: ii) which, though it might appear specific to Keo, in fact articulates a representation, predicated on a value placed on 'origins' and connection through affinal alliance, which increasingly is being revealed as

---

[4] Liberally interpreted, all six of Almagor's components (1989*b*: 144) can in fact be identified in Keo society. One is a division of society 'into one or more sets of halves', which I take not to require comprehensive moieties (nor indeed 'division' in any strict sense) but simply a pervasive inclination to combine social units in pairs.
[5] A similar conclusion has been drawn in regard to certain South American dual organizations which, according to Maybury-Lewis, 'are not rooted in descent, nor are they functions of kinship' (1989*b*: 109; see also Rivière 1993).

widespread in Indonesia (see, for example, Fox 1980*b*; Barraud 1990; McKinnon 1991; Reuter 1992; Beatty 1992; Forth 1994*c*). As some of these studies suggest, 'origins'—whether identified with wife-givers or ancestors—are moreover conceived as encompassing derivatives.[6] At the same time, Keo 'descent' strikes a seminal contrast with common anthropological applications of the same metaphor. In this way, it facilitates further consideration of the comparative utility of descent as an analytical category, not just in regard to Austronesian-speaking societies but generally as well.

2. *A Synopsis of Keo Geography, Economy, History, and Language*

How far 'Keo' refers to a distinct cultural and historical unity has been discussed elsewhere (Forth 1994*a*). Before the Dutch established a colonial administration early in the twentieth century, the Endenese people, who reside to the east of Keo, applied the name to inland as well as coastal populations located immediately to the west. Evidently because maritime Endenese had more direct dealings with coastal groups, the Dutch, who were introduced to people in more westerly parts of Flores by Malay-speaking Endenese intermediaries, reserved the name 'Keo' for the population residing to the south of the Ebu Lobo volcano, while initially reserving 'Nage' for the population residing to the north of this prominent peak (see Map 1).[7]

From the beginning of the colonial period, the Dutch intended eventually to include the Keo region as part of the district or 'kingdom' (BI *kerajaan* or *swapraja*) of Nage. Owing to greater instability in Keo (Dietrich 1989; Forth 1994*a*), however, the region was temporarily maintained as a separate 'kingdom' with its own raja, resident in an eastern village named Kota (later to become known as Kota Keo). In 1931, after resistance to colonial incursion had subsided, Nage and Keo were joined to form a single administrative entity under the Nage leader in Bo'a Wae. What had been Keo and Nage then came to be known simply as Nage (Swapraja Nage) or alternatively as 'Nage Keo', a compound name consonant with a characteristically dualistic form exemplified in indigenous place-names as well as in numerous other local usages (Forth 1996*a*).

After the amalgamation with Nage, 'Keo' no longer designated a separate unit

---

[6] The Polynesian extension of this principle is illustrated by Sahlins's observation that, in Hawaii, descendants are represented as specific instances of inclusive, or 'generic', ancestors (1981: 13).

[7] According to E.D. Lewis (pers. comm. 1996), in the Sikkanese language of eastern Flores 'Soge', a name for Ende, is combined with 'Keo' to form 'Soge Keo', a reference to the entire south coast of Flores. Also referring to Sikkanese usage, Tule ([n.d.]: 9) cites a poem recorded in Petu's *Nusa Nipa* (1969: 35) which includes a similar pairing, 'Tonggo Keo'. Tonggo (dialectal, Togo) is the coastal settlement located in the extreme eastern part of Keo that has long been connected with Ende. Illustrating an earlier application of the name which included Nage as well, the first detailed map of 'Keo' appears in Riedel (1886: 70). This records several coastal settlements in western Keo, including Ma'u Kota and Ma'u Waru (Ma'u Wayu), associated respectively with the inland villages of Paga (II: 1: vi) and Wulu Wayu (II: 4: iv).

of colonial or independent Indonesian administration. As inhabitants of the region probably did not use the term to identify themselves prior to the colonial era, its currency was thus evidently short-lived, both as a territorial and an implicitly ethnic designation. It is an intriguing circumstance that 'Keo' occurs as the name of one of the older villages of western Keo (Forth 1994*a*: 304; see also II: 4 below). Yet how this instance might inform the later application of the name to a much larger region, and thence to a division of the Dutch colonial administration, remains unclear. In its more inclusive senses, 'Keo' is still known but is no longer often heard, its administrative referent long having been superseded by newer political divisions that cross-cut both the former colonial districts of Nage and Keo. To their northern Nage neighbours, Keo are known as *ata ma'u*, 'people of the (south) coast' (*ma'u*, 'coast, coastal settlement'), a designation which, because many Keo reside some distance from the sea, is to be understood in a relative sense. Similarly, Keo and others call their language *sara ma'u*, 'coast language' (*sara* also means 'way, manner'), while western Keo sometimes employ this term to specify the language of east-coastal Keo.

Despite these qualifications, the people whose society I explore in this book possess a sufficiently distinct culture to merit a separate designation. 'Keo' presents itself as by far the best option, not least of all because I have been able to obtain for it the approval of the people themselves. At present, Keo in the broadest sense are divided between the administrative subdistrict (BI *kecamatan*) of Mauponggo and the southern part of the subdistrict of Nangaroro, immediately to the east.[8] Both subdistricts are among the eight that make up the Indonesian Regency (BI *kabupaten*) of Ngada (thus distinguished from the ethnic, or ethnographic, designation 'Ngadha'), which occupies a large part of the central area of the island of Flores and which in turn forms part of the Indonesian province of Nusa Tenggara Timur. The population I distinguish as 'western Keo' inhabits part of the Mauponggo subdistrict located to the west of Ma'u Nori (see Map 1). More specifically, the study concerns over thirty traditional villages included in seven of the twenty-three 'administrative villages' (BI *desa*) that make up the subdistrict. Proceeding roughly north to south and east to west, the seven *desa* are Jawa Pogo, Ulu Loga, Loda Olo, Wolo Telu, Sawu, Loka Laba, and Wuli Walo. Although seven is a valued total among Keo, this consideration has not affected the present geographical delimitation which, being partly due to the limitations of space imposed by a book, is somewhat arbitrary. With regard to colonial divisions, the area comprises a continuous territory largely coinciding with the former subdistricts (BI *haminte*) of Sawu and Maukeli, with over 90 per cent of component villages falling within Sawu. In terms of Catholic Church divisions, it is similarly conterminous with the parish of Wolo Sambi.

---

[8] When referring to modern subdistricts, I follow the transcription employed by the Indonesian government. Ma'u Ponggo (actually Ma'u Pogo)—originally the name of a coastal hamlet—thus becomes Mauponggo, Ma'u Kéli becomes Maukeli, and so on.

PLATE 1. Ebu Lobo volcano and the double settlement of Pau Lundu taken from the lower village (Pau)

Ethnographically, the area I describe encompasses the original territories of four of a larger group of ancestral siblings. To be sure, villages to the west and east in many respects resemble those treated here, and many are moreover linked with these through marriage. Yet adjacent areas also reveal differences, thus further justifying the boundaries described above. Villages immediately east of the area (including Lédho Ngule, Lédho Woru, and Dhoki), for example, reveal a social order in which a village is represented as a single clan (*suku*) divided into a number of segments consistently named after ancestors. With few exceptions, villages located within the focal area by contrast include two or more clans distinguished by names other than those of ancestors, which in most cases recognize branches in one or more other villages.

Keo territory comprises a rugged, highly accidented terrain that in several places gives way to a narrow coastal plain. All settlements treated in this book are located on or below the southern slopes of Ebu Lobo, the active volcano which the Dutch called 'Keo Peak' (Keopiek; see Plate 1). With an elevation of 2,149 metres, Ebu Lobo is by far the highest mountain in the entire Keo region. In western Keo, the second highest is Mount Nata (Kéli Nata), with twin peaks measuring 983 and 910 metres respectively. Located southwest of Ebu Lobo, and forming a single range with several lower mountains and hills that extend towards the Sawu Sea, Kéli Nata figures prominently in Keo history and mythology. Its lower slopes also define the western extent of what Keo call the 'Sawu Valley' (Yobo Sawu), the northeastern side of which coincides with the lower reaches of the great volcano itself. Although evidently a usage dating only from colonial times, and referring to the colonial subdistrict of Sawu rather than the older village of that name, this entity serves further to define my geographical focus. Interestingly enough, local people speak of Yobo Sawu as including seven *desa* (modern administrative units); yet this reckoning excludes *desa* Wuli Walo, the component settlements of which I describe in Part II (Ch. 6), while it includes Wolo Ede, a *desa* I mention only incidentally.

Because of its relatively high elevation and location to the south of Ebu Lobo, western Keo receives more rainfall than areas north and east of the volcano and, indeed, most other parts of Flores Island and the province of Nusa Tenggara Timur. In highland regions, rain falls during every month of the year, and even in the drier months (from June to September) one often experiences heavy downpours, morning or late afternoon mists, and relatively cool, damp, and overcast conditions. Combined with volcanic soils, abundant rainfall produces a generally fertile landscape somewhat reminiscent of Bali. As Keo themselves remark, even a stick thrust into the ground will sprout and grow in the Sawu Valley. All the same, there is noticeable variation in both rainfall and temperature between higher and lower elevations. Particularly in the drier months, temperatures close to the coast can be quite oppressive, even at night, while just a few kilometres inland one needs a blanket to sleep comfortably.

Keo territory includes no large rivers, only a number of springs and streams. Larger streams nowadays feed several wet-rice complexes developed after the Second World War. One water course, the river Koya, divided the colonial districts of Nage and Keo and nowadays forms the boundary of the modern divisions (*kecamatan*) of Mauponggo and Boawae. Owing to the clearing of forests on higher slopes to extend cultivation and obtain wood for construction, some springs and streams have disappeared in recent decades, thus reducing the availability of water for drinking and bathing (cf. Bosselaar 1932). Near the inland settlement of Pajo Mala, insufficient water has recently led to the abandonment of stream-fed rice fields, some of which have been replaced by small coffee plantations.

Consistent with soil fertility, the Keo population is dense by eastern Indonesian standards. Within the study area, data provided by officials in the subdistrict office of Mauponggo in 1996 indicated a population of 8,693 inhabiting some 52 square kilometres, and thus a density of about 167.[9] While the foregoing pertains to total population, not quite all residents of the region with which I am specifically concerned are ethnically Keo. Since precolonial times,

---

[9] The total population of Keo—that is, Mauponggo plus part of the Nangaroro subdistrict to the east—numbers somewhere between 37,000 and 39,000. Population figures from the first half of the twentieth century are recorded in Forth (1994a: 315).

Muslim Endenese from the port of Ende and the Isle of Ende (Pulau Ende) have settled along the Keo coast, engaging in fishing, maritime trade, and occasional cultivation on land owned by Keo clans. This Endenese minority is encountered in Ma'u Wayu (Ma'u Waru, II: 4: iv) and to a lesser extent in or near other Keo coastal hamlets (*ma'u*), including Ma'u Bajo (II: 1: i) and Ma'u Kéli. Although local people reckon that Endenese make up three-quarters of the Ma'u Wayu population, their total number is difficult to determine. Nevertheless, it is quite clear that they form but a small part of the total population, and, moreover, have regular dealings only with a similarly small minority of Keo who live on the coast and have converted to Islam. In addition to hamlets occupied by Endenese immigrants, the territory of the *desa* named Sawu includes the modern settlement and administrative centre of Ma'u Ponggo—thus named identically to the subdistrict (Mauponggo)—occupied by resident officials and others who derive from outside Keo. Among the latter are several Chinese merchant families who own shops and engage in an import–export trade.

Traditional Keo are subsistence cultivators and livestock breeders. Hunting, most notably of wild pigs, is practised but contributes little to the diet. Freshwater fishing is negligible, while sea fishing is almost exclusively a pursuit of Endenese immigrants, who sell part of their catch to both highland and coastal Keo. Although Keo—even the inhabitants of villages located close to the coast—are described as never having made or owned boats or having gone to sea, the ethnic division of labour this implies may be relatively recent. Apical ancestors of a number of clans are described as sailing to western Keo in seagoing vessels. In addition, several indigenous territories include both coastal and inland areas, the former being traditionally used by Keo for salt and lime production, and in some places weir fishing.[10]

Major Keo staples include rice (*pae*), grown in dry and nowadays irrigated fields, and maize (*yolo*). In higher regions two maize crops a year can be expected, in March or April and July or August. Planted at the same time as maize in October or November, dry rice is ready for harvesting in April, while wet rice is now cultivated the year round. Former cultivars, including millet (*wete*) and Job's tears (*ke'o; Coix lacryma-jobi*), are rarely planted any longer. Supplementing or complementing cereals are a variety of tubers, pulses, fruits, and vegetables. As elsewhere in Indonesia, extensive use is made of coconuts. Even the briefest description of the Keo economy would be incomplete without

---

[10] That the present pattern was already established in the nineteenth century is suggested by Weber's (1890: 21) characterization of relations between coastal itinerants and indigenous inland villagers as marked by mutual fear and distrust, despite their involvement in a transitory trade. In particular, he refers to the then palisaded village of Mbawa (or Bawa), which he describes as falling within the territory of Keo. Located about a quarter of an hour's journey from the coast, Mbawa is linked with the coastal settlement named Ma'u Mbawa, which I mention again below. Interestingly, Freijss (1860: 467) was warned by traders from Tonggo about reputed 'murderers' called '*orang-bawa*', a possible reference to the same Mbawa people. Both of these authors provide other information on people they call Keo, including details of physical features, hairstyles, clothing, and other items of material culture (see also Riedel 1886).

mention of palm tapping. Especially in highland regions, the Arenga palm, *lo moke* (*Arenga pinnata*), provides a juice which Keo ferment to make palm wine or toddy (*tua bhaya*) and then distil to produce a potent gin (*tua ara*). In drier coastal regions, the Arenga is largely replaced by the Lontar palm, *lo koli* (*Borassus sundaicus*). A requisite part of informal prestations to wife-givers, toddy or gin is essential to any ritual undertaking, and the stills of western Keo produce some of the finest gin anywhere in Flores.

Keo livestock includes water buffalo, horses, pigs, goats, dogs, and domestic fowls. With the exception of pigs (which form part of a wife-giver's counter-prestation), all the mammalian kinds are used as bridewealth and, like fowls, are slaughtered and consumed on ceremonial or festive occasions. Buffalo and, to a lesser degree, horses are the animals most prized in affinal exchange, while buffalo, pigs, and fowls (in this order) are the most valued sacrificial animals. Only recently have Keo begun to employ buffalo as draught animals. At present, they also raise cattle introduced by the Dutch from Madura, as well as the more recently imported Balinese variety.

Although the drier and warmer climate of the coast renders this region less productive than the interior, Keo agriculture is limited more by terrain than by precipitation or soil fertility. Because of high population density, demand for arable land often outstrips supply, a situation which, for some time, has regularly given rise to disputes that have sometimes led to violence (Forth 1994*a*: 310, citing Karthaus 1931). During the past two decades, a solution to pressure on land has been sought through a policy of voluntary transmigration. Recently, several western Keo families have moved to central Sulawesi and Kalimantan, while a greater number have participated in relocation schemes in Mbai, on the north coast of Flores, and in the Golewa subdistrict of eastern Ngadha, immediately west of Mauponggo.

Like other eastern Indonesians, Keo are increasingly involved in an emerging monetary economy, requiring cash to pay taxes, school fees, and modern medical costs, and to purchase a variety of non-traditional items. Responding to external development initiatives, Keo people have begun producing cash crops, including coffee, cloves, candlenut, and more recently vanilla and cacao. Coffee was the earliest introduced, while clove planting began in Mauponggo in 1969. Occasionally, commercial planting of perennials has compromised traditional rules of land tenure, as for example when people entitled only to cultivate annual crops on land owned by others have planted clove trees. In addition, the government has begun promoting the registration of lands collectively held by clans or houses in the names of individuals. For the most part, however, relations involving land continue to be governed by the local social order, and Keo villagers still devote most economic effort and resources to subsistence production.

As money comes more into use, Keo increasingly participate in weekly markets where they sell and buy produce and purchase a variety of processed foods and manufactured items. Trading and markets, however, are by no means new to Keo, as shown by Arndt's description of the coastal market at Ma'u Mbawa, near the extreme southwestern limit of Keo territory (1963: 183–85). Formerly, the Ma'u Mbawa market was a centre for the export of slaves. Conducted mostly by Goanese, Buginese, and Endenese slavers—the latter from the port of Ende and Pulau Ende (Isle of Ende)—this cruel trade was once also prosecuted at Ma'u Wayu (II: 4: iv). In return for slaves, Keo vendors received metal currency, gold, and gunpowder. Other local products exported from Ma'u Mbawa included rice and maize. As Arndt notes, during the colonial period the market was closed, more recently to be revived as a weekly event featuring very different commodities.

Other than as suppliers of local produce and slaves, some Keo may once have been more actively involved in export. Reporting on a voyage to Flores in 1854–56, Freijss (1860) mentions 'Keo's' as well as 'Tonggo's' (that is, people from Tonggo; see Map 1) conducting an itinerant trade along the island's south coast. While the people Freijss describes as 'Keo's' may actually have been Endenese settled in coastal Keo (Forth 1994a: 306), it is also possible that they included indigenous Keo. In Keo Ondo (II: 1: i), I was told how men of that village and the neighbouring village of Nua Nage had formerly travelled in Buginese vessels to Ujung Pandang (on Sulawesi) to trade coconuts for pottery. From genealogical evidence, one such trip appears to have taken place about the middle of the nineteenth century. Internally as well, western Keo engaged in trade with other parts of Flores. People from the north-coastal region of Mbai, sometimes referred to as Goanese (*ata goa*), at one time visited Keo to obtain betel and areca in exchange for salt, while Keo people are described as journeying to areas to the northeast to conduct the same trade. Nowadays regional produce from all over central Flores is transported by motor vehicle to a variety of weekly markets, including one in the administrative centre of Ma'u Ponggo.

Apart from evidence that Keo regularly traded with outsiders during the nineteenth century, little is known about the precolonial history of the region. Local traditions recount how people identified as Majapahit Javanese settled temporarily at Jawa Pogo, a summit near Mount Nata, which they supposedly levelled in an aborted attempt to erect some sort of structure (I: 1: ii). In view of Portugal's presence in more easterly parts of Flores from the sixteenth to the eighteenth century, including missionary activity in parts of eastern Keo and Nage (*Sejarah Gereja Katolik Indonesia* 1974; Lehmann 1984, 1987; Lame Uran 1987; Heurnius 1855), it is likely that, during this time, Portuguese also entered what is now western Keo.

Europeans seem, however, to have made no lasting impact on local culture before the twentieth century. In several western Keo villages and former village sites, one still finds brass cannon reputedly obtained from the Portuguese. According to a local tradition, a Portuguese priest, whose name is usually pronounced as 'Don Juan' (with the /j/ rendered as in English), once built a chapel at a spot called Lebi Wolo Wea, near the double settlement of Pau Lundu (II: 1: vii; II: 3: iii). Fearful of his putative spiritual power and the possibility of his stealing their land, Pau villagers murdered the man while preserving his clothes and a book as relics. Although such objects seem more often encountered in eastern Keo and parts of the Nage region, garments, banners, swords, and other items of Portuguese manufacture have similarly been maintained in other western Keo villages besides Pau Lundu. Interestingly, the name 'Don Juan' (sometimes in the Portuguese transcription 'Dom João') further occurs in the published history of Ende and Tonggo as a reference to a 'Muslim renegade' who lead a Makassarese fleet in an attack on Pulau Ende in 1602 (van Suchtelen 1921: 9; Rouffaer 1923–4: 145). But, other than the name, there is nothing to link this man with the priest who is claimed to have founded a chapel near Pau Lundu.

The Netherlands Indies government took effective control of central Flores in 1907. From the beginning, a major concern of the Dutch administration was extinguishing rebellions resulting from the imposition of taxes and road construction employing corvée labour (Forth 1994a: 308–10). Colonial reports dating from the 1930s (for example Koster 1938) mention the need to improve roads to facilitate a more effective administration and to promote economic development. Owing to the rugged terrain, transportation remains difficult in many places to the present day. The recent widening and paving of the main road leading from the administrative centre in Ma'u Ponggo to the junction with the Flores highway has, however, greatly improved road travel between a number of villages in western Keo, reducing considerably the former isolation of the region.

Following the establishment of the colonial district in 1912, the Dutch formally divided Keo into ten subdistricts, later designated as *haminte* (from Dutch *gemeente*, 'municipality'). Leadership of these was assigned to headmen (*kepala mere* or *kepala haminte*) who, as far as possible, were selected from the oldest landowning groups (Forth 1994a: 310).[11] Coinciding with most of the area considered here, the subdistrict of Sawu was among the largest of these. Another region incorporated in this study coincides with part of the former subdistrict of Maukeli, which included the villages of Liwo, Wulu, and Wagha (II: 6) and was centred in the coastal hamlet of Ma'u Kéli. Like other colonial subdistricts, Sawu was divided into a number of 'villages' called *kampong* (Malay for 'village'), or *kepala kampong*, a term that literally means 'village head' and, indeed, referred to their appointed leaders as well. Though all bore the names of traditional villages, in most cases a *kampong* comprised two or three traditional villages (*nua*). Many such amalgamations, however, occurred

---

[11] *Kepala* is the Malay word for 'head, headman, leader'. *Mere*, more correctly *mére* (cf. Nage *méze*), is the word for 'big, great, major' employed throughout central Flores.

only as a later administrative development, and many more villages were recognized as independent *kampong* at the beginning of the colonial period than towards the end (see Hamilton 1918, who lists twenty-three *kampong*). During the early national period, the colonial *haminte* and *kampong* were maintained by the Indonesian government, but in 1957 both were replaced by the units called *desa* (BI 'villages'). Usually comprising between three and six traditional villages (*nua*), these *desa* are intermediate in size between the two kinds of colonial unit. Somewhat later, the administrative entity named Nage, or Nage Keo, was dissolved altogether and replaced by four modern subdistricts (BI *kecamatan* Mauponggo, Nangaroro, Boawae, and Aesesa), each headed by a government appointed official (*camat*).

Although the Portuguese established Roman Catholic communities in more easterly parts of Flores as early as the sixteenth century, conversion to Catholicism in Keo reflects missionary activity by the Society of the Divine Word initiated during the 1920s. At present, over 90 per cent of the population of the Mauponggo subdistrict are reckoned to be Catholic. The remainder, including Endenese migrants as well as ethnic Keo who mostly converted during the twentieth century, are Muslims.[12] The port of Ende and Pulau Ende appear to have been the sole sources of Keo Islam (Tule [n.d.]: 10). Associating regularly and sometimes intermarrying with Endenese, Keo Muslims generally reside near the coast, where all mosques are located. Although converts from inland villages tend to move to coastal settlements, many maintain ties with their places of origin; hence it is not unusual to find Muslim Keo continuing to co-operate in collective undertakings with Catholic members of the same village, clan, or even house. Although coastal settlements include Keo Catholics as well as Keo and Endenese Muslims, according to popular reckoning, which seems correct, the former usually reside 'above', that is landward of the main coastal road, while Muslims live 'below' the road, closer to the beach. Replicating the landward–seaward contrast fundamental to the indigenous direction system as well as to the form and disposition of traditional villages, this residential distinction explains the phrases *wawo rala* and *au rala* ('above' and 'below the path') as references to followers of Catholicism and Islam respectively.

As accords with a local Catholic practice of designating Muslim Keo as *ata Ende*, or 'Endenese' (Tule [n.d.]), Christians describe converts to Islam as adopting Endenese language, clothing styles, and mannerisms. A few have also taken up maritime occupations. While conversion may be motivated by marriage, either with Endenese or Keo Muslims, it is not clear how far a preference for religious endogamy affects current marriage patterns. Adherence to world religions, however, certainly has implications for traditional marriage as

---

[12] Keo Muslims of longer standing are found only in eastern Keo, particularly in the vicinity of Tonggo, where a mosque was first built around 1820 (Tule [n.d.])

PLATE 2. The village of Keo Ondo showing the chapel at the landward extremity and a shrine at the seaward end

well as for other aspects of local culture, most notably in regard to the Catholic Church's ban on marriage with MBD and other cousins, and on plural marriage. Although Islam, of course, presents no barrier to either cousin marriage or polygyny, there is, interestingly enough, a perception that Catholicism accommodates local custom more than does Islam. One obvious difficulty for Muslims is the traditional requirement that wife-taking affines be served with pork; another is the use of live pigs as counter-prestation to bridewealth. In this regard, one of my regular hosts, a Muslim, recounted how he had found a solution by arranging for one of his sons to become a Catholic so that he could take care of customary affairs, including the raising of pigs to give to non–Muslim wife-takers.

If there are now any Keo confessing neither Catholicism nor Islam, they are not formally recognized as such. Although some Catholics attend church irregularly, most appear to participate in the Sunday service, sometimes travelling considerable distances to do so. Apart from the church in Wolo Sambi, three villages within the study area (Keo Ondo, Kuyu Wulu, and Pajo Mala) contain chapels, constructed in each case at the 'head' (the landward extremity) of the settlement. These villages, like several others, also include shrines with statues of the Virgin Mary, usually placed at the opposite end (see Plate 2). Despite conversion, the majority of Keo still maintain indigenous beliefs pertaining to local spirits and ancestral benevolence and continue to conduct traditional sacrificial and other rites. If such rituals are performed less often than formerly, this would appear to reflect new demands on resources, especially livestock, more than an altered conviction. Since I first visited western Keo in 1984, several villages have initiated or completed the lengthy and expensive ritual undertaking of replacing sacrificial posts (*peo*) and other ceremonial structures.

Linguistic research is little advanced in central Flores. No dictionary yet exists, either for dialects spoken in Keo or in neighbouring Nage. Provisionally classifiable as an Austronesian language belonging to a Central-Malayo-Polynesian grouping (Blust 1979), the language of western Keo is closely related to dialects spoken in eastern Keo, Nage, and eastern Ngadha. Following local opinion, the language is also mutually intelligible with at least one dialect of Endenese. At the same time, phonological and lexical differences are noticeable even within the area of the present study. To cite just two instances: the /c/ sound (as in English 'chart') heard in highland villages is replaced closer to the coast by an /s/, while the /d/, encountered in some northern and western villages (for example, in Kuyu Wulu and Liwo), elsewhere becomes /nd/. Unlike Nage and Ngadha, western Keo speech possesses a /y/ sound, corresponding variously to the /h/ and initial glottal in Nage and some instances of /r/ in Ngadha and Endenese. Similarly, the /z/ found in Nage and Ngadha is replaced by /r/ in Keo. In official usage, and nowadays sometimes in local speech, place-names, especially, diverge from indigenous pronunciation by the replacement of /y/ with /r/, /g/ with /ngg/, and /b/ with /mb/. Thus the settlement name Bolo Yoga becomes 'Bolo Rongga', Ma'u Pogo becomes 'Ma'u Ponggo', Ma'u Wayu becomes 'Ma'u Waru', and Wolo Sabi becomes 'Wolo Sambi'. As Keo themselves recognize, all these usages reflect the influence of Endenese, and more particularly the colonial employment of Endenese interpreters, who lent their own pronunciation to terms cognate with words in their native language.

3. Outline of the Volume

Consistent with the focus on dualism (though not consciously inspired by it), this book comprises two parts. In Part I, I discuss general features of Keo society. The way Keo explicate present patterns and relationships with reference to notions of 'origin' is reflected in the first chapter, which describes the historical or mythical derivations of major groupings and introduces the fundamental relationship of 'land mother' and 'defender'. Chapter 2 then deals with the spatial ordering of local society, outlining the organization of villages and hamlets and the ceremonial structures that distinguish the former. Since a village is essentially a sacrificial site, the chapter also reviews forms of dual leadership focused in sacrificial instruments (*peo*) and ritual performance. Beginning with a discussion of land tenure, Chapter 3 considers in turn property-holding groups I call 'estates', the larger clans that comprise these, and the 'house' considered as both a residential entity and a kind of social unit. The next chapter (4) comprises an analysis of kinship and marriage. After describing the polysemous category *ka'e ari* (elder–younger), I review Keo practices and ideas relating to marriage and affinity, bridewealth, and the alliance relation. Several major metaphors informing fundamental social relationships are then considered in detail in Chapter 5, as are practices of adoption and incorporation constitutive of Keo corporate groups.

Part II comprises a series of case studies illustrating, elaborating, and qualifying general features of western Keo society outlined in Part I. Describing connections between specific groups and local historical accounts of processes illuminating present forms and relationships, the contents of this second half are more directly responsive to the interests of my Keo hosts. This second set of chapters thus incorporates the sort of information that Keo people themselves expected me to record, partly for posterity, and partly, they hoped, to illuminate more obscure aspects of present-day social relations.[13] Distinguished with reference to a territory associated with one of several ancestral founders, each chapter describes a collection of linked clans and villages, in this way composing a sort of 'mini-ethnography'. In addition, each highlights one or more specific organizational or conceptual themes outlined in Part I.

Variation found in western Keo village organization further informs the reference to 'combination' in the subtitle of the present work. As noted, dualistic social unities are typically represented as the outcome of a process of combination rather than of division within pre-existing wholes. At the same time, each community reveals a particular combination of organizational forms and principles, rather than a replication of a completely uniform, empirical pattern characteristic of the region as a whole. In this respect, the study does not isolate a single institutional model of Keo society so much as it demonstrates why no such model may be possible.

---

[13] Some Keo even expressed the hope that my enquiries could lead to a definitive resolution of local conflicts, for example, over rights to land. Although I endeavoured to disabuse them of this prospect, I was probably not entirely successful. Even so, I trust that anyone from Flores who reads this account might be able to appreciate why it cannot be construed as a final statement about 'the correct order' of Keo society or of any of its component relationships.

PART I

Social and Cultural Dualities

1

Ancestors and Descendants:
'Mothers' and 'Children'

1. The Earliest Ancestors

Following a tradition widespread in central Flores, the earliest ancestors of the Keo people were a group of siblings, all surnamed Ga'e, who came from the So'a region, to the northwest. From these derive the principal 'land mother' (*ine tana*) clans as well as their 'defenders' (*ana tuku*), among whom the former divided their territories in an initial partition.[1] Although the entire population ultimately recognizes an external origin (a notion of local autochthony being absent from their mythology), Keo reserve the term 'immigrant' for a number of clans that arrived in the region significantly later. In addition to Defenders of the Land Mothers and these later immigrants, four or five long-established clans share no known or recognized relationship with the Land Mothers and are not counted among their Defenders. Generally, though, Keo consider the territories of these clans as falling within the domain of the Ga'e siblings, more particularly that of the eldest brother, Lape Ga'e; and they do not expressly recognize them as an aboriginal population.

Several traditions speak of an original set of seven Ga'e siblings, most of whom were male. Since Keo elders are often able to recite a greater number of names than seven, and since different sets of names are recognized from place to place, the numeral—associated in various ritual contexts with life and the possibility of sustained growth—is to be understood as a symbolic usage. Comparable representations include the idea that sufficient genealogical knowledge involves the ability to trace back seven generations (*pi lima rua*) and the notion that a Land Mother should possess a set of seven Defenders. In fact, some Land Mothers have more than seven, while others have considerably fewer.[2] As a name of revered ancestors, Ga'e probably derives from *ga'e*, meaning 'lord, master, owner (of slaves)'. In other languages of central Flores the word similarly denotes the highest social rank, while in Keo and Nage it further occurs in *moi ga'e*, a compound term for 'wife-givers' incorporating the partly synonymous *moi* ('owner, possessor'). The association of 'Ga'e' with early ancestors would also seem to be connected with its use in designating a supreme being, called Ga'e Bapu in Keo and Ga'e Déwa in Nage. In both

---

[1] In order to indicate these special senses of the terms, I hereafter capitalize their English glosses.
[2] Further uses of the number seven are described below. The appearance of the numeral in various contexts of local history is well illustrated by Pajo Mala traditions summarized in II: 2: ii.

regions, this entity is further designated with the parallelistic expression *ndéwa (or déwa) réta, ga'e rale* ('*déwa* above, *ga'e* below').

The area of the present study (see Map 2) comprises territories associated with four of the Ga'e siblings. All male, these are Lape Ga'e (the eldest), Géra Ga'e, Gewo Ga'e, and Lobo Ga'e (the youngest). As the eldest brother who, in accordance with present practice, divided the land among his younger siblings, Lape Ga'e is further recognized as the ancestral owner of the entire territory, called Tana Lape. Only he, and by extension his descendants, are therefore known as 'Mother Lape' (Ine Lape), a designation that identifies the male forebear as the ancestor of the principal Land Mother clan. In accordance with the practice of appending the mother's name to a child's own name, the Ga'e siblings are recognized as offspring of an ancestress named Ine Ga'e (Mother Ga'e). The most complete genealogy I recorded for Ine Ga'e was provided by M. Dhae Menge, headman of the clan Pajo in the village of Pajo Réja.

According to this genealogy, the earliest ancestors were a pair of brothers named Téru Téna. Consistent with an extensive pattern of binary naming, the phrase actually designates an elder brother named Téru and a younger named Téna. Instancing another recurrent pattern of Keo genealogy, only one brother, in this case the elder, had issue. Téru sired Re and Réna, alternatively named Ghe and Ghéna. Following the same pattern, only Re, the elder, has links with subsequent generations. Although the exact connection cannot be specified, Re eventually gave rise to a female named Rire, or Rie. Underlining the mythological character of this lineage, Rie refers to the volcano Ine Rie (Mother Rie), located in Ngadha country, well to the west. Rie then married Lobo, which is to say Ebu Lobo (Grandfather Lobo), the great smoking volcano that dominates most of Keo and Nage territory.

Mother Rie bore a daughter named Liru (Sky). She in turn had a daughter named Leke ('(house post which) rests on the ground'). Leke was the mother of Ine Ga'e. In this mixture of male and female ancestors, one glimpses another feature of Keo genealogical reckoning. All the major Ga'e ancestors, the children of Ine Ga'e, were male. Yet the great majority of clans that claim to derive from them do so by way of a sister, daughter, or other female relative of a male Ga'e. Expressed another way, most western Keo clans are linked with the mythical lineage by way of male ancestors who were 'wife-takers' of the Ga'e.

Keo have little else to say about the early ancestors named above. The myths include no mention of wives in the first two ancestral generations, while the husbands of Liru and Leke seem to be unknown, and evidently unimportant. Accounts vary concerning the husband of Mother Ga'e (Ine Ga'e). According to the narrator from clan Pajo, this was a personage named Kolo, who took the form of a dove (*kolo, Streptopelia* sp.) which defecated on the forehead (*waka*) of Mother Ga'e and thus made her pregnant.

For the remainder of the tradition, I rely more on narratives provided by G.

Jago Uko, who claims dual membership of the clans Kate and Pajo Wolo in the village of Lower Pajo Mala (II: 2: ii). According to this account, Mother Ga'e was married to a man named Nau, and it was he who fathered the several Ga'e siblings. This version, too, begins with Téru and Téna. Lending the story a somewhat more historical cast, this pair are described as having come from Lopo Bata (= Lompobatang) in southern Sulawesi, from where they fled by sea when the volcano Lompobatang erupted.[3] Sailing without direction, they eventually landed at Leke Ratu. A small island lying off the south coast of Manggarai (in western Flores), Leke Ratu—speculatively glossed by one commentator as 'chief house post' (apparently from BI *ratu*, 'monarch')— receives mention in several Keo and Nage traditions as a temporary place of landing of early ancestors coming from overseas. What might account for its mythological prominence I was unable to illuminate.[4]

After remaining on Leke Ratu for some considerable time, the children of Téru and Téna, named Ghe and Ghéna, moved north and eastward to a place called Wolo Wio, in Ngadha territory. There they gave birth to another generation, a brother and sister pair named Wijo and Wajo.[5] Evidently by way of an incestuous coupling, this pair in turn gave birth to a son named Ngenga. Ngenga then moved to Mount Léna (Kéli Léna) in the above-mentioned So'a region, thus becoming known as Ngenga Léna. In this version of the myth, Ngenga is the father of Ine Ga'e, the mother of the Ga'e siblings. Apparently following the lead of her paternal grandmother, she, too, is described as marrying her brother, the man named Nau. Owing to strife within the family of Ngenga connected with the incestuous union of his children, Mother Ga'e and her husband removed from So'a. They fled in a southerly direction until they reached the coast. Proceeding eastwards they arrived at Kéka Yégha, the first place from where Mount Léna, their former abode, was no longer visible. Mother Ga'e and Nau then began to ascend the ridge of hills that defines the western side of the Sawu valley, the locus of the present study. Finding the region fertile, they finally settled in Nata (Nua Nata), atop Mount Nata (Kéli Nata). This was the birthplace, and first residence, of the various Ga'e siblings. Most closely associated with Mount Nata is Lape Ga'e, the eldest of the group and the principal male ancestor in the western part of Keo.[6]

---

[3] Gunung Lompobatang, known to the Dutch as Piek van Bonthain, is located in southwestern Sulawesi, just east of Makassar. Since it is described as a long dormant volcano (*Encyclopaedie van Nederlandsch-Indië, Part 1 (A–G)*, 1917: 352; see also *Atlas van Tropisch Nederland* 1938), the Keo myth, if it has any historical basis, would appear to reflect experience of a very distant past.

[4] Called Toreneiland by the Dutch, the island is known in Manggarai as Nutja Mules or Nutja Atju, 'Dog Island' (Verheijen 1967: 21, s.v. *atju*; 339, s.v. *mules*), the second name (Atju) evidently being reflected in Keo as 'Ratu'. The island is now inhabited by a small Muslim community.

[5] Arndt (1954) records variants of these several pairs of names in his description of Ngadha traditions.

[6] Remarking on the status of the Ga'e ancestors as offspring of an illicit union leading to the removal of their parents from their place of origin, modern Keo recognize parallels with the biblical story of Adam and Eve and their expulsion from Eden.

2. *Myths of Mount Nata*

As the birthplace of the Ga'e siblings, Mount Nata, a relatively flat hilltop with an elevation of over 900 metres, figures as the local place of origin of the Keo people. Other mythical traditions connect the place with other origins. In a variant of a myth distributed widely in central Flores and elsewhere in eastern Indonesia (see Blust 1981*a*, 1991; Forth 1989*b*), Keo relate how, in the time of the original village of Nata, there were once two women who had just given birth. One morning, when everyone else had left to work in the fields, one of the women found she was without fire. As they lived on opposite sides of the village plaza, her companion could not help her; for neither had reached the fourth day after delivery and so they could not leave their houses. The woman who had fire found a solution by lighting a piece of coconut fibre and tying it to the tail of her dog. The other woman then called the animal, which, with the firebrand dangling behind it, scurried to her house. Later in the afternoon, when other villagers began returning home, the two women related what they had done. The story spread throughout the village, and on the third telling there arose great laughter. The result was a natural catastrophe (*wuya wando*) involving a flood and massive landslide which destroyed the village of Nata and gave rise to a spring, the source of the river Koko which flows into the sea near Ma'u Bajo.

At the time of the catastrophe, there was an unnamed pair of siblings, a brother and a sister, who had remained outside the village. They had been busy digging tubers and stopped to rest near a grove of bamboo. When they saw the land around Nata subsiding, they grasped on to the bamboo. The collapsing earth carried them as far as the coast, where they were washed out to sea. They drifted as far as the island of Sumba, called Wio throughout central Flores. There the siblings contracted an incestuous marriage, and the woman became pregnant. At this time, the people of Sumba were reputedly ignorant of natural methods of delivering children. They cut open the woman's abdomen, saving the child but always causing the mother to die. When it came time for the woman from Nata to deliver, the man—her husband and brother—sealed up their house, so that no one could witness the delivery. Later, when both parents emerged unharmed with their infant, the Sumbanese were amazed. The pair from Nata then taught them how to deliver children naturally, and they came to be widely recognized as powerful healers. After acquiring great wealth, the Nata siblings became the rulers (rajas) of 'Kanata' (Kanatangu); their present descendants are said to retain a remnant of the bamboo on which their ancestors floated to Sumba.

Traditions such as this commonly specify the complete destruction of all but one or a few favoured survivors. In this case, it seems that rather more were spared, including of course children and descendants of the Ga'e siblings, who later took up residence elsewhere in the vicinity of Mount Nata. Following one

PLATE 3. An elder of clan
Ebu Pata with a metal object
identified as the headgear of
the Wulu ancestor Raga Wea
(Raga Kico)

account, the destruction of Nata occurred about five generations after the birth
of the Ga'e ancestors. Descendants of Lape Ga'e eventually founded a village,
also named Lape Ga'e (or, simply, Lape). Naming both landscape features and
settlements after early ancestors is instanced elsewhere in the Keo region. For
example, a hill adjoining Kéli Nata is named Raga Kico, after the male ancestor of the clan Ebu Pata (more correctly named Raga Wea), who like numerous
others also derives from Lape Ga'e (see Plate 3). Not far away, another hill, and
a former place of settlement, is called Céla, the name of the wife of Lape (II:
1: i). Linking prominent peaks with beings identified as early ancestors of
humans is, of course, further exemplified by genealogical ideas noted just
previously, concerning the volcanoes Ebu Lobo and Ine Rie.

Yet another hill mentioned frequently in Keo traditions, especially in
accounts of clan origins and changes in settlement composition, is the peak
named Jawa Pogo. At present, Jawa Pogo is the name given to the modern
administrative unit (BI *desa*) coinciding with a large part of the territory of the

ancestor Lape Ga'e. Located close to Kéli Nata, the level summit of the hill is said to have been 'cut' or 'chopped' (*pogo*), and thus rendered flat, by an expedition of people from Jawa (*ata Jawa*), nowadays identified as Majapahit Javanese. The effort is described as part of a plan to construct a bridge linking Flores, again with Sumba. According to another, apparently more modern, version the 'Javanese' intended to erect a Hindu–Buddhist temple, or a city, on the levelled site. In order to reach the summit, the invaders formed a human ladder on the back of a large water buffalo. But to foil their plan, a local man slaughtered the beast, so that all came tumbling down. In so far as the slaughter of buffalo is central to Keo culture and society, the idea that this particular act proved decisive in thwarting the construction efforts of foreign intruders seems highly appropriate. Thus defeated, the people of Jawa returned directly to their vessels and sailed for home.

Reminiscent of a Sumbanese tradition concerning the former existence of a stone bridge at Cape Sasar that once linked Sumba with another land mass, sometimes specified as Flores, the story of Jawa Pogo, and especially the theme of cutting or chopping, suggests further parallels with a more general creation myth. The region of So'a, whence derived Ine Ga'e and her children, is also known in western Keo as the site of a great liana (*tali léke*) that once connected the earth with the sky (cf. Forth 1998, Ch. 10). At that time, sky and earth were much closer together than at present, and both were inhabited by people who, by way of the huge vine, would regularly visit and give assistance to one another. Owing to a conflict (the variable details of which cannot be given here), a person of the earth chopped down the liana, so that the link between the two parts of the cosmos, as well as a mutual beneficial relationship between their inhabitants, was severed once and for all.

Subsequent to this event, populations once united in So'a began to disperse. Although explained specifically with reference to another negative act—namely, sibling incest (thus an undesirable joining rather than a severing)—the removal of Mother Ga'e and her family to western Keo provides an instance of the general mythological dispersal following the cutting of the great liana. The 'chopping' of the peak named Jawa Pogo also accounts for changes in population distribution, albeit in a different way. The myth largely endures in accounts of the arrival of several Keo clans from the north and east, whose ancestors, hearing of the spectacular project of the men from Jawa, came 'to watch Jawa chopping' (*moni jawa pogo*). On arrival they discovered the region to be exceptionally fertile. As expressed in a typical mythical formula, while roasting maize to stay their hunger, the spectators observed that kernels which fell to the ground germinated immediately. Thus impressed, they decided to remain. Some moved into areas that were previously uncultivated. Others were given land by direct descendants of the Ga'e ancestors—the Land Mother clans—or by groups that had received territory in the original division following the dispersal from Mount Nata, the earliest Defenders of the Land Mothers.

Worthy of separate mention are western Keo groups that claim derivation from other islands, or from ancestors hailing from other parts of Flores who arrived in the region by sea (II: 4, 5 and 6). Among these is a small remnant group named Wio (the local name for Sumba) who are widely, though not invariably, reckoned originally to have come from Sumba. In a similar vein, a part of the clan named Keo, in the village of Keo Bélo (II: 4: ii), claims to derive agnatically from a pair of Sumbanese named Ja'e Mata and Umbu Temburu, who initially settled in Borong, in southeastern Manggarai, before moving to Keo. One of these men was a forebear of the second wife of the last colonial raja of Nage, J. Juwa Dobe, whose sons thus also claim descent from Sumbanese—as well as from Keo.

Another three groups, now resident in the villages of Sawu, Dhawe Yoja, and Wagha, locate their original homeland on the island of Savu, usually specified with the binary name 'Sabu Rote'.[7] The large and prominent clan named Sawu, now occupying the village of the same name, descends from an ancestor named Jara Waju (also pronounced as Jara Wadu). Reflecting a widespread mythical theme, Jara was the elder son of a Savunese ruler who, following his father's death, contested with his younger brother, Mélo Waju, over the succession. To decide the issue, the two brothers held a competition, in which the younger, through a deceit, proved victorious. Shamed by his defeat, Jara Waju left Sawu with his wife and a group of followers and set sail for a destination unknown. They also landed at Borong, in Manggarai, later moving eastward to Ae Mére in the Ngadha region. From Ae Mére, Jara Waju proceeded to Ma'u Mbawa, the coastal location near the extreme southwestern corner of Keo, on the boundary with Ngadha territory. Later he moved on to several places, including Watu Pésa (near the present coastal settlement of Ma'u Ponggo), Bo'a Nage (a place just seaward of Lui), and from there to Wudhi (a village near Wolo Sabi; see Map 2). In Wudhi, Jara Waju's descendants established themselves permanently in the Keo region, thus founding the clan now known as Sawu. Other reputed Savunese immigrants remained in Ma'u Mbawa, with one later founding the highland village of Dhawe Yoja (II: 5: v). The ancestor of clan Wagha, by contrast, is described as sailing directly from Savu.

Portrayed as a warrior who provided military assistance to various local populations as he moved eastward from Borong, Jara Waju obtained rights to lands in several places. Territory to which he laid claim in Ae Mére is said to be more extensive even than lands held by his descendants in western Keo. In Ae Mére and Ma'u Mbawa, as well as in the Keo territory occupied by clan Sawu, Jara Waju also left wives and offspring. After remaining for a while in Keo, the Sawu ancestor moved on to Ende, where he founded another settlement of Savunese (now known by the Indonesian, or Malay, name 'kampong Sabu'). Late in life, he returned to the island of Savu, where he died.

---

[7] Rote—rendered in Nage dialects as 'Ote—is the island of Roti. The /b/ in 'Sabu' apparently reflects the influence of Malay or Bahasa Indonesia.

One interest of the history of Jara Waju is the way it parallels other mythical accounts. Noteworthy in this regard is the story of Bi Tua, the ancestor of the Bamo people of Kéli Mado, in southeastern Nage (see Map 1). Also a militarily superior outsider, Bi Tua is similarly described as an immigrant from Minangkabau in Sumatra, who, driven by shame, left his homeland following a dispute with his brother over the governance of his father's kingdom. Like Jara Waju, he is moreover described as landing in southern Manggarai, indeed on the above-mentioned island of Leke Ratu, before proceeding eastwards to the Nage and Ende regions (see Fontijne 1940, who gives the island's name as Loke Atu.)

The story of Jara Waju and clan Sawu bears on another feature of Keo ancestral traditions. Mentioned at least as often in clan histories is a Sawu ancestor named Goa Mére. Some genealogies give Goa Mére as the name of the son of Jara Waju, and thus in effect the founding ancestor of Sawu in western Keo. Yet my most regular Sawu informant described Goa Mére as an alternative name for Jara Waju himself. In this connection, it may be relevant that the name can be construed as an epithet meaning 'major foreign invader'. Often paired with Jawa (interpreted as a reference to the island of Java), Goa, from the settlement of that name in southern Sulawesi, functions as a generic for non-European foreigners, while *mére* means 'big, great, major'. However the name is to be understood, it is remarkable how genealogies and local narratives often depict Goa Mére as contemporaneous with ancestors of other groups who, by most other indications, lived much earlier. Goa Mére is thus described as the father-in-law of Léwa, the ancestor of clan Guyu Wolo resident in the village of the same name (II: 3: ii), and hence apparently a generation mate of the ancestral couple named together as Boa Maga (most closely associated with clan Bindi Wae in Pajo Mala, II: 2: i). In addition, the Sawu ancestor appears in the genealogy of clan Leka as the husband of Pae Molo, a woman elsewhere specified as the ZDD of Lape Mére (often identified with the above-mentioned Lape Ga'e), who in the longest genealogical account appears seventeen generations before present adults. By contrast, the genealogy of clan Sawu shows Jara Waju as living five or six generations prior to present-day adult descendants, thus suggesting that this ancestor—and hence his putative son, Goa Mére—arrived on Flores no earlier than one hundred and fifty to two hundred years ago.[8]

---

8 The discrepancy may not be so pronounced in the case of Goa Mére's relationship with Léwa, since my records locate the Guyu Wolo ancestor just seven or eight generations before the present. Moreover, less elaborate genealogies represent Lape Mére as living just eight to ten generations ago. Since immediate descendants of Lape and Léwa are generally spoken of as having lived rather earlier, however, it would seem more likely that their genealogies are contracted. Otherwise the bulk of Keo history that I describe below would have had to have occurred after the arrival of clan Sawu's ancestors on Flores.

It is questionable how far historically unlikely genealogical claims, such as that specifying Goa Mére himself as the wife-giver of clan Guyu Wolo, can be explained as reflecting present social arrangements. Clan Sawu seems at least as often to have taken wives from Guyu Wolo and, in any case, is not a prominent affine of either sort. The same applies to Goa Mére's reputed marriage to a woman of clan Leka.

As I demonstrate later, this sort of anachronism colours other Keo ancestral traditions (see II: 1: iv and II: 4: i, regarding the Bolo ancestor, Dhoi Léwa). In part, it may be ascribed to a tendency to identify famous forebears with derivative groups, so that the action of a whole clan or individual descendant is attributed to an apical ancestor. Such anachronism would be problematic for a study aimed at an accurate reconstruction of western Keo history. What is important for the present enquiry, however, is only the order in which ancestors of particular groups are claimed to have established themselves in particular territories; and in this respect Keo hold quite definite ideas. Jara Waju of clan Sawu, for example, is widely recognized as a relative latecomer in western Keo; hence despite their political prominence, the Sawu people are considered subordinate to older groups in regard to both land and ceremonial precedence (II: 5: iii).

3. *Land Mothers and Defending Children*

Paralleling the mythical tradition of a primordial Mother (Ine Ga'e) and a group of mostly male children (the Ga'e siblings) is the previously mentioned relation of *ine tana*, or Land Mother, and *ana tuku*, Defender (more completely, 'defending child'). In western Keo the principal Land Mothers are groups that descend in the male line from sons of Ine Ga'e. In contrast, their various Defenders are clans tracing agnatic descent from male ancestors who were born of women, mostly sisters and daughters, of the male Ga'e siblings. Thus while Defenders ultimately trace their descent to the Ga'e through women, the opposition of 'mother' and 'child' pertaining to the first and second generations (Mother Ga'e and her sons) is replicated in the second and third (the sons, considered as Land Mothers, and their defending children).

Just as certain groups are Defenders of one of the several Ga'e siblings, so groups that are in turn subordinate to the former are themselves *ana* (children) who regard the original Defenders as *ine* (mothers). Subordination in this context refers in the first place to territorial partition. Thus each of the original Land Mothers, being the first to occupy a particular territory, is the original 'owner of the land' (*moi tana* or *ngaya tana*) who initially divided it among a number of defending children (*ana tuku*). The number of Defenders recognizing a common 'mother' is quite various. By far the largest cluster in western Keo comprises about a dozen clans that trace territorial and genealogical connections to the eldest of the Ga'e siblings, Lape Ga'e. By contrast, clan Liwo, descending agnatically from the youngest sibling, Lobo Ga'e, can claim only three Defenders (II: 6), as can clan Keo, which descends from Géra Ga'e (II: 3). As might be expected, the several Defenders of a single Land Mother are ranked in an order of precedence. Particularly when 'mother' and 'child' inhabit a single settlement, this order is then manifest in the sacrificial sequence observed in the collective slaughtering of water buffalo.

Granting land to Defenders entailed the right to found villages of their own and thus to erect separate sacrificial instruments, or *peo*. Keo describe this as a process located squarely in the past, during a formative period distinct from present or recent times. New Defenders, therefore, can no longer be created; nor can new villages or sacrificial instruments—except of course for those that renew or replace established ones. Territory granted by Land Mothers was formally transferred by way of an oath, to the effect that, should the donor group ever try to take back the land, they would suffer horrible illness and death and would eventually become extinct. Despite the territorial subordination of Defenders, therefore, these groups enjoy full rights to ceded lands and so can themselves be called 'owners of the land' (*moi tana*).

To distinguish original from secondary owners, Keo speak of 'large' (*mére*) and 'small' (*co'o*), or 'major' and 'minor', *moi tana*. By the same token, Defenders (*ana tuku*) who have themselves ceded land to yet more recently arrived groups may be designated as Land Mothers of the latter. Yet Keo tend to reserve the title of *ine tana* for the original owners, and then largely for the clans of the Ga'e siblings. (Another way of specifying these principal Land Mothers is *ine pu'u*, 'trunk mother', a term comparable to *ine peo* and *peo pu'u*, which I discuss presently.) At the same time, observed usage suggests that people more readily employ *ana tuku* not only for principal Defenders but also for territorial subordinates one degree removed (that is, Defenders of Defenders).[9] Similarly articulating relations between members of paired groups, another use of 'mother' and 'child' should be specified. When questioned directly, Keo usually claim that, in regard to territorial connections, *ine* and *ana* always refer to the relationship of Land Mother and Defender ('defending child'). Yet as I often noticed—and as informants' remarks confirmed—Keo also distinguish clans as 'mother' (*ine*, *ta ine*, *yoga ta ine*, 'mother people, people of the mother') and *ana* (or *ta ana*) simply on the basis of temporal precedence within a given locale, regardless of the source of lands claimed by the junior group. In some such cases the earlier established group is traditionally described as having invited another, sometimes a segment that split off from the main body of a clan in another village, to join it in the same settlement and share in its lands. In these circumstances, Keo speak of the former as 'detaining' or 'holding' (*te'o tange*) the later arrival.

As this variable application of *ine* and *ana* might suggest, one encounters conflicting reports regarding the status of particular groups as Land Mothers and Defenders. Indeed, some Keo tend to apply the title of Defender to any group that has obtained a sizeable area of land from another, even if it was acquired by purchase or simple occupation rather than by formal grant. The relevance of these distinctions will become clearer in later chapters. Suffice it

---

[9] The relationship appears not to go any further than this. Thus I did not encounter groups recognized as Defenders of Defenders of Defenders of one of the Ga'e siblings.

to note here that true Defender status, as it may be called, involves the conferral of a separate sacrificial instrument (*peo*), and often the initiation of an affinal connection in addition to a grant of land.

More completely designated as *ine tana, ame watu*, 'mother of the land, father of the stones' (see *tana watu* as a standard pairing, Forth 1996*a*), the title of Land Mother, applying equally to an ancestor and a derivative clan (*suku*), is roughly equivalent to the *tuan tanah* (BI 'lord of the land') of other Indonesian societies. Combining the terms for 'mother' and 'father', the complete title qualifies the manifest femininity of the designation. It thus reduces the initial curiosity of the common reference to Lape, the ancestor of the seniormost *ine tana* clan, as Ine Lape, 'Mother Lape', and to present representatives of the Land Mothers as 'mother people' (*yoga ta ine*). Even so, the fact that only the term for the female parent occurs in mundane usage accords with the mythological prominence of the Mother of the several Ga'e siblings, through whom their descent from earlier ancestors is traced. As I later show, it further agrees with Keo conceptions of the relationship of affinal alliance (I: 4). Closely bound up with territorial connection, Keo expressly describe the affinal tie, quite contrary to the English idiom, as one of 'descent' by way of— or, indeed, with—the female parent (I: 4: iv, I: 5: ii).

As the standard term for subordinate Defenders of a Mother's territory, *ana tuku* also invites closer scrutiny. Although *ana* is 'child, offspring', it further refers to things that are relatively small or form part of a larger collectivity. The two shorter surfaces of a rectangular house, for example, are called the *ana*, 'children', whereas the longer surfaces are called the *ine*, 'mother(s)'). Since the 'child' sides normally coincide with the two lateral surfaces of a dwelling while the 'mother' sides form the front and back, an inversion of this arrangement is described as a 'child embracing, cradling the mother' (*ana ka'o ine*).[10] Clearly, the idiom implies that in the usual way of things, the shorter sides are 'embraced', which is to say, contained, by the longer. As I show later, the same applies to 'defending children', who as territorial subordinates and frequently as wife-takers are encompassed by a particular Land Mother.

Keo regularly refer to *ana tuku* simply as *tuku*, particularly in possessive contexts when describing a group as Defender of another. Otherwise, *tuku* denotes an embankment or retaining wall, a dam, or a weir. The word thus generally refers to something that lends support as well as creating or maintaining a limit. In the same vein, *tuku* can be construed verbally, in the sense of 'to hold up' and 'to retain'. To appreciate its sense in the present context, *ine tana* and *ana tuku* should be considered as a pair comprising two parallelisms. Whereas the connection of 'mother' and 'child' is relatively straightforward, this particular mother is identified with the 'land' or 'earth' (*tana*), which is

---

[10] This idea seems curious in view of evidence for an earlier practice whereby houses were constructed with the short surfaces at the front and back of the building. Formerly, though, it may have been the longer right and left sides that were designated as *ine*.

then held up by the children, identified as retaining devices (*tuku*) that prevent collapse or erosion. At the same time, *tuku* can denote something which serves as a barrier against an external force, hence further informing the status of *ana tuku* as Defenders of a Land Mother.[11]

Consistent with all senses of the term, Keo identify groups designated as *ana tuku* with the peripheries or boundaries of the entire territory of a Land Mother. In ritual speech, they are described as people who 'dwell at the side, live at the end' (*ndi'i singi, mera sepu*), thus occupying the 'periphery of the land, the extremity of the stones' (*singi tana, sepu watu*) of the Mother's domain. Alternatively, Defenders are characterized as 'dwelling at the edge' (*ndi'i dhi*) of an originally undivided territory. As I later show, the phrase recalls the specification of subordinate, wife-taking affines as forming the 'edge of the blood' (*dhi ya*) in relation to a wife-giving source (I: 5).

In contrast to the association of Defenders with peripheries, a Land Mother is identified with the centre of an entire territory. 'Mother people' (*yoga ta ine*) are thus those who 'dwell in the middle, and reside at the centre' (*ndi'i kisa, mera ora*)—an expression applied in other contexts to a mediator or arbitrator. In the nature of things, some Defender clans are always more centrally located within the Mother's domain; hence the same phrases can further distinguish certain Defenders from others. In the course of time, some *ana tuku* have come to share a single village with their *ine tana*, or to found with them a double settlement. In this instance, Keo describe Defenders as 'dwelling as one, residing united' (*ndi'i 'ili, mera mogo*) or 'dwelling side by side, residing intermingled' (*ndi'i ipi, mera kamo*) with the Land Mother (I: 2: iii). In a few cases, movement of settlements has resulted in a Land Mother becoming incorporated into a village established by one or more Defenders. Keo then speak of 'the mother changing places with the child' (*ine yaka ana*), an expression reminiscent of 'child cradling the mother'.[12]

Regardless of the actual location of Defender clans within the domain of a Land mother, *ana tuku* and *ine tana* are categorically contrasted as parties respectively occupying the periphery and centre of a single, albeit divided, spatial whole. Correspondingly, where two or more Defenders occupy the same village as their Land Mother, the Mother's houses tend to be more centrally located, while those of the 'children', the Defender clans, are situated towards the landward and seaward extremities. As I describe in the next chapter, erected in the centre of the village plaza is the *peo*, the sacrificial instrument whose possession secures and signifies rights to territory. Accordingly, where Land Mother and Defenders occupy the same settlement, either both of the two

---

[11] Were it not for the fact that the English word normally denotes one who is retained rather that one who retains, *tuku* and *ana tuku* might be glossed as 'retainer(s)'.

[12] Some people wished to distinguish *ndi'i singi, mera sepu*, described as groups that guard the boundaries of a Land Mother's territory, from *ana tuku*, denoting more centrally situated Defenders who are especially obligated to protect the Mother. In general usage, however, the former phrases also refer to a particular instance of *ana tuku* (Defenders), understood as a broader category.

major ceremonial statuses associated with this object are maintained by the Mother, or the Mother retains the senior position and assigns the junior one to a Defender.

The centrality of both *peo* and Land Mother further illuminates the phrases *ine peo*, 'peo mother' and *peo pu'u*, 'trunk, source or original *peo*'. Although *peo pu'u* can also be glossed as 'original *peo*' (as opposed to a 'branch *peo*', *peo taya*, erected by a segment that has split off from the main body of a clan), both expressions specify a sacrificial instrument belonging to a Land Mother. *Ine peo* can, moreover, refer to Land Mothers themselves, conceived as possessors of the oldest *peo* and as the source of their Defenders' *peo*, while according to another interpretation, '*peo* mother' might further distinguish the seniormost of the two statuses associated with a sacrificial instrument. Since *peo* belonging to Defenders are mostly erected in separate villages, which are themselves spatially peripheral, the most central instrument in a domain is, of course, that of the oldest occupant and original owner, the group of the Land Mother.[13]

As accords with their relatively peripheral position within a territory, Keo characterize 'defending children' (*ana tuku*) as warriors and military allies who guard and maintain the boundaries of the Land Mother's domain. Employing the same parallelistic elements encountered in phrases denoting Defenders themselves, their principal task is specified as ensuring that 'the end is not broken, the edge is not torn' (*sepu ma'e betu, singi ma'e boyo*), that is, that the boundaries of the Mother's territory are not violated or transgressed. Also referring to their role as protectors of the domain of the Land Mother, Keo further describe *ana tuku* as a 'strong embankment, stout foundation' (*tuku nu'u, tuye nemo*). Relevant to this imagery is the sense of *tuye* as a fundament of stones encircling and buttressing the trunk of a *peo*. Exploiting the same imagery, Keo also describe Defenders as *tuke yeko*, meaning roughly 'support (*tuke*) for what bends or folds' (*yeko* here refers particularly to the back of the knee), and thus referring to something which prevents falling or collapse.

More elaborate phrases portray *ana tuku* as 'heads used as retaining walls, bones supporting earthen terraces' (*ulu tau tuku tuye, toko tau pale yape*), alluding to the military obligation of Defenders to safeguard the territory of their Land Mother. Should warriors of these groups be killed, the Land Mother, as the principal, is not obliged to pay a reparation (*tobo*) of the sort required when less permanent military supporters fall in battle. For their 'wounds (should) bandage themselves, (and their) blood wipe itself away' (*neka kebhe beki, ya yasi dhato*). As regards their defensive function, it is also worth noting that local

---

[13] Central and peripheral components of a single whole are further distinguished as 'mother' and 'child' where a *peo* consists of a forked post of Cassiawood (I: 2: iv). Such posts are carved in a way that preserves the remnants of an odd number of roots (three, five, or seven). Whatever the number, the most central and largest 'root', designated as the *kamu pu'u*, 'trunk, or source, root', is also called the 'mother' (*ta ine*), while the smaller, surrounding 'roots' are conceived as 'the children' (*ta ana*).

histories reveal how groups have sometimes been assigned as *ana tuku* as part of the resolution of a violent dispute between two Land Mothers, in order to ensure the peace and secure their boundaries against further violation.

While Defenders enjoy independent rights to part of a Land Mother's territory—and, especially since they possess *peo* of their own, ceremonial independence as well—the Land Mother's connection with the territory as a whole nevertheless finds expression in ritual and mystical ways. Suggesting that the mere presence of an *ine tana* ensures the well-being of the earth, Keo claim that, should a Land Mother clan desert its territory, be driven out, or become extinct, then 'the stones would have no mother, and the land would lack a father' (*watu ine mona, tana ame gédhe*), and crops would be destroyed by birds or insects. Land thus lacking a mother and father is also described as 'like a young *kuku* (*Schoutenia ovata*) tree, and a new lontar palm shoot' (*tana bhoka kuku, watu loge koli*), that is, devoid of branches and without fruit. Although plants may apparently continue to thrive, should a Land Mother leave a domain, all food derived from the land will become bitter, and drink will be sour (*ka ba'i, inu bela*).

In a more active vein, a Land Mother ensures the welfare of the land by annually planting a 'ritual garden' (*uma gua*), usually some time in October.[14] After determining that the rainy season is near, partly by observing the evening rising of the Pleiades (*ko*), the leader of the *ine tana* clan prepares a tiny plot, just a metre or two square. Dividing the area into seven sections or terraces (*yape*), he plants a variety of crops—including rice, maize, millet, and Job's tears—and in the central section (*yape kisa*) erects a stake. The crops are conceived as the share for birds and other pests, which should then spare the produce of other fields. For this reason, it is of no consequence if the plants do not thrive, and once planted no care is taken to promote their growth (cf. Fontijne 1940, who describes similar practices in southeastern Nage). Only after the Land Mother has prepared a ritual garden may regular fields be planted, with cultivators belonging to the Land Mother clan preceding all the others.

Although one or two people still plant *uma gua*, the custom has now largely fallen into disuse. To what extent secondary landowners, that is, Defenders who are recognized as Land Mothers by yet later arrivals, also plant ritual gardens is no longer clear. Some, however, claim to do so, or to have done so in the past, planting the tiny plots directly after the leader of the principal Land Mother clan has planted the principal ritual garden (see II: 1, 5, 6, regarding the clans Yoga, Sina, Obo, Tongo, and Pata). Should anyone plant out of turn, that is, before one's Land Mother has planted, he can be required to provide a pig which is then slaughtered as part of a compensatory rite.

---

[14] *Gua* variously means 'rite, ceremony', 'custom', or 'prohibition, a taboo observed by a specific group'. In regard to ritual, it may especially refer to calendrical or life cycle rites (Forth 1998: 295).

Keo similarly conceive of collective buffalo sacrificing (*pébha*) as ensuring the well-being of the land, particularly by way of the blood that falls and thus 'washes the earth' (*basa tana*). Especially important in this regard are sacrifices performed at the *peo* of the Land Mother, to which all Defenders can be called upon to contribute. At the same time, Defenders slaughter, to the same effect, at their own *peo*. Inasmuch as Defenders are primarily conceived as providing military and political support, while Land Mothers maintain the land primarily in ritual and mystical ways, the contrast of *ine tana* and *ana tuku* is the closest one comes to a division of spiritual and temporal power among Keo. Yet from this it should not be inferred that the Land Mothers are specifically or exclusively religious figures; nor are they in any sense politically subordinate to their Defenders. In addition, the contrast is obviously a relative one, as Defenders can be Land Mothers in relation to Defenders of their own. Indeed, Keo social order does not admit a division of religious and worldly authority between discrete groups, as was indicated in the Introduction with regard to the paired statuses associated with a *peo*.

As detailed in later chapters, transferring independent rights to land was often accompanied by a transfer of women in marriage. In this way the status of Defender, or 'defending child' (*ana tuku*), frequently coincides with that of 'wife-taker' (*ana weta*), and the position of Land Mother—or '(original) owner of the land' (*moi tana*)—with the affinal status of 'wife-giver' (*moi ga'e*). But while the Ga'e siblings, especially, are often represented as primal wife-givers as well as major Land Mothers, affinal connection is by no means exclusive to *ine tana* and *ana tuku*. Nor, indeed, are the latter always affinal allies. At present, the contracting of marriages is largely independent of relations of occupational precedence within shared territories; and in a few instances, rather than 'wife-givers', Land Mothers have for a considerable time been related as 'wife-takers' to their Defenders.

Nevertheless, in regard to conceptual content, the two relations remain closely identified. As I show later, wife-givers are intimately associated with the category *pu'u* ('trunk, origin, source'). Just as the sacrificial instrument of the Land Mother—the 'peo mother' (*ine peo*) or 'trunk peo' (*peo pu'u*)—is considered the 'source' of all other *peo* within a domain, so *ine tana* similarly denotes a 'source' in relation to groups classified as *ana tuku*. One therefore encounters considerable overlap between three categorical contrasts, pertaining respectively to territorial subordination and subsumption, affinal relationship, and distinctions conceived in an idiom of biological growth. A further point of similarity lies in the encompassing nature of the senior term in each case. In the Keo idiom, wife-takers are not only conceived as a part of the wife-giving group; they 'descend' (*poro*) from them as well. In the same way, just as a 'tip' (*lobo*) grows out and forms an extension of a 'trunk' (*pu'u*), so the territory of a Defender clan, regardless of its affinal status, remains comprised in the wider territory of the Land Mother.

How precisely these category pairs have coincided in given historical instances, jointly informing particular social, territorial, and ceremonial formations, is reviewed in later chapters. In considering the spatial framework in which these relations are realized, attention must first be given to the organization of villages.

2

Localized Unities and Dualities

Although the relation of Land Mother and Defender involves spiritual and
political links between groups often resident in separate settlements, in most
respects the largest unit of social and ceremonial action is the village (*nua* or,
in parallelistic form, *nua ola*).[1] Villages are also the most inclusive social and
territorial units that Keo distinguish by proper name.

Forming the centre of a wider territory that includes subordinate and derivative hamlets (*bo'a*), a village is most clearly defined by the possession of a
sacrificial tree, post, or column (*peo*) as well as several complementary ritual
structures. In contrast, hamlets lack these objects. Possession of a *peo*, in
particular, is crucial not only to the ceremonial integrity of a village but to its
political and territorial independence as well. For it is only by sacrificing water
buffalo at the *peo* that residents periodically reaffirm their rights to land within
the village territory. While much of what follows concerns the form of settlements, it should therefore be kept in mind that, as much as anything, a village
is defined by an activity, namely, sacrificing.

1. Villages (nua)

Throughout western Keo, major residential sites are typically located atop long
ridges or spurs that extend from the lower slopes of the volcano Ebu Lobo and
other, surrounding peaks. Beneath these lie cultivated lands, pasturing areas,
and forests exploited by villagers. The need for defence in precolonial times is
the reason Keo most commonly give for siting settlements in relatively elevated
places. During the twentieth century, a number of villages occupying the tops
of hills or cliffs relocated to lower-lying and hence more accessible sites,
usually closer to roads. Although encouraged to do so by colonial and later
national governments, such movement is, however, largely continuous with a
traditional pattern of shifting settlement.

Genealogies and local histories reveal how, after occupying a site for several
generations, a whole village will commonly move to a new site, often not far
from the earlier location. Keo mention several reasons for such moves. Some are
attributed to military defeat. Others appear connected with the requirements of

---

[1] *Ola* has the more general meaning of 'place, location', as well as several other uses. The word *one*, meaning
'inside, interior' and 'home, homeland, place of derivation' is contextually synonymous with *nua*. The former settlements named Nua Bale and Nua Bajo, and the present village of Keo Bélo, are thus alternatively called One Bale, One
Bajo, and One Keo.

swidden cultivation. Illness and other misfortune, usually interpreted as reflecting the opposition of local spiritual forces, are cited in yet other instances. For example, several traditions refer to invasions of caterpillars (*ngota wika*; *wika*, 'to drive out, expel') that rendered villages uninhabitable (II: 1: vi; 2: i; 4: iii).

Most village histories record three or four former locations of a *nua*. Frequently, local migration has resulted in previously separate settlements combining to form new, more complex wholes. At present, nearly all Keo villages contain two or more clans (*suku*). Virtually all multi-clan villages reflect this process of combination, rather than an internal segmentation of single village populations. Where an entire village migrates to a previously uninhabited site, villagers often retain the original village name. Otherwise, they will adopt a new name, typically one describing physical or other features of the new site. Similarly, when an immigrant group becomes incorporated into another, pre-existing village, it commonly retains the name of its former village as its clan name. Whatever name is used, the old village is distinguished as the immigrants' *nua tenge*, their 'original' or 'true' village. In contrast, *nua olo* (*olo* 'old') describes a village that has moved entirely to form a 'new village' (*nua muri*) occupying a different site but often bearing the same name.

If a *nua* is the centre of a territory usually inhabited by two or more co-resident clans, the centre of a *nua* is the *peo*, the sacrificial post or other instrument erected, or 'planted' (*toni*), in the middle of the village plaza (*kisa nua*). Equally exclusive to villages are 'houses' (*sa'o*), relatively permanent residential structures arranged in two rows placed either side of the central plaza. Apart from sharing ownership of the *peo*, resident clans usually possess two or more houses within a village. Stressing the importance of houses as more than practical habitations—and addressing the fact that many people spend most of their time away from village houses—one man pointed out that having a house in a village serves as a visible sign (BI *lambang*) of permanent rights within a village territory. While the point is well taken, land tenure in Keo is corporately exercised neither by villages nor by the occupants of individual houses, but by component clans and, in more specific ways, by divisions (*ngapi*) of these clans which are usually more inclusive than single houses (I: 3: ii). Keo often describe all groups sharing a single village as the collective owners of sacrificial structures (*peo*) and ceremonial buildings (*nde yenda*). But this too requires qualification, as we shall see later.

More elaborately designated as *wawi wodhi, manu kae* '(place where) pigs root and fowls scratch', the space behind rows of village houses (*la'e sa'o*) is ordinarily called the *biri* (roughly 'outside') or *logo* ('back'). Formerly, Keo would site granaries (*bo*) in this area. In contrast to the traditional practice of placing hearths inside houses, it is now more common to build structures serving as separate kitchens behind or beside village residences, or to construct a new house in front of an old one, which then becomes the kitchen. Marked by a pile of stones, graves (*yate*), too, are located behind rows of village houses, though some are built in the spaces between adjacent buildings. Where graves are placed in the village plaza, directly in front of associated houses (*mewa sa'o*), these will belong only to the most prominent of deceased villagers (see Plate 13).

Whereas, in the past, villages were often enclosed by walls (Weber 1890: 21), nowadays they are less clearly bounded. Although paths and main entrances located at the two shorter sides are plainly visible, a village is more readily identified as a collection of houses arranged either side of a central sacrificial instrument. Roughly rectangular in shape, the shorter sides, or extremities, are designated as the 'head' (*ulu*) and 'tail' (*éko*). Since a village is normally disposed on a slope, or at any rate with one extremity pointing approximately towards the volcano Ebu Lobo or another peak, the head of a *nua* is the part disposed *réta*, 'up', 'upstream' or 'landward'. Accordingly, the tail is always *lau*, 'down', 'downstream' or 'seaward'. Alternative terms for 'up' and 'down' in this context are *réle* and *rili* (cf. Forth 1991*a*: 140).

Coinciding with a secondary axis, the two longer sides of a village—and thus the two rows of houses placed either side of the plaza—are disposed *mena* and *rale* (see Fig. 1). Reckoned from a position facing *réta* ('landward'), or towards the 'head', these are general terms of direction glossable as 'towards the right' and 'towards the left' respectively. Thus, the two rows of houses placed either side of the plaza are called the *padhi mena* and *padhi rale* (*padhi*, 'row, line', is sometimes substituted in this context with *bhisu*, also meaning 'corner'). Particularly outside of villages, *mena* and *rale* refer in effect to a direction proceeding around a focal peak, either to the right or left. For locations close to the coast, on the other hand, Keo apply the terms differently, using *rale* to indicate 'to the right' and *mena* to mean 'to the left', in both cases facing towards the sea.

For expository convenience, I hereafter refer to the *mena* side of a village as the right side, and the *rale* side as the left. The terms are not, however, synonymous with the usual words for 'left' (*leu*) and 'right' (*wana*). Nor are *mena* and *rale* consistently associated with the moral and symbolic values pertaining to the lateral terms. How far they might do so in specific contexts will be taken up later, in reference to the disposition of particular buildings and ritual structures. Further defining the spatial organization of villages is a second pair of coordinates, *wawo* and *au*. Translatable as 'above' and 'below', the terms distinguish parts or sections of a village in regard to their proximity to the 'head' and 'tail' ends respectively. In several instances, Wawo and Au express a diametric dualism, contrasting landward and seaward components of single villages or double settlements. The opposition can further define and distinguish social units both within and between villages, especially where *wawo* and *au* are incorporated in group names (as in the Upper and Lower—Wawo and Au—villages of Pau Lundu, or the clans Bolo Au and Bolo Wawo). The contrast of *mena* and *rale* serves a similar function, but to a lesser extent. Social contrasts within *nua*, therefore, are mostly articulated in the vertical dimension, that is, in respect of the opposition of head and tail and the landward–seaward axis. It is consistent with this that, when a village expands, Keo never build new houses behind existing ones. Instead, the settlement is extended longitudinally, in the landward or seaward direction, or the community will remove to a larger site.

In accordance with their valorization of the head/tail contrast, Keo employ *ulu éko* to specify village communities as social wholes. In formal speech, *nua* are thus named with parallelistic expressions incorporating the anatomical terms, as, for example, in Ulu Céla, Eko Bolo, the formal name of the village of Nua Nage (see Appendix 2). Combined in the same way, 'head' and 'tail' occasionally designate larger territories as well. Thus the domain of the ancestor Gewo Ga'e (II: 5) is known as Ulu Lowo Koto, Eko Ngalu Loya (Lowo Koto and Ngalu Loya name a river and a headland respectively.). *Ulu* and *éko* are similarly paired in generic expressions denoting territorial unities and associated social groups. The entire domain of a Land Mother, for example, is described as a 'large head, long tail' (*ulu mére, éko léwa*), while *ulu pulu, éko pongo* ('bundled head, bound tail') depicts a village community as a ritual and political unity.[2] Also noteworthy in this connection is *mosa ulu, laki éko*. Referring to the high-ranking leaders (*mosa laki*; see Section 6 below) of a village, the expression contrasts with *mosa tana, laki watu*, which denotes persons who own or control a larger territory—thus a Land Mother or, more generally, any party recognized as the owner of an area of land, otherwise designated as *moi tana*, 'landowner'.

Being mostly built on inclines, a Keo village typically consists of two or more terraces, called *tenda* or *yape* (or parallelistically, *yape tenda*).[3] Especially where they differ considerably in elevation, these are reinforced with stone retaining walls (*kota*), and access to adjoining terraces is provided by a sloping walkway of stones and earth called *ngi'i kojo*, literally 'crab's teeth (pincers)'. In the steepest village sites, only a pair of houses, one on either side of the village plaza, occupies a single terrace. Less accidented sites may include four or more. As earlier remarks concerning the contrast of higher and lower (*wawo* and *au*) parts of a village should suggest, a division into terraces (*yape*) sometimes coincides with a social partition, a pattern that finds its clearest expression among the Bale people of Pajo Mala, who comprise two clans named 'Higher Terrace Bale' and 'Lower Terrace Bale' (Bale Yape Wawo and Bale Yape Au, II: 2: ii). Yet by no means is this always the case. Often a single terrace

---

[2] Comparable to the first pair of phrases is *tana ghégha mére, watu légo léwa*, 'land of large extent, stone(s) of long expanse'. Although generally denoting land that is 'boundless', or so vast that its boundaries cannot be clearly defined, the phrases can contextually refer to the territory of a Land Mother before it is divided among a number of Defenders. Another expression conveying the more general sense is *tana mére manga, watu léwa jawa*. (*Manga*, 'to exist, be available', serves mostly to emphasize *mére*, 'big, large'; *jawa* can mean 'foreign, distant (place)', but its exact sense here is uncertain.)

[3] While *yape* and *tenda* are synonymous in this context, *yape* more specifically denotes a terrace or level viewed horizontally, a flat area situated below another. In contrast, *tenda* can specify a level in its vertical aspect, as in *taku tenda* 'to be wary of a ledge, the possibility of falling off a ledge'.

includes houses belonging to different clans, while in a number of villages, constructed on less accidented sites, a division into terraces is hardly apparent. All the same, there is a general notion that a single terrace should ideally be occupied by a single clan (*suku*), an arrangement reputedly more common in the past. Whatever the historical value of the assertion, it at least shows how Keo tend to conceive of clans, if not always as physical parts of villages, then at least as comparable spatial or territorial entities. Indeed, as I discuss later, the distinction of 'clan' and 'village' is somewhat relative and, particularly where both are designated with the same proper name, can tend towards practical insignificance.

In one or two instances, Keo commentators noted how the relative disposition of groups occupying higher (*wawo*) and lower (*au*), or landward and seaward, parts of a settlement was consistent with status differences between earlier and later arrivals, or senior and junior houses of a clan. This, however, has at best a situational relevance, and as often as not the opposite association obtains.

2. *Hamlets* (bo'a)

While the focal sense of *nua* is a single settlement containing a sacrificial instrument (*peo*), houses (*sa'o*), and graves, the term is also employed in slightly different senses. Sometimes Keo speak of a pair of conjoined villages, thus a double settlement, as a single *nua*. Conversely, they occasionally refer to sections of a village, exclusively occupied by separate clans, as distinct *nua*. The latter application seems always to reflect a former state of affairs in which the two sections were indeed separate villages. In local histories, *nua* is occasionally applied to former settlements that seem to have lacked sacrificial instruments. How far this usage can be attributed to the fact that the communities in question have since established themselves in villages which possess such instruments is not clear. It may, alternatively, reflect an earlier period when possession of a *peo* was not essential to the definition of a *nua*, or simply the circumstance (which seems to apply in most, if not all, cases) that the village in question is regarded as the place of origin of a clan or other grouping, now established elsewhere.

Strictly speaking, settlements that have never possessed a *peo*, and which therefore have never been ceremonially and politically independent, are called *bo'a* (hamlets). Although also bearing individual names, hamlets can be described as extensions of *nua* in so far as residents of *bo'a* always claim membership of clans possessing houses (*sa'o*) within a particular village. As this should suggest, *sa'o* refers to more than a physical dwelling and, as I demonstrate in the following chapter, is regularly employed to denote a social group whose members normally reside in two or more buildings. Most hamlets are located a short distance from their associated village. In fact, a few are immediate physical extensions of villages. In accordance with the subsidiary status of *bo'a*, no matter how large or permanent their component dwellings may be, these are not designated as *sa'o* ('houses') but rather as *kéka* ('huts, field houses'). The formal distinction of course underlines the exclusive association of *sa'o* and *nua*. In accordance with their lack of sacrificial structures, residents of *bo'a* must return to their houses in the *nua* on ceremonial occasions. Especially where villages are located close to Catholic chapels, Christian residents of hamlets commonly return to their village on Saturday afternoons, spend the night there, attend services in the morning, and return to their hamlets later in the day.

Often located closer to cultivated fields than are villages, *boa* ('hamlets') mostly consist of several dwellings occupying a single site. Where one encounters a single hut or more permanent residential structure, or maybe two, Keo tend to speak simply of *kéka* or *kéka uma* ('field huts') rather than *bo'a*, even though these sites, too, are individually named. Besides lacking *peo* and ceremonial buildings, hamlets are further distinguished from *nua* inasmuch as component dwellings need not be arranged in rows or built either side of a clearly demarcated village plaza. Whereas villages are pre-eminently ordered spaces, clearly oriented in terms of the two pairs of major direction categories (landward and seaward, and 'right' and 'left'), hamlets thus manifest a far less regular disposition. Nowadays, dwellings located near roads or paths tend to be oriented towards these thoroughfares, either facing them or being disposed perpendicularly.

More southerly villages, whose territory extends to the Sawu sea, possess what Keo generically call *ma'u* or 'coasts' (see Introduction). Included in these coastal areas are one or more seaside hamlets occupied, like other *bo'a*, by members of clans centred in the associated village. In some cases, coastal hamlets are named after their associated villages or after component clans. Thus Ma'u Keo ('coast of Keo') is linked with the village of Keo (Keo Bélo), Ma'u Wayu with the clan Wayu (now established in the village of Bo'a Ora—formerly called Wulu Wayu), and Ma'u Bajo with the clan Bajo (in Nua Nage). Members of villages other than the one recognized as the owner of a *ma'u* may reside in these coastal hamlets—as, for example, do Munde and Lui people in Ma'u Keo—while several of the largest seaside hamlets also incorporate groups of migrant Endenese seafarers.

Although coastal hamlets, like other *boa*, normally lack sacrificial instruments, an exception is found in the case of Ma'u Béna, a settlement whose unusual ritual status—and effective transformation into a *nua*—is explained in Part II (II: 6: iv). The exceptional nature of this settlement highlights another general feature of Keo residential organization. Indigenous histories indicate that hamlets (*bo'a*) do not normally develop into *nua*. As we have seen, Keo history describes new *nua* as being formed as a function of ancestral land grants to wife-takers and other Defenders. The founding of more recent villages, on the other hand, is attributed to clan fission within established settlements or, more often, to village communities moving in their entirety to new sites—some of them formerly occupied by *bo'a* that were effectively replaced in the process.

As I show later, these observations bear on the question of Keo 'descent groups'. Simply stated, villages (*nua*) are independent units that are not hierarchically related as senior and junior segments of non-localized patrilineal clans, even though, as I show in the next chapter, inhabitants of many villages recognize agnatic connections with residents of other villages.

3. Double Settlements

As noted previously, of particular interest for this study is the pattern whereby two villages (*nua*) are paired to form 'double settlements'. Although *nua* is sometimes applied to the entire settlement, the status of each member of a pair as a separate village is indicated by its possession of a separate *peo*. Inhabitants of paired villages often exploit land deriving from the territory of the same Land Mother, and may even be related as Land Mother and Defender. But whatever their relationship, the two need be no more dependent on one another, ceremonially or otherwise, than are any two other villages. Keo designate each component of a double settlement with a distinct *ulu éko* name. Only in a few instances is a name of this sort additionally applied to an entire double settlement. A more common pattern involves naming the 'head' (*ulu*) of one settlement identically to the 'tail' (*éko*) of its partner (see, e.g., II: 1, 3, 4; Appendix 2). Nevertheless, the possibility of conceiving components of a double settlement as a unity is further attested by the claim of a Keo Ondo man who described his village and the adjoining village of Nua Nage (II: 1: i–ii) as forming a single 'head and tail', even though, as he acknowledged, the pair were not designated by any single *ulu éko* name.

As the anatomical terms should suggest, a double settlement always comprises two villages located landward and seaward of one another, conjoining parts distinguishable as above and below (*mawo* and *au*; see Fig. 1). Sometimes one village directly adjoins the other, being separated only by a stone retaining wall (*kota*). In other cases a short distance, usually not more than fifty metres, intervenes between the two. Despite this variation, the pairing of villages in double settlements regularly finds expression in ordinary naming. Names such as Bolo Yoga and Pau Lundu (see Plate 1) thus denote settlements where the two terms of a compound name each designate separate villages. At the same time, an identical form of naming pertains to some single villages, where the names of two clans (for example, Kota Pau, Suga Bhoja, Wulu Wayu) designate the village as a whole. In several instances, the pattern reflects the transformation of a former double settlement into a single *nua* (for example Kate Bale, Pau Leka, Sawu Obo). But this is not invariable.

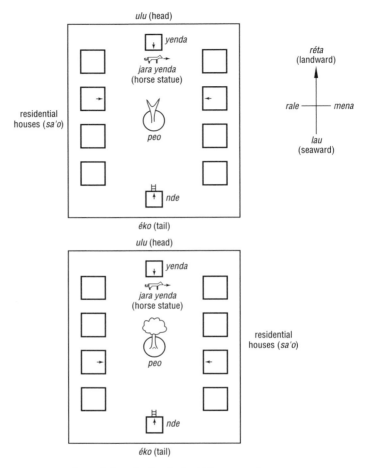

Arrows indicate the direction in which structures face.

FIG. 1. Stylized representation of a double settlement with major terms of direction

Always distinguishing the two as older and younger, Keo historical traditions explain double settlements simply with reference to an earlier established community having invited another to join it. In this way, double settlements appear always to have been constituted by combination, and never by a division of pre-existing local wholes. To formalize their pairing, the older group should transfer at least one plot of land to the invitee. A standard expression invoked in this context characterizes two such villages as becoming 'bleating goats that can hear one another, crowing cocks that answer each other' (*yongo bhe papa léle, manu kako papa walo*). Sometimes the expression is elaborated with the phrases *kuba tau tunda, bhondo tau dhogo*, 'toddy jars set in a row, baskets piled on top of one another'.

For Keo, the foregoing expressions imply an expectation that the two communities, because of their close physical proximity, will act co-operatively and provide one another with mutual assistance. Such reciprocity is most evident in the context of funerals. Traditionally, villages composing double settlements were responsible for arranging the digging of the grave when a person of the other village died. More recently, since the introduction of log or plank coffins and Christian ritual, this obligation has been transferred or extended to the provision of coffins and other materials. It must be stressed, however, that mutual assistance of this sort is not exclusive to double settlements. In some instances it applies to groups sharing a single village, while in others it involves two, or sometimes three, less proximate villages. Particularly in regard to double settlements, it should also be noted that mortuary reciprocity, like other forms of generalized mutual assistance, entails symmetrical exchange between units asymmetrically distinguished as older and younger. Hence the exchange of funerary services can hardly be considered fundamental to the constitution these local dualities.

Other phrases describing double settlements refer to common defence as a historical motive for their formation (e.g. *bani papa kapi, tego papa geu*, 'companions in bravery, equals in strength'). Again, however, Keo usage reveals additional applications, most notably in reference to outsider groups that have become incorporated into a single village and have come to share a *peo* with prior residents (an arrangement described as *peo pinda, nabe faya*, 'shared *peo*, common altar stone'). While closely associated with double settlements, even the expression referring to bleating goats and crowing cocks can be similarly employed. In fact, there may be no term or phrase that exclusively and unequivocally denotes a double settlement. One of my most knowledgeable informants argued that the expression *ulu pulu, éko pebu*, a variant of phrases recorded above (*ulu pulu, éko pongo*, 'bundled head, bound tail'), specified a double settlement whereas a similar parallelism, *ulu mogo, éko pulu* ('united head, bundled tail') described a single village. Yet other commentators claimed the two expressions were synonymous, and that both could equally refer to a single village—an interpretation consistent with the component terms of each not revealing any clear difference of sense. Following another opinion, the inhabitants of two adjoining villages can be distinguished as 'dwelling side by side, residing intermingled' (*ndi'i ipi, méra kamo*), while groups occupying the same village 'dwell as one, reside united' (*ndi'i 'ili, méra mogo*). But this distinction, too, appears not to be consistently observed in actual usage.

During the colonial period, administrators encouraged residents to transform the *nua* of some double settlements into single villages. The two clearest examples of this process concern Pajo Mala and Pau Lundu (II: 2: i; II: 1: vii; 3: iii). In Pau Lundu, ceremonial structures (*yenda* and *nde*) marking the head of the seaward village, Pau, and the tail of the landward village, Lundu, were moved. All structures were then concentrated at the landward extremity of Lundu and the seaward end of Pau, while the stone wall that separated the two *nua* was dismantled and replaced by a ramp of earth and stone (*ngi'i kojo*). Described as an effort to 'create a single village' (BI *bikin satu kampung*), a similar project was undertaken in Pajo Mala. But while the bounds of the two villages—Upper Pajo Mala and Lower Pajo Mala—were altered, the ceremonial buildings situated respectively at the tail of one village and at the head of the other, were never relocated as in Pau Lundu. In both Pau Lundu and Pajo Mala, component villages moreover retain their own *peo* to the present day, so that in this major respect, the amalgamations were not nearly complete. Similarly, while new *ulu éko* designations were coined for the projected unities (for example, Ulu Rala Oto, Eko Rita Léwa, 'Head at the motor road, Tail by the *rita* tree', for the whole of Pajo Mala; II: 2: ii), villagers yet retain separate designations of this sort when referring to the individual *nua* (for example, Ulu Kota Papa, Eko Rita Léwa, a specific reference to Lower Pajo Mala).

To some degree, this movement to merge paired villages may reflect a colonial organization of two—or, in a few cases, three—villages into a single administrative unit, designated in Malay as *kampong*, or *kepala kampong* (see Introduction). Given that *kampong* ('village') translates into Keo as *nua*, native administrators appointed to lead such units may, in other words, have been inclined to effect a physical unification concordant with an administrative one. Be that as it may, the merging of formerly separate villages, including the components of former double settlements, is a process that evidently has a long history in Keo, and certainly precedes the colonial period. What is more, in the cases mentioned, amalgamation was never completed. In fact, there is an irony here. For the two *peo* that remain standing in Pau Lundu, like the two instruments still found in Pajo Mala, derive from separate Land Mothers and thus signify attachment to different major territories—a state of affairs tending to prevent a total merging of separate sacrificial communities within a single village, though not precluding it entirely (see for example II: 6: ii, regarding clans Tongo and Pata).

4. Instruments of Sacrifice

More than a mere collection of houses, a Keo village is a social unity largely by virtue of its central sacrificial focus, the *peo*.[4] A few villages contain two such structures, erected side by side (and thus disposed *mena* and *rale*) and belonging to separate clans. Yet in these instances the unitary significance of the objects

---

[4] Although local people offered several etymological suggestions, the derivation of *peo* is obscure. The similarity of the term to *peu*, 'to tie up, bind', is interesting in view of common sacrificial practice but is perhaps not significant linguistically.

PLATE 4. Forked sacrificial post (*peo yebu*) surrounded by short upright stones in Upper Pajo Mala

is preserved in the sacrificial act, and more specifically by the requirement that whenever buffalo are slaughtered at one, animals must simultaneously be killed at the other. Standing adjacent, moreover, two such *peo* usually share a single pedestal of stones.

Western Keo villages display an interesting mixture of four kinds of *peo*. One sort is a forked post carved from the trunk of a *yebu* tree (*Cassia fistula*), variously designated as *peo yebu* ('Cassiawood peo'), *peo tu'u* ('dry peo'), or *peo mata* ('dead peo'; see Plate 4). In contrast, there are two varieties of 'living peo' (*peo muri*, *peo ngeta*). The more common is a planted *kesi* tree (perhaps *Lannea* sp.; Verheijen 1990), a durable hardwood with reddish bark and dark wood (see Plate 5). Sacrificial *kesi* trees may be the oldest sort of *peo* in this region. Many Keo identify them with the Ga'e siblings, ancestors of the oldest Land Mothers who required their Defenders (*ana tuku*) to erect *peo kesi* as well. However, since forked Cassiawood *peo* occur throughout the Nage region to the north, as well as in eastern Keo, it is also possible that *peo* of this sort preceded

PLATE 5. Sacrificial *kesi* tree (*peo kesi*) in Nua Nage

the sacrificial *kesi* trees. In this connection, it may be significant that when Keo plant *peo kesi*, they first remove all secondary branches and carve the tree to a bifurcate shape identical to that of a forked, 'dead' *peo*. Also, once the branches have grown again and the tree has become luxuriant, it must be pollarded (*toa peo*)—an act accompanied by rites involving the slaughter of a goat or pig—which in effect returns the living *peo* to its original bifurcate form (see Plate 17). Being partly a practical matter, pollarding is usually done in preparation for a buffalo sacrifice (*pébha*), so that the animals can more easily be tethered before the tree in a manner I describe below.

While most *kesi* tree *peo* stand alone in the village plaza, in a few instances they have been paired with the other kind of 'living peo', a sacrificial *dheyo* tree (BI *dadap*, *Erythrina* sp.) planted to the right or left of the first. In other cases, the two sorts of trees have been planted separately in two villages composing a double settlement. Keo explain such pairs as symbolizing an affinal alliance between an older, or 'original', wife-giving group and a more recently arrived wife-taker. Having a darker, more durable wood, the *kesi* always belongs to the wife-giver, while the *dheyo*, being softer, less durable, and possessing a light-coloured wood, belongs to the wife-taker. As we shall later see, an identification of hardness and softness with the two sorts of affines, and more generally as 'male' and 'female' qualities, finds further expression in bridewealth and counter-prestation goods, which Keo distinguish as 'hard things' (*ta ndego*) and 'soft things' (*ta meku*) respectively.

While individual cases largely bear out the local interpretation of *kesi* and *dheyo* pairings as expressions of affinal alliance, in the village of Liwo (II: 6: i) a sacrificial *dheyo* tree stands alone and, according to villagers, has always done so (see Plate 18). Belonging to the clan Liwo, and thus to the direct descendants of the ancestor Lobo Ga'e moreover, it is not the sacrificial instrument of a later arrival but, indeed, one of the original Land Mothers, albeit the youngest. Liwo's present *peo dheyo*, planted in 1988, is in fact the only such *peo* now standing in western Keo. Others that have died during the last several decades have yet to be replaced. The relationship of the clans Yoga and Bolo, as former possessors of *dheyo* and *kesi* trees respectively, and once co-resident in the now abandoned settlement of Bolo Yoga, is also noteworthy in this context. As Yoga is the older group, its ownership of an inferior *peo dheyo* does not accord with the order of arrival of the two clans. But since the older in this case is, somewhat unusually, the wife-taker, the division of sacrificial trees between the two groups is consistent with their respective affinal status.

In two other cases where a pair of affinally related clans inhabit the same village and each possesses a *peo* of its own, the two sacrificial instruments are not of *kesi* and *dheyo*. Thus, in Paga one finds two adjacent *kesi* trees (see Plate 11). Similarly, in Munde there are two sacrificial columns of stone (*peo watu*), the fourth variety of *peo* encountered in western Keo (see Plate 6).

At present, seven villages within the study area possess, or recently possessed, forked Cassiawood *peo*. By contrast, about sixteen have at one time had sacrificial trees of *kesi* or *dheyo*, while seven now possess *peo* of stone. Although the rule has been breached in at least one instance, Keo claim that owners of living *peo* should never replace them with 'dead' (or forked) *peo*, or vice versa. As this might suggest, particular kinds of sacrificial instruments are conceived as inextricably linked to particular territories and ancestral land dividers. In several instances where groups distinguished as Land Mother and Defender differ in their respective possession of living sacrificial trees (*peo muri*) and 'dead' *peo* (*peo mata*), local commentators construe the contrast as definitively reflecting this difference of status. Yet while it is sometimes 'dead' *peo* that people link with the senior position, at other times the same sort of sacrificial instrument is, on the contrary, identified with the junior status. There is thus no absolute symbolism in this regard, even though the contrast is sometimes adduced in representations of particular local hierarchies (see II: 3: vi).

Decorated with elaborate carvings and with a height of two metres or more, forked Cassiawood *peo* are constructed of a durable hardwood of deep red. In regard to colour, this type of *peo* apparently shares the same symbolism as the sacrificial *kesi* tree—red (*toyo*) being a colour generally associated with spiritual power among Keo as among Nage (Forth 1998). In other respects, though, forked posts mostly differ from other sorts of *peo*. Only a forked *peo* or, more particularly, the Cassia tree from which it is carved, is spoken of as a woman and designated with a female name (for example, Bu'e Pau, 'Maiden of Pau', Pau being the group from whose territory this tree was obtained). Accordingly, when villagers take such a tree from another group's territory, as they regularly do, they must provide a 'bridewealth' (*ngawu*) consisting of buffalo and golden ornaments, which the landowner must reciprocate with a counter-prestation. It may also be consistent with the femininity of a Cassiawood *peo* that, when the object is first brought into the village, it is ridden (*saka*) by male functionaries designated as 'trunk rider' (*saka pu'u*) and 'tip rider' (*saka lobo*). Relevant here is the use of the same word, *saka*, for sexual mounting (see Forth 1998: 283). By contrast, *kesi* or *dheyo* trunks are not 'ridden' when they are carried into a village. In Guyu Wolo (II: 3: ii), where a new *kesi* tree is customarily provided by the owners' Land Mother, the gift is reciprocated with a parang, a procedure reputedly also followed when two stone *peo* were erected at the founding of the village of Munde (II: 4: ii). Yet while a parang is always included in a bridewealth, it is uncertain how far Keo themselves recognize this sort of transaction as analogous to a marriage payment.

In several other respects as well, forked Cassiawood *peo* are associated with a more elaborate symbolism and ritual than are other kinds of sacrificial instruments. While this is not the place to detail all usages involved in erecting and inaugurating the several sorts of *peo*, it may be sufficient to note that only the *yebu* (Cassia) tree is identified with a particularly powerful kind of spirit (*ga'e bapu*) which, although partly brought under human control, remains inside the forked post when it is erected in a village. Sacrificial *kesi* trees and stone *peo* also possess such spirits. But they are said not to appear, or not to take up residence in the *peo*, until the tree or column is planted and ritually inaugurated (*reme*) by smearing it with blood. Interestingly, some people I questioned were, in this regard, even more doubtful about the spiritual property of the soft, less durable *dheyo* trees.

Prior possession of a powerful, and potentially malevolent, spirit illuminates practices required specifically when obtaining a Cassia trunk. Among these is a series of acts, conducted by seven functionaries (including the above-mentioned trunk and tip riders), which depict the acquisition of the tree as a military venture intended to counter resistance from a malign spiritual force.[5] In this connection it may also be relevant that only *peo* of Cassiawood are regularly employed in a form of ritual slaughter known as *paya* or *sése*. More characteristic of the neighbouring Nage, this involves tying buffalo to the post and allowing the beasts to run loose on the end of a long cable while subjecting them to repeated wounding (see Forth 1998). On at least one occasion, this

---

[5] Apparently contradicting other ideas, Keo speak of this action as driving out (*wika*) undesirable spirits. In contrast, I was told that when a *kesi* or *dheyo* tree is excavated no spirits are expelled. The implications of this sort of seeming inconsistency, which will be familiar to many ethnographers, is discussed with reference to very similar ideas in my study of Nage religion (1998). In much the same vein, while Keo speak of *peo yebu* as female, other ideas suggest a decidedly masculine character.

type of sacrifice is reported to have been performed with a *peo kesi* in the village of Lédho Ngule, just east of the present study area. Similarly, the people of Loka Kayo (II: 5: v) claim once to have conducted *paya* using temporarily erected bamboo poles, while conversely, people of Kota Pau (II: 3: i), who do possess a forked Cassiawood *peo*, told me they have never employed this method of slaughter. Even so, as western Keo generally speak of *paya* sacrifice as a practice exclusively connected with posts of spiritually powerful Cassiawood, the foregoing appear to be exceptions to a widely recognized pattern.

Owners of other sorts of *peo* employ another method of sacrifice, called *pébha*. The term is also applied to buffalo sacrificing in general, otherwise expressed with the compound *paya pébha*. *Pébha* involves tethering several buffalo close to a sacrificial tree or stone column with stout ropes. The ropes are so attached to the *peo* that the heads of the animals are raised ('suspended, hung up', BI *gantung*, a local gloss of *pébha*) and their necks exposed, thus further rendering them immobile and facilitating their dispatch with, ideally, a single chop to the throat (*toa*). Villages with forked posts may perform *pébha* as well, in addition to the *paya* method.

The powerful spiritual nature of the Cassia tree (*yebu*) is further imputed in another ritual peculiarity of villages that possess forked *peo*. While groups that employ living *peo* of *kesi* or *dheyo*, or columns of stone, cut the front teeth of women only after marriage, and when they become pregnant, the owners of *peo yebu* insist that this be done as soon as a woman becomes nubile. As I witnessed in 1991, the matter assumes an urgency when a new forked post is to be erected, since then all unmarried female residents must undergo the operation before the *yebu* trunk is brought into the village. Villagers who possess living sacrificial trees, by contrast, merely require that women and children avoid the *peo* once it is planted. In view of the strict general prohibition on sex with girls whose teeth remain unfiled, possibly pertinent here is a belief that only forked Cassiawood *peo* can assume the form of a human male and have intercourse with women.

This distinct character of *peo yebu* is one of several indications that Keo conceive of the forked posts as standing in opposition to their owners, and thus as requiring more ritual control. 'Living *peo*' are, on the contrary, identified with their human possessors. When a forked post becomes old and neglected, the object is thought to manifest itself as a malevolent spirit, moving about at night and endeavouring to harm villagers. Should this be determined to have occurred, villagers should consider obtaining a new *peo yebu*, a procedure that involves ritually 'killing' and burying the old one. Also, should any part of the Cassia tree from which a new forked *peo* is cut revive, then villagers consider themselves in danger of extinction. They therefore take great care when excavating the trunk in order to ensure that no living roots are left in the ground, to which end they may burn any that remain. By contrast, when a living sacrificial

PLATE 6. Sacrificial stone column (*peo watu*) in Kuyu Wulu with *ia* stone in the foreground

tree, a *kesi* or a *dheyo*, falls in a windstorm or simply withers and dies, Keo see this as a direct reflection of some undesirable state of affairs among its human owners. In this case, then, it is obviously the death of the *peo*, rather than its survival in an excessive spiritual condition, that bodes ill for human well-being.

Much of what concerns living sacrificial trees also applies to *peo* consisting of single upright stone columns, or 'stone *peo*'. In a number of instances, the columns, usually between 1.5 and two metres high, have been erected as replacements of sacrificial *kesi* trees. In one village this was done several decades ago in an attempt to cure a leading man of a persistent illness, and in another, following the destruction of a living *peo* in apparently inauspicious circumstances.[6] Residents of other villages, however, say they have always possessed stone *peo*—thus in two or three cases contradicting the express principle that

---

[6] Villagers in Wulu erected a stone *peo* early in the twentieth century to replace a sacrificial *dheyo* tree that had become so large that it could not be pollarded. In so doing, however, they claimed to have been reverting to an original practice of employing a *peo* of stone.

descendants of Ga'e siblings and their Defenders should always employ *peo kesi*, or living *peo*. Erected in some instances reputedly by the apical ancestor of the Land Mother, *peo* consisting of stone columns require the least ritual expenditure since, unlike forked Cassiawood posts and living *peo*, they never need to be replaced. In this regard one encounters various evaluations of *peo watu*. Not surprisingly, people who employ such instruments claim they are superior to sacrificial trees and forked posts, marking their owners as the earliest inhabitants of a region. Obviously, this is another contention contradicting a categorical association of the Ga'e siblings with living *peo*. In contrast, other Keo characterize stone *peo* as decidedly inferior.

In spite of differences in form, substance, and associated rites and customs, all *peo* are identical in regard to their use as sacrificial instruments essential to maintaining territorial integrity and rights to land. Occasions for sacrifice are the same for all *peo*. The most important of these are collective sacrifices inaugurating a new *peo* (*pébha reme peo*; *reme*, 'to make firm') and periodic sacrifices performed once in a number of years to celebrate and promote the fertility of the land (*pébha tua ae, uta lebo*, 'slaughtering for flowing palm wine and abundant crops'). In both instances, all groups sharing the sacrificial instrument must provide a buffalo for slaughter, lest their claims to lands connected with the *peo* be challenged. Less collective in character, other sacrifices performed at *peo* serve as the high point of critical rites conducted to alleviate illness and other affliction (*pébha rio weki*, 'slaughtering to wash the body'), to celebrate victory in land disputes (*pébha poto tana*, 'slaughtering to elevate the earth'), or to formalize the transfer of individual plots (see I: 3: i, regarding traditional possibilities of land alienation).

Peo of all sorts are commonly erected in the centre of a circular or rectangular platform of stone slabs piled to a height of a metre or more, and variously called *tuye peo*, *tuye tiko*, *kota peo*, or *ligo peo*. Larger flat stones at the top of the platform, designated as *nabe*, then serve as altars where offerings of food and drink are placed for ancestors and other spiritual beings. Where a platform is lacking, one or more altar stones are laid on the ground at the foot of the *peo*. Also surrounding a sacrificial post, tree, or stone column, one usually encounters a series of shorter upright stones, sometimes erected on top of the pedestal (see Plate 4). Described as 'supports' (*sipe*, *sipo*, or *lipi*) of the *peo*, the stones are generically designated as *ia* or *ngusu*. Just as their arrangement varies from village to village, what they signify is similarly subject to a variety of interpretations. In some settlements the stones advertise the presence of the several separate landholding groups (or 'estates', *ngapi*) that rightfully slaughter at the *peo*. Erected after a new *peo* is inaugurated, or subsequently on the occasion of another major sacrifice, the stones are then called *watu ngapi* ('estate stones'; see further I: 3: ii). Alternatively, such stones can signify a number of separate clans (*suku*) sharing the sacrificial instrument.

Whereas *peo* symbolize the unity of a group, usually an entire village, the *ia* (or *ngusu*) thus represent individual parts that make up the social whole. In addition to 'supporting' the *peo*, Keo sometimes describe the vertical stones as 'guarding' (*jaga*) the sacrificial instrument. In this regard, one man wanted to equate the stones with Defenders and the *peo* with a Land Mother. The equation is by no means exact; for although *ia* can represent a Defender clan, in some instances one of the stones surrounding the *peo* is linked with the Land Mother group itself, while in others the groups signified are not related in this way at all. Nevertheless, there is an obvious parallel between, on the one hand, a central *peo*—always most closely associated with the seniormost group in the village—and peripheral stones, and, on the other, a Land Mother clan, identified as the original owner of an entire territory, and Defender clans, spatially or conceptually linked with its peripheries. Also noteworthy is an interpretation proposed by another man, who identified the *ia* stones, as objects that support a *peo*, with the residual 'roots' (*kamu*) of a forked deadwood post, things also described as lending strength to the sacrificial post and, especially, as preventing it from 'turning'. (In this respect, it may be recalled how central and peripheral roots of forked *peo* are distinguished, like Land Mothers and Defenders, as *ine* and *ana*, or mother and children.)

Ia also refers to upright stones erected to commemorate a military victory. Sometimes placed near sacrificial posts or trees, at other times in front of village houses, the monuments are specified as *ia lawa* (cf. BI *lawan*, 'enemy') or *ia tego bani* (*tego bani*, 'strong and bold'). Keo speak of the stones, reputedly taken from the villages of defeated enemies, as signifying rights to land acquired in war. In this respect, their significance obviously converges with that of similar stones representing component groups united in the possession of a single *peo*. In fact, Keo describe all stone objects (including altar stones, or *nabe*) as 'evidence' (BI *bukti*) of territorial rights, just as they do other ceremonial objects, including of course the *peo* themselves.[7]

In a third application, *ia* refers to a similar upright stone which in some villages is planted several metres landward of the *peo*. In connection with the method of buffalo sacrifice called *pébha*, these stones are complemented by a temporary lattice of bamboo commonly called *yaka* (see Plate 14). A more complete designation is *yoka yaka*, the first term of which specifies the vertical bamboos, and the second the horizontal. Erected seaward of the *peo*, the structure is provided with as many gaps as there are buffalo to be slaughtered. By way of tethers attached to the heads of the animals, the buffalo are positioned so that they face landward, thus towards the *yaka* and *peo*, and indeed towards the 'head' of the village. Each tether is then placed through a gap in the lattice, and all are brought together and passed through the crotch, or

---

[7] Another stone classified as *ia*, which stands in the plaza of the village of Bale Wolo, commemorates the grave of the founding ancestor, who is actually buried in a former village. This, however, is an unusual usage, and may reflect other peculiarities of Bale Wolo as a settlement occupied by a branch of a single clan derived from the village of Lower Pajo Mala (II: 2: i).

central point of branching, of the sacrificial post or tree. In the case of stone *peo*, two stout bamboo poles lashed vertically or diagonally to the column of stone serve this purpose. After being passed through the *peo*, the several tethers are wound once around the *ia* (located landward of the sacrificial instrument) and then tied to a bamboo stake planted next to the upright stone. Keo call the temporary stake *madhu*, a term that is otherwise—and perhaps more accurately—applied to a permanent wooden post (cf. Ngadha *ngadhu*, referring to a structure functionally equivalent to a *peo*). Decorated with carvings in the same way as a *peo* of Cassiawood, permanent *madhu* are only employed with forked posts. Within the area of the present study, one encounters a carved post of this sort only in the village of Kota Pau; however, other examples are found further to the east.

5. *Ceremonial Buildings*

Keo conceive of *peo* as facing towards the head of the village. Thus, in *pébha*, the common manner of slaughtering described just above, the sacrificial instrument, the victim, and indeed the settlement itself (which is to say, the human community) all share a single orientation consistent with a hypothetical identification of all three. The head of the village, the landward extremity, is also the location of a special ceremonial building called *yenda* (or *sa'o yenda*; *sa'o*, 'house'). In fact, a complete village possesses two ceremonial buildings, the second one, called *nde* (or *sa'o nde*), then occupying the seaward extremity, or 'tail', of the settlement.[8] When a village is founded, the *nde* is constructed after the *yenda*, which is erected after the central *peo*. Underlining the connection between the two structures and the central sacrificial instrument, the few villages that contain two *peo* also possess two *yenda* and two *nde*, a pair of buildings of the same kind standing next to one another at either end of the settlement. At present, the clearest instance of this variant arrangement is to be seen in the village of Paga (see Plate 12). Suggesting a connection between *yenda* and *nde* and forked Cassiawood *peo* in particular, in all cases the post supporting the right front corner of each building is of the same spiritually powerful wood (*yebu*).

   As complements of the central *peo*, Keo similarly characterize the two buildings as symbolizing the possession of independent rights to land. Accordingly, groups that have *peo* but no *yenda*—for example Bale in Upper Pajo Mala and Yoga in Keo Ondo (II: 2: ii, 1: ii)—remain partly dependent, particularly in ceremonial contexts, upon related groups established in other villages. Being closely identified, even conflated, not only are the two buildings commonly named as a pair—*nde yenda*—but Keo often apply the compound

---

[8] Occasionally a residential house is built at the head or tail of a settlement. However, this seems to be done only when the extremities have never been occupied by a *yenda* or *nde*, as in the villages of Muka (II: 1: iv) and Wulu (II: 6: ii).

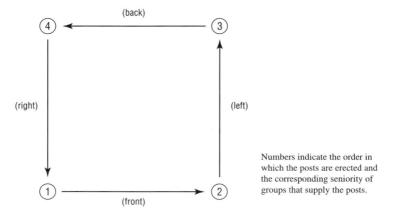

FIG. 2. Order (*gili molo*) followed in erecting posts of *yenda* and *nde*

indiscriminately, in reference to either building. Indeed, many people seemed not to know that one is specifically named *nde*, and the other *yenda*.

Like the *peo*, Keo usually consider *yenda* and *nde* as common possessions of all clans resident in a village, and only in a couple of instances are the buildings considered the exclusive possession of a component clan. Where they are owned in common, co-resident clans share in their construction, with different groups supplying different components, as well as animals for slaughter. According to a general formulation, the right-front and left-front posts of both buildings should be provided respectively by holders of the two major statuses connected with a *peo*—the trunk and tip riders of a forked *yebu* post, and the earth breaker and excavator in other cases—while the back pair should be contributed by two immediately junior estates sharing the same sacrificial instrument (see II: 1: iv, 2: ii).[9] Each member of the quartet also provides a sacrificial pig. The order of erecting the posts thus follows a spatial and temporal sequence, corresponding to a social order of precedence, locally defined as 'turning, proceeding to the right' (*gili molo* or *kago molo*; see Fig. 2).

Usually no more than two metres square, *nde* and *yenda* are both considerably smaller than residential houses and always face inwards, towards the centre of the village. Although simpler forms of the buildings include just two posts (see Plate 20), most are supported by four. More elaborate forms of both *yenda* and *nde* are decorated with carving, similar to that found on forked *peo*,

---

[9] In villages employing a forked *peo*, these posts, located at the left back and right back corners of the building, would be provided respectively by the third and fourth members of the series of seven ritual statuses involved in obtaining the sacrificial post. Named respectively as *yanda yiwu* (dialectal *yada yiwu*, '(one who) guides the masses') and *lando bépi* (*lado bépi*, 'one-sided head-dress'), the significance of similar ceremonial positions among the neighbouring Nage is discussed in Forth (1998: 281–2).

PLATE 7. Wooden horse statue (*jara yenda*) in Lower Pajo Mala

and also with plumes (*lando*) of plaited Imperata grass stuck in either end of the roof ridge. While generally similar in size and shape, the two buildings nevertheless differ in both form and function. Serving as a place to store trophy horns of water buffalo slaughtered at the *peo*, as well as pigs' jaws and goats' skulls, the *yenda* is readily distinguished by a wooden statue of a horse (*jara yenda*) set atop two posts and erected directly in front of the building (see Plate 7). The statue can be made from various woods (including *oja* (*Toona sureni*), *ta'u*, and *mesi*, both unidentified). As indicated by its ever erect penis, the horse is clearly male; the wooden stallion is also mounted (*saka*) by a male human rider in a similar state of arousal. Without embarking on a full discussion of the possible significance of the statues (see Forth 1998: 140–2; 1999), it may be noted that these unambiguously sexual features suggest some connection with fertility. Indeed, most Keo say that in order to ensure the fertility and well-being of the village, the horse and rider should face towards the rising sun, which in this part of central Flores coincides with the direction of *mena* (contextually interpretable as the 'right' side of the settlement). Yet this disposition is reversed in the far western part of the study area. Here, moreover, the *yenda* is erected at the tail of the village, or in another spot seaward of the *peo* (II: 6: i, ii).

Consistent with these several features, including the decidedly masculine

PLATE 8. Detail of the rider
and horse statue in Lower
Pajo Mala

character of buffalo sacrificing for whose product the building serves as a repository, Keo describe the *yenda* as the male counterpart of the female *nde*. Also in agreement with their gender attributes, a *nde* is usually slightly smaller than a *yenda*. A *nde* recently erected in the village of Oja (II: 5: v) furthermore includes carvings of female breasts at either side of the door, a detail also encountered in Nage cult houses (*sa'o waja*, Forth 1991*b*: 12, pl. 3). Located at the tail of the village, the *nde* is clearly distinguished by a ladder or wooden platform that provides access to the building as well as by two anthropomorphous statues, called *ana ndeo*, erected either side of the ladder. These comprise a naked male figure, in some villages carved from Cassiawood and always placed on the (heraldic) right, and a naked female who always appears on the left (see Plate 9). Since over most of the study area, the *nde* occupies the tail of the village while the statues face towards the head, this disposition links the male member of the pair with the *mena* ('right') side of the village and with what Keo determine to be the right side of the building. The female,

PLATE 9. Modernized (clothed) *ana ndeo* statues in Lower Pajo Mala

accordingly, is associated with both left and the direction called *rale* (see Fig. 1).

While Keo distinguish *yenda* and *nde* as respectively masculine and feminine, the presence of a male statue in the female building indicates how both subsume their gender opposites. Similarly, in some villages to the east, the *yenda* horse carries a female as well as a male rider, while in Lower Pajo Mala (II: 2: i), on the back of the wooden steed, one encounters a carving of a vagina conveniently placed in front of the penis of the single male rider. In addition, the withers of this horse, which the rider clutches, are exaggerated so as to resemble female breasts (see Plate 8). Keo commentators vaguely identified *ana ndeo*, the anthropomorphous statues kept in a *nde*, with the earliest, unnamed, generic male and female ancestors (cf. Arndt 1944: 159, Forth 1998: 129, regarding Lio and Nage respectively). Others compared the figures to free spirits called *nitu*, citing this identification in support of a rule against bringing them into an ordinary residential building. Simply providing a home for the *ana ndeo* is thus one discernible function of the *nde*.[10] Otherwise, a *nde* serves as a place to store 'old rice' (*pae olo*), a small portion of the harvest ritually replaced each year with a container of 'new rice' (*pae muri*) in order to ensure that a portion of the crop (which may or may not be consecrated to spiritual beings) always remains inside the building.

Although the rites are now mostly in abeyance, Keo also employ *nde* as the site of first-fruits rituals generically called *ka gua*. For this purpose some of the buildings are provided with a tiny hearth, built in the left front corner. In the past, similar rites were performed in the *nde* just prior to harvesting. Owners of ritual gardens (*uma gua*) further used the buildings for storing recovered seed, to be planted in these special plots the following year. Golden heirlooms, also, were sometimes kept inside a *nde*. When this was done, the buildings were guarded night and day by members of the lower class (see Section 7 below), special male servants called *ana susu* (*ana*, 'child, person'; *susu* is 'breast, milk' but possibly has a different sense in this context). In the rituals just mentioned, such servants were privileged to consume the first fruits of the rice harvest, and, according to some accounts, might actually take up residence inside the *nde*. Be that as it may, they were the only people allowed to enter either a *nde* or a *yenda*, as they were in fact required to do when placing trophy horns inside the latter.

Since gold and buffalo are the major forms of Keo traditional wealth, *nde* can be seen to complement *yenda* as storage places of metal valuables and trophy skulls respectively. Keo further describe both *yenda* and *nde* as places of divinity (*ga'e bapu* or *ga'e ndéwa*) and ancestral spirits, and hence as 'restricted' (*piye*) areas. Women may never enter them, lest they become infertile. Nor should persons of either sex approach the buildings idly, especially after dark. Also, if the structures are not maintained, then the welfare of villagers can suffer. At the same time, Keo do not distinguish the buildings, nor either of them from the *peo*, with reference to particular categories of spirits. On the ground in front of both *yenda* and *nde*, one usually finds a stone altar (*nabe*). As this should suggest, offerings may be placed before both sorts of buildings, as is done in rites performed to alleviate illness or other affliction within a village, or in the context of any major sacrifice at the *peo*. Yet rites incorporating food offerings are more frequently conducted inside residential houses (*sa'o*), at the foot of a special pillar (*nduke*) located in the corner of the hearth. *Nde* and *yenda*, therefore, are by no means the only traditional buildings that serve Keo as ritual sites.

Particularly for the alleviation of illness, Keo also make offerings to ancestors and the divinity (*ga'e bapu*) at special structures called *joto*.[11] Although

---

[10] Neither *nde* nor *yenda* has a sense that might illuminate their application to the two ceremonial buildings. Whether *nde* could be connected with *ndeo* is a matter for linguistic investigation, as is a possible relation between either term and *ndéwa*, 'divinity, spirit'.

[11] The meaning of *joto* is variable. Sometimes the term refers to what are otherwise called *bhaga* (see below) and other ritual structures that are supported by one or two posts and lack statuary.

they are rarely encountered at present, many villages formerly contained one or more of these. Erected before a particular house, and thus specifically serving people resident in or otherwise associated with the dwelling, a *joto* consists of a single post, about a metre in height, planted beside a flat altar stone (*nabe*). Leaning against the post is a miniature bamboo ladder with an uneven number of rungs, usually three (see Plate 16). The post itself is surmounted by a round thatched roof, giving the entire structure the appearance of an umbrella.[12]

Resembling *joto* in their simplicity, small structures supported by just two posts and provided with altar stones have recently taken the place of *nde* and *yenda* in Lower Pau Lundu (II: 3: iii), a village presently lacking these larger buildings. While the designations are somewhat variable, buildings of this sort erected at the 'tail' end of a village are called *bhaga* (also meaning 'to bar, to shut, block off'), and those at the 'head' *wondi* (see Plate 15). In Pau Lundu, men of the clan Bo Bana constructed the buildings in 1992 for the specific purpose of making offerings to counter a series of recent afflictions and for storing horns of sacrificial buffalo. The major difference between *wondi* and *bhaga* and their larger counterparts is that the former pair are not provided with *ana ndeo* or a wooden horse statue. Accordingly, *bhaga*, or *joto bhaga*, was given as a more correct term for the *nde* located in Upper Pajo Mala (II: 2: ii) since, although this building stands on four posts, it lacks anthropomorphic statuary. A similar application of *bhaga* is encountered in the village of Wulu (II: 6: ii).

Formerly some villages also included buildings called *bo piye* ('restricted granary') or, less often, *bo buti* (*buti* denotes a plaited container of pandanus leaf used for storing rice seed). As the names may suggest, these structures were exclusively employed for storing the special, ritual portion of new rice, and in this respect replaced the *nde*. Groups employing *nde* for this purpose therefore did not possess *bo piye*. Circumstances in which certain groups in the past erected buildings of the latter sort are discussed in later chapters. So, too, are yet other ritual buildings named *boge ipu* and *dhoke piye* (or *joto dhoke piye*) which occur only in the extreme western part of the area under study and which, in functional terms, appear mostly to correspond to *bo piye* and *nde* in more easterly villages (II: 6).

6. Dual Leadership

Thus far I have reviewed several major instances of social and spatial dualism. A binary principle is further instanced in Keo village leadership, especially in what might be distinguished, albeit somewhat arbitrarily, as ritual leadership.

---

[12] In this respect, the posts resemble the sacrificial structures that the Ngadha call *ngadhu* or *madhu*. In the village of Lower Pau Lundu (II: 3: iii), a *joto* is reputedly built on the site of the grave of the earliest ancestor of the clan Bo Bana, but this seems not to be a regular practice.

As a community united around a *peo*, a Keo village comprises a hierarchy of groups headed by a pair of statuses, the previously mentioned *saka pu'u* and *saka lobo*, or 'trunk rider' and 'tip rider'. While belonging to particular houses, in ceremonial contexts the statuses are represented by individual male leaders, or by appointed surrogates. In a strict sense, 'trunk rider' and 'tip rider' refer specifically to forked *yebu* posts. Yet Keo further apply the terms to a comparable pair of statuses associated with living sacrificial trees and *peo* of stone. In these cases the more accurate designations are *ta koe*, which denotes the senior partner (equated with 'trunk rider') and *ta kabhe*. Translatable respectively as 'earth breaker' and 'excavator', the names allude to the ceremonial roles of breaking the earth—the initial act when villagers plant a new *peo*—and scooping a quantity of soil from the ground broken by the senior partner. As might be expected, when a forked peo is planted the tasks are undertaken by the trunk rider and tip rider respectively; hence the distinction of *koe* and *kabhe* applies to these two positions as well.[13]

It should be noted straight away that 'earth breaker' and 'excavator' are merely convenient glosses of the Keo terms. In ordinary usage, *koe* and *kabhe*, both meaning 'to dig (the earth)', are virtually synonymous. Indeed, the contrast between the two acts is primarily a temporal one, the task of *koe* being executed first and that of *kabhe* following directly afterwards.[14] What this suggests, then, is that, rather than denoting a pair of functionaries defined by distinct and complementary actions, the two statuses serve as a kind of dual metonymy representing an entire community, comprised of numerous components (variously conceived as clans, estates, or houses) united around a single *peo*. The same applies to the statuses of 'trunk rider' and 'tip rider', although in this case the names implicate opposed physical extremities of a botanical whole standing for a sacrificial unity. While the first ceremonial contrast is defined temporally—with regard to who digs first—the second is therefore conceived more as a spatial opposition. Nevertheless, since a botanical trunk always appears before a tip, the most recently emerged extremity of a plant, a temporal distinction is implied here as well.

Whether designated as earth breaker or trunk rider, the senior partner and principal owner of a *peo* is also accorded sacrificial precedence and is thus further identified as *ta pébha wunga*, 'the first to slaughter (a buffalo)'. As all these idioms suggest, leadership in Keo, and especially ritual leadership, is expressed less with reference to individual birth order or any other sort of genealogical seniority than with regard to sacrificial practice and the instrument of sacrificial killing. In collective sacrificing, the second victim is the

---

13 The function of *koe* is more completely designated as *toke koe*. Informants glossed *toke* as 'to stick (in), implant', an act initially carried out with a parang, and 'to indicate', referring to the spot where the hole for the *peo* is to be dug. A context in which *toke* was represented as a partly separate task from *koe* is described in an account of the village of Guyu Wolo (II: 3: ii).

14 The observation equally applies to Ngadha cognates of the two terms. See also Ngadha *kabhe koe*, 'to dig a hole' (Arndt 1961: 227, s.v. *kabhe*).

animal provided by the tip rider or excavator. After the second sacrifice, the leaders of other houses then slaughter in an order determined in advance and reflecting a negotiated hierarchy founded on residential priority and agnatic seniority. In the case of forked *peo*, the series includes five other statuses which, together with the trunk and tip riders, are associated with the seven ceremonial duties entailed when obtaining a new Cassia trunk (see n. 9 above). Where the statuses of trunk and tip rider, or earth breaker and excavator, belong to separate clans, the senior position belongs to the group that first occupied the village. Where they belong to the same clan, then the senior position should be assigned to the senior house, the agnatic descendants of a forebear older than the founder of the next junior house, whose descendants become the tip rider or excavator. How relations of seniority and precedence have been worked out in particular cases is described in later chapters.

While the first of a series of sacrificers is normally the trunk rider or earth breaker (*ta koe*), a partial exception is found where the task of first breaking the ground to erect a new *peo* is assigned not to the principal owner but to the Land Mother (*ine tana*). Of eight cases, four pertained to sacrificial *kesi* trees (belonging to clans Nila, Guyu Wolo, Dhawe, and Se); two to stone *peo* (belonging to clans Béle Jawa and Welu, both in the village of Munde); and two to forked *yebu* posts (erected by the Dhawe Yoja people and the clan Néso in Wulu). Regarding the last two instances, it should be recalled that with *peo yebu*, breaking the earth is a ritual task separable from riding the trunk. Sometimes the Land Mother also formally obtains the new *peo* for the Defender, while in three instances for which I have detailed information, the Land Mother receives a parang (*topo*) in recognition of performing the initial ritual duty. Having a man of the Land Mother clan carry out the first task in planting a Defender's sacrificial instrument is, of course, consistent with the former group's ancestor having granted the latter the right to erect a separate sacrificial instrument in the first place. Yet with all other *peo* in western Keo, the Land Mother is not involved in this way, and most Defenders continue to replace sacrificial instruments quite independently of their *ine tana*. Furthermore, even where a Land Mother serves as earth breaker, it is still the principal owner, the leader or most senior segment of the Defender clan, who sacrifices first. With regard to the eight cases mentioned above, it may also be relevant that as many as seven concern Defenders resident in the same village or double settlement as the Land Mother.

Standing for an entire local society, the pairing of leaders identified as 'trunk' and 'tip' especially is comparable to the parallelistic use of 'head' and 'tail' (*ulu* and *éko*) to refer to an entire village or more inclusive territory. At the same time, it is particularly the senior member of the pair—the trunk rider or earth breaker—who Keo identify with the social whole, and who therefore encompasses the entire series of sacrificial agents articulating the internal hierarchy of a territorial unity. As the overall leader of a village, the trunk rider is thus designated as the one who 'calls the head, summons the tail' (*wuku ulu, énga éko*). Suggesting an association with both extremities of the village, the expression also recalls how 'trunk' encompasses 'tip' in Keo representations, a matter to which I give more attention later on.

Although largely defined in ritual terms, the status of trunk rider or earth breaker (where the second task is not assigned to a Land Mother) is the closest one comes among Keo to a traditional position of village headman. Where a village comprises a single clan, the position moreover coincides with that of clan headman. On the other hand, when two or more clans share a village, and hence, usually, a single *peo*, these groups and their headmen exercise a high degree of autonomy; and the authority of the trunk rider is then largely confined to ceremonial matters.

Indeed, in the traditional order of Keo society political and economic leadership is only indirectly connected with formal positions associated with the *peo* or precedence in ritual matters. In most contexts authority is exercised by the *mosa laki*, a formally endogamous yet rather loosely defined group of wealthy and respected male elders, often described by Indonesian-speaking Keo as 'nobility' (BI *bangsawan*).[15] To be sure, trunk riders and tip riders, or earth breakers and excavators, should always be *mosa laki*, and are normally counted among the leading members of the category within a given village. In order to maintain their positions, therefore, it is essential that occupants of the named ritual statuses command sufficient wealth, particularly in sacrificial animals. Nevertheless, people identified as *mosa laki* are far more numerous than are the ritual offices. Also, while Keo characterize the latter as ascribed on the basis of agnatic succession, political and economic prominence—and hence a major place among *mosa laki* on these grounds—is often largely achieved.

Partly because the term has a largely attributive ring, it is doubtful how far *mosa laki* denotes a formal social rank. What is clear is that the category forms a mutually exclusive contrast with *yo'o*, a term denoting slaves—war captives and their descendants—as well as subordinates better described as hereditary retainers.[16] Since slavery is now outlawed, the distinction of course no longer has legal force; yet it is one that in various ways continues to be recognized by Keo. For present purposes, we should particularly note that *yo'o* are still not accorded independent rights to land, nor, as this should suggest, are they allowed to sacrifice buffalo at the *peo*. Attesting to yet another dualistic feature of traditional social order, Keo strictly speaking recognize no middle rank. A category named *uta tua* ('vegetables (and) palm wine') comprises poorer people disparagingly characterized as living only to eat and drink. Drawing on a

---

[15] Apparently cognate with words in other Indonesian languages meaning 'male, masculine', and 'husband', *laki* can be glossed as 'brave, bold', and 'noble'. *Mosa*, on the other hand, denotes adult males of large animals, including buffalo, horses, and pigs.

[16] *Yo'o* (cf. Nage *ho'o*) may be related to *co'o* or *so'o*, 'small'. Euphemistic expressions for slaves include *ana ebu*, a term comprising the words for 'child' and 'grandchild' which can also mean 'descendant', and *ana rale tana* (see I: 4: iv).

contrast of meat and less valued, mundane foods (generically designated as *uta*), Keo further describe them as persons who do not regularly sacrifice or properly contribute to other rituals, even though they have the right to do so. In these respects, *uta tua* obviously diverge from the model of the *mosa laki*, the principal sacrificers, and ceremonial as well as political leaders. In the same context it seems more than a coincidence that *mosa* denotes large male animals, including bull buffalo, which are the sort preferred, if not always required, as sacrificial victims. Yet, even though their life-style may resemble that of slaves, *uta tua* are not *yo'o*. Formally, they are classifiable as members of the upper rank, albeit marginal ones.

Partly by way of the dietary metaphor, the foregoing contrasts conceptually locate *mosa laki*—or the category as ideally conceived—in the centre of villages, the place of sacrificial posts, trees, and stone columns, and hence the *uta tua* in the hamlets and fields, the locus of subsistence activities. Being completely subordinated to higher-ranking members of the clans and houses into which they are inducted, *yo'o* traditionally played no part at all in the ceremonial order centred on sacrifice and the *peo*. It should be clear that the hierarchical order internal to Keo villages and articulated by sacrificing buffalo bears little relation to the binary division of ranks, since the sacrificial order concerns only the upper rank. As I later show, this order pertains, moreover, to groups defined as 'houses' (*sa'o*), or in another aspect as 'estates' (*ngapi*), and as such is distinct from a stratification of society based on wealth and political standing that ultimately applies to individuals. In so far as I continue to speak of hierarchy, I therefore use the term in a sense approaching Dumont's, referring to an order of ritual inequality which, while not completely divorced from economic realities, is not directly defined by them.

7. Sacrificing and the Articulation of Local Communities

While Keo spend most of their time in fields and hamlets, the village (*nua*) remains the centre of ritual activity and especially sacrifice. The sacrificing of water buffalo, in particular, is central to the *nua*, not just conceptually but also materially, as an activity embodied in the *peo*. Organizationally as well, buffalo sacrifice serves to articulate and reinforce internal social divisions—the clans, estates, and houses—that compose a village. It does so because, as Keo themselves aver, sacrificing as a performative activity confirms rights to land and membership of land-holding groups. Referring to a recent decline in sacrificing, owing in large measure to other, newer demands on water buffalo, Keo further claim that, if people sacrificed more regularly, the numerous current disputes over land—which they judge to be excessive by a more traditional standard—would be significantly reduced or disappear. By the same token, parties claiming ownership of land have an obligation to contribute buffalo to collective sacrifices. Keo emphasize the principle to the extent of arguing that anyone who fails to fulfil this obligation can lose such rights, particularly if another is able to substantiate a competing claim by sacrificing in his place.

The last point mostly refers to sacrifices formerly conducted at a given *peo* once every ten to twelve years (according to local estimates) and designated as *pébha tua ae, uta lebo*, 'slaughtering for flowing palm wine and abundant crops'. Further specified as *pébha nai ngapi*, 'slaughtering estate by estate', the periodic sacrifices require the participation of all groups connected to a single *peo*. In this way, these several collectivities in effect constitute or reconstitute themselves, just as they bring about a revival of the whole *nua*. Yet despite expressions of unity, this whole is always a hierarchical one. By way of the sacrificial sequence among groups sharing a single *peo*, Keo express and affirm an order which ultimately refers back to relations of territorial and genealogical precedence. The nature of the collectivities thus ordered forms the subject of the following chapter.

3

Clans, Estates, and Houses

Keo conceive of relations among clans (*suku*) and villages (*nua*) largely as relations among male ancestors. As noted, recipients of territory granted by original Land Mothers were frequently male affines, husbands of female relatives, who then founded villages and erected sacrificial instruments of their own. In this way, their children and descendants formally established themselves as separate clans. Hence clans have their origin in, or as, villages. In the course of time, however, settlements have split, moved, and merged with others, so that at present a single village can comprise two or more clans.

Of the twenty-eight villages described in Part II, twenty-four (or 85.7 per cent) contain two or more clans. The largest number is five clans, a total found in just four villages (14.3 per cent). As for the rest, over 35 per cent include just two clans, 25 per cent have three, while the remaining 11 per cent have four clans. As regards the four *nua* comprised of a single clan, it should be remarked that three are found in the extreme eastern part of the study area, and that this pattern is usual even further to the east.

Just as clans residing in the same village periodically reaffirm rights to portions of the village territory by sacrificing buffalo so, by fulfilling obligations to contribute to sacrificial rituals, individuals (or, more exactly, heads of families) are able to confirm their membership of corporate land-holding groups, both clans and divisions of clans (*ngapi*). Belonging to these groups thus incurs obligations which, if not fulfilled, can place membership in question. Clanship is partly an ascribed status inasmuch as children formally belong to the clan of one of their parents, usually the father. Yet as already indicated, clanship needs continuous ritual affirmation, particularly in so far as it is a matter of rights to land.

1. Land Tenure

As populations have expanded and groups ramified, the majority of Keo clans have divided their lands into social units here called 'estates' (*ngapi*). Exercising land rights largely independently of other divisions of the same named clan, separate estates have arisen in part through internal segmentation. Yet genealogies also reveal instances where new estates have emerged from formal adoption and the incorporation of outsiders. In this, as in other respects documented below, Keo clans can be characterized as possessing a modular structure, based as much on processes of combination as on division within existing wholes.

While people gain access to agricultural and other lands by virtue of birth into corporate clans and estates—or, in the case of women, by marrying into them—in precolonial times as well parcels could be transferred between individuals through purchase, in discharging debts, and in payment of fines and reparations.[1] To a degree, therefore, Keo treat land as an alienable good, as well as the hereditary property of notionally permanent human groups. In principle, purchased land (*tana beta, watu geti*; *beta*, 'to buy', 'to sever'; *geti*, 'to break up, tear', 'to take away, transfer to another') should be kept separate from corporately held clan land, designated simply as *tana suku* or *tana pu'u peo* (see Section 3 below). Keo thus assert that an individual may freely dispose only of land he has himself acquired through purchase or otherwise. Hereditary clan land, by contrast, can never be sold. Nevertheless, it may be assumed that, in the course of time, individually owned land gradually passes into collective possession. Conversely, individually owned land, or much of it, would appear to have its origin in territory which at one time was collectively held by some larger group.

Purchase, either from Land Mother clans or their Defenders, is also the means by which clans deriving from more recent immigrants have obtained permanent title to lands. As mentioned earlier, land can also pass between clans when small gifts of one or more plots accompany invitations to join the donor, in either a single or double settlement. Often, land obtained by purchase is acquired from more than one previous owner, so that clan territories can comprise an amalgam of plots derived from several sources. Since older clans, established at the original division of lands, have often, through various means, similarly expanded their original territories, this situation—which parallels the composite, modular character of clans noted above—is by no means peculiar to more recent immigrants.

In the past, Keo say, land was plentiful and cheap. Clan traditions describe parcels of land being exchanged for trifling values: seven chicken heads, pet monkeys, a quantity of tubers, palm gin or gunpowder, or a single buffalo. Nevertheless, these transactions conferred on purchasers full territorial rights. As accords with the double sense of *beta*, which means both 'to purchase' and 'to sever, break', buying land results in the severance of all connection with previous owners. Like formal Defenders, immigrant groups acquiring land in this way founded new villages and erected sacrificial instruments (*peo*) of their own. In the latter connection, they are however distinguished as 'breaking the earth alone, excavating by themselves' (*koe beki, kabhe dhato*). The phrases may appear to express an admirable independence; yet they also imply that neither

---

[1] Examples recorded in local histories concern land given as compensation for false accusations of witchcraft and land used as collateral on loans or as a wager. There was also a peculiar case in which a husband was required to give a parcel of land to the brother of his two wives, a pair of sisters who both gave birth to septuplets and consequently died in childbed. This transaction exemplifies a variant of mortuary payments (*tobo*), described in the next chapter (I: 4: iv).

the immigrant clan nor the land they acquire is bound to any Land Mother. *Peo* erected by such groups are similarly described as being without a 'mother'. One man—significantly, perhaps, the leader of a major Land Mother clan— even went so far as to claim that, in this circumstance, there was actually little point in erecting a *peo* or in 'washing the earth with blood'. As this last phrase refers to sacrificing buffalo for the benefit of the land, the imputation is that such shedding of blood is ineffective when the connection between the land and the Land Mother has been broken. In any case, the status of clans occupying purchased land is obviously different from, and evidently inferior to, that of Defenders who, by virtue of having been freely granted a part of a Land Mother's territory, as well as a *peo*, preserve a connection with the donor.[2]

Possessing a similar status are other immigrants who are reputed simply to have occupied part of a territory not previously brought under cultivation, and so not effectively claimed by earlier groups. Exemplified especially by clans established in the northernmost part of the domains of Lape and Gewo Ga'e (II: 1: iv; 5: ii), such groups are described as having 'chopped down thick forest, hacked through ancient vines' (*pogo kaju tébe, yota are una*). As neither the land nor their sacrificial instruments were formally granted by a Land Mother, these clans as well are not fully recognized as Defenders (*ana tuku*). All the same, employing the term in a looser sense, Keo sometimes describe them as such, in relation to the Land Mother notionally holding dominion over the wider territory in which their lands are situated (see I: 1: iii).

Similar, yet distinct from original land grants made by Land Mothers to Defenders, are gifts of one or more plots sometimes made to wife-takers, or more precisely to a bride and her husband. Keo designate such land as *tana ka tuka*, or 'belly food land' (cf. Nage *tana tuka foko*, 'belly and throat land'). Named after the woman given in marriage (see, for example, Tana Tuwa, 'Tuwa's land'; Kuyu Wulu, 'Pasture of Wulu'), the phrases imply that a wife-giver, or wife's father, provides this land in order that the couple may sustain themselves. Since land is given in this way only when bridewealth is paid, *tana ka tuka* normally becomes an inalienable possession of the husband's group. Yet it does so only so long as his children and descendants continue to fulfil obligations to the wife-giver, or, as Keo say, so long as the wife-taker continues to provide the wife-giver with 'palm wine and fowls'. If they do not do so, or if wife-takers should abandon the land, then the wife-giver may demand its return.

Actually, there was some disagreement on this point. Several people claimed that, because the donors are bound by oath never to take the land back, *tana ka tuka* should never be reclaimed. This opinion, however, appears to conflate land given as a marriage prestation with original grants made by Land Mothers

---

[2] Purchasers, too, may contribute animals for slaughter at the *peo* of a Land Mother. However, they do so as invited guests, and not as a matter of right or obligation.

to Defenders. Although original Defenders were often wife-takers as well, Keo generally distinguish these ancient grants from marital transfers of land that continue to be given in the present day. It is important to recall that Keo locate the former, as part of a permanent and irreversible division of territory, in a formative era that is definitely past, when new clans and villages were founded and new sacrificial instruments were erected. On the other hand, it is quite possible that land ceded long ago to wife-taking Defenders originated in something like 'belly food land' which in the course of time has acquired a different interpretation. By no means all marriages involve prestations of land by wife-givers. The practice is also described as less common nowadays, owing to a present shortage of land. Where *tana ka tuka* is provided, its purpose is evidently to ensure that recipients, as hereditary wife-takers, have the means to keep supporting the donors in subsequent generations, for example, by assisting them in raising bridewealth for their own sons and grandsons.

Outsiders may acquire temporary usufruct of land. If this is corporate clan land, the owner should seek the approval of other members of his estate (*ngapi*). In return for land use, once every five years cultivators should provide a buffalo, or a large goat or pig, the size of the animal depending on the area cultivated. The payment, called *fedho*, can be waived in certain circumstances, and is not required when land is cultivated by members of other estates within the same clan. From time to time, owners might also ask tenants to assist with small animals, palm wine, or other foodstuffs on ritual occasions. In this way, outsiders may enjoy indefinite usufruct, until owners, with sufficient notice, decide to resume cultivating the land themselves.

In times past, clans were able to augment their territory through warfare. Keo tend to speak of particular clans, rather than villages or groups smaller than clans, as antagonists in former wars, though this may simply reflect the historical process whereby what are now named clans, usually components of multi-clan settlements, were once independent village populations bearing the same name (see Section 3 below). All divisions of a clan had to concur before military action could be undertaken. Often, several clans—including, of course, Land Mothers and their Defenders—united against a common enemy. In addition, individual men of unaffiliated clans, known for their martial or strategic skills, might be specially engaged as warriors or military commanders, and it was once common practice to hire Lionese mercenaries as well.

Sometimes, victors would return a portion of conquered lands to the original owner as a reconciliatory gesture. Otherwise, land won in war was divided among a clan's constituent estates or among a number of allied clans. Sometimes the resolution of violent conflict has resulted in other modifications of land tenure arrangements. In several cases two clans occupying adjoining territories have effectively dissolved their common boundary by allowing members unrestricted usufruct within each other's territories as part of an ongoing relation of mutual assistance sometimes included in the category of 'land siblingship' (see II: 4: i). Employing a standard idiom, Keo describe this sort of territorial pairing as 'bounding the land (only) with stems of maize and stalks of rice' (*bhondo wai toko yolo, lange wai ku pae*). The component groups are also depicted as jointly possessing 'a single clump of earth, a single piece of stone' (*tana a bhabha, watu a li'e*) or 'shared land, common stone' (*tana pinda, watu faya*). As local commentators explained, members of the two clans should refrain from 'revealing borders, searching for boundaries' (*nono bhondo, gae lange*) and, within their combined territories, should define fields only by planting annual crops—a notion that implicates the contrary practice of planting coconut and areca palms (*nio* and *yeu*) in order to mark a permanent partition of lands among different clans or different estates of a single clan. Indeed, it is claimed that if palms were planted to mark boundaries, the trees would not thrive. As this may suggest, the principle of completely unrestricted access actually applies only to lands of two clans that have yet to be divided among component estates, though members of the other clan may be granted usufruct of divided land as well.

What appears most remarkable about these arrangements is that, with one possible exception, the territories thus combined belong to the domains of different Land Mothers. In fact, in all instances the two groups continue to maintain separate villages, and hence separate *peo*, thereby preserving their independence in ceremonial affairs. Various circumstances that have led to a dualistic sharing of rights to land by otherwise distinct clans are documented in village studies included in Part II.

Consistent with the maintenance of distinct clan identities even when land boundaries are dissolved or obscured, Keo society reveals a pronounced preference for preserving clans and their component estates as distinct territorial, and at the same time sacrificial, entities. When a group dies out, therefore, rather than allowing its lands and moveable property to be taken over by outsiders, an heir will be adopted from another clan—usually, and by preference, a sister's son or another male from a wife-taking group (I: 5: iv). As a possible entailment of this principle, an individual may acquire permanent rights to lands belonging to the territories of two or more clans, and thereby in effect claim membership of more than one clan, a matter I explore later on.

2. *Estates* (ngapi)

Before dealing further with clans, it is useful to describe the component collectivities that Keo call *ngapi*. In view of their significance for land tenure and connected ritual activities, these I have chosen to call 'estates'. From another perspective, clans can also be seen as comprising a number of 'houses' (*sa'o*). The social referents of this term are described in Section 4 below.

Considered as a social group, an estate consists of several male family heads, mostly close agnates, holding permanent, hereditary rights to a number of plots of land (*ngoya*). Assigned to particular families (or, in one sense, 'houses'), plots constitute shares in an estate distinguished as *ngia*, a term also meaning 'face'—and, as was explicitly pointed out in this context, 'responsibility'. Some informants described *ngia* and *ngapi* as synonyms which, when compounded as *ngapi ngia*, refer to what is otherwise simply called *ngapi*. Other terms denoting individual shares of agricultural land are *bhaco*, 'plate, eating vessel', and *ku* (or *ku tana*, 'parcel of land'). Bounded by large trees or other natural objects, the area of a plot is variable, though Keo describe one to two hectares as a usual size.

Keo name plots with reference to natural features or a historical or cultural association of the place. In contrast, whole estates are usually named after male ancestors, that is, as the *ngapi* of a particular forebear who was accorded partially independent title to part of a clan's land. Very occasionally, estates are named after women. As accords with local descriptions of these as wives whose names happen to have survived in public memory longer than those of their husbands, such designations appear to reflect the practice whereby widows hold trusteeship of their husband's estate until infant sons become adults.[3] Whether they might alternatively reflect the attainment of separate *ngapi* status by the children of uxorilocally married men (I: 4: iii) is doubtful, since such children are normally inducted into the estate group of their mother's brother.

The territory of an estate forms part of the total territory of a given clan, permanently assigned to one of its constituent segments. Referring to the rule that one may plant palms and other perennials only on such hereditary land, the territory of an estate (*tana ngapi*) is designated as 'land surrounded by coconut trees, encircled by areca palms' (*tana nio tiko, yeu tako*), an expression that can further denote the entirety of a clan's lands that have been divided among constituent estates. Several clans are described as still possessing some territory not assigned to any component estate—land which may thus be used by any clan member—but most clan territory is now completely apportioned. All matters concerning the cultivation of land within an estate are decided by the *ngapi* under the leadership of its most senior male member. As noted, in consultation with other estate members, a man may allow an outsider usufruct of a plot. Tenants may cultivate tubers and vegetables, as well as rice, maize, and other cereals, and they may also be allowed to tap palms growing at the edge of fields. But in accordance with the above-mentioned phrases designating hereditary estate land, only the owners may plant productive trees such as coconut and areca palms. It perhaps goes without saying that members do not

---

[3] In such cases, Keo also speak of widows as group leaders and holders of ceremonial offices. The widow of the former leader of the clan Upper Bale was recognized as the 'trunk rider' of the new sacrificial post erected in 1991 in Upper Pajo Mala (II: 2: ii), since her eldest son was considered too young to replace his dead father. As a woman, however, she was unable actually to execute the duties of the position and on this occasion was replaced by another man of Upper Bale. This man, moreover, is inclined to described himself as the 'trunk rider'.

have the right permanently to alienate estate land, which is to say, clan land. In so far as alienation is possible, a decision to this effect could only be taken by the clan as a whole.

Stressing the hereditary nature of rights in estates, Keo commonly translate *ngapi* with BI *waris*, in the sense of 'inheritance'. In view of Arndt's gloss of the same word in Ngadha (1961: 375), *ngapi* would appear simply to denote a division of a larger whole, or a share of a limited good. Nevertheless, it is significant that informants first explained the term to me as referring to the several spaces in a bamboo lattice, or *yaka*. As mentioned in the previous chapter, at major buffalo sacrifices each estate contributes a single animal whose tether is passed through a hole in the *yaka* before it is tied to the *peo*.[4] Provided with a particular number of gaps each representing a particular estate, a *yaka* thus constitutes a vivid representation of a clan, or set of clans, comprising a specific number of *ngapi*. As also noted in the previous chapter, in some villages vertical stones called *watu ngapi*, erected around the central *peo*, present a similar image.

Nearly 40 per cent of clans consist of just two estates, while others possessing a larger number are described as originally comprising a single pair. Especially when a clan incorporates both of the major statuses linked with a *peo*, two is indeed the minimal number of component estates, since trunk rider and tip rider, or earth breaker and excavator, should always possess separate *ngapi*. Of sixty-six clans for which *ngapi* numbers could be reliably determined, 39.4 per cent had two estates, 25.75 per cent had three, while others consisted of four (seven cases), five (five cases), six (four cases), or seven (two cases). Five named clans constituted a single *ngapi*, but as this would suggest none now independently maintains a *peo*, and indeed two of these (Wani Wona and Wio; II: 5) are regularly described as estates subsumed by other named clans.

Closely connected with their significance for land tenure, estates function primarily as units of buffalo sacrifice, and it is mainly in this context that Keo speak of *ngapi*. When all members of a clan, or of several clans, come together to slaughter at a *peo*, each estate is thus obliged to provide, minimally, a single animal for *pébha nai ngapi*, 'slaughtering estate by estate'. Sacrificing is, furthermore, the arena in which Keo local communities constitute or affirm a hierarchical ordering of *ngapi*. Just as the victim contributed by the earth breaker or trunk rider is always slaughtered before buffalo belonging to other members of a clan or village, so the animal provided by the seniormost estate within a clan, the 'trunk (or stem) *ngapi*' (*ngapi pu'u*), should be dispatched before buffalo brought by other estates, which are then killed in a fixed order.

---

[4] *Ngapi* also denotes a declivity or narrow ledge on a hillside or cliff face, but this sense is probably not relevant to its use in the present context. A possible connection with *yape*, referring to a 'terrace' or 'level' within a village is sociologically interesting, but is probably not sustainable etymologically. More likely is a relationship with *kapi*, 'member of a pair, mate, accompaniment', which occurs in phrases I discuss presently in reference to connections among hereditary land, *peo*, and heirloom gold.

For this reason, the 'trunk *ngapi*' is also designated as the 'first estate' (*ngapi wunga*), while other estates are similarly designated with ordinal numbers referring both to the order in which they slaughter and to the order of their formation, largely on the basis of agnatic segmentation. *Ngapi* may be assigned specific functions in other ceremonial undertakings as well, for example, when groups sharing a common *peo* each provide one of the four posts and a sacrificial pig when erecting a *yenda* or a *nde*. (Examples pertaining to the villages of Bolo and Upper Pajo Mala are described in the first two chapters of Part II).

Where several estates compose a single clan, the seniormost is normally the one associated with the apical ancestor or the eldest of a set of brothers. Because *ngapi* composing a clan are not always related agnatically, however, inequality among estates does not always coincide with a strict genealogical seniority. Again, buffalo sacrifice provides the context in which this hierarchy is negotiated, or renegotiated. Preparing for and expediting major sacrifices can result not only in alterations to the order of slaughter. It may also entail a revision of a single clan's component estates themselves, by reassigning members or even inaugurating new estates. Accordingly, when responding to my enquiries Keo frequently had difficulty determining the number of *ngapi* within a clan or their (ancestral) names. When determinations were made, people often referred explicitly to divisions recognized and procedures followed at the last collective sacrifice (*pébha nai ngapi*). As was sometimes pointed out, since in many villages sacrificing on this scale has not been conducted for thirty or more years, how precisely clans are, or should be, divided into *ngapi* may no longer be clear. It is therefore not an exaggeration to describe estates as being constituted anew with each major buffalo kill.

In addition to sacrificial precedence, and in accordance with Keo patterns of inheritance whereby older brothers usually receive more than younger brothers, more senior estates (including of course the 'trunk *ngapi*' of a clan) normally contain more plots (*ngoya*) and so are larger than junior ones. At the same time, members of senior *ngapi* do not possess special rights to land allocated to junior estates. Thus, should they wish to cultivate fields belonging to the latter, they must seek permission like anyone else. Within estates, leadership is accorded to the most senior men. Nowadays identified with the partly Malay expression '*kepala ngapi*' ('estate headman'), it is these leaders who are mainly responsible for providing the buffalo to be killed at collective sacrifices; and it is formally in their names that the animals are slaughtered. Other adult males belonging to the same *ngapi*, that is, younger brothers or cousins of the estate leader, may augment the slaughter by providing additional animals. Distinguished by placing their tethers on either side of the trunk of the *peo* rather than through the crotch (*tali piye*) of the tree, forked post, or other object serving as the sacrificial instrument, these additional victims are then designated as *kesa boge*, '(those that) add to the meat'. The same term is applied to subordinate members of the *ngapi* themselves, or in so far as an estate can be conceived to comprise two or more houses (*sa'o*; see Section 4 below) to houses junior to that of the *ngapi* leader.[5] While it is especially wealthy estates that slaughter more than the minimal single buffalo, any man who has the means can use the occasion of a large-scale sacrifice to offer an animal on his own behalf, for example as a means of dealing with illness afflicting himself or his immediate family.

3. *Clans* (suku *or* woe)

Named groups I call clans are usually designated as *suku*, an evident borrowing from Malay. Following a common opinion, a more traditional term is *woe*, or in parallel form, *'ili woe*, words also used for 'clan' in eastern Keo, Nage, and Ngadha, and apparently more often employed in the far western part of Keo, which borders on Ngadha country.[6] When referring to particular clans, *suku* often prefixes the clan name, as for example in 'Suku Kate' or 'Suku Sawu'. Where a clan name is the same as a village name, this sort of usage then serves to distinguish the *suku* from the *nua*.

Keo historians are able to recite clan genealogies deriving all members, or at least a core of members, from a single ancestor or ancestral couple. Details of men's marriages are more often remembered than women's; the usual ratio, I would estimate, is something in the order of five to three. Following a ubiquitous pattern, apical ancestors (who in ways already indicated may themselves descend from earlier Ga'e siblings) comprise a pair of brothers, or less often, a husband and wife or a brother and sister pair. The two names are then juxtaposed, so that the second is interpreted as a 'surname' (*sabhe*) of the first—a function most often subserved at present by the mother's name. Particularly where two brothers are thus designated, as for example in the pairing Pogo Raga (II: 5), Keo genealogists regularly specify one, either the elder or the younger, as having been without issue (*ana mona*). In this way, what may be described as a binary origin is transformed into one that is effectively unitary, thus permitting a single succession. In some genealogies, male sibling pairs also appear later in the lineage, where more often than not they similarly represent founders of branches of a clan. On the other hand, where a brother and sister appear at the apex, they figure as ancestors of two distinct clans. In the second

---

[5] *Kesa boge* can include lines of co-resident wife-takers, which do not form independent estates of the wife-giving clan. Indonesian-speaking Keo nowadays often describe junior members of an estate, or houses other than that of the estate leader, as *anggota*, in the sense of 'followers' (see n. 11 below).

[6] *'Ili* generally denotes a number of things of the same kind brought together to form a palpable collectivity. In the phrase *ndi'i 'ili* (I: 1), it has the sense of '(living, residing) united, as one'. Among Nage, *'ili* is sometimes identified with BI *jenis* ('kind, species'; Forth 1995*a*). Arndt (1961: 212) partly glosses the Ngadha cognate, *cili*, as 'bush, shrub, stem' and 'things possessing a common root', thus suggesting the general idea of a collectivity sharing a single origin (or 'trunk, source', *pu'u*). Although I recorded no other locally recognized meaning of *woe*, both Nage and eastern Keo usages (P. Tule, pers. comm. 1997) suggest that the word may also mean 'to bind, wrap or wind around' and 'binding, connection'. Whether *woe* might allude to the practice of tying a number of sacrificial buffalo simultaneously or in succession to a single *peo*, although unconfirmed, remains an intriguing possibility (see I: 2: vi).

instance, the clan, though possessing a female forebear, is normally perpetuated by a son.

In standard anthropological parlance, Keo *suku* may be described as
predominantly agnatic 'descent groups'. At the same time, many clans include
genealogically unrelated outsiders, including remnants of other named clans
unable to preserve economic or political independence, which may then be
incorporated as separate estates (*ngapi*). Keo commentators sometimes spoke
of estates as existing prior to clans. This seemed to refer to the occasional
report that what are now considered clans were formerly *ngapi* of a single clan
(see, for example, the two clans of Bolo, II: 1: iv, and the two clans of Keo Bélo,
II: 4: ii), and possibly the fact that in order to function as an independent sacrificial community, a clan must comprise at least two estates. Even so, it must be
stressed that the development of clans through lineal ramification and segmentation is not typical of Keo society. Instead, the historical appearance of new
clans is usually ascribed to immigration of groups from elsewhere or, as in the
traditions of the Ga'e siblings, by wife-takers gaining recognition as separate
clans when granted territory and sacrificial instruments by wife-giving Land
Mothers. Keo clans further diverge from a strict model of unilineal descent
groups in so far as membership requires the payment of bridewealth, the children of marriages without bridewealth being incorporated into their mother's
clans. In the local idiom, 'descent' (*poro*), although an accurate translation of a
Keo category, does not refer to a relationship conferring membership of a
common unilineal group—or indeed any sort of group—but, as I explain
below, denotes a relationship between persons belonging to distinct groups,
and normally different clans.

Although 'clan' is its best single gloss, Keo in fact employ *suku* in a relative
sense. While, on the one hand, the term commonly denotes named groups
comprising a number of partly independent estates, Keo sometimes apply *suku*
to individual estates as well as to entire clans. Contextually, they also use the
term to refer to the entire population of a village, thus seemingly ignoring
named internal divisions. In several instances, named groupings described as
'clans' sharing a village with one or more other clans comprise moieties, each of
which is itself called a *suku*. Usually recognizing no agnatic connection, these
moieties are in turn composed of two or more estates. The degree of independence between the two halves is quite various. Although always sharing a
common *peo*, they sometimes function as separate clans, while in other cases
they practically form a single clan. The first possibility is exemplified by clans
Bolo Wawo and Bolo Au (II: 1: iv), and the second by the clan Bajo Léwa—a
merging of once separate groups named Bajo and Léwa (II: 1: vii).

A comparable pattern occurring at a lower level involves clans dually
composed of two originally unrelated estates (*ngapi*) recognizing different
genealogical or geographical origins. For example, clan Kota in the village of
Kota Pau comprises an 'original' (*tenge*) estate plus a later addition (II: 3: i). In

a variant of this pattern, the clan Bindi Wae consists of *suku* Bindi and Wae, a group of co-resident wife-takers originally from the village of Wae, who are now fully incorporated as an additional estate. Further contributing to the pervasive dualism of Keo social organization, where two quite separate clans residentially or otherwise form a recognized pair, Keo also occasionally represent these as a single *suku*. Thus one often hears people describing their clan, for example, as Wulu Dhaga or Koyu Yéwe, whereas in fact they specifically belong to Dhaga or Koyu, or Wulu or Yéwe.[7] Worth recalling in this connection is the formally identical method of naming settlements mentioned in the last chapter, whereby a number of villages, both past and present, are designated with the names of just two component clans (e.g. Kota Pau), a form of nomenclature that also applies to many double settlements (for example, Pau Lundu).

Several clans have segments bearing the same name localized in two or three different villages and therefore associated with separate *peo*. These, too, are designated simply as *suku*. Nowadays, Keo sometimes use Malay terms for 'branch' (*cabang* or *ranting*) to refer to residentially dispersed clan segments. In the indigenous idiom, however, 'branch' (*taya*) applies to the relation between two *peo* rather than parts of a clan, as when the sacrificial instrument of a group that has split off from another is described as an 'extended branch, spreading root' (*taya so, kamu lana*) of the older, or 'original', *peo* (*peo tenge*). Segments, or 'branches', of a clan established in different villages are not to be confused with estates (*ngapi*). Estates are components of clans (*suku*) resident in one or more houses (*sa'o*) within a single village and linked with a single *peo*; whereas each separately established clan segment itself comprises two or more estates.

Apart from the foregoing, there are several separately named clans, established in different villages, which recognize an agnatic connection to common ancestors. When these are added to identically named but residentially dispersed clan segments, it becomes clear that the majority of western Keo villages—77 per cent (twenty-four of a sample of thirty-one)—are agnatically linked by way of their component clans (see Fig. 3).[8] Sometimes Keo distinguish localized segments of clans by compounding the clan name with that of a co-resident clan. Thus Leka Yoga, for example, denotes Leka people residing with a branch of clan Yoga in the village of Keo Ondo. (Senior segments of these groups are resident respectively in Pau Leka and Kuyu Wulu, also called Bolo Yoga.) Otherwise, one may simply specify the village concerned, while in some instances the direction terms *mena* and *rale*, roughly coinciding with

---

[7] 'Wulu Dhaga' also distinguishes this group of Wulu, resident in Nua Nage (II: 1: i), from Wulu people in other villages.

[8] Nine villages (29 per cent of the thirty-one) are thus connected agnatically with one other village, seven (23 per cent) with two others, two (7 per cent) with three, five (16 per cent) with four, and one (3 per cent) with five others.

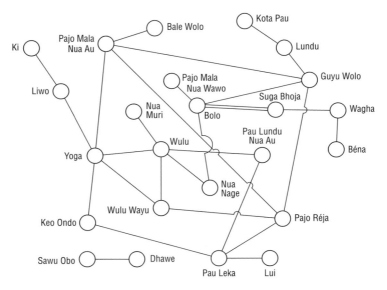

FIG. 3. Agnatic links among villages

'east' and 'west' in most of Keo, can be used to distinguish the relative locations of two villages containing groups bearing the same clan name.

Distinct from these methods of naming, several localized clans, or clan
segments, all of them junior groups in their present places of residence, are
partly designated with the name of the village, which is identical to the name
of a more senior clan. This name is then qualified with the actual clan name.
Resident with the older group, Bolo, in the village of Bolo (also called Muka),
clan Suga is thus referred to as 'Bolo Suga' (II: 1: iv). Another instance is
'Wagha Yéwe', designating the segment of clan Yéwe resident with clan Wagha
in the village of Wagha (II: 6: iii). The two compounds, of course, distinguish
these groups of Suga and Yéwe from members of the same clans resident in
other villages. Formally similar to this pattern are the names 'Pajo Kayo' and
'Pau Ngodho' (II: 2: i, 3: iii). Yet these denote subordinate clans, otherwise
known simply as Kayo and Ngodho, which are found only in the villages of
'Pajo' (actually Pajo Mala) and Pau (Lower Pau Lundu) respectively. Hence in
these cases the naming practice is more reflective of a subsumption of each by
a senior clan—an implication which is not absent in Bolo Suga or Wagha Yéwe
either. Separate from all these usages is the pattern just noted above, whereby
compounds comprising the names of two clans are applied to whole villages, or
where paired clan names (for example, Wulu Dhaga) refer to both groups
simultaneously, or as a unit.

Although otherwise operating like clans localized in a single settlement, residentially separate clans or clan segments recognizing a shared agnatic origin—and thus derivation from a single ancestral territory—are generally obliged to assist one another, especially in ritual undertakings. In the same vein, they reciprocally transfer members from one group to another when a component estate is lacking heirs. Agnatically connected clans can also call upon one another for support in land disputes, a notion evidently linked with their designation as 'land siblings' (*ka'e ari tana watu*, I: 4: i) and the division, between their ancestors, of an original common territory. In a few cases, moreover, junior segments, even ones possessing *peo* of their own, yet display a degree of ritual dependence on senior groups resident elsewhere, as I illustrate later (II: 1: ii, v; II: 2: ii).

In spite of diverse applications of the term *suku*, one can discern 'clan' as a focal sense, specifying a social group distinct from estates (*ngapi*) or villages (*nua*) and, indeed, intermediate between these. Whereas estates are usually distinguishable only by reference to founding ancestors, most clans are named in the same way as villages, for the most part with reference to trees or plants or other natural features of the landscape (see Appendix 3).

Of a sample of 73 western Keo clan names, 54 (74 per cent) bear the same name as a village or other location where the group resides or formerly resided. Of the 54 clan names, 35—thus nearly two-thirds—have geobotanical or topographical referents, or otherwise describe a feature of a settlement (see, for example, the clan Nua Muri, 'New Village', not to be confused with the present village of the same name). In contrast, only seven of the 73 clan names—less than 10 per cent—are names of ancestors. Since plant totemism is scarcely attested among Keo, it may be inferred that the possession of plant and tree names by many clans reflects their original status as names of villages, themselves named after botanically identified sites. Of 38 names designating extant villages, 25—again nearly two-thirds—can be construed as references to associated flora or other features of the location.[9] In addition, a total of 26 of the 38 village names—thus 68.5 per cent—are simultaneously the name of a clan resident in the village in question.[10]

Complementing the evidence of local histories, then, all these figures suggest that what are now clans were once villages—in some cases, perhaps,

---

[9] The 38 include names paired with others to designate villages (for example, Wulu Wayu), all of which are simultaneously clan names. Of the 25, 14 are also clan names, while a different 14 are names of plants and trees (as opposed to other landscape features). Eight of the 14 plant names denote both a village and a clan, while 9 of the clan or village names are plant names.

[10] Since the above figures refer to names, and since some villages have more than one name while others are designated with compound names, one might instead apply the foregoing analysis to a sample of thirty villages. In that case, it is found that twenty (two-thirds) of the villages have at least one name which is simultaneously the name of a component clan. With compound names, the village name comprises the names of two component clans. Of the thirty villages, moreover, twenty-three are designated with names of plants or trees (sixteen instances) or of other natural features of the landscape (seven instances). These results, therefore, do not differ significantly from those obtained when enumerating names rather than settlements.

comprising further divisions that are no longer recognized—and that they have lost their status as exclusive localized groups through a combination of fission, resulting in branches of clans becoming established in other villages, and fusion with other clans (or localized segments thereof).

An identification of clans with villages is also suggested by a tendency to represent sacrificial instruments (*peo*) as the possession of a single clan—then designated as *moi peo*, 'owner of the *peo*'—even though the instrument is commonly shared by two or more clans. In the latter case, members of this group, always the older or oldest in the village, are further described as the 'true' or 'original' (*tenge*) people (see Rosaldo 1975: 6, who records a similar usage among the Ilongot of Luzon). In a similar vein, Keo refer to land over which an entire clan, or a clan localized in a particular village, exercises corporate control as 'land at the stem of (or deriving from) the *peo*, (and from) stone monuments and altars' (*tana pu'u peo, ngusu nabe*). A comparable expression is 'land accompanied by a *peo* and altar stones, by golden ornaments and chains' (*tana kapi ne'e peo nabe, kapi ne'e wea londa*). The phrases allude mostly to the acquisition by clan ancestors of independent rights to land jointly with the right to erect a *peo* and associated stone objects. The reference to gold jewellery is partly explained by the decorative use of heirloom gold in sacrificial ritual focused on the *peo*. Like Nage (Forth 1998: 82–5), Keo speak of the possession of such objects, many of which have now disappeared owing to sale or theft, as legitimating a clan's rights to land.

Consistent with the foregoing, Keo describe junior clans that now share a *peo* with more senior co-residents as once having possessed sacrificial instruments of their own. By the same token, they further assert that, in the past, all clans (*suku*) occupied separate villages (*nua*). Whatever the historicity of these generalizations, as noted earlier it is possible, indeed likely, that separate clan identities hypothetically maintained in former villages have sometimes dissolved with the movement of village populations and their amalgamation with like groups elsewhere. It is also worth remarking that the linking of corporate clan rights with possession of a *peo*, as in the expressions given above, does not strictly require that every clan possess a sacrificial instrument of its own, but merely that clan members have the right, and indeed an obligation, to participate in sacrifices at the post, tree, or stone column erected in the village where the clan resides.

Wherever a clan is the sole or principal possessor of a *peo*, the clan headman is the person occupying the status of trunk rider or earth breaker. Similarly, where the second ceremonial status is assigned to another clan, the leader of that clan will be the tip rider or excavator. Although distinguished only by the partly Malay term *kepala suku* ('clan head'), single leaders of other clans are also recognized among Keo. In all cases, clan headmen, who generally operate as *primus inter pares* within a larger group of clan elders (*mosa laki*; I: 2: vi), are normally the most senior males of a clan's senior estate (*ngapi pu'u*) and senior house (*sa'o pu'u*). While not all clan headmen occupy specific ceremonial functions in connection with the *peo*, it is nevertheless these men who have custody over the gold heirlooms (*wea kapi peo*, 'gold paired with the *peo*', or *wea kapi ne'e tana watu*, 'gold paired with land') that Keo associate with the exercise of independent land rights.

Recognizing single leaders is thus another feature marking clans as unitary social groups. A few clans also observe special food taboos (*gua*, a term also meaning 'custom, ritual'; cf. *uma gua*, I: 1: iii). In contrast to the widespread clan taboos found among neighbouring Ngadha (Arndt 1954), however, only a minority of western Keo *suku* possess such prohibitions. In two instances (clans Kayo and Béle Jawa, II: 2: i, II: 4: iii), moreover, the taboo applies only to women of the clan. Similarly, a prohibition on pork consumption, observed by Yoga, Yéwe, and three clans in the village of Wulu, concerns only a single male and female member of a family, selected to uphold the taboo in each generation. Several ancestral narratives account for the adoption of this prohibition, but their details are contradictory (II: 6, n. 8). The only other instance where a food taboo is rationalized in myth concerns clan Wagha's prohibition on dog flesh, which is explained by the founding ancestor's special attachment to his dog (II: 6: iii).

Keo regularly speak of entire named clans as exogamous groups. Nevertheless, among numerically large groups one occasionally encounters intra-clan marriages, and these are not disapproved. In this context, people often describe an absence of ties of 'blood' (*ya*) as permitting marriage within a clan. As this would suggest, not all members of a single *suku* are regarded as sharing common 'blood', a category I discuss more fully in a later chapter (I: 5: iii). In so far as one can speak of 'alliance units' (or 'alliance groups') among Keo, it is furthermore houses (*sa'o*) rather than entire clans that are required to observe the rule of asymmetric marriage. Where a marriage involves two different clans, by far the more common circumstance, all other houses of the husband's clan may be asked to assist with the bridewealth, as may agnatically related branches resident in other villages. Yet the clan is not exclusively implicated in the exchange of marriage prestations either. For one thing, members of other clans can contribute to a bridewealth. Indeed, where a marriage concerns two villages, all residents of the wife-taking village may participate, as may inhabitants of paired villages in the case of double settlements. For another, other divisions, or houses, of the prospective groom's clan may be prevented from assisting with bridewealth if they are closely related as wife-givers to the bride's group. Occasionally, Keo describe named clans as linked in an enduring alliance, and as obliged to contract at least one further marriage in every generation (see, e.g. II: 2, 6). Yet on closer inspection the relationships are found to apply more specifically to the senior houses of the clans in question.

Earlier I mentioned the possibility of a man simultaneously claiming rights in more than one clan, or what might be called 'multiple clanship'. Writing in

English, it is convenient to refer to individuals as 'members' of clans, even if the usage is not entirely unavoidable. However, as the possibility of multiple clanship as well as certain other kinds of evidence suggest, rather than viewing individual persons as parts of clans (or of other, less inclusive groups), it may be more accurate to describe Keo clanship as a part, or possession, of individuals.[11] As indicated, clanship is not determined once and for all by parentage or the circumstances of the parents' marriage, but can be acquired during one's lifetime—for example, through adoption—and, indeed, augmented or multiplied. A point to appreciate here is that, while birth to particular parents provides a sufficient, if not a necessary, basis for clan affiliation, having rights in a clan—including rights to lands collectively held by clans and clan segments—is a status that must be maintained through the fulfilment of obligations, and especially by contributing to clan sacrificial ritual. In this last respect, Keo clanship appears to be as much a matter of shedding animal blood as of possessing and sharing human blood.

While multiple clanship is one among several features of Keo society signalling a pronounced divergence from classical anthropological models of unilineal descent (Rivers 1924; Leach 1962; see also Holy 1996: 73–4), it is not particularly common. Thus, by far the majority of men claim affiliation to a single clan—and hence a single estate. As mentioned earlier, multiple clanship can occur when adoptees retain, or reclaim, rights in the clans of their genitors, or when a man provisions a funeral and thus acquires rights to the estate of a man who dies without economically capable heirs. Keo also state that rights to land of another clan can be acquired by slaughtering buffalo in place of parties who may have more legitimate claims, but who are unable to fulfil their sacrificial obligations. By this means, a man in the village of Lui (II: 3: v), who died several generations ago, is reputed to have become affiliated to no fewer than five clans in five different villages.

It perhaps goes without saying that clanship in Keo is one among several components of social identity that is more relevant in some contexts than in others. With regard to various aspects of marriage, for example, residence in a village or other local entity can be more important—in contributing to bridewealth, for instance. So, too, can membership of a 'house', where maintaining a proper affinal asymmetry is concerned. These points are amply supported by Keo genealogical knowledge. Regarding the derivation of spouses from other villages, Keo usually know the village of origin and also the affinally related

---

[11] This is supported by local usage. Thus one says of a person, *imu suku X*, 'he (has) clan X', meaning that X is his clan and not, strictly speaking, that he 'belongs' to X. Compare *imu fai ga'e rua*, 'he (has) two wives', and *imu jara mona*, 'he (has) no horse'. By the same token, in this context there is no term that exactly translates 'member'. Modern Keo do use BI *anggota* ('member') with reference to group affiliation; yet they employ the term in the sense of 'follower, supporter, appendage', or someone (or something) that augments something else. Rather than specifying an unequivocal part–whole relationship, this usage thus implies instead a contrast of principal and subsidiary, or even of centre and periphery, an image that is of course also relevant to the relation of Land Mother and Defender—and, indeed, originally to English 'member' as well.

house (specified either with the name of an ancestor or a present occupant), but often will be unable accurately to identify the clan. Similarly, in sacrificial orations (*bhea*), speakers always identify affinal houses that have given wives to a sacrificer's own house (see I: 4: iv, regarding the 'maternal line of origin') and either the village or clan to which affines belong. Yet in this context as well, village names are mentioned more often than are clan names (see Appendix 4).

In this connection, it is also relevant that Keo, including recognized experts in traditional matters, often display an incomplete knowledge of the clan composition of neighbouring villages. Outsider accounts tend, moreover, to take the form of a dualistic simplification of a more complex state of affairs, so that three or more co-resident clans, for example, may in effect be reduced to just two, sometimes by construing two paired clans as a single *suku*. In addition, where clanship is not accurately attributed, a person is often identified as a member of a clan which bears the same name as the village, or which is otherwise better known. In both cases the clan given recognition is normally older than co-residents, a circumstance that in turn usually involves a closer connection with the *peo*. Better known, or consistently recognized, clans are accordingly ones occupying the status of trunk rider or tip rider (or earth breaker or excavator).

Particularly where a clan holds the principal ceremonial status, there is a tendency to identify it with the village as a whole, regardless of whether it bears the same name as the entire settlement. Not only do local representations effectively reduce villages of three or more clans to a duality, therefore, but a duality or larger collectivity may in the same way be reduced to a unity. Sometimes the reductions appear quite deliberate, not merely an innocent simplification—particularly where they form part of a discourse internal, rather than external, to a village. In this circumstance, interested commentators will give other groups token recognition yet deny them the status of separate clans, describing them instead as parts of another clan. Denial of separate clanship, or even the simple failure to recognize it, can thus operate as a mechanism of subordination. As I illustrate in later chapters, whether a group is represented as a separate *suku* is often a political question hinging on whether it is recognized as possessing independent rights, especially to land. As the representation of some clans as parts of others would suggest, this aspect of relations among Keo clans closely approximates Dumont's model of 'hierarchical opposition', or encompassment. So do other relationships, as I show later in a discussion of affinal alliance. At the same time, rarely if ever is duality completely obscured by a subordinating unity, whether in regard to relations among clans or in other areas of Keo social and conceptual life.

4. The House (sa'o)

While clans are composed of estates, they also comprise a number of houses. The observation applies even more tangibly to villages, which can be seen both as a collection of social groups and a collection of objects, including sacrificial instruments, ceremonial buildings and, indeed, residential houses arranged in a definite spatial order. Mediating between these two series—the social and the physical—the 'house' (*sa'o*) can thus be called pivotal to Keo social order. Entailed in this are two partly distinguishable referents of *sa'o*. First, the term designates a physical building, especially a residential building, located inside a village (*nua*). Secondly, it refers to a group of people resident, at least nominally, in one or more such buildings in the same village. In this second sense, *sa'o* is conceptually expandable, being further applied to larger groupings. Stressing the unitary aspect of the clan, Keo will describe an entire *suku* as a single house (*a sa'o*), an entity implicitly identifiable with the clan's seniormost or 'trunk house' (*sa'o pu'u*), the one most closely associated with the founding ancestor. Two localized clans derived from a single clan and resident in separate villages (for example, Pajo Kayo in Pajo Mala and Bale Wolo), may also be described as a 'single house', as in effect can two houses of different clans linked in a special relationship (see I: 4: i, regarding *ka'e ari sa'o ténda*, 'house siblings'.)[12]

As the foregoing may suggest, the relation between *sa'o* and *ngapi*—the categories of 'house' and 'estate'—is somewhat complex. Not uncommonly, people belonging to the same estate will collectively possess a single village house, even though some may reside most of the time in a hamlet, outside the village. Yet even when estate members own two or more physical houses in a village, they will, in the way described just above, often speak of themselves as composing a single *sa'o*. To describe a house as a division of an estate would, therefore, be inexact. *Ngapi* and *sa'o* are not straightforwardly related by taxonomic inclusion, as in a segmentary lineage model, but figure instead as two complementary aspects of the constitution of clans. As shown, a *ngapi* is first and foremost a sacrificial entity operating publicly to affirm rights to a division of a clan's territory, or better said, a collection of lands connected to a single sacrificial instrument (*peo*). Being itself a 'division' of a larger whole, an estate can only be conceived in relation to another, so that a clan cannot strictly speaking be described as consisting of a single estate, but only of two or more. In the few instances where named clans do appear to admit a single estate, they may be considered as remnant groups linked with *peo* more closely associated with more senior clans; and where such a clan is said formerly to have maintained a sacrificial instrument of its own, it must be inferred that the group once comprised at least two *ngapi*. With *sa'o*, by contrast, the emphasis is much less on division and very much on unity—so much so that the concept can be applied to a series of successively encompassing social levels (physical houses, estates, clans, and so on).

---

[12] Varying applications of *sa'o* replicate usages reported elsewhere in Indonesia, for example, by Traube (1986: 70) for the Mambai of Timor. Much further afield, they also recall Tallensi applications of 'house' (Fortes 1949, cited in Holy 1996: 76–7).

Typically coinciding with a group of close agnates, an estate is *de facto* an exogamous entity. Yet only occasionally do Keo speak of *ngapi* as units to which marriage rules apply. Particularly in regard to affinal alliance, Keo instead specify 'houses' (*sa'o*), rather than estates, or indeed clans, as the units bound to maintain a required asymmetry. As previously remarked, a man can take a wife from a clan to which his own clan has given wives, so long as the marriages involve different houses (*sa'o pésa*). In so far as *sa'o* is polysemous in the ways indicated above, its use in this context is, of course, quite ambiguous, and one can never be certain *a priori* of the sort of grouping, genealogically or otherwise defined, to which it might refer. On the other hand, whenever thus employed to rationalize particular marriages, 'house' implicitly denotes a group smaller than the clan (*suku*). Hence, conceptually at least, it serves well enough to preserve the asymmetry of affinal relations that Keo require.

Also articulating marital connections, Keo represent the houses (*sa'o*) from which a person's mother and other female ascendants came—thus the natal houses of ego's mother, mother's mother, and so on—as the individual's place of origin (*pu'u*). In the last section I mentioned genealogical orations called *bhea*. Performed on the occasion of major buffalo sacrifices, the orations provide the main public context in which such relations of derivation are announced and reaffirmed. Reciting what in effect are series of alliances reckoned through the mother and the father respectively, and thereby recounting his father's places of origin as well as his own, a male sacrificer (or a speaker representing him) records a continuous series consisting not of clans or estates but, as indicated just above, of 'houses' (see Appendix 4). Referring to a person's place of 'affinal origin', as it might be distinguished, the image of a house also figures crucially in the Keo notion of 'descent' (*poro*), as I elaborate later.

Further revealing the stress on social unity implicit in their concept of house (*sa'o*), Keo represent division within social wholes as parts of a house. For example, where *sa'o* denotes a larger collectivity (which may be a clan or estate) comprising members inhabiting two or more village dwellings, the former is said to be divided (*bagi*) into *lika wunu*, 'cooking hearths', or *kana wawi*, 'pig troughs', which then denote the individual physical dwellings. The same idiom is used to describe the partition of a clan into several estates. The expression *lika wunu* is actually a contraction of *lika ne'e pondo wunu*, 'hearth stones and leaf pots'. *Pondo wunu*, 'pots of leaves' refers to vegetable matter used to feed pigs, animals traditionally kept near houses and cared for by women. Referring especially to female labours, these phrases, interestingly enough, thus depict single residential houses—or *sa'o* in the sense of individual buildings—as purely domestic places, which only in combination form a larger public, ritual or political, whole.

Considered as a social grouping smaller than a clan, or even an estate, *sa'o* are not named except contingently, with reference to a forebear (who was not necessarily the founder of the house) or to a more recent inhabitant. In so far as the distinction may be relevant, the same applies to physical dwellings.[13] Especially when conceived as components of estates and clans, Keo do, however, distinguish the most senior house as the 'trunk (or origin, original) house' (*sa'o pu'u*). In one sense, *sa'o pu'u* denotes the house of the leader of a clan (or a segment of a clan linked with a particular *peo*), and especially the *sa'o* of a principal sacrificer, that is, a 'trunk rider' (*saka pu'u*) or 'earth breaker' (*ta koe*). In this context, then, 'trunk house' (*sa'o pu'u*) is virtually synonymous with 'trunk estate' (*ngapi pu'u*). However, where an estate (*ngapi*) is conceived as comprising two or more houses, *sa'o pu'u* also refers to the most senior of these, thus to the house of the *ngapi* leader. Keo further use the term synonymously with *ngapi*, so that a clan that includes, for example, seven estates (a rather high number, but attested in two cases, see II: 2: iii; 3: ii) is alternatively described as comprising seven *sa'o pu'u*. Suggesting an identification of the estate leader with the entire estate, these usages further illustrate the partial identification of *ngapi* and *sa'o*, mostly effected by the polysemous character of the second term.

As mentioned earlier, a clan's senior house is identified with the entire group where an obligation to perpetuate an affinal alliance, conceived as linking two whole clans, falls specifically on the *sa'o pu'u* of each. Villagers in Nua Muri (II: 5: ii) similarly claimed that segments of a clan localized in different villages may contract marriages so long as these do not involve partners belonging to their respective trunk houses. Genealogical and other evidence, however, suggests that this rule (if such it is) is not widely observed elsewhere, and that some Keo even tolerate marriages between *sa'o pu'u* and other houses of the same clan in the same village. *Sa'o pu'u* further occupy a special status in relation to a whole clan in so far as groups affinally related to other houses—in this context sometimes specified also as 'estates'—participate in exchanges of goods required, for example, when the trunk house inaugurates a new residential structure (*nalo sa'o*). By contrast, when junior *sa'o* similarly receive guests, exchanges are more often restricted to specific affines of the host.

Although the differences are no longer observable, Keo say that the distinction between 'trunk houses' and junior houses was formerly marked by the outward form of their associated buildings. More particularly, *sa'o pu'u*—that is, the residences of clan leaders—and sometimes houses of senior men of other estates (including especially 'tip riders' and 'excavators'), were built as 'ladder houses' (*sa'o tangi*). As the name suggests, the most distinctive feature of these buildings was a ladder placed in front of the entrance. Nowadays, this contrast is obscured by the fact that most village houses possess ladders, whereas formerly access to ordinary *sa'o* was provided by a single beam or stout

---

[13] In this way, Keo houses differ from the 'cult houses' (*sa'o waja*) of the neighbouring Nage, some of which are named, for example as 'sailing vessels' of an apical ancestor, or as a particular clan's 'pool' or 'head-dress' (Forth 1998).

bamboo pole (*padha*) attached horizontally just before the raised front verandah (*ténda*), to serve as a step.[14] Trunk houses, which is to say 'ladder houses',
were also once decorated with plumes (*lando*) of Imperata grass erected at
either end of the roof ridge. As noted, this kind of ornamentation is also characteristic of the ceremonial buildings called *yenda* and *nde* (I: 2: v). In fact,
many informants identified the name *sa'o tangi* with *nde*, buildings which, as
noted, also possess ladders. These resemblances thus suggest a general identification, now obscured by changing house styles, of the residences of clan leaders and other prominent men with one sort of ritual structure. Since wealthy
owners employed their 'ladder houses' to store heirlooms, including items of
gold, weapons (spears, shields), and war jackets (*dupu*), they would assign
slaves to guard the buildings, something also formerly done with *nde*.

Also relevant in this respect are associations of ladder houses with spiritual
beings, associations that are absent, or at least not explicated, in regard to other
village residences. Decorating the front interior wall of a *sa'o tangi*—and still
found in the more modern dwellings of some trunk riders and earth breakers—
was a piece of ornamental plaitwork called *mata nitu*, roughly 'eye, source, or
focus of *nitu* spirits'. Beneath the raised floor of such a building, and more
particularly below the hearth, was placed a stone, variously called a 'spirit
stone' (*watu nitu*), 'naga (snake) stone' (*watu naga*), or 'prohibited stone' (*watu
piye*). Keo commentators identified both objects with the partly tutelary spirit
of the house called *ga'e bapu* (or in parallel form, *ga'e sa'o, bapu ténda*, 'lord of
the house, powerful spirit of the verandah'). As mentioned earlier (II: 2: iv),
ga'e bapu spirits are also thought to inhabit *peo*; and one form they can assume
is that of a *naga*, a large snake or snake-like being. Owing to the presence of
this *ga'e bapu*, women were formerly forbidden to give birth inside ladder
houses, since the voracious spirit might then 'eat' the child. As noted in the
previous chapter, similar restrictions, intended to preserve women's fertility,
apply to the buildings called *nde* and *yenda*.

It is not clear whether the prohibition on childbirth has any bearing on the
phrase *sa'o mara*, once glossed as 'dry or clean house', and possibly used in
some places as a synonym of 'ladder house'. Although I first recorded the term
in Muka (or Bolo, II: 1: iv), later enquiries indicated that it is all but unknown
elsewhere. Also, if it was ever used to describe *sa'o tangi* in general, the component *mara* may have alluded instead to the link between these prominent
houses and particular banyan trees called *nunu tu mara*. Specially planted just
outside the village, such trees are the object of elaborate rites addressed partly
to external *nitu* spirits in the event of illness or affliction (see plate 19). In this
context *tu mara* denotes the act of conveying (*tu*) offerings to an altar located

---

[14] Local accounts suggest that 'ladder houses' were not always significantly larger than other houses. Keo also say
that, formerly, all houses were smaller than at present. Even so, it seems likely that the 'ladder houses' of prominent
leaders were also classified as *sa'o bale*, a term explained as referring to especially large and well-constructed houses
built of more durable woods than other dwellings.

beneath a banyan, a meaning further evidenced in *pébha tu mara*, referring to buffalo sacrifice aimed at curing a particular sufferer. Although *mara* may designate an offering made with this purpose, it seems also to have the sense of something like 'complete, finished, ended'.

Whatever the import of these particular usages, many of which are no longer readily observable, it is quite clear that houses of leaders of clans and estates, which is to say houses identified as 'trunks' or 'origins' (*sa'o pu'u*), possess—or formerly possessed—a distinctive spiritual character. Senior components of estates, clans and, indeed, whole villages, are distinguished from more junior affiliates in the same way. Again, however, this contrast does not pertain to a complementary opposition of religious and worldly power or authority. It derives from a conception of 'trunks' as wholes subsuming parts ('tips', *lobo*), whose greater spirituality is a function of temporal precedence ritually reproduced in a sacrificial hierarchy, the units of which are estates (*ngapi*) or in one sense, 'houses'.

As a physical structure linked with several kinds of collectivities, and as a symbol of unity, the Keo house (*sa'o*) provides an obvious source of social metaphor. One example has already been noted, namely, the use of 'house' and 'hearth' to distinguish houses in the sense of inclusive social groups from divisions associated with individual dwellings. As this is not the place for a comprehensive description of the physical house, it may be sufficient to mention a few basic features (see Fig. 4). Always rectangular, the building is longitudinally divided into two halves by a central wall in which is set a single doorway. The front half forms a gallery, *ténda*, which nowadays is itself usually enclosed with a wall with doorway and windows provided with shutters. Behind the central wall lies the back half of the house, the *tolo*. On the heraldic left side of this section, one finds the area of the hearth (*lapu*). Related to this positioning of the hearth, the *tolo*—the more enclosed and private, inner part of the house— is largely associated with women. As a more public area where guests are received and matters pertaining to relations between groups (bridewealth, for example) are discussed and negotiated, the gallery (*ténda*) by contrast is more closely identified with men. Yet by no means is the *tolo* an exclusively female place. In fact, in various ways this posterior section is identified with the house as a whole (see Forth 1991*b*, regarding the similarly constituted Nage house). Conversely, where *sa'o* forms a parallelism with *ténda*, as it regularly does in ritual idioms, the first term particularly connotes the more private back section, as opposed to the more public gallery. As regards the bisexual character of the *tolo*, especially relevant is the use of the hearth, located in this part of the house, not only for cooking but also as a ritual focus. Here, food offerings are dedicated to ancestors and other benevolent spiritual beings, and this is always done by men.

Two other structural features inform metaphorical uses of 'house' (*sa'o*). First, all traditional houses are raised off the ground on wooden posts or piles,

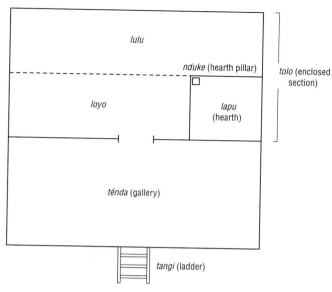

FIG. 4. Schematic diagram of a house

thus creating an opposition between the floor and the ground, a metre or more below. Since a person must thus move vertically when leaving or entering a house, this feature is crucial to Keo notions of 'descent', as I show later on. Secondly, while the division of gallery (*ténda*) and inner house (*tolo*) produces a bifurcate order within the building as a whole, the *tolo* is itself dually divided into a front section called *loyo* (denoting the area that includes the hearth) and a rear section called *lulu*.

Against this background, one can better understand parallelistic expressions such as *sa'o mére, ténda léwa*, 'large house, long gallery'. Opposing 'gallery' and 'house'—a contrast implicitly identifying the entire building with the enclosed back section—the phrases refer to a group larger than the occupants of a single building but usually less inclusive than an entire clan. That the expression might also be applied to an entire clan or even some larger kinship grouping is supported by information from eastern Keo (P. Tule, pers. comm. 1997). Indeed, *sa'o mére, ténda léwa* appears to have no absolutely fixed structural referent, functioning partly as a rhetorical device for stressing or promoting the unity of various sorts of collectivity. In regard to this flexibility, of course, the expression immediately recalls the polysemy of *sa'o* ('house') itself.

The parallelism of 'house' and 'gallery' further occurs in *ka'e ari sa'o ténda*, roughly 'house siblings', applications of which I describe in the next chapter.

Contrary to what the gloss may suggest, this expression does not refer exclusively to members of a single house. The latter collectivity Keo specify instead with the phrases *ulu lulu, éko loyo*, 'a head and tail formed of the back and front (of the *tolo*)'. Implicitly equating an entire house with its enclosed rear section (*tolo*)—the more private part of a residential building consisting in turn of front and back subsections (*loyo* and *lulu*)—the expression can indeed refer to a 'house' in the sense of a single dwelling. Even so, in other usages the combination of *lulu* and *loyo* conveys a broader, or more ambiguous, sense of 'house', as a reference to a larger social entity. Thus a standard phrase commits an oath-taker to a course of action on pain of 'death from the *loyo* (of his house), all the way to the *lulu*', an allusion to the ultimate extinction of his entire group.[15]

While all these expressions apply mostly to social categories whose core is agnatic kinship, the Keo house conceptually informs relations of affinal alliance as well. It is especially in this respect that Keo might be seen as conforming to Lévi-Strauss's model of 'house' (or 'house-based') societies, which he describes as founded on the marital pair and as allowing the substitution of affinity for 'descent' (1982: 187; see also Carsten and Hugh-Jones 1995). In the Keo idiom, both *ana sa'o*, 'children, people of the house', and *ana réta tolo*, 'children, people up in the inner house', denote persons claiming full membership of one's own kin group, normally and by preference traced through males. In contrast, the children of natal women married without bridewealth, as well as co-resident wife-takers mostly descended from the former and similarly occupying a secondary status within the group, are designated as *ana rale tana*, 'children, people down on the ground', referring to the area beneath the raised house floor. A variant expression is *ana rale ténda*, which locates wife-takers 'down—that is, out—on the gallery', thus distinguishing them from people who conceptually occupy the 'inner house' (*tolo*).

In much the same vein, Keo distinguish wife-givers and wife-takers as *wawo lapu* and *au lapu*, '(people located) above and below the hearth'. Accordingly, correct marriage for a man is described as 'taking from above the hearth, above the hearth pillar' (*ala wawo lapu, wawo nduke*). Also linking the hearth with marriage alliance is the expression *leo pu'u nduke*, 'travelling around the hearth pillar', referring to a three-unit cycle. As *nduke* (or, more completely, *nduke lapu*) denotes a wooden pillar situated in one corner of the hearth, and since the hearth arguably forms the conceptual centre of a dwelling (Forth 1991*b*), the image conveyed is thus one of women moving in marriage around a fixed object, yet remaining inside a unitary social formation, again represented by

---

[15] As it specifies the back part of the *tolo* as a 'head', the expression *ulu lulu, éko loyo* is consistent with my interpretation of the Nage house as involving an orientational reversal as one moves from the front gallery into the enclosed back section (Forth 1991*b*). By the same token, in relative spatial terms, Keo specify the front subsection (*loyo*) as 'below' (*rili*), and the back subsection (*lulu*), linked with 'head', as 'above' (*réle*).

the house.[16] The identification of the relation of wife-giver and wife-taker with a single house implicit in the foregoing expressions is basic to Keo social order. So, too, is the concomitant idea that wife-takers derive from wife-giving 'houses' and, in a sense, always remain part of those houses. The last principle finds further expression in such terms as *ndi'i sa'o*, '(those who) reside, remain in the house', referring to wife-givers (I: 4), and *ana ndi'i*, 'children who remain (in the house)', denoting the issue of uxorilocal marriages (compare *ana rale tana*, mentioned above). At the same time, an image of marriage as involving a departure from one house and removal to another is expressed in *nuka sa'o* ('to enter a house'), referring to a wife's incorporation into her husband's group following the payment of bridewealth. Extending the idiom, Keo refer to the children of such a marriage as *ana nuka* 'children who have entered', a phrase than can further be glossed as 'wife-takers'.

An identification of women, particularly married women, with the hearth is also revealed in a Keo expression describing the remarriage of widows. When a deceased husband's survivors allow a man of another clan to marry his widow in exchange for bridewealth, Keo describe the process as 'digging up the hearthstones, lifting out the hearth' (*wuka lika, legha lapu*; cf. Ngadha *vuka*, 'to transplant', 'to throw away', Arndt 1961). Further explained by one commentator as meaning 'prying up and discarding the instrument for cooking food', the phrases refer to an arrangement considered a poor alternative to widow inheritance, since the woman is then lost to the group (or the 'house') as a provider of both cooked food and new members. Identifying wives with the hearth further lends coherence to the representation of wife-givers, male affines from whose 'house' a wife-taker is conceived to derive, as 'those who light the hearth (or hearthstones), and make the flame hot' (*ta mia lika, bana ara*), and 'those who ignite the firewood, and fan the fire' (*ta tuki tune, yangi api*). Following local interpretations, the phrases depict wife-givers not only as a past source of women married to wife-takers, but also as a continuing source of life. If fire refers metaphorically to the life of the wife-taker, then the wife-giver, as the one who lit the fire, is the originator of that life. In addition, the wife-giver's maintaining a fire in the hearth can be construed as preserving the house itself, as a place of origin in which derivative wife-takers also continue to have a part.

As should become clearer in the following chapter, it is scarcely possible to discuss marriage and affinity in Keo without reference to the house. It is significant, therefore, that the process of marriage is completed only when wife-takers—a married couple or the husband's parents—construct a new house or

---

[16] In some traditional rituals, I was told, a male functionary should circumambulate the hearth pillar (*nduke*) before placing offerings for ancestors and other beneficent spirits in the corner diagonally opposite the pillar, called *dhogi*. As this area is designated as 'above the hearth' (*wawo lapu*), the phrase further applied to wife-givers, it makes sense that only persons claiming full membership of a house may enter this part of the hearth. Wife-takers are prohibited from doing so.

renovate an existing one. Final marriage prestations are then exchanged 'to open the path' (*kota rala*), thus formally allowing the wife-giver access to the wife-taker's new residence. Once this is done, the services of the man who served as intermediary in marriage negotiations (*wa'a rala*) are terminated, and the two groups can thereafter meet and exchange goods without any external mediation. Consolidating their union, a married pair thus create a new house (dwelling), which in time can become a new clan segment—a 'house' in the wider sense, or even a new estate—and eventually, albeit rarely, a new 'clan'.

In addition to its prominence in representations of marriage and affinity, especially as a reference to a unit maintaining regular connections with like units, the concept of *sa'o* is equally implicated in the more encompassing relation Keo call *ka'e ari* (elder–younger). Relevant here is the way the category of 'house' is expandable, applying to levels of social grouping and relationships that are otherwise opposed. For Keo, 'house' thus pertains in different contexts to both 'wholes' and 'parts'—clans and divisions of clans—and inclusive kinship and exclusive affinity. In the following chapter I show how the same observation applies to the relation of *ka'e ari* itself.

4

Kinship and Marriage

1. The Relation of Ka'e Ari (Elder–Younger)

Partly employed as a kin term for siblings, *ka'e ari*, a pairing of the terms for 'elder' and 'younger' or 'senior' and 'junior', is of considerable analytical import. The expression obviously comprises categories articulated by an asymmetric contrast based on relative age or some other kind of temporal precedence. Yet, especially in reference to groups or collectivities, Keo further apply *ka'e ari* to a variety of social relationships characterized by reciprocity and mutual assistance. Consistent with their recognized equality or symmetry, parties involved in these relationships (for example, members of groups that regularly assist one another in ritual) are not distinguishable respectively as 'senior' (*ka'e*) and 'junior' (*ari*). Not being contrasted as 'elder *and* younger', they recognize one another simply as *ka'e ari*, or as one might say, as—or as being like—'siblings'.

As an expression composed of two terms indicating inequality but contextually specifying equality (or at least, 'undifferentiation'), *ka'e ari* is the inverse of *éja* (WB, ZH), a single term applied reciprocally to unequal affines—wife-givers and wife-takers. In its most specific, genealogical sense, *ka'e ari* denotes the relation of same-sex siblings and thus contrasts with *weta naya*, designating the relation of siblings of opposite sex (*weta*, Z; *naya*, B; see Appendix 1). Yet when applied to reciprocal relationships between social groups, *ka'e ari* implicitly includes people of opposite sex as well. Also, with regard to relative age, even opposite-sex full siblings can address or refer to one another as *ka'e* and *ari*. Hence *ka'e ari* can be seen to subsume *weta naya* ('sister-brother'). Although Keo employ a special term for WZH (*coghe* or *soghe lae*)—men who are wife-takers of the same third group—being neither wife-givers nor wife-takers to one another, these relatives, too, can be classified as *ka'e ari*.

For Keo, the relation of opposite-sex siblings can be called the source of affinal alliance in so far as proper marriage joins the child of a 'sister' with the child of a 'brother'. Hence the relation of alliance is similarly encompassed by the relation of *ka'e ari*. In this way, the encompassing category approaches the meaning of 'kin' (or 'kinship'), particularly as the English word can include affines as well as kin in the narrower, or consanguineal, sense. Here I use 'encompassment' in a way similar to Dumont, as a reference to a relation between whole and part identified with terms otherwise construed as contraries. While in a broad sense *ka'e ari* encompasses affinal alliance, therefore, in some contexts the expression specifies relationships as precluding affinity, most notably when it refers to the children of same-sex siblings, or indeed to brother and sister. A further symptom of this subsumption of one relationship by the other is the previously mentioned possibility of marriage within the clan. Another is the occasional incorporation of wife-takers, as a separate estate (*ngapi*), in the clan of a wife-giver, as exemplified by Bindi and Wae in Lower Pajo Mala (II: 2: i).[1]

Applied to relations between whole groups, *ka'e ari* generally describes parties who share a positive social relationship involving a generalized reciprocity. In view of the mutual obligations such relationships entail, their symmetry contrasts with the asymmetry of the relation of wife-giver and wife-taker. Yet in accordance with the encompassment of affinity by *ka'e ari*, individuals can participate in relationships falling contextually under both rubrics. The most vivid instance of this possibility is when different houses of the same clan intermarry.

In addition to full siblings and parallel cousins (see Appendix 1), members of the same house (*sa'o*) and clan (*suku*) are classified as *ka'e ari*, regardless of whether they are considered to share ties of 'blood' (*ya*; see I: 5: iii) or any exact genealogical connection. Also included in the category are groups counted as separate *suku* yet regarded as sharing a common agnatic or geographical origin. In other cases, *ka'e ari* is not predicated on any putative common origin but is simply rationalized by a long-standing agreement, initiated by particular ancestors, and requiring two groups (commonly houses belonging to different clans) to provide one another with material assistance. In this situation, participants are sometimes unable to articulate the basis of their relationship, but classify one another as *ka'e ari* nonetheless.

Keo employ several expressions to distinguish specific instances of *ka'e ari*. One is *ka'e ari dhadhi dhore*, roughly 'siblings in birth and succession'. This refers to full siblings of the same sex, whose identical origin is further indicated by the supplementary expression, *a bau, a kubu bo'i*, 'of one umbilical cord, of one afterbirth container'.[2] The first expression can also be applied to segments of a clan whose male ancestors were full siblings. Exploiting the same imagery—derivation from a single womb—another phrase describing brothers or their agnatic descendants is *ka'e ari puse pinda, bau dhawi*, 'siblings sharing a navel cord, connected by placentae'. Bound up with local notions of blood connection, particularly blood transferred through females, a phrase with a similar reference is *ka'e ari dhi wini*, roughly 'siblings of the seed'.

Used to describe members of the same house, estate, or named clan, the phrase *ka'e ari sa'o ténda*, 'siblings of the house and gallery'—or 'house

---

[1] Evidently because Wae no longer takes wives from Bindi, members of the clan were reluctant to classify the two segments as wife-giver and wife-taker (see Section 4 below); yet they also thought *ka'e ari* should not be the sole alternative to the affinal designation. Interestingly, they settled on *meta naya*, 'sister (and) brother', as the best way to characterize their relationship.

[2] *Kubu* is a kind of gourd used as a container for the placenta, while *bo'i* refers to a bamboo knife used to cut the umbilical cord.

siblings'—is further applied to separate clans that share a common agnatic ancestry.[3] One example concerns the clans Sina in Kuyu Wulu and Pajo Wolo in Lower Pajo Mala, who descend from a pair of brothers (II: 1: iii). Also characterized as 'house siblings' are segments of different clans, especially their senior or 'trunk' houses (*sa'o pu'u*), whose forebears contracted to provide one another with regular material assistance (*kura kesa, bora penu*, 'augmenting what is insufficient, making full what is diminished'), particularly in ritual undertakings. Such groups also provide one another with heirs when natal successors are lacking. As I was able to observe in one such case, involving clan Kate in Upper Pajo Mala and clan Suga in Bolo (II: 2: ii), men of the two houses count one another as full brothers when exchanging material goods with affines. As the leader of the Kate house described the commitment, it is as if each house simultaneously possessed membership of the other clan. Especially in this context, *ka'e ari sa'o ténda* may be better understood as referring to parties whose houses are related 'like siblings', that is, like components of a single clan (conceived as a single house), rather than to people mutually obligated like members of a single house. The same observation applies to a slightly different application of the expression, as a reference to two houses or, more exactly, estates of the same or different clans linked by the adoption (*ghawe*) of a member of one group by the other (see I: 5: iv).

Similar to the foregoing in regard to both form and variety of reference is the expression *ka'e ari tana watu*, 'siblings of land and stone', sometimes rendered as *ka'e tana, ari watu* (approximately 'land seniors, stone juniors'). Whereas 'house siblings' largely denotes people belonging to a single clan localized in the same village—and thus sharing a common sacrificial instrument (*peo*)—'land siblings', on the other hand, usually describes groups which, though sharing a common agnatic origin, are considered separate clans (*suku*) and possess separate *peo*. Some Keo further construe *ka'e ari tana watu* as including whole clans which, at some point in their history, notionally dissolved common boundaries and began sharing rights in one another's territories, thus 'bounding their fields with maize stems and rice stalks', *bhondo wai toko yolo, lange wai ku pae* (I: 3: i). With both sorts of relationship, participants are further described as *ka'e ari tana pinda watu faya*, 'siblings of shared land and common stone'.

Based on a territorial connection of another kind is the bond Keo call *ka'e ari nua ola*. Since *nua ola* is the parallelistic term for 'village' (*nua*), the expression may be translated as 'village siblings'. In fact, it is more accurately glossed as 'village mates' or 'fellow villagers', as it usually denotes people belonging to different clans and possessing separate agricultural holdings. Regardless of clan affiliation, Keo expect village mates to provide mutual assistance much as

---

[3] The expression is occasionally rendered as *ka'e sa'o, ari ténda*, roughly 'house elder, gallery younger', without any change of meaning.

do agnates and others classified as *ka'e ari*. As previously indicated, a diffuse reciprocal assistance is also characteristic of the two components of double settlements (I: 2: iii). Accordingly, even though double settlements comprise two villages (*nua*), residents of one village further apply *ka'e ari nua ola* to residents of the village paired with their own. In yet other instances the same phrase can express a specific bond—for example, a long-standing military alliance—between two villages that do not compose a double settlement.

Territorial connection, rather than 'kinship' in any consanguineal sense, is also entailed in the relationship of *ka'e tuku wutu, ari wina lima* (or *ka'e ari tuku wutu, wina lima*). Translatable as 'elder siblings of four clumps of palm fibre, younger siblings of five pales of bamboo (or coconut wood)', the phrases characterize two groups that form an alliance after concluding a military conflict and making peace. In this process, the two parties sometimes exchange parcels of land, so that each possesses a plot within the territory of the other—an arrangement exemplified by clan Pajo Wolo in Lower Pajo Mala and clan Late in Nua Muri (II: 2: i; II: 5: ii). As an alternative to exchanging land, reconciled enemies may acquire the right to help themselves to produce (tubers, fruits, maize) when passing through the territory of the other. This arrangement is illustrated by people of Bolo and Keo Bélo (II: 4: i), who in this context further describe themselves as 'land siblings' (*ka'e tana, ari watu*). Referring to materials used to construct fences, the terms *tuku* ('fibre used in binding') and *wina* ('palings') in the phrases recorded above allude to the re-establishment of boundaries following the resolution of war, as well as an agreement to maintain and assist in defending these boundaries against third parties. Possibly taking a cue from the word *tuku*, which occurs as well in *ana tuku*—the formal Defenders of a Land Mother—other commentators stressed military support as the reference of the longer expression. One man even interpreted *wina* in this context as referring to sharpened bamboo used as a weapon rather than a paling.

With other relationships classified as *ka'e ari*, the emphasis is on mutual support in ritual undertakings rather than territorial or military co-operation. Members of different clans that regularly attend one another's ceremonies and help one another in the provision of rice, and animals are described as *ka'e kegu, ari boge*. While not susceptible of a literal translation, the two qualifiers respectively denote a 'handful (of rice)' (*kegu*) and a 'piece of meat' (*boge*). Some groups thus related are also 'ritual partners'. Described as *papa ne'e téngu lo'u, ulu kaba*, or 'partners in respect of necks (and) humps, (and) buffalo heads', this particular relationship requires that each side give the head of the buffalo victim to the other whenever either engages in sacrifice.[4] Where groups possess forked *peo* of Cassiawood, and thus practise the method of slaughter called *paya*, it should, moreover, be a member of the opposite group who 'turns

---

[4] *Téngu* is 'neck'; *lo'u* refers to the fleshy area, or hump, behind the neck of a male buffalo.

the rope' (*ghéle tali*), that is, attends to the long cable by which the buffalo is tethered, ensuring that it rotates freely around the sacrificial post. Although it can refer more generally to reciprocal assistance in sacrificial matters, another expression denoting ceremonial reciprocity of this sort is *paya papa kaka, wela papa geu*, 'sacrificing (buffalo) mutually, slaughtering (pigs) reciprocally'.

Whereas the foregoing concerns clans resident in different villages and possessing separate *peo*, comparable ritual partnerships also occur within a number of villages and even within some clans, between different houses or estates. Usually classified under the rubric of *ulu* (or *téngu*) *geu, kage sabhe* (or *bale*), 'exchanging heads (or necks) and jaws', partners in this case actually slaughter animals on one another's behalf. The practice especially concerns pigs, of which the heads—and thus the trophy jaws (*kage*)—are later given to the sacrificer by the beneficiary (or 'sacrifier', to use the term coined by Halls to translate Hubert and Mauss's *sacrifiant*, 1964: ix). Occasionally, however, the arrangement may extend to the slaughter of buffalo as well, in which circumstance the sacrificer can request the animal's hump.

As the existence of these ritual partnerships within as well as between clans should indicate, this sort of reciprocal relationship is by no means exclusive of other instances of *ka'e ari*. Indeed, most groups linked in this way appear also to be related, in one or another sense, as 'house siblings' (*ka'e ari sa'o ténda*), a connection which, as noted, can also concern houses belonging to different clans. At the same time, not all houses, or all clans, possess ritual partners. Following the observation of a major informant, where such partnerships link divisions of the same clan, they are more characteristic of junior houses than of 'trunk houses' (*sa'o pu'u*), whose connection with junior segments is ensured by the simple fact of their seniority. Although this assessment appeared not to be entirely borne out by the evidence of particular cases, Keo do recognize ritual partnerships as serving to increase solidarity between groups at the same time as they allow others to share in the meat of slaughtered animals. While thus creating and maintaining what are sometimes called 'debts of meat', the practice in a sense further maintains sacrificial standards, in so far as groups are obliged to sacrifice animals at least as large as those previously offered for sacrifice by their partners. If the portion of meat given is smaller than what the donor earlier received, the recipient may demand compensation—even, I was told, a plot of land. There is also a belief that ritual partnerships, and more particularly, the practice of having another party slaughter one's animals, ensures that meat and rice will be sufficient to feed all who attend a feast.

While ritual partnerships between clans typically involve social units linked with different villages and *peo*, within an association of groups sharing a single sacrificial instrument the two principal statuses—earth breaker and excavator or trunk rider and tip rider—are similarly conceived as *ka'e ari*. In this instance, however, the terms do not define a reciprocal relationship so much as a hierarchical order whereby the superordinate position is defined as the 'elder' (*ka'e*) and the subordinate as the 'younger' (*ari*). Where the two positions are vested in a single clan, the former is of course occupied by the estate (*ngapi*) which is senior in terms of agnatic descent. Where they are assigned to separate clans, it is normally the one deemed to have arrived first in the territory or village that occupies the senior status.

Since Keo also distinguish earlier and later arrivals in a territory as 'mother' (*ine*) and 'child' (*ana*) (I: 1: iii), in this context the contrast of 'elder' and 'younger' coincides with an opposition further applied to parties which, as noted, are quite regularly related as wife-giver and wife-taker. In a similar vein, one group usually represented as a single clan, Liwo (II: 6: i), comprises two segments distinguished as earth breaker and excavator, and hence contrasted as *ka'e* and *ari* in respect of their common *peo*, but which derive from a brother and a sister and so to that extent recognize an original relationship by marriage (see also II: 1: v, regarding Koyu and Yéwe). Both possibilities, of course, bear out the more general point, that most relationships Keo categorize as *ka'e ari* do not preclude affinal connection. By the same token, it should be clear that whether two groups act as *ka'e ari* or as wife-giver and wife-taker is a matter of context. This is further seen in regard to the collectivities formed when amassing bridewealth (see Section 3 below). Indeed, in accordance with the subsumption of affinity by *ka'e ari*, it is mostly in connection with particular marriages that the distinction becomes practically relevant.

2. Marriage and Affinity

Keo regularly make normative statements concerning the possibility of marriage between categories of kin. A union between a man and a woman related as *naya* (B, FBS, MBS, MZS, w.s.) and *weta* (Z, FBD, FZD, MZD, m.s.), or otherwise stated, the 'children of same-sex siblings' (*ana ka'e ari*), is forbidden (*piye*). In contrast, marriage between their offspring—the 'children of sister and brother' (*ana weta, ana naya*)—is not only permitted but, in the traditional scheme, is enjoined.[5] Although this local formulation might appear to permit marriage between FZD and MBS, these relatives, who classify one another as opposite-sex siblings, are in fact proscribed as spouses. Hence among siblings and first cousins, only MBD (m.s.) and FZS (w.s.), reciprocally classified as *li ana*, remain as possible marriage partners. It perhaps goes without saying that people who do not recognize any previous relationship are allowed to marry. This of course is equivalent to stating that marriage is permitted between groups related as *ka'e ari* in a more inclusive sense. Keo describe marriage between previously unrelated parties as 'cutting through

---

[5] See Barraud's description of Kei affinity as 'subordinated to the brother–sister relationship' (1990: 209; cf. 1979: 142–8). A similar characterization is proffered by Erb (1987) for the Rembong of western Flores.

Imperata grass, trampling down giant reeds' (*ke'a ki, dera kela*), that is, following a route where a clear path, an affinal alliance, has yet to be created.[6]

Consistent with the prohibition of marriage between FZD and MBS is the previously mentioned prohibition on direct exchange. Conceived as an illicit reversal of proper affinal relations, the negative evaluation of such marriages is revealed in several standard expressions. Among these are *ala malo pora*, 'taking back the (pig's) flesh', and *topi mela mando, luka sapu sunda*, 'parang cutting backward, sarong fastened with the ends twisted around'. Since pork is the only meat wife-givers can serve to wife-takers, while parangs and textiles are major items of bridewealth and counter-prestation respectively, the phrases describe a reversal of the direction in which prestations should be transferred between the two sorts of affines. In the same way, *sonde po'o tua*, 'puncturing the palm wine container', depicts direct exchange marriages as destroying the alliance relation by allusion to a wife-taker's continuing obligation to provide a wife-giver with palm wine. On the other hand, the synonymous phrase *nganda ngi'i ki*, 'looking up at the teeth of the thatch', refers to a woman's illegitimate re-entry on marriage into a house from where she, directly or indirectly, originates. 'Teeth of the thatch' denotes to the ends of bamboo slats which, being arranged in horizontal rows, resemble teeth and are visible only from the interior of a dwelling. Since these are best viewed by a woman lying on her back, a specifically sexual interpretation is also possible. However that may be, the phrase provides yet another instance of the general Keo use of house imagery in articulating proper affinal relations (I: 3: iv).

In other eastern Indonesian societies, including the neighbouring Nage (Fontijne 1940), two groups are sometimes permitted to reverse the direction in which wives were previously transferred so long as no marriages have taken place during a number of intervening generations. Questioning failed to elicit any definite rule of this sort among Keo. People generally insisted that reversing the relationship between wife-giver and wife-taker was never possible, with some remarking how the injunction sometimes made it difficult for groups with many wife-takers to find groups from which they could themselves take wives. On the other hand, one local authority claimed it should be possible to take a woman from a previous wife-taker with the payment of a 'fine' (*maja*; or *ti'i tulu ngia*, 'to provide a screen for the face'). Similar disagreement is encountered regarding the possibility of marriage between genealogical MZD and MZS. In accordance with their being classified as 'sister' and 'brother', a union between these relatives can be construed as incestuous, a view that is buttressed

---

[6] Now possible only for non-Christians, polygyny seems to have been uncommon even in pre-Christian times. Although genealogies reveal several instances of men with two, three, or four wives, and in one case six, it is not always clear how often the women were married simultaneously. If polygyny still occurs among the majority Catholic population of western Keo, it does so rarely. Although informants' comments suggested the arrangement was not preferred, a man may marry two sisters, as may two brothers. Following traditional practice, which was continued at least until the 1950s, prospective spouses might be betrothed as infants, and even before birth. Betrothal was described as most appropriate for children related as MBD and FZS.

by the present Catholic Church ban on all first-cousin marriages. However, replicating a provision found among other eastern Indonesians (including Nage, see Forth 1993a: 96), marriage between matrilateral parallel cousins is deemed possible when the groom is the son of the younger sister and the bride the daughter of the elder, and when the relation between the fathers of the prospective spouses does not otherwise preclude their union. Keo described such unions as most appropriate where no matrilateral cross-cousin is available for a man to marry. Like marriage with MBD, moreover, marriage with MeZD counts as 'taking blood' (*ala ya*), and is regarded as preserving a valued connection of blood between wife-taker and wife-giver (see I: 5: iii)

While 'children of *ka'e ari*' (*ana ka'e ari*) denotes people who may not marry, as indicated earlier, the offspring of many people related in one or another way as *ka'e ari* are quite free to do so. Within his own genealogical level, it is in fact only a man's Z, FBD, FZD and MyZD, as well as the daughters of other close agnates (for example FFBSD) who are unequivocally prohibited. Women belonging to other terminological generations are also generally proscribed. Yet more distantly related members of these generations as well may be allowed as spouses, especially if they are not considered to share 'blood'.[7] In regard to marriageability, Keo sometimes speak of degrees of relationship. For example, by contrast to first cousins, second matrilateral parallel cousins (for example, MMZDD–MMZDS), defined as people whose grandparents (*ebu*) classified one another as same-sex siblings, were reckoned to be marriageable. On the other hand, so far as agnatic relationship is concerned, there appears to be no precisely defined genealogical limit beyond which people can marry without more ado.

As noted, Keo state as a generalization that people belonging to the same named clan should not marry, and the majority of marriages do, indeed, involve different clans. At the same time, marriage within several larger clans— thus within one of several social fields defined as *ka'e ari*—does occur. As this would suggest, it is in fact more accurate to speak of houses rather than clans as both exogamous groups and alliance units. Yet it would not be correct to say that Keo simply permit marriage between houses of the same clan. Affinal, or matrilateral, connections also have a bearing on this issue. Thus, to the extent that distant agnates (typically members of the same clan but reckoned as belonging to different houses) are distinguished by the possession of different wife-givers, marriage between them will be more acceptable than when they share the same wife-givers. This, of course, is consistent with the usual misapprobation of marriage between MZS and MZD, even where the two are distant agnates, or for that matter not agnatically related at all. The consideration further accords with the regularly articulated idea that some people, though

---

[7] As in eastern Sumba (Forth 1981: 331), a man may marry polygynously with a woman and her BD, an arrangement described as *due ine ana*, 'to have "mother" and "child" as co-wives'.

belonging to the same clan, do not share ties of 'blood', or have 'different blood' (*ya me'a*). As is further discussed in the following chapter, 'blood' in this context refers to a quality transferred through married women (I: 5: iii).

Regardless of how it is construed in regard to specific marriage possibilities, *ka'e ari* always denotes what may be called a reduplicative relationship. While in its widest sense it encompasses affinity (the relation of wife-giver and wife-taker, or of *éja*, WB, ZH), where the two categories are unequivocally in contrast (for example, when the former applies to siblings and close agnates), *ka'e ari* involves a prohibition of marriage which is reproduced in successive generations. Thus, just as eB and yB cannot become in-laws (*éja*), neither can their sons, their sons' sons, and so on. In contrast, the relation of opposite-sex siblings, in a sense the basis of Keo affinity, can be called transformative. While siblings are themselves prohibited from marrying, a sister's son and her brother's daughter are on the contrary the most appropriate marriage partners. More exactly, they are considered so when the sister was married with bridewealth.

3. Bridewealth and Counter-prestation

As a full account of bridewealth components and transactions could easily occupy an entire chapter, here I confine my remarks to aspects of marriage payments relevant to alliance, affiliation, economy, and sacrificing. Although marriage with bridewealth is strongly preferred, not all negotiated marriages involve marriage payments. Keo describe men who marry without bridewealth as 'residing separately' (*ndi'i dhato*). The phrase refers to the husband's obligation to remain with the wife's group and his consequent separation from, and effective loss of membership of, his natal group. Children of such marriages, specified as *ana ndi'i* (roughly 'children who remain, stay (in place)') are then counted as members of their mother's group, though their status therein is lower than that of agnatic members. Although the descendants of uxorilocal marriages may be recognized as distinct lines—or even in a sense, houses—within the female ancestor's clan, they do not form separate estates (*ngapi*). Designated as *ana rale tana* ('children down on the ground', I: 3: iv), they are subsumed by other *ngapi* and possess no independent right to sacrifice buffalo at the wife-giver's *peo*. Accordingly, they enjoy only a right of usufruct in regard to lands in the wife-giver's estate.

The incidence of *ndi'i dhato* marriages varies from village to village. People of Pajo Mala (II: 2) say that nowadays they always allow uxorilocal husbands who cannot pay a formal bridewealth to return home with their wives and affiliate children to their own clans once they have provided the wife-giver, over a number of years, with material assistance. Such assistance is then, in effect, counted as bridewealth. Even in recent times, however, uxorilocal marriages involving permanent induction of children into the maternal group have regularly been contracted in other places. The village of Nua Muri (II: 5: ii) is particularly known for the practice. Outsiders speak disapprovingly of the frequency with which Nua Muri people have incorporated husbands from elsewhere by dispensing with bridewealth. Apparently linked in this instance with relative poverty, *ndi'i dhato* marriages among Keo are not a regular means by which agnatic groups acquire new members when natural sons are lacking; for heirs can always be adopted from among the children of sisters for whom bridewealth has been paid. Nevertheless, uxorilocal marriage is particularly appropriate in certain circumstances, for example, when an outsider wishes to marry a widow. It is worth stressing as well that such marriages are positively contracted, and are not simply the result of a husband defaulting on negotiated marriage payments. Partly for this reason, the offspring (*ana ndi'i*) enjoy a higher status than do illegitimate children (*ana lora* or *ana la'a lora*, 'children from wandering'), who are generally subordinate in all matters to agnatic members of their mother's natal group.[8] As one man put it, while *ana ndi'i* have fewer rights in the maternal group than do natural children or adoptees, the illegitimate children of unmarried women have none at all (see further I: 5: iv).

Although Keo men may marry without paying bridewealth, only an exchange of goods can fully initiate or affirm an affinal alliance between two groups. While contextually classified as 'wife-takers' (*ana weta*), children and descendants of women for whom bridewealth was not paid are thus at best marginal to the category. Residing matrilocally, they never leave the wife-giving house, which formally speaking is the only group to which they belong. By the same token, men in this situation may not normally marry a MBD. As Keo pointed out, not only would the woman then be classified as a 'sister', but there would be no one to pay or receive bridewealth for her. The same applies to male adoptees (*ana ghawe* or *ana pendo*) related as ZS to their adoptive fathers, who are similarly excluded from marrying a MBD or another woman of the house of the maternal uncle. In one case a woman had cohabited with, and borne a child by, her FZS, who was an *ana ndi'i* of her natal clan, Guyu Wolo. The match was not, however, recognized as a legitimate marriage.

The importance of bridewealth exchange in defining affinal alliance is thus evident. Keo call bridewealth *ngawu*, a word with the wider meaning of 'goods, material wealth'. Alternative terms are *weli ngawu* and *weli fai*, 'price of a wife' (cf. Valeri 1994: 2, who records a similar usage among the Huaulu of Seram). As accords with its general sense, *ngawu* can also refer to goods of the same sort

---

[8] The designation 'children from wandering' implies that such offspring derive from illicit affairs conducted when people stroll or relax away from habitations. Further reflected in the reference to an unmarried mother as a 'free, loose wife' (*fai welu*), the same imagery is encountered in the Sumbanese phrase *ana mbawa* (Forth 1981: 336, n. 13). Other expressions for illegitimate children include *ana wea wonga, londa koba*, 'children of flowers used as golden ornaments and metal chains made of vines', and *ana kisa kobe, manu kako*, 'children of midnight and the cock crow'. Implying a lack of constraint, even a wildness, in the circumstances of an illegitimate conception, the first expression sardonically suggests that an absent bridewealth was replaced by wild plants. The second may allude as much to the metaphorical darkness of the child's paternity as to premarital liaisons being conducted at night.

that the recognized genitor of a child, usually a male child, might give to the family of an unmarried mother. In this way, a man is able to adopt (*ghawe*) a natural son as his legitimate heir without thereby marrying the child's mother, who indeed by this time may have married someone else. Despite the common designation, therefore, a payment of this sort does not result in marriage. Nor by the same token does it initiate or perpetuate an affinal relationship between two groups.[9]

Consistent with both the ritual and economic value of water buffalo, Keo usually express the amount of a bridewealth simply in terms of the number of buffalo included. Even so, each buffalo is normally given with a horse and metal valuables, and the wife-taker's prestation always additionally includes a number of goats and dogs. In fact, the total bridewealth might include any sort of animal, with the exception of pigs—since pigs always form part of the wife-giver's counter-prestation. The pre-eminence of buffalo among bridewealth valuables parallels their value as sacrificial victims (cf. Bloch 1992: 66–7). In both cases, an expenditure of the animals—through slaughter in one context and through giving in the other—serves to constitute and define fundamental groupings and relations. Just as offering buffalo for slaughter is the way estates (*ngapi*) affirm their identity as social entities with definite rights, so exchanging buffalo for brides is constitutive of the relation of affinal alliance. In both contexts, moreover, buffalo provide a means to life, by securing access to agricultural land and replenishing the earth with their blood on the one hand, and by obtaining wives to maintain or increase the human membership of the husband's group on the other.

Keo say bridewealth was generally higher during the early decades of the twentieth century than it is at present. Nowadays, a bridewealth comprising five buffalo is considered usual, though as many as ten animals can be requested. As in sacrifice, male animals are valued over females; and the majority of animals given as bridewealth should be male. While totals of five and ten are mentioned most often, the figures do not take into account additional animals which are provided for slaughter, to feed members of the wife-giving party who attend marriage negotiations. Nor do they include the horses and other goods given with buffalo. Dogs and goats are mostly slaughtered by the recipients (that is, the wife-givers) and consumed during the marriage proceedings. Likewise, most pigs provided by wife-givers serve as meals for wife-takers. In this context, Keo speak of pigs as 'soft things' (*ta meku*) and buffalo, goats, dogs, and other livestock as 'hard things' (*ta ndego*). The two phrases further describe the entirety of the counter-prestation and

---

[9] Nage call this procedure *tau ana ame*, 'to make (a relationship of) child and father', a phrase also known to Keo but possibly not indigenous to them. The standing of such children is described as somewhat lower than that of children born of mothers married with bridewealth. The arrangement appears most feasible when a man engages a woman as a temporary mistress (*ana bu'e*), a relationship traditionally requiring a payment to the woman's parents, which thus lent a degree of public recognition to the biological parentage of any resulting offspring.

PLATE 10. A woman from the groom's party places the parang (*topo*) in the back section of the bride's house

bridewealth. In so far as goods thus classified represent their donors—or more particularly the persons of the bride and groom—the expressions suggest a sexual reference, namely, the female and male genitalia in intercourse, although they may conceivably point to other contrasting male and female qualities as well (cf. McKinnon 1991: 177).

Also included in bridewealth are items of gold jewellery, designated simply as *wea* ('gold') and usually consisting of pairs of decorated or undecorated ear pendants. One pair should be given with one buffalo. Formerly, golden chains (*londa*) and other metal items, including foreign coins, were also employed as bridewealth. Nowadays, the objects serve only as decoration on ceremonial occasions, including major buffalo sacrifices. Another essential bridewealth component minimally comprises a single parang (*topo*) presented with a quantity of palm wine. When the wife-takers first enter the house of the bride, a female member of the party (who may be the groom's own mother) places the parang on a shelf at the back wall of the enclosed posterior section (*tolo*) of the building (see Plate 10). Designated as 'pushing forward the parang, inserting the lance' (*soyo topo, seli bhuja*),[10] this act marks the point at which Keo consider a

---

[10] Since Keo do not actually give a lance, the phrase more accurately reflects the practice of Nage, who do, indeed, present a lance, as well as coconuts and a fowl, with the parang.

marriage contract binding and signals an intention to continue the proceedings until the exchanges are complete. The transfer of the parang also confirms subsequent children of the marriage as full members of the father's group and as his legitimate heirs—a status designated as *ana soyo topo, seli bhuja*. Keo further link the parang with the groom's duty to protect and provide for the bride, as well as his obligation to her parents, for whom he must perform temporary bride service. Placing the object in the innermost part of the bride's parent's house, therefore, can be understood as signifying a temporary incorporation of the groom in the group of the wife-giver—an interpretation consistent with the general representation of wife-takers as part of the wife-giving group. At the same time, since symbolically this is the most female part of the house, the 'insertion' of the parang, a decidedly male object, might be understood as an act of penetration paralleling sexual intercourse (cf. Bloch 1992: 71).

Always required in reciprocation for bridewealth, the wife-giver's counter-prestation is called *sunda*, or *sunda seke*.[11] In addition to pigs, the goods mainly comprise decorated textiles. A quantity of cloths, in some instances minimally a man's and woman's cloth, reciprocate major portions of bridewealth. Any individual who contributes one or more large animals to a bridewealth can expect to receive textiles in return. Apart from specific counter-gifts, the bride's family also provides additional cloths intended for the bride herself. Figuratively designated as 'leaves for wrapping up meat' (*wunu toba*), these are presented with quantities of pork and rice. In the past, wealthy groups of high rank also transferred one or more female slaves (called *dhoko yipe*, '(those who) carry the betel basket') with the bride. The women were then eventually married to male slaves belonging to the groom's house. Keo further relate how at one time slaves were also employed as bridewealth, just as they could similarly be exchanged for land. The practice of a wife-giver providing a newly married couple with a parcel of land (*tana ka tuka*) was discussed in the preceding chapter.

Although the amount of counter-prestation is expected to match the quantity and quality of the bridewealth items, the total number of cloths is not fixed but, as Keo say, should reflect the bride's parents' regard for their daughter. Keo do speak of particular cloths being given in return for buffalo and other valuables forming particular parts of a bridewealth. Yet they avoid representing the two sorts of goods as units of a strict economic exchange whose quantity must strike a precise balance; and they further deny that bridewealth involves a measure of the woman in purely material terms.[12] On the other

---

[11] Described as synonymous, the components of the last expression seem not to be further analysable. The term *sunda*, however, suggests the idea of reverse action, as in *luka sapu sunda* ('sarong fastened with the ends twisted in opposite directions'), the earlier mentioned phrase referring to direct exchange. As applied to counter-prestation, *sunda* and *seke* refer as much to the act as to the items given (see also *sunda bhalo*, 'to give and receive'; cf. the Ngadha cognate *suda*, glossed by Arndt (1961) as 'to repeat, reiterate').

[12] One encounters similar ideas in other parts of Indonesia, including Sumba (Onvlee 1973: 89; Forth 1981: 367, 372) and Seram (Valeri 1994). As Valeri argues with regard to the Huaulu, whereas wife-takers may regard bridewealth as a purchase price, wife-givers consider the bride as a gift and accordingly reckon the counter-prestation in the same way (cf. Forth 1981: 372–3).

hand, there is the idea that as much as was received for a mother should be given for her daughter. Keo also remark that, nowadays, counter-prestation is usually so low in value relative to the bridewealth that wife-takers lose out according to a strict economic calculation.

Indeed at present, Keo regularly evaluate the total cost of a man's marriage in monetary terms and often speak of bridewealth as a heavy financial burden. They also claim that, in the past, marriage payments were fewer and schedules simpler, describing bridewealth as having become inflated during the colonial period. On the other hand, the usual amounts of animals and golden ornaments have reputedly decreased during the last two or three decades. Yet expectations have not always been reduced accordingly. Bridewealth may be given all at once or, as is more common, in stages. Typically, the two parties negotiate a total bridewealth to be given over a period of time in named instalments. '*Ulu liwu*, an apparently hyperbolic expression meaning 'forty-four', is sometimes used to refer to this total, though it more exactly denotes the quantity of buffalo and golden ornaments, usually the largest part of the entire prestation, which complete a bridewealth.

As mentioned in the preceding chapter, collectivities that form to raise bridewealth do not always coincide with clans, houses, or estates, but are variably composed in relation to particular marriages. Where bride and groom belong to different villages, all members of a village, regardless of clan affiliation, can be invited to contribute to the bridewealth or counter-prestation. So, too, may agnatically related yet separate clans resident in other villages. On the wife-taking side, contributors might even include other wife-givers of the groom's clan or house. Only contrary affinal ties of quite specific kinds should preclude participation. For example, people should not contribute to a bridewealth if they previously received counter-prestation goods at the marriage of the bride's brother.

According to an explicit local formulation, when amassing a bridewealth a man's father should first call for assistance from other members of his house (*sa'o*) and, immediately thereafter, his own wife-takers (*ana weta*). Only then will he approach other houses of his clan. Later still, he may call on other clans in the same village or in a paired village (linked with his own in a double settlement) and perhaps related clans resident elsewhere. Expressed another way, one can say that, with the exception of wife-takers, a man seeks support from various categories of *ka'e ari*, beginning with the most closely related agnatic kin and, as it were, extending outwards. How consistently these guidelines are followed in practice is, however, difficult to determine. As Keo pointed out, who is called upon to assist depends as much on whom the principal has himself assisted in the past. Nevertheless, they do fairly reflect the importance in this context of wife-takers—the husbands of sisters and daughters of the groom's father—who are bound by a continuous obligation to assist to much the same extent as are agnatic kin. In fact, it would not be going too far to say that, in the context of a man's marriage, wife-takers are counted as belonging to his own group, a representation that is of course consistent with a general subsumption of affinal connection in the category of *ka'e ari*. Furthermore, while this encompassment is mostly asymmetrical, the inclusion among contributors to a bridewealth of parties that have in the past given wives to the house or clan of a groom, shows how wife-givers, too, can contextually be treated as *ka'e ari*.[13]

Bridewealth and counter-prestation may be returned only when a wife dissolves a marriage, usually by deserting her husband. When it is, by contrast, the husband who initiates divorce, and particularly when he formally banishes the wife, he can only recover the bridewealth after she remarries;[14] and I was told that most men would be reluctant to marry such a divorcee. Genealogical evidence and local statements suggest that, even before Keo conversion to Catholicism, separation of spouses involving a return of marriage prestations was uncommon. Returning bridewealth does not absolutely determine the subsequent affiliation of offspring. Children might all remain with one parent or they may be divided, with infants for obvious reasons more often remaining with the mother. At the same time, if bridewealth is not recovered, then the husband's group have a greater claim on children of divorcees when they reach adulthood. Those who remain with the mother usually occupy a status comparable to that of children of marriages without bridewealth (*ana ndi'i*) or children of widows who return with their mother to her natal group when a deceased father's agnates fail to provide her brother with required mortuary goods (see Section 5 below). Although dissolution of marriage involving return of bridewealth and remarriage of divorcees was evidently possible in the traditional social order of western Keo, its comparative rarity, like the resulting status ambiguity of both female divorcees and their offspring, is consistent with a view of marriage as a union connecting two groups in an enduring alliance.

4. Givers and Takers of Wives

As should by now be evident, 'wife-taker' and 'wife-giver' do not invariably coincide with the collectivities formed to exchange marriage prestations. Nor do they apply to the most inclusive kind of exogamous grouping, generally

---

[13] That collectivities formed to amass bridewealth can be based as much on common locality as on descent group affiliation was especially suggested by one instance where a man and his wife, both from eastern Keo and now permanently resident in a field hut near Pau Lundu (II: 3: iii), received contributions at the marriage of their son from a variety of men from Pau Lundu and neighbouring villages, none of whom was agnatically or affinally related to the groom's parents. It should be noted, however, that residing a long distance from agnates and other relatives, as in this instance, appears to be a relatively recent development which may encourage a greater recourse to ties of locality (as opposed to kinship) than was usual in the past.

[14] Called *tu malo fai*, 'to send a wife back', banishment involves the ritual act of suspending the woman's sirih basket from her forehead (*teo ne'e yipe oka*), which is how a woman carries the item when she sets out on a journey. Also, a device called a 'bamboo cannon' (I: 5, n. 16) is fired. Both acts mark a definitive separation of the couple.

defined as clans (*suku*). Instead, the alliance categories refer to parts of clans, usually specified as 'houses' (*sa'o*), that are linked to like units mostly comprised in other clans, by virtue of specific marriages.

Although not entirely satisfactory in all contexts, 'wife-giver' and 'wife-taker' provide reasonable glosses of the Keo terms *moi ga'e* (or *moi mame*) and *ana weta*. Analytically, two kinds of wife-givers need to be distinguished. Describable as 'immediate' wife-givers, the first includes houses that have directly given wives to ego's house, thus those of WB and WF, MB, FMB, FFMB, and so on. The second variety comprises what Fox, referring to the same entity on Roti, terms the 'line of maternal affiliation' (1980*b*: 119; see also Traube 1986: 86; McKinnon 1991: 107; Beatty 1992: 69–73), but which, with respect to a local idiom, I would prefer to call ego's 'maternal line of origin'. Although unnamed among Keo, the category evidently corresponds to what in different parts of the Tanimbar Islands is called a 'ladder' (Pauwels 1994: 82) or a 'row' (McKinnon 1991: 103). As elsewhere, the Keo maternal line comprises the houses of MB, MMB, MMMB, and more distantly related groups indirectly connected to one's own, over as many generations, by a series of women's marriages. It is thus as much a line of affinity as a line of origin. In a similar regard, it should be noted that the MB, as both the immediate wife-giver of ego's father and as the closest link in the maternal line—or closest point of origin—belongs to both categories of wife-giver.[15]

Keo themselves distinguish wife-giving groups in the maternal line of origin inasmuch as they specify these as a person's *pu'u*, his or her 'source', '(place of) origin', or 'trunk'. The line is also given special recognition at funerals, when the house of the deceased's MB—or, in its absence, that of his MMB—is owed goods called *tobo*, an institution I describe in the next section. Following the Keo idiom explicated in the following chapter, a person is moreover considered to 'descend' from (*poro pu'u*) the house of his MB as well as less immediately connected houses in this maternal line. In so far as a man, as it were, inherits his father's maternal line of origin, and indeed obligations pertaining thereto, Keo wife-givers further include the houses of his FMB, FMMB, FMMMB, and so forth.[16] Accordingly, sacrificial orations (*bhea*) commonly record forebears in the maternal line of origin of the speaker's father (*logo ta ema*; *logo* is 'back', thus also 'background, genealogy'), as well as those comprising his own maternal line which, of course, is also his mother's (*logo ta ine*).

In the view of some commentators, *moi mame* should be reserved for members of ego's maternal line, while immediate wife-givers—such as WB,

---

[15] It should be stressed that the maternal line of origin is not a matrilineage, nor indeed any sort of 'group'. Recent research among the Lio (Sugishima 1994), however, suggests that, in some parts of Flores, named matrilineal groups may have developed from this sort of unnamed category.

[16] If MBD marriage were consistently practised, then FMB and FFMB would, of course, belong to the same house as MB. Also, the group of the MMB would be the same as that of WMB and MBWB, relatives also classifiable with MB as *moi* and thus included as wife-givers in the broadest sense.

WF, FMB, and FFMB—are properly classified only as *moi ga'e*, construed as a broader category subsuming *moi mame* as well. Observation, however, revealed that Keo often employ the two terms synonymously; and indeed the two sorts of wife-giving affines are generally treated in the same way, in regard both to material exchange and marriage possibilities. In both expressions, the element *moi* can be understood either as the term for MB (also designated as *ame moi*; *ame*, F) or in the sense of 'owner, possessor'. The second component of the first expression, *mame*, is identical to the western Keo term for FZ (also MBW, MBWBW, WMBW). Yet, in view of the general asymmetry of the system, its appearance in this context may reflect an eastern Keo use of *mame* as the term for MB (see Forth 1994*b*, 1995*b*), as some local commentary indeed seemed to confirm. In the expression *moi ga'e*, by contrast, the paired term *ga'e* is virtually synonymous with *moi* in the sense of 'owner'. Since *ga'e* refers, among other things, to a master of slaves, one might accurately translate the resulting compound as 'lord and master'.

It is, therefore, quite clear how both expressions represent wife-givers as superior affines, an evaluation that accords both with Keo ideology and ritual practice. Combining *mame* with the word for 'grandparent, ancestor', another term for wife-givers is *ebu mame*, sometimes identified as a usage deriving from coastal and more easterly dialects. Although often equated with *moi mame*, as the element *ebu* ('grandparent, ancestor') would imply the expression can refer more specifically to wife-givers in the second and higher ascending genealogical levels (including MMB) and their present heirs and successors. Consistent with this, *ebu mame* seems to be employed most often in funerary contexts, where a dead man's surviving children apply it to the house of their father's MB.

Invoking house imagery, Keo further designate wife-givers as *ndi'i sa'o* or *mera sa'o*, '(those who) reside, remain in the house'. (The first term, especially, should be compared to *ana ndi'i*, a reference to the offspring of uxorilocal marriages, who remain with their mother's groups.) As suggested in the preceding chapter, these phrases are illuminated by the idea that a person derives from the house of his wife-giver and, in a sense, still belongs to it. A similar implication is contained in the contrast of *ana réta tolo*, 'children (people) up inside the house', and *ana rale tana*, 'children (people) down on the ground' (I: 3: iv), which conceptually locate wife-givers in the enclosed, innermost section of the house, and wife-takers beneath the raised house floor. This contrast of above and below recurs in the synonymous phrases *wawo lapu* and *au lapu*, also discussed in the preceding chapter. Yet another instance is the pair *wawo yape*, '(people) above the terrace, on the higher terrace', and *au yape*, 'below the terrace, on the terrace below', referring to wife-givers and wife-takers respectively. More commonly heard among their Nage neighbours, Keo deemed this pair of phrases as inappropriate in the modern era in so far as they connote—some would say denote—a relation of master (*ga'e*) and slave (*yo'o*).

In one opinion, however, the same applies to *moi ga'e*, while the phrase *ana rale tana* similarly refers to slaves as well as wife-takers. Whatever the present propriety of the usages, the associations they evoke are obviously consistent with the superiority, in affinal contexts, of wife-givers, and the recognized dependence and subordination of wife-takers.

As the reciprocal of *moi mame* and *moi ga'e*, the standard expression for 'wife-taker', *ana weta*, comprises the terms for 'child' and 'sister (m.s.)'. A closely comparable usage is *ana naya* (*naya* is 'brother, w.s.'), which women employ to refer to their natal group, that is, their husbands' wife-givers, and which is thus identically articulated with regard to the relation of opposite-sex siblings. Although primarily meaning 'child', in these contexts *ana* can be further understood as 'descendant' or 'people, member (of a group or category)'. Corresponding to terms for wife-takers in several other Indonesian languages (see, for example, Karo *ana beru*, Singarimbun 1975: 113; eastern Sumbanese *ana kawini*, Forth 1981: 285), *ana weta* may, therefore, be understood as 'children or descendants of sisters'. In accordance with this gloss, some Keo doubted the applicability of the term to DH, ZH, or FZH, that is, affines who are not 'descended' in the maternal line from one's own house (like DC, ZC, or FZC), or who do not reckon ego's group as a component of an inherited maternal line (as for example do FFZCC). The contrast this implies obviously corresponds to the distinction of the two sorts of wife-givers outlined above. Yet, as in that case also, the interpretation is contradicted by observed practice, which indicates that both sorts of connection are comprised in a single, general category of 'wife-takers'.[17]

At present, Indonesian-speaking Keo often refer to wife-takers as 'descendants of females' (BI *turunan wanita/perempuan*), or alternatively as 'people descending indirectly' (*turunan tidak lurus/langsung*) from one's own group. Yet another expression is 'descendants on the side' (*turunan samping*). The last phrase, in particular, recalls the representation of Defenders (*ana tuku*) as people who occupy the peripheries of a Land Mother's domain (I: 1: iii), and who are frequently reckoned as wife-takers of the older, and conceptually central, group. In the same national-language idiom, Keo accordingly specify agnatic kin as 'direct descendants' (*turunan lurus/langsung*) of the male ancestors of a house or clan.[18]

While these several idioms may appear to emphasize lineal connections rather than relations of marriage alliance, the accuracy of this assessment hinges on the Keo concept of 'descent', a subject explored in the next chapter. Just as important is an implicit conception of wife-takers as a subsidiary part, extension, or derivative of a wife-giving group (cf. Barraud, 1990: 200, who

---

[17] In so far as this distinction is expressed in local terminology, ZC, as it were the most focal sort of wife-taker, can be specified as *ana ane*, or alternatively *ane ana*. Both compounds, as well as *ane* alone, are common kin terms for ZC (Forth 1994*b*: 98).

[18] As used in this context, 'direct' and 'indirect' have no equivalents in Keo. Nor, in regard to its cognatic application, does Indonesian *turunan*, 'descent, descendant'.

describes wife-taking houses in Kei as 'a constitutive part of the (wife-giving) house', and McKinnon, 1991: 95, who in this regard speaks explicitly of 'encompassment'). Consistent with this characterization, Keo describe wife-takers—particularly, though not exclusively, co-resident wife-takers—as people who, although in a sense belonging to the wife-giver's house, are not 'true', 'authentic' or 'original' (*tenge*) members, a status occupied only by agnatic descendants.[19] Their lack of full standing of course relates to the fact that their only link to the group is through females. Accordingly, wife-takers might alternatively be described as a feminine extension of a wife-giver.

Further supporting the feminine character of wife-takers is the Keo application of *ana weta* not only to the husbands, children, and descendants of women who have married out, but also to the women themselves. The symbolic femininity of the category is also underlined when affines exchange goods in ritual settings. As I was able to observe from feasts celebrating the inauguration of a new house (*nalo sa'o*), by far the majority of animals and other goods provided by *ana weta* are nominally donated by females, including young unmarried girls and female infants related to the principal male householder as, for example, ZD, FZD, FZCD, or FZCCD. At the largest house inauguration I attended, nearly 70 per cent of over one hundred wife-takers' gifts were formally brought by females. Where males are recognized as donors, moreover, they are frequently husbands or brothers of female donors. Such pairing appears to reflect a more general preference for attributing parts of a total gift (for example, one of a pair of goats or one of a number of containers of palm gin) to individual members of a donating couple or family. Thus, where male wife-takers contribute animals to a wife-giver's bridewealth, they are sometimes given in the names of the donors' wives. Inaugurating a wife-giver's new residence, however, is probably the major occasion on which wife-takers affirm their connection to—one might also say their 'participation' in—the wife-giving group, a circumstance that is of course fully in accord with the importance of the house in Keo representations of affinal alliance.[20]

5. *Alliance and the Perpetuation of Affinity*

Corresponding to the contrast of above and below evidenced in expressions referring to wife-givers and wife-takers, and further indicated by the appearance

---

[19] Regularly equated with Indonesian *asli*, Keo *tenge* is similarly used to distinguish the founders of a village from more recently arrived residents, as was noted earlier (I: 2: iii).

[20] Suggesting a view of a house as the joint property of a married couple, the exchange of prestations at house inaugurations can, moreover, include persons related to the male house-holder as, or through, WZ, WZH (and perhaps especially WyZH), and WZD. Other possibilities, attested in particular instances, include WBD, WMBD, WMBDD, MMZD, and MMZDD. Although all these relatives are in this context classified as *ana weta*, and bring goods of the sort appropriate to that category, reckoning them as 'wife-takers'—or even as spouses, children, or descendants of women classified as *weta*—is in most instances obviously problematic; and it is therefore significant that, in the view of some commentators, all or most are more accurately conceived as *ka'e ari*. In this regard, it should be pointed out that goods provided by *ana weta* are not different in kind from those supplied by parties classified, with agnates, as *ka'e ari*.

of *ana* ('child') and *moi* ('mother's brother') in standard terms for the two sorts of affines, affinal alliance among Keo is largely represented as a vertical relationship between higher and lower genealogical levels. Accordingly, in its focal sense the Keo category of wife-takers refers to children or descendants of women (D, Z, FZ, FFZ, and so on) who were transferred from the wife-giver's house in marriage, rather than to components of a horizontal, and notionally synchronic, chain of perpetuated marriage connections. From this, it follows that alliance consists not so much in marriages repeated between the same two groups in successive generations, as in the ramification of wife-taking groups themselves—and, indeed, of *their* wife-takers.

Nevertheless, one must not forget that Keo marriage rules do encourage the perpetuation of affinal ties through further unions. As noted, Keo also describe particular clans, or more accurately their seniormost houses, as being obligated to take at least one woman from an established wife-giver in each generation, or as having been so obliged at some unspecified former time. Referring to an enduring alliance with wife-givers in clan Céla (II: 1: i), men of clan Pajo Wolo in Lower Pajo Mala (II: 2: i) thus claim that prospective spouses who refused a marriage that perpetuated the tie would be mystically punished by a deterioration of the genitalia (*lasu mese, puki pota*, 'disappearing penis, vanishing vagina').[21] In addition, some clans (II: 6: ii) are locally recognized as maintaining three-unit alliance cycles (*leo pu'u nduke*, I: 3: iv), even though cycles are not a particularly favoured arrangement and, in one opinion, are tantamount to direct exchange.

The value Keo place on perpetuating alliances is further evident from their representation of widow inheritance. A brother or other agnate who assumes the spousal responsibilities of a dead man is said to 'ascend to (his) widow' (*nai walu*).[22] Men of different clans related as 'house siblings' (*ka'e ari sa'o ténda*) may also inherit one another's widows, as in one famous case in Pajo Mala where the childless headman of clan Kate was succeeded by the son of a Pajo Wolo man born to the former's widow (II: 2: ii). Described metaphorically as 'repairing a broken fence, rebuilding a collapsed stone wall' (*yasa boka wake, kota beghu tuye*), widow inheritance is characterized as securing affinal connections and preventing outsiders from marrying women for whom bridewealth has been discharged.

Although he replaces the deceased husband, Keo do not fully regard the inheritor as the widow's legitimate spouse. At the same time, they do recognize him (and not the dead man) as the father of any children the widow may bear him. While it is possible for another man to marry a widow by paying

---

[21] This was also described as a consequence of Céla taking women from Pajo Wolo, thus reversing the relationship.

[22] *Nai*, 'to ascend', can also refer to successive action by members of a series (see *pébha nai ngapi*, I: 3: ii). As accords with Arndt's glosses of the Ngadha cognate (1961: 345, s.v. *naci*), in this context the term may have the further sense of 'to hold in high regard' or 'to honour', an interpretation supported by the Nage phrase *he walu*, 'to show consideration for, think (well) of a widow'.

bridewealth to the deceased husband's group, such an arrangement, negatively characterized as 'disassembling the hearth' (*wuka lika*), is generally disapproved and appears always to have been uncommon. A better recourse, where there is no one in the dead husband's group to replace him, is to allow an outsider to contract a uxorilocal union without bridewealth, particularly as this ensures that any children the widow may subsequently have will belong to the dead man's house and clan.

Yet another expression of the value placed on maintaining affinal alliances is the standard admonition *tua ma'e pota, manu máe 'ila*, 'let not the palm wine (or gin) cease, let not the fowls disappear'. Referring to goods wife-takers are obliged to provide to wife-givers, the phrases specify an obligation to continue the material transfer over the generations.[23] Especially noteworthy here is the way the idiom highlights material assistance owed by wife-takers, rather than the women provided by wife-givers. So long as this assistance is not discontinued, Keo aver, people can still consider themselves as affinal allies regardless of whether they continue to contract further marriages. By the same token, the two parties should not controvert the asymmetry of the original relation by contracting unions in the opposite direction. Affinal alliance can thus endure simply as a hereditary connection between groups, as indeed in some instances of the relation of Land Mother and Defender. As this latter association should suggest, whether or not alliances are given effective recognition, and for how long, can depend on a variety of social and political considerations unrelated to the degree to which members of the two groups continue to marry.

A view of alliance as a tie extended simply by virtue of the ramification of wife-taking lines pertains especially to wife-giving houses comprised in a 'maternal line of origin' (those of the MB, MMB, and so on). It is thus from these groups, and especially from the house that provided a female forebear initiating a series of women's marriages traversing several successive generations, that a person is conceived to 'derive' (*pu'u*), and even to 'descend' (*poro*). Formed once and for all from unions linking a number of agnatic groups, this genealogically diagonal tie obviously does not depend on further marriages between different pairs of affines, though these of course are not ruled out. It only requires public recognition of a continuing relationship, through women, to an original house, or group of wife-givers, regarded, like more immediate components of the maternal line (for example, MB, MMB), as a 'source' or 'trunk' (*pu'u*). In this maternal line of origin, it should be noted, successive 'nodes', as they might be called, are subsumed by preceding ones, so that all are ultimately encompassed by, or identified with, the original wife-giver, the source or origin of the line. By the same token, the MB (or his house), as the

---

[23] Since providing fowls is actually more characteristic of Nage, in this context *manu* may be understood as a synecdochal reference to livestock in general. Alternatively, though Keo never mentioned the connection, the reference could conceivably be to a practice I describe below, whereby a wife-giver provides a fowl in order to effect the recovery of an ailing wife-taker.

most recent or proximate node, is considered a person's origin (*pu'u*) in a metonymic sense. As will be elaborated later, an individual 'descends' (*poro*) not just from his MB, but also from his MMB in so far as the maternal uncle 'descends' from *his* MB. Just as wife-takers are conceived as parts of wife-giving houses, therefore, an entire line, including the ego that is its most recent terminus, is ultimately encompassed—by way of a conceptual process comparable to a telescope—in the original house, the very first wife-giver in a line constituted of women's marriages.[24]

Other aspects of Keo alliance are illuminated by the funerary obligations of wife-takers, or what may be called mortuary payments. When a man dies, his sons or other heirs are required to give a quantity of goods to the deceased's MB and WB, who should be notified immediately after the death occurs. When a married woman dies, her husband or sons (if she was a widow) must similarly make payments to her brother and her MB. Consisting of goods of the same sort as are used as bridewealth, the payments are generally designated as *tobo*, a term that more specifically refers to the portion owed to the MB. If for some reason the MB (or his successors) are not available or willing to receive the goods, then representatives of the house of the deceased's MMB may be called instead.[25] Other wife-givers—for example the group of a dead man's FMB—are also invited to funerals. But while they, too, receive goods, reciprocating alliance prestations which they customarily provide, these are not classified as *tobo*.[26] Nor do the goods have the obligatory character attaching to mortuary payments owed to the deceased's MB—the most proximate connection in the maternal line of origin—and to the brother-in-law (or the brother, where the deceased is a married woman). Keo regard it as a source of considerable shame if no one comes forward to request *tobo*. If no one were to claim the part owed to his MB, this would imply that the deceased lacked a place of 'origin' or 'derivation' (*pu'u*). Similarly, if no one were thus publicly to acknowledge his status as the deceased's WB (or a married woman's B), the legitimacy of surviving children would be called into question.

Comparative evidence suggests a relation between *tobo* and *tebo*, 'body, corpse' (cf. Ngadha *tobo*, 'corpse', Arndt 1961: 534). In reference to the portion owed to the MB, Keo also speak more elaborately of *tobo mata* (*mata*, 'dead,

---

[24] This aspect of Keo affinity recalls Barraud's evaluation of alliance in the Kei Islands, and particularly her claim that 'what is transmitted from generation to generation in marriage alliance is a relationship of affinity rather than an obligation to exchange women' (1990: 194).

[25] Mortuary payments are reciprocated with pigs, cloth, and rice, things given by wife-givers by way of formally requesting the payments. While subject to negotiation, the amount of *tobo* given to the deceased's MB should include at least one large male buffalo, or two smaller animals, and either a horse or items of gold (designated *peri lu mata*). Further included is a parang called *dhoi toko* ('(what) carries the bones') or, in its place, a goat or dog. The deceased's family also slaughters at least one buffalo for the group of the MB, who later take away the head (*ulu mata*, 'head of death') together with another parang, notionally used to sever the head (*sae ulu*). The portion owed to the deceased's WB is smaller, comprising a single buffalo given with gold or a horse and, possibly, a single parang.

[26] Instead, they are called *yoko* or *yoko yupa*, terms applied to all goods brought by both wife-takers and wife-givers to affinal funerals, as well as goods given in reciprocation for these. Alluding to the process of mortuary exchange in general, the terms more literally denote textiles in which a corpse is wrapped in preparation for burial.

death'), *tobo weki* ('body *tobo*'), or *weli weki*, 'price of the body'. Another name is *ulu mata*, roughly 'dead head', a phrase more specifically denoting a buffalo slaughtered for the deceased's MB (see n. 25). In contrast, *ulu muri*, 'living head(s)', distinguishes live buffalo given to the same party. Especially the characterization of *tobo* as the 'price of the body' might imply that a person, or his body, is in effect possessed by his MB (*moi*), who must therefore be compensated by the deceased's agnates (or husband's agnates, in the case of a married woman) before they can dispose of it (see Fox 1971, with regard to comparable Rotinese usages). If not an actual purchase of the corpse, *tobo* can alternatively be viewed as compensation for a death that has occurred, as it were, outside of a person's house of origin, in accordance with the representation of wife-takers as continuing participants in the wife-giver's house. Also relevant here is another use of *tobo*, as a reference to goods owed to the survivors of a man for whose death one is somehow responsible—for example, recruited warriors who fall in battle.[27]

Several additional points support these interpretations. First, when a ZC is actually incorporated in the MB's house—either because his father did not pay bridewealth or because of adoption (*ghawe*) by his maternal uncle—*tobo* is not required. Secondly, although nowadays the debt is usually not paid until well after the completion of mortuary rites, Keo state that, formerly, burial could not take place before mortuary payments were discharged. The suggestion that surviving kin must make a payment to the deceased's MB before disposing of the corpse is further consistent with the fact that the term *moi* (MB) can also mean 'owner' (see also *moi ga'e*, 'lord and master', 'wife-giver').

Noteworthy in this connection is the Keo notion, comparable to ones encountered in several other parts of Indonesia, that wife-givers, and especially the MB, have power of life and death over a person. If a person suffers serious or persistent illness, it may be determined that a cure can be effected only by slaughtering a fowl provided by a maternal uncle, in a manner imitating a buffalo sacrifice (*paya manu*). Blood of the fowl is then placed on the patient's feet, a practice reminiscent of what is done when a wife-taker first enters a wife-giver's new house. By refusing to provide a fowl for this purpose, Keo say, a MB can ensure the death of a ZC, and by swearing never to do so in the future, he poses a serious threat to a wife-taker's well-being. In much the same vein, angered wife-givers are able to invoke a powerful curse, ensuring the extinction of a wife-taking house, livestock failure, and other sorts of misfortune.

Although subsumed by *tobo* in the broader sense, the mortuary payment owed to the WB (or a deceased woman's brother) has a somewhat different significance. Distinguished as *tudhi bu'a, léko bhéka*, 'breaking of the (palm-tapping) knife, splitting of the palm juice container', the payment is specified with reference to a wife-taker's obligation regularly to supply wife-givers with

---

[27] Since surviving kin of war recruits and mercenaries could demand compensation in the form of land (*tana*), this kind of payment is sometimes specified as *tobo tana*. A similar compensation, connected with the extraordinary deaths of two women in childbirth, was mentioned in the previous chapter (I: 3: i, n. 1).

palm wine or gin. As Keo themselves recognize, the phrases thus describe death as causing this flow of a valued liquid to cease, at least so far as the individual producer is concerned. Yet they are further understood as referring to the person of the deceased, identified with instruments employed in obtaining the juice of the palm. Accordingly, Keo sometimes construe 'broken knife' (an alternative gloss of *tudhi bu'a*) as a specific reference to a deceased married man, and 'split container' (*léko bhéka*) as a reference to a deceased married woman. (Noteworthy here is the fact that only men use knives for palm tapping, while wine or gin in bamboo containers is frequently carried and presented to wife-givers by women.) Combining the two phrases can then describe a situation where both members of a spousal pair have died and all debts to the woman's natal group are discharged.

As indicated above, if no one comes forward to claim *tudhi bu'a*, *léko bhéka*, doubt is cast on the legitimacy of the deceased's offspring. Accordingly, if a dead man's heirs fail to discharge the amount required, his widow's natal house can demand that the woman and some or all of her children be returned to them (see further I: 5: iv). Mortuary payments owed to the WB might thus be understood as a final stage of bridewealth, and, indeed, Keo speak of them as facilitating widow inheritance. The possibility of a dead man's wife and children being reclaimed by her natal house when mortuary obligations are not met may further suggest that a man fully belongs to his own agnatic clan or house only when these are discharged, thus after his death (cf. Bloch, 1992: 86, who describes Merina as never being 'completely a member of a life-transcending descent group' while they are alive; see also Holy, 1996: 156, glossing Fox, 1987: 174–5). For if the goods are not given after his death, and after the death of his wife, then a man forfeits his patrimony and becomes in effect like a husband married uxorilocally without bridewealth, who thus 'remains separate(d)' (*ndi'i dhato*; see Section 3 above) from his agnates.

Somewhat in accord with the foregoing, employing the Indonesian phrase *putus hubungan*, 'breaking a connection', Keo describe mortuary payments owed to both the MB and the WB (or B, w.s.) as severing ties between wife-taker and wife-giver. The notion is interesting as it evidently contradicts the more widely attested representation of affinal alliance as a relationship that should endure beyond death. In so far as the transaction can be seen as completing bridewealth, this notion of disconnection may appear to concern more the brother-in-law's portion, a specification further suggested by metaphors of breaking and splitting in the name of the latter payment.[28] Yet

---

[28] The idea of severance is also revealed in the phrases *peo bu'a, nabe* (or *madhu*) *bewu*, 'breaking of the sacrificial instrument, smashing of the altar stone (or *madhu* post)', referring to a quantity of goods a man can request at the death of his ZHF. This prestation is, however, additional to the payments designated as *tobo* and may even be a recent innovation. Although it is unclear why the deceased affine, or the relationship affected by the death, should in this case be designated by terms denoting ritual instruments, the fact that Land Mothers commonly grant these to Defenders (who often are simultaneously wife-takers) is conceivably relevant to this usage. Among Nage, I recorded a similar expression describing the death of a man of very high rank.

Keo make no distinction in this regard. What is more, the notion of affinal severance is expressed not only in local statements but in rites focused on the relation of MB and ZS. Exceptionally, a very wealthy man may undertake to discharge his own mortuary payments (*tobo*) before his death, a practice and status called *logo sia* ('clear, clean back (biography, genealogy)'). In one opinion, to do so he should transfer goods to all recognized wife-givers (*moi ga'e* or *moi mame*), not just to the houses of his MB and WB, thus freeing himself from all further affinal obligations.[29] In order to formalize the disconnection, a representative of the house of the man's MB must sprinkle him with a mixture of foxtail millet and ash (*wéca ne'e wete toyo ne'e awu lapu*) from a punctured half coconut shell. Significantly, the same practice figures in rites effecting banishment. In this way, as well as by means of other ritual procedures (including shearing the head and remaining naked in confinement for four nights), a *logo sia* in effect reverts to a premarital condition, as a function of what Keo statements suggested is a symbolic rebirth and return to infancy.

While providing a telling instance of a more general ritual theme, *logo sia* denotes an obviously exceptional practice. It is, furthermore, one that Keo do not entirely approve of, linking it with excessive pride and an arrogant individualism. Indeed, by discharging his own mortuary payments, a man effectively usurps the position of his sons and heirs. It may be in this light that, according to a respected, albeit unusual, local opinion, a man who 'clears his (own) back' should forbid his sons from marrying women related as MBD, so as not to revive a severed alliance. In contrast, when surviving children discharge mortuary debts on behalf of a dead man, they arguably reaffirm their relationship both with representatives of their father's maternal line of origin—more particularly, the house of their FMB—and the house of the deceased's WB, who is the children's own MB. (When a married woman dies, groups receiving mortuary payments are of course those of her children's MB and their MMB.) In this light, then, mortuary payments can be seen as part of an ongoing material exchange which perpetuates rather than cancels affinal alliances, but specifically in respect of the living rather than the dead person, who it may be assumed is the real subject of mortuary separation.

Nevertheless, if all deceased persons are ritually disconnected from the houses of their MB, as Keo statements proclaim, then one is left with the question of how a man's sons can inherit the connection, thus continuing to recognize the group of their FMB (the closest 'node' in the father's maternal line) as a wife-giver. Even more to the point, if the mortuary payment for a deceased woman, the *léko bhéka*, disconnects her from her natal house, it remains unclear why her children are not similarly disattached from their MB and other ascendants in the maternal line of origin. One can only conclude that alliance,

---

[29] In the general representation, men who become *logo sia* are absolved not only from ritual restrictions (*piye*) to which wife-takers as a class are subject but also from other prohibitions, including clan food taboos where these apply.

or inherited affinity, somehow transcends the separation associated with mortuary payments, which is the same as saying that marriage alliance transcends death. The affinal disconnection that Keo posit is, therefore, best understood as a temporary state of affairs pertaining solely to the mortuary period—the several days between burial and final mortuary rites when, significantly enough, Keo (like their Nage neighbours, Forth 1993*b*) treat the deceased soul as though it were an intrusive, malevolent spirit (*nitu*). Coincident with the dead later attaining the status of a benevolent ancestor who is reunited with living kin, the alliance—to the extent that it ever was truly nullified—is accordingly resumed once the mortuary context no longer prevails. Here it should be noted that Keo and Nage funerals are overwhelmingly concerned with separating the dead from the living in general. Hence in relation to the wider theme of affinal continuity, the idea that death and mortuary payments sever maternal lines of origin reflects this specific ritual setting rather than an aspect of Keo alliance *per se*.

Regardless of local evaluations of the purpose of mortuary payments, Keo ideology further entails an enduring connection between a person and his maternal line of origin by virtue of a posited transfer of maternal blood (*ya*). Earlier I noted how this maternal connection, like the relationship of wife-giver and wife-taker more generally conceived, is bound up with notions of 'origin' or 'derivation' (*pu'u*) and 'descent' (*poro*). The articulation of these several concepts, all referring to relations through women, in a society composed of basically agnatic groups is further explored in the following chapter. Also dealt with are related issues bearing on inheritance, incorporation, and group composition.

5

Metaphors of Social Process:
Origination, Derivation, and Incorporation

Social relations discussed in previous chapters are informed by several complementary or mutually reinforcing metaphors. After exploring these in turn, I
consider how the relations they articulate bear on incorporation and the standing of individuals within social groups. For students of Indonesia and other
Austronesian-speaking societies, these metaphorical themes may appear all too
familiar. Yet to obtain a fuller understanding of western Keo society, and to
explore how they illuminate a more widespread symbolism, it is necessary to
review the Keo variants in some detail.

1. Pu'u: *Origin, Source, Place of Derivation*

Denoting the stem or trunk of a tree or plant, the application of *pu'u* to social
relations constitutes a botanical metaphor of a sort encountered in both western and eastern Indonesia (Fox 1980*a*, 1996; Sather 1996: 81, citing Freeman
1981: 31). In the same contexts, the term conveys the general sense of 'source'
or 'origin'. As previously shown, Keo associate *pu'u* with the senior member of
several major binary relations—including Land Mother (*ine tana*) and
Defender (*ana tuku*), and 'trunk rider' (*saka pu'u*) and 'tip rider' (*saka lobo*).
Similarly, the most senior house and estate of a clan are designated as *sa'o pu'u*
('trunk house') and *ngapi pu'u* ('trunk estate'), while in several idioms Keo
describe wife-givers (*moi mame*) as the *pu'u*—the trunk, origin or place of
derivation—of wife-takers. Regarding this common designation of both senior
houses and wife-givers as 'trunks' or 'sources', it should be remarked how *pu'u*
applies to otherwise contrasting relations of agnation and affinity, as does the
same idiom in other eastern Indonesian societies (see e.g., Forth 1981: 289).

Pu'u articulates more than synchronic relations between social statuses or
groups. In fact, the term's most frequent appearance is in such ordinary statements as *nga'o pu'u ena X*, 'I have come from X'. Since X denotes a spatial location from which one has recently travelled, in this context *pu'u* is most simply
glossed as 'from' (*ena* is a general preposition usually replaced by a direction
indicator, such as *réle*, 'above', or *rili*, 'below'). Yet the same statement can also
be translated as 'my source (trunk) is at X' or 'I have (had) X as my source'.
For Keo, therefore, simple movement from one location to another implies a
recognition of the former as a trunk or origin. By the same token, rather than
merely describing the superior member of a hierarchical pair, *pu'u* suggests

movement or growth in a particular direction, as well as an encompassment of ends by beginnings.

As regards alliance, a person or group derives from another, or recognizes another as its *pu'u*, specifically in the sense that the latter has provided a woman in a previous generation. This specification thus corresponds both with the peripheral character of wife-takers documented in the preceding chapter and the more general association of 'trunks' with 'centres' demonstrated earlier in regard to territorial and ceremonial relations. The idiom also accords with the 'vertical' representation of Keo alliance signalled by the appearance of *moi* (MB) and *ana* ('child') in terms denoting wife-givers and wife-takers. Similarly, in botanical contexts, *pu'u*—the lower, and relatively central, portion of a plant—contrasts with *lobo*, designating the 'tip', or most recently emerged part.

Conceived in terms of this binary contrast, the asymmetric, unidirectional, and in a sense linear nature of affinal alliance may account for a negative local evaluation of alliance cycles. In a couple of instances, a closed cycle involving three groups residing in the same village is not only locally recognized but approved (II: 2: i; II: 6: ii). Nevertheless, an especially knowledgeable commentator argued that all cycles, regardless of length, are undesirable, since they entail a wife-taker returning women to an ultimate source (*pu'u*), a situation further described as a 'turning back' (*bhando walo*) or 'circling (and) returning' (*kili walo*). As pointed out with regard to a similar assessment of cycles in another eastern Indonesian society (Forth 1981: 409–13), such a view may seem inconsistent with the fact that, unless new units are continually being created, asymmetric marriage rules make closed cycles of some length inevitable. By the same token, one could say that this cyclical aspect inherently contradicts any absolute distinction of wife-giver and wife-taker, especially where, as in western Keo, the kin classification is transitive. Yet local knowledge of actual affinal connections is often sufficiently restricted so as to conceal longer cycles. Furthermore, in the established cycles mentioned just above, the circular arrangement is expressed, as it were synecdochally, with reference to entire clans (*suku*), whereas series of asymmetric affinal connections, or maternal origin lines, are of course normally articulated with regard to component houses (*sa'o*). As noted, the same focus on houses as parties to alliances equally permits unions resulting in symmetric exchange when viewed at the level of whole clans. What the negative opinion of cycles evidently expresses, then, is a particular value placed on maintaining the distinction of 'source' and 'derivative' with regard to particular maternal lines of origin.

When in reference to affinal connection Keo claim to 'derive from X' (*pu'u ena X*)—or from the 'house of X' (*pu'u ena sa'o ko X*, where X denotes a particular named forebear)—the 'trunk' (*pu'u*) in question can be the person's MB, MMB, or MMMB, and so on. In other words, an individual can specify as his 'trunk' or 'origin' any group forming part of his maternal line of origin.

By contrast, a person is not normally reckoned as deriving from the house of his FMB or FFMB—immediate wife-givers of ascendants in his own agnatic group—unless of course this happens also to be the house of his own MB. At the same time, affinal forebears like FMB may be conceived as a person's place of origin (*pu'u*) to the extent that an individual (and for obvious reasons more particularly a man) is identified with his own house and thus with male ascendants belonging to this house. Here, it should be recalled that a deceased man's sons, or other heirs, inherit obligations towards the former's maternal line of origin, and so in this way treat it as their own. In contrast, a man's WB is not regarded as his own 'source', though of course, in time, the former becomes so for the latter's own children, and thus for his house if not for himself.

The crucial point is that, whenever applied to social relations, *pu'u* always refers to a connection traced through one or more females. Thus never can a person be said to derive, for example, from his FFF, or locate his 'trunk' in a group in which he claims membership solely by virtue of male links. The principle is further evident from several other expressions incorporating *pu'u*. Elaborating a more general botanical imagery, *pu'u bheto*, 'stem of *bheto* bamboo (*Dendrocalamus asper*)', denotes the group of a man's MMB or, according to a broader definition, wife-givers in the maternal line in the second ascending generation or higher. Evidently invoking the image of a segmented structure consisting of three or more nodes, *pu'u bheto* can more specifically refer to the group summoned to receive the mortuary payment (*tobo*) normally owed to heirs of the deceased's MB when these are not available or for some reason refuse to recognize the deceased as a wife-taker.[1]

Another expression applied to wife-givers of more than one remove is *pu'u kamu, logo lighu*, 'source of the root (or 'trunk and root'), back and dull side (of a knife)'. In their most specific sense, the paired phrases denote the earliest known wife-giver in a maternal line of origin. Thus, if one could trace back six generations, for example, the *pu'u kamu* would be the house of the MMMMMMB. Consistent with the pairing of *pu'u* with *logo* ('back, hind part, behind') in the foregoing idiom, *logo*, a term often employed in the senses of 'history, biography' and 'genealogy', further occurs in several other expressions referring to wife-givers. As shown in the previous chapter, *logo sia*, '(a person with a) clear back', describes a man who during his lifetime is able to free himself of obligations towards wife-givers by discharging his own mortuary payments. Similarly, *logo ta ema*, 'father's back', and *logo ta ine*, 'mother's back', respectively denote the father's and the mother's maternal lines of origin (the latter of course, also being a person's own). Other instances include *dhéko logo*, 'following the back, behind', and *ala logo*, 'taking (from)

---

[1] An alternative expression is *pu'u muku*, 'banana stem', equated by one informant with *ulu muku*, 'banana stool' (cf. *ulu* as '(anatomical) head'). Among the Nage, *ulu muku* denotes an additional mortuary payment owed to the deceased's MMB, as distinct from the MB.

the back', both referring to marriage with a MBD or another woman born to a group classified as *moi mame* (wife-giver).[2]

Substituting the contrast of back and front for the vertical opposition of trunk and tip, *logo* articulates the same social relations as does *pu'u*, while expressing with at least equal clarity the temporal location of Keo wife-givers in a structural past and hence their identification as origins, beginners, or initiators. This last aspect of the status finds further expression in ritual. When a new house is built, the principal male householder invites the leader of a wife-giving group—either the senior representative of the group of his MB or of the MB of the householder's deceased father—to perform an act described as *teka bega, koe kowo*. Translated as 'to cut and split, to break and go right through', the phrases recall the term *ta koe* ('earth breaker'), denoting the senior member of the pair of statuses—also called 'trunk rider' (*saka pu'u*)—associated with a sacrificial tree (*peo muri*) or stone column (*peo watu*). The ritual service involves the wife-giver making the first incision at the trunk end (*pu'u*) of the length of wood that is to serve as the main post of the house, a component called the 'hearth post' (*posa lapu*) or nowadays 'ruling post' (*posa raja*, from BI *raja*, 'ruler'). Just as significant is the further designation of this post as the 'trunk post' or 'post of origin' (*posa pu'u*). Before the component is planted in the ground, the wife-giver should also perform a speech blessing (*nete niro*) the wife-taker and requesting that obstacles be removed and negative forces countered, both during the building process and subsequently (*niro* is 'spittle'; see Forth 1998). In this way he provides the wife-taking house with the prospect of unity, fertility, and longevity. To the same end, blood from a pig provided by the wife-giver is smeared on the post, and the animal's liver is used as an augury, to determine how the wife-takers will fare in their new abode and what precautions they might have to take in order to avert affliction. When the house is later thatched, the first pig slaughtered is similarly obtained from a wife-giver, thus further ensuring that the inhabitants of the new dwelling will thrive.

The significance of wife-givers—and more particularly the maternal line of origin—as the source of wife-taking houses and, in a sense, of wife-takers themselves, could thus hardly be made plainer. Consistent with the emergence of a botanical 'tip' from the 'trunk', and the unification of the two extremities in a single whole more closely identified with the 'trunk', these particulars also accord with usages representing a wife-taker as part of the wife-giver's house. Recalling the identification of a marriage with a house, as well as the wife-giver's status as originator or initiator, the first pig slaughtered during marriage proceedings, too, is provided by a maternal uncle, more specifically by the mother's brother of the bride. Indeed, only from the liver of this animal can

---

[2] From the woman's point of view, marriage to FZS or another man of the house into which her FZ married is called *siwo kote*, ' to hang on to the clothes (of the FZ)'. The phrase turns on the image of a small child following an adult female while tugging at her garments.

the success of a marriage be divined. Among Keo, therefore, both marriage and house construction are processes originated by wife-givers. The two processes converge, moreover, in so far as a couple's building a new house formally completes their marriage (I: 3: iv).

Whenever a new house is completed and ritually inaugurated, it is again a wife-giver who should provide the first of a series of pigs for slaughter. In this context, however, I encountered disagreement as to whether this party should be the principal male householder's MB (or his heir)—apparently the more usual donor—or, as in one observed instance, an agnatic descendant of his FMB (for example, FMBSS). In fact, one of my most knowledgeable informants insisted that it should always be someone of the house of the principal's FMB, his *logo ta ema*, who provides the animal. As indicated above, as an alternative to the house of the own MB, a representative of this group may also be called to make the first cut in a new 'trunk post'. Hence this difference of opinion may reflect no more than very specific local, or even individual, preferences. However that may be, it should be noted that an association of the FMB with house construction is perfectly consistent with the normally agnatic composition of groups called 'houses', as well as with the common circumstance that new buildings regularly replace ones erected, on the same site, by the householder's father.[3] Also worth recalling here is the possibility, entailed by the preference for MBD–FZS marriage, that MB and FMB may belong to one and the same house. In the context of house ritual, one in fact confronts a more general equivalence of wife-givers representing the maternal lines of origin (or 'trunks', *pu'u*) of all men composing an agnatic line of succession coinciding with a social entity designated as 'house' (*sa'o*). As I show below, this equivalence further illuminates Keo conceptions of agnatic groups as communities of blood.

In addition to derivation from forebears traced through women, or a maternal series of affinal connections, as already noted, *pu'u* can also pertain simply to spatial movement. Consequently, Keo describe geographical derivation and removal—for example of a clan from another village or region—in precisely the same way as they express affinal ties predicated on the physical transfer, over several generations, of a series of out-married women. In accordance with the classification of such women, as well as their children, as *ana weta* (wife-takers), individuals, regardless of sex, are in this context identified with their mothers and higher female ascendants. Thus Keo men sometimes describe themselves—or the predominantly agnatic groups to which they belong—as having moved from one village or clan to another, whereas what they more exactly refer to is the movement of women in marriage over a number of generations between groups established in different places. Representing a series of

---

[3] Barnes (1974: 268) notes how in Kédang, an honorific applied to MB also distinguishes FMB or FFMB from MB, thus suggesting that in this society as well, the two sorts of wife-giving affines are sometimes identified and other times contrasted.

affinal alliances (or a maternal line) as a journey can therefore sometimes give rise to ambiguity.[4] As I demonstrate in the following section, the same sort of metaphor of movement, particularly as it concerns the movement of women entailed by marriage, also underlies the Keo notion of 'descent'.

2. 'Descent' (poro)

Keo not only describe themselves as 'deriving' (*pu'u*) from wife-givers. They also speak of wife-takers as 'descending from' (*poro pu'u*, cf. Nage *dhodho pu'u*) wife-givers by way of maternal lines of origin comprised of successive MB–ZC bonds. This conceptualization of the relationship thus coincides with what Barraud, describing Kei alliance, refers to as 'descendance' (1990: 200)— although, interestingly enough, this term seems not to reflect a Kei idiom comparable to Keo *poro*.[5] In regard to the partial synonymity of its component terms, as a reference to human derivation *poro pu'u* might simply be understood as a more elaborate version of *pu'u*. That the phrase appears to compound words denoting movement in opposite directions—downwards and upwards—is perhaps curious, but not problematic. As shown, *pu'u* ('trunk, stem'), though primarily a botanic usage connoting upward growth, can in fact refer to spatial derivation from any direction. In affinal contexts, the term thus denotes a source or starting point from which, in the Keo view, an individual or group 'descends' (*poro*).

Keo obviously resemble English-speakers—and, indeed, anthropologists— in employing a word denoting downward movement to describe social relations between people belonging to higher and lower generations. They do so, however, in a very different way. To begin with, Keo 'descent' describes in the first instance the relation between MB and ZC, and can thus involve just two generations. From here, relations of *poro pu'u* are traced upwards to the MMB, MMMB, and so on. In this way, Keo 'descent' designates a process of derivation involving links traced entirely through females. By the same token, what we might call a line of 'descent' in Keo comprises, beyond the relation of MB and ZC, a series of affinal links traversing two or more generations, or a kind of alliance chain. Keo speak of 'descent' (*poro*) as connecting not just individual relatives—ascendants and descendants—but also agnatic groups, more especially houses. Even entire clans can be described, synecdochally, as 'descending', or, indeed, deriving (*pu'u*), from specific other clans, that is, from groups which in previous genealogical levels directly or indirectly gave wives to their own.

---

[4] This initially became apparent when recording genealogies. Occasionally, when I asked about the derivation (*pu'u*, or in BI *asal*) of a married woman, respondents gave not her natal group but rather that of her own M, and thus MB. As I later discovered, a less equivocal formulation of the question is *bu'e apa imu?*, or 'of what (group) was she an unmarried woman', thus 'what was her natal group'.

[5] Barraud describes this 'descendance' as something that 'diffuses through different houses, generation after generation, binding together each man and his sister's children, or, in other words, the descendants of male and female children' (1990: 200).

While in their sociological uses both Keo and English 'descent' figure as metaphors of downward movement, the former is the more obviously motivated. As indicated previously, the Keo usage can be construed as referring ultimately to a woman's physical descent from the interior of a raised house subsequent to her marriage and incorporation into another group. Owing to the form of residential buildings, in order to go out, a new bride—more specifically, one for whom a bridewealth is paid—necessarily goes down as well. Thereafter she both 'ascends to' and 'enters' (*nuka*), that is, becomes incorporated into, the house of her husband. Hence Keo describe a woman married with bridewealth as having 'entered (another) house' (*nuka sa'o*), and her offspring as 'children who have entered' (*ana nuka*).[6] In this connection, an intriguing comparison is found in the Tanimbarese (Selaru) practice of denoting what I have called the Keo maternal line of origin with the local term for 'ladder', a concept that Pauwels (1994: 82) defines as a 'whole row (of affinally linked houses) except Ego'.

The grounding of the Keo idiom in a physical movement of women makes it quite clear why, in this society, 'descent'—a downward spatial progression—cannot serve as an appropriate metaphor for intergenerational relations traced through men, or lineal relations within agnatic groups. For, as local commentators pointed out, after marriage men usually 'do not travel anywhere'. By the same token, in the Keo usage wife-takers do not 'descend' *from* the women provided by wife-giving groups (their mothers, MM, and so on), but rather *with* them. Put another way, both wife-takers and out-married women descend from the groups of (male) wife-givers from which these women in an initially different sense 'derive'. This much, of course, is fully in accord with the general identification of wife-takers, or 'children of sisters' (*ana weta*), with women married out of a wife-giving group. It also makes sense in relation to the notion of individuals or groups 'descending' from houses whose cores are agnatically related males—those who 'remain inside the house' (*ndi'i sa'o* or *mera sa'o*; I: 4: iv).

Although Keo 'descent' concerns all links in a continuous chain of women's marriages, in at least one context it pertains especially to the relation of an individual or group to the house (*sa'o*) considered as the initial, or original, wife-giver. In the genealogical orations (*bhea*) performed on the occasion of buffalo sacrifice, a man may expressly claim 'descent from' (*poro pu'u*) only the first wife-giver in a maternal line, his *pu'u kamu, logo lighu* (see Section 1 above). Later transfers of women in this line, and in a sense also of wife-takers themselves, are then mostly described with a variety of other verbs specifying movement from one place to another (see Appendix 4). Even so, Keo otherwise represent themselves as 'descending' from more immediate wife-givers as well,

---

[6] That these children 'descend', or have descended, from their mother's natal house illuminates an initially curious local BI equivalent of *nuka sa'o*. This is *jatuh di* X, 'to fall into X', which describes a woman's marrying into another group and hence her children's incorporation therein.

the most immediate of course being the house of the MB. As was suggested with regard to the cognate concept of 'trunk' or 'origin' (*pu'u*), this possibility of recognizing various 'descents' allows groups to claim alliance connections with a variety of others, emphasizing or ignoring particular relationships as context demands.

While the indigenous idiom is thus perfectly coherent, the issue of Keo 'descent' is now potentially confounded by a modern use of *turun*, the BI word for 'descend', and its derivatives (*turunan* and *keturunan*, 'descendant', 'descent') to describe relations reckoned through males as well as females. When used genealogically *turun* ('to go down') has much the same meaning as its English equivalent. Hence when speaking the national language, Keo in effect conflate agnatic descent and the quite different sort of social relationship indigenously expressed with *poro*. At the same time, they are able to distinguish traditional 'descent' as *turunan perempuan* ('descent through females'), thus contrasting it to agnation, specified as *turunan laki-laki* ('descent through males'). As mentioned in the preceding chapter, nowadays Keo also use Indonesian expressions meaning 'direct' and 'indirect descent' to distinguish agnatic members of a house from descendants through women, or wife-takers.

Even without the complication of modern national language idioms, the use of 'descent' in Keo sociology presents the analyst with an expository dilemma. As previously shown, the organization of clans and component groupings in this society diverges considerably from classical models of unilineal descent. To the extent that some correspondence can be found, Keo clans and houses might be described as reflecting ambilineal and for the most part patrilineal descent. Yet, when speaking their own language, Keo use 'descent' to refer to an affinal relation rather than a principle of group composition. Conceived as a series of intergenerational female links, Keo 'descent' may appear to involve matrilines; yet as should by now be obvious, it would be inaccurate to describe the social order as matrilineal, or even as double unilineal (as van Wouden, 1968, might have been inclined to do).

Because 'descent' is ineluctably associated in anthropology with corporate group formation, I refrain from using it exclusively to refer to the marriage-based complex of relationships Keo describe with *poro* (or *poro pu'u*). Nor am I inclined to resort to a special term, like Barraud's 'descendance', to gloss the Keo word, which straightforwardly translates as 'descent'. On the other hand, since Keo clans and houses are not consistently agnatic or patrilineal in composition, I avoid referring to them as 'descent groups'. One could conceivably abandon 'descent' altogether in this last context and replace it entirely with another concept. 'Derivation' might suggest itself as one alternative (see Fox 1988: 14, who similarly speaks of 'origin structure'), partly because *pu'u* reveals an agnatic association in the designation of senior clan segments as 'trunk houses' (*sa'o pu'u*). However, quite aside from the term's reference to geographical derivation and physical movement not directly connected with social relationship, Keo do not in fact speak of a person or group 'deriving' (*pu'u*) from ancestors exclusively through males, since in reference to ancestral connections, *pu'u*, like *poro*, always involves at least one female link. One should also not lose sight of the fact that, employing the national language, modern Keo do, indeed, use a word meaning 'descent', applying it moreover in a completely cognatic way. In effect, I have chosen to follow their present usage, while always specifying descent in the male line as 'agnatic descent'.

3. Blood and Seed

Keo describe the contribution of both parents to a foetus as *ya mina*, 'blood (and) grease (fat, oil)'. Suggesting their basic equality in this context, paternal and maternal components of a person are distinguished respectively as *ya mina ema* and *ya mina ine*. In the same vein, Keo speak of blood (*ya*) as a substance uniting or connecting ancestors and descendants through both male and female links, thus implying a thoroughly bilateral view of 'consanguinity'. They further claim that for a marriage to be fertile, both spouses must possess blood that is not too 'hot' (*ya bana*) or 'cool' (*ya eta*), or that husband and wife should complement one another in this respect.[7] At the same time, adopting a more analytical view of *ya mina*, Keo interpret *mina* ('grease') as an allusion to male semen (*ae loe*; *loe* is also 'pus, matter in the eye'), and *ya* ('blood') as a specific reference to blood in the womb that is discharged during menstruation. The same equations are made with regard to *ya mina ema* and *ya mina ine*—the father's' 'blood and grease' then being identified with seminal fluid.

One may therefore conclude that Keo mostly conceive of blood as a female substance, even though it is also a property possessed and shared by males. A similar equivocality—or, better said, multivocality—appears in their use of *dhi ya* to refer to descendants (*turunan* in BI) traced through both men and women. As *dhi* means 'edge, side', 'extremity, limit, extent, end', and 'close to, right beside', the expression might be glossed as 'edge, extent of the blood (of a particular forebear)'. In this way, the phrase specifies a living person, of either sex, as the present terminus of a notional flow of blood outward from a centre identified with a particular ancestor. Even so, Keo often interpret *dhi ya* as describing genealogical connection specifically through females. In this contrast, a person tracing descent through one or more male links (for example, from his FFF) is specified simply as being 'of the blood' (*ko'o ya*) of an ancestor. Similarly, agnates (*ka'e ari*) sharing common male forebears describe themselves as being of 'one blood' (*a ya*). In a related idiom, groups based on a consistently agnatic succession are said to preserve 'true (or original, authentic) blood' (*ya tenge*), in contradistinction to groups which in one or more

---

[7] Details of the theory vary. Although the meaning is not necessarily relevant in this context, *ya bana*, 'hot blood', also describes someone who is hot-tempered, bold, or aggressive.

generations have maintained internal continuity partly by means of female links—for example, through extensive induction of children born to natal women. Accordingly, one man, speaking Indonesian and employing a loanword from European languages, explained *ya tenge* as meaning 'patrilineal'! As noted in Chapter 3, *tenge* also describes the oldest clan of a village occupied by two or more clans. In this context, then, the term implies a definite precedence, just as it does in regard to connection through males as opposed to females. Keo further use *tenge* when specifying genealogical as opposed to classificatory relatives; thus a man's genealogical MBD, for example, is called *li ana tenge*.

As these distinctions suggest, in a strict sense, individuals and groups (especially houses) are 'connected' in the Keo view only by blood transferred by women in marriage. People belonging to a single agnatic group, on the other hand, are not actually 'connected' by blood, and blood is not in any exact sense 'transferred' over the generations through males belonging to the same group.[8] Instead, father and son, like FF and SS, are united, and even identified, by virtue of shared blood, as of course are siblings and other agnates of the same generation. Borrowing a phrase from Sperber (1975: 39), who describes the ritually unmarked transfer of a Dorze title from father to son, one might thus speak here of 'continuity without transition'.[9] What is more, the blood which constitutes the common property of Keo agnates ultimately derives not from a man but from a woman.[10]

In view of this conception of blood sharing by male kin, it becomes clearer why, especially in the context of affinal exchange, a man treats the maternal lines of origin of male ascendants—the houses of FMB, FFMB, and so on—as he does his own. Different relations involving blood also bear upon Keo marriage prohibitions. While brother and sister are identical in regard to blood associated with both parents, FBS and FBD share at least the blood of a common FM and FMB. In partial contrast, MZS and MZD are prevented from marrying because, like agnates, they have derived the same blood, identically transferred through women, from the same wife-giver. At the same time, the intervention of two different female links evidently permits the previously noted dispensation in the case of MyZS and MeZD. With FZD and MBS, on the other hand, marriage is excluded by the prospect of an illicit reversal—a return of female blood to its source. As noted earlier, the representation of proper marriage and affinal alliance as a unilateral flow of blood transferred through a woman and thus connecting distinct groups (or 'unities of blood') finds expression in the phrase *ala ya*, 'to take blood' (or *ala walo ya*, 'to take blood again'). This, of course, refers to the valued union of a man and his

---

[8] Although agnatic ascendants and descendants are described as sharing 'blood relation(ship), connection' in the national language idiom *hubungan darah*, this expression has no exact equivalent in Keo.

[9] See also the idea that intergenerational continuity in certain South American societies involves 'substitution' rather than 'descent' (Rivière 1993: 509, citing Da Matta 1979).

[10] A similar, though not identical, situation has often been recorded for classic African patrilineal systems, including the Nuer (see Holy 1996: 77).

matrilateral cross-cousin or a similarly related woman in the category of *li ana*, although in accordance with the qualification registered above the privileged marriage of MyZS and MezD can also be considered as an instance of 'taking blood'. Closed cycles, too, are represented in an idiom of blood, that is, as instances of *ala ya*, or *papa ala ya*, 'mutual taking of blood'.[11]

Connections of blood passed through females are relevant as well to a marked preference for selecting adoptees from among a man's sister's sons (see Section 4 below). Adoption, however, does not displace other consanguineal bonds. Apart from his obligations as a wife-taker, the father of a man adopted by a MB may, by virtue of their shared blood, be especially motivated to contribute to the son's bridewealth, even though it is the adoptive father, the maternal uncle, who is principally obligated. By the same token, in one case a large portion of a man's bridewealth had been provided by his natural father's younger brother. Genealogical evidence also suggests that, through their own marriages or their children's, adoptees may perpetuate marriage alliances of their natal houses rather than those of the adopting group (which is normally included in a different clan), so long as this does not involve marriage between a ZS and his MBD.[12]

Not only do blood ties thus retain a significance following changes of house membership or clanship, but as was earlier remarked, persons of the same clan (*suku*) are not always regarded as sharing blood, even to the extent that Keo use distinctions of blood to rationalize marriage within clans. In a more general frame, it should also be recalled that many relationships classified as *ka'e ari* do not involve blood, and indeed, that some varieties explicitly do not. Worthy of mention in this connection are several cases where different estates or houses of the same clan were claimed not to be united by blood, even though genealogical records revealed traceable, albeit distant, links between them. In such instances, denial of blood relationship may be understood simply as confirming the relative independence of estates and houses, in marriage as in other collective affairs. Yet the idea also accords with a view of blood as a connector identified specifically with women taken in marriage, since in the cases just cited, components of a single clan recognized 'derivation' (*pu'u*), or 'descent' (*poro*), from different wife-givers.

As regards the above-mentioned phrase *dhi ya* as a reference to descendants through females, the 'edge' (*dhi*) of a person's blood (*ya*) quite obviously identifies *ana weta*, 'children of sisters' or 'wife-takers'. It should be stressed,

---

[11] Although *papa* can denote a reciprocal action or relationship (cf. BI *baku*), it does not always do so. Indeed, Keo use *papa ala ya* and *ala ya* ('to take blood') interchangeably when describing a marriage between two people who are considered to share blood. As in this context, therefore, *papa* often emphasizes the binary quality of a relationship rather than specifying symmetry or reciprocity.

[12] The genealogy of clan Béngi in Pau Leka (II: 3: iv) provides examples of this. A Béngi man adopted by the co-resident clan Pau Tenge contracted a marriage with a woman from clan Pau Padhi Rale, a wife-giver of his natal group. In addition, the same man's daughter was given in marriage to a long-standing wife-taker of Béngi rather than to a wife-taker of his adopters.

however, that the party with whom an outward flow of blood originates is necessarily a man—a male ancestor identified with a particular house. In other words, although blood is transferred from mother to child, and is in this respect feminine, it is ultimately derived from a masculine source (*pu'u*). As accords with the general peripherality of wife-takers, as people separate from the core of the wife-giving group yet at the same time are subsumed by it, 'edge, extremity, limit of the blood' in this acceptation describes parties who receive, and thus participate in, blood issuing from a particular source (or 'trunk') and yet are distinct from that source. By the same token, one is reminded of the relation of Land Mothers, associated with an entire domain but more specifically with its centre, and Defenders, clans that occupy more peripheral parts of the same domain but are recognized as independent groups. As well as their characterization as people occupying the 'edge, limit' (*dhi*) of the former's territory, also worth recalling, then, is the frequent recognition of Defenders as original wife-takers of a Land Mother.

In the sense of 'extremity', *dhi* also appears in *dhi téke* (or *dhi ya*), *naka yani*, approximately translated as 'limit (beginning) of the binding, producer of many (*or* one who flourishes, has flourished)'. Since Keo equated the phrases with *pu'u kamu*, *logo lighu* (see Section 1 above), however, the expression appears to refer not to wife-takers but to a wife-giver, more specifically the earliest wife-giver in a maternal line of origin. Also relevant in the present context is the phrase *dhi wini*. Although translatable as 'edge, limit of the seed', in formal speech the two terms are sometimes disjoined. Thus, a person may be described as the 'edge' of X and the 'seed' of Y (*dhi X, wini Y*), referring to derivation from two wife-giving houses included in a single maternal line of origin, or possibly in a person's own and in his father's maternal line. (In the same idiom, *dhi* can be identically paired with *kamu*, 'root'.) Accordingly, Keo commentators generally equated *dhi wini* with *dhi ya*, 'edge of the blood', noting that the first phrase similarly referred, exclusively or especially, to consanguineal ties reckoned through women. Here, then, one encounters the replacement of 'blood' by a botanic metaphor reminiscent of the coincidence of female blood connection with derivation, or 'descent', from wife-givers specified as 'trunks' (*pu'u*). Indeed, since *pu'u* further refers to an entire tree or plant, wife-givers may also be conceived, in the botanic idiom, as a source of (female) seeds.[13]

As indicated in the previous chapter, *dhi wini* also occurs in the expression *ka'e ari dhi wini*. While denoting full siblings of the same sex, particularly brothers, the phrase is also explained as referring to the children of two sisters (MZC) in respect of their sharing, like full siblings, the same MB, or a single

---

[13] Although I seem to have recorded them just once, it is worth mentioning the phrases *dhi wini ta ema* and *dhi wini ta ine*. These appear to refer to derivation traced from the father's (*ema*) maternal line of origin and from the mother's (*ine*) maternal line, which is of course one's own. Comparable expressions are *logo ta ema* and *logo ta ine*, discussed in Section 1 above.

place of origin. By the same token, when requesting a woman in marriage Keo refer to the prospective bride as *yolo wini*, 'seed maize, maize kernels for plant-ing'. In this context, 'seed' evidently refers to the woman herself; yet it might also be taken to mean the children and descendants that in-married women provide. A usage that bears out the second possibility is *wini wete, ngawu pae*, 'seeds of millet, rice seed left over from planting'. Although some people thought this expression could refer equally to descendants through either males or females, Keo also equated it with *dhi wini*, identified particularly with children born to, or descended from, out-married women or, in other words, wife-takers. Corresponding to *dhi X, wini Y* in genealogical orations, one thus encounters the mostly synonymous parallelism *wini X, ngawu Y*.

Further supporting this interpretation is a prohibition wife-takers are obliged to observe in respect of wife-givers. Under no circumstances may a wife-taker (*ana weta*) eat remnant rice seed (*ngawu pae* or, simply, *ngawu*) of a wife-giver (*moi mame* or *moi ga'e*), and especially seed belonging to a maternal uncle (*ame moi*), lest they suffer affliction. Partly to preclude this possibility, owners therefore ceremonially consume all left-over seed immediately after planting. In so far as wife-takers are designated by the same term as the rice, breaching the prohibition would be tantamount to their consuming them-selves, or something regarded as identical to themselves, thus effecting the gravest sort of reversal. Although possibly reflecting another root (see *ngavo* in Arndt 1961: 376), it may also be significant that *ngawu* further denotes 'bridewealth', goods which, of course, should be received and 'consumed' not by wife-takers but only by wife-givers.

In combination, Keo metaphors of origin and derivation (*pu'u*), descent (*poro*), blood (*ya*), and seed (*wini*) articulate a view of wife-givers and wife-takers as respectively central and peripheral parts of a single whole. Since payment of bridewealth secures for them separate status, however, wife-takers can be described as existing outside as well as within conceptual spaces identi-fied with wife-givers. In the remainder of this chapter, I demonstrate how this encompassment of wife-takers by wife-givers affects standing within corporate groups, by reference to a person's degree of independence from his or her 'trunk' or 'source'.

4. Degrees of Encompassment: Adoption and Incorporation

Evoking the image of a newly-married woman going down and hence depart-ing from her natal house, the notion of wife-takers 'descending from' wife-givers may imply a greater separation than does either the botanical or consanguineal idiom. Yet various usages affirm the principle that wife-taking affines retain a place in wife-giving houses of origin—just as junior segments of a clan are encompassed by another kind of 'origin house' (*sa'o pu'u*), that is, the seniormost agnatic segment, which is closely identified with the clan as a

whole. Accordingly, in several contexts, Keo speak of wife-takers, though actually born elsewhere, as 'returning' (*walo*) to a wife-giving house. Only in this
light do Keo practices of adoption become fully intelligible.

Keo describe inheritance and succession as *suyu fu, mula ngi'i*, 'replacing the
hair, (re)planting the teeth'. The phrases connote a prospective heir's obligation to provide for the deceased's funeral and discharge mortuary payments,
while in context they can also refer to widow inheritance. Since *mula* is 'to
plant', the expression also exploits a botanical or horticultural imagery.
Ordinarily, a man is succeeded by his own sons, the eldest becoming his principal heir. When a man lacks male offspring, however, and there is no one
else—a BS, for example—left in his own house or estate (*ngapi*), he normally
adopts an heir, usually from another clan (*suku*). For the adoption to proceed,
all members of both clans should be in agreement, as the resulting reassign-
ment of persons to estates can have implications for both sides.

Although most men who adopt heirs are without sons of their own, or lack
sons able to marry and themselves produce offspring, in a few instances men
with married sons, too, have adopted additional sons. By far the most preferred
sort of adoptee is a son of a sister married with bridewealth and thus incorporated into her husband's clan. The usual term for adoptees is *ana ghawe*.
Although *ghawe* means 'set aside' or 'separated from a larger collectivity', Keo
also translated it as 'to take back', again suggesting the idea of a wife-taker as
originating from, and in a sense still belonging to, a wife-giving house. When
necessary, children may be adopted from other houses or estates within the clan
or from other clans regarded as 'siblings' (*ka'e ari*). It is perhaps significant,
though, that Keo were often reluctant to recognize *ghawe* as the correct term
for adoption where the adoptee was not a sister's son.[14]

While it is also possible to adopt females, both Keo statements and the
genealogical record (which revealed just two clear instances) show this to be
rare. Women are said to be adopted only when no men are available, and then
mainly in the hope that they will bear sons who can themselves be adopted in
order to perpetuate the group.[15] Another commentator, describing the adoption of females as a practice of the past, suggested that adopters may also be
motivated by the prospect of receiving a woman's bridewealth when she
marries. As noted in the last chapter, like other men incorporated into their
mother's groups, adopted sister's sons may not marry their MBD. In a couple
of cases, an *ana ghawe* had taken a woman from the adopter's clan, but not his

---

[14] Apart from ZS, genealogical records show adoptees related as DS, classificatory BS, DH, BWZS, WFZDS,
WFZS, and WS (the son of a widow married to a childless adopter). The last five specifications were each instanced
only once, and some (notably WFZS) may be considered odd. Although men usually adopt just a single male heir, very
occasionally two may be adopted.

[15] As the only person available to look after his estate, the leader of a *ngapi* of clan Bale Yape Au in Pajo Mala (II:
2: ii) adopted the daughter of a Bolo man, after he and his agnates had all moved to Ola Bolo in the eastern part of the
Ngadha region (see II: 1: iv, n. 17). The present heir is the woman's son, who bears the same name as his mother's
natural father (Gogo Wéwe).

house, and in at least one instance the adoptive father, the man's MB, had provided the bridewealth. (Marriage with a MBD is of course not precluded when a man is adopted by a clan other than that of his maternal uncle.)

When a wife-giver adopts the child of a wife-taker, he presents the parents with a gift of pigs and textiles. Called *ae susu, eba wua*, 'milk and cradling cloth (baby sling)', the prestation suggests a means of compensating the natural mother for having raised the child in infancy. The adoptive father may also provide a gift for the adoptee himself. These gifts are not formally reciprocated by the child's parents, who merely provide a goat or dog to feed the wife-giver. The subsequent entry of an *ana ghawe* into the house of his adoptive father is further celebrated with dancing, the playing of gongs and drums, and the firing of 'bamboo cannons' (*bo lengi*).[16] When an adopter takes a child from another estate (*ngapi*) of his own clan, a gift of pigs and cloths is not required. Should they request it, however, the adoptive group may cede a piece of land to the child's parents. Appropriately enough, the transfer would then reduce the territory of an estate lacking in heirs while increasing that of one that can afford to give up children for adoption. Land may also be given when an adoptee is taken from a clan that is not a wife-taker, as in one case where as many as five plots were provided. In this circumstance, it is also usual for the adoptive group to provide golden jewellery and other items of the sort used as bridewealth (*ngawu*).[17]

Another term for an adoptee is *ana pendo*. Although described as a synonym of *ana ghawe*, strictly speaking the expression alludes to a partly distinct process of adoption. Similarly applied to the son of a sister married with bridewealth, and usually to her first born, *ana pendo* refers to a child whose adoption may be arranged provisionally, before a sister gives birth. In contrast, *ana ghawe* are usually older, even mature, when they are adopted. Evoking the image of a child 'remaining' in the house of his MB even though he is likely to have been born in the house of his father, *ana pendo* translates as 'child who is left behind'. As this representation may suggest, whether one can accurately speak of 'adoption' in this case is moot. Mother's brothers who request sister's sons as *ana pendo* are recognized as having some claim on a nephew. They are not required to make any payment to the child's parents nor to relinquish any part of the mother's bridewealth. Furthermore, not always are such men, actually or prospectively, without sons (and therefore heirs) of their own.

Even so, a child's parents may not readily acquiesce to a maternal uncle's request for a nephew. Nor are they absolutely required to do so. As I was told, many people are reluctant to have children designated as *ana pendo*. Although

---

[16] Constructed of thick stems of bamboo, these 'cannons' are exploded with kerosene to create a loud noise. Among both Keo and Nage (who call the instruments *bo mina*), they are most often employed just prior to a funeral, to signal that a death has occurred. Formerly, brass cannons and firearms were also used for these purposes.

[17] In one instance, such goods were described as *soyo topo, seli bhuja*, the phrases normally applied to the crucial portion of bridewealth that effects the incorporation of a woman into her husband's group.

in principle an uncle is as obligated to an adopted ZS as he is to his own offspring, if the adopter should later have sons of his own the latter may push the ZS aside, especially in matters of inheritance. For the same reason, giving up children as *ana pendo* is reputedly rare in western Keo at present, in contrast to the continuing practice of adopting sons as *ana ghawe*, where the male adoptee is normally the adopter's exclusive heir.[18]

While parents obviously have some say in a son's adoption, the preference for adopting sisters' sons—both as *ana pendo* and *ana ghawe*—is evidently bound up with Keo conceptions of affinal alliance and the relation of opposite-sex siblings. For in this regard, a sister's son is in a sense already subsumed in the house of the mother's brother and, indeed, may be required to return there should affinal obligations, especially mortuary payments, not be discharged after his father's death. By the same token, rather than as a simple material compensation, the prestation called *ae susu*, given for an *ana ghawe*, can be understood as a wife-giver's acknowledgement of this manifestation of the affinal bond. That wife-takers are under some obligation to wife-givers in matters of adoption is moreover suggested by several cases where the transfer had left a genitor sonless, and he had therefore later adopted (*ghawe*) an heir from among the sons of his own sisters. Not always, however, does an *ana ghawe* lose all connection with his natal group—as indicated earlier with regard to fathers contributing to an adoptee's bridewealth. Also, where after an adoption the natal group finds itself without male members, an adoptee may be called back to his house of birth. As noted earlier, provided he does not relinquish his inheritance of his adoptive estate, a man and his agnatic descendants may in this way come to hold rights in, or membership of, two clans.

Adoption by a maternal uncle also affects the institution of mortuary payments (*tobo*) described in the last chapter. When an adopted ZS (*ana ghawe*) dies, payment is made only to his WB. Nothing is owed to the house of his MB, since this of course is his adoptive group. In addition, the adoptee's own heirs are not required to make a payment to the house of the deceased's adoptive mother's brother (the natal group of his adoptive mother), nor, apparently, to the house of the adoptive father's MB, who was of course the deceased's own MMB. On the one hand, this dispensation can be seen to confirm the deceased's separation from his natal house. On the other, it indicates that the brother of his adoptive mother (the adoptive father's immediate wife-giver) is not reckoned as taking the place of the deceased's own maternal line of origin. As regards the theme of funerary separation discussed in the last chapter, an adoptee can be presumed sufficiently disconnected from his actual, or natal, maternal line by virtue of his adoption. Ironically, however, this is accomplished by incorporating him into the group that constitutes its most proximate

---

[18] *Ana pendo* are said to be more common further east, and particularly in the region of Ma'u Nori, where they are called *ana mera* (*mera*, 'to remain'). There, I was told, a woman's first child, regardless of sex, is always given to her brother. A similar custom is reported from the eastern Ngadha region of Sara Sedu (Molnar, forthcoming).

node. As might be expected, the mother's brothers of illegitimate children and offspring of uxorilocally married women (*ana ndi'i*), who are similarly inducted into their mother's groups, also do not receive mortuary payments.

The practice of adopting sister's sons further reflects a preference for obtaining heirs from outside rather than from within the clan. As indicated earlier (I: 3: i), in this way the demographic—and sacrificial—strength of clans is maintained, as is their internal division into houses and estates (*ngapi*). Not only would transferring male members from other *ngapi* reduce their membership, but it could compromise the separate existence of these territorial and sacrificial divisions inasmuch as adoptees might more readily be torn between their natal and adoptive groups. Quite often, when an estate is perpetuated by an heir obtained from outside the clan, the *ngapi* in question is renamed after either the heir or, more often, his adopter. Occasionally an adoption initiates a division producing a new estate, designated in the same way.

It should be stressed that adoptees (*ana ghawe*, but with qualifications, *ana pendo* as well) formally acquire the same rights as natural children. Consistent with this, surnames of adoptees are commonly changed by replacing the first name of the natural mother with that of the adoptive mother (thus, for example, a man of clan Bo Bana originally named Bhoko Se'i later became Boko Toyo). Nevertheless, Keo still express a preference for natural over adoptive succession. Members of lines deriving from an adoptee may thus continue to be described as *ana ghawe* by other divisions of the same clan who, in contrast, specify themselves as 'true, original' (*tenge*) members. In the modern idiom, they further distinguish themselves as 'direct' as opposed to 'indirect' descendants of agnatic forebears—a contrast which, as noted, also applies generally to wife-givers and wife-takers (see Section 2 above). Such attributions are especially apparent where relations within a clan are acrimonious. Not surprisingly, a particular misapprobation obtains where, as in several cases I recorded, a group has resorted to adoption (*ghawe*) in more than one generation. Despite the possibilities of non-agnatic incorporation, therefore, Keo still place a higher value on patrifiliation and the perpetuation of houses and clans exclusively by agnation.

The superiority of what may be called natural heirs over adoptees forms part of a more inclusive order of precedence affecting standing within Keo corporate groups. As noted, adoptees designated as *ana pendo* are most secure where the adoptive father has no other, natural heirs. The same applies when a recognized genitor adopts an illegitimate child who, although he acquires rights of inheritance, may still be challenged by the sons of the man's legitimate wife. On the other hand, when there is no one to perpetuate a house or estate other than an *ana ndi'i*—the son of an uxorilocal wife-taker and a natal woman married without bridewealth—then this person can claim the status of sole heir and successor to childless uncles or grandfathers. Among kinsmen, the only status lower than *ana ndi'i* is *ana lora*, a child born outside any contract of marriage whatsoever. Yet Keo history reveals instances where, in the absence of more rightful claimants, even illegitimate nephews have acquired full membership in the houses of their mother's brothers and, partly through force of character, a high social standing within more inclusive communities. By the same token, where free members of a group die out completely, the right to replace them is recognized as falling to hereditary slaves (*yo'o*).

At first glance, it may seem odd that the preferred heirs of childless men are sons of sisters incorporated into other groups, rather than the offspring of uxorilocal unions who have no claim to membership of their fathers' house or clan. The preference, however, only underlines the value placed on patrifiliation, and the concomitant valorization of marriage with bridewealth. Not only does an exchange of marriage prestations complete a marriage, it also creates a complete person—someone who, in the peculiarly Keo sense, has 'descended' (*poro*) from a place of origin and who, potentially, is both a wife-giver and a wife-taker. As indicated earlier, the children of women married without bridewealth are not in a full sense wife-takers. They have no social existence independent of the wife-giving group and, after their deaths, no mortuary payment can be made to their mother's brothers. The mother's natal house is not a 'trunk' (*pu'u*) from which they have grown. Nor, remaining subordinate to agnatic members of the group, can they themselves become 'trunks' in respect of *their* sister's children. While in one respect they may appear to be subsumed within the mother's house to a greater degree than other wife-takers incorporated into other groups, as 'children down on the ground' (*ana rale tana*, I: 4: iv) they are not so much 'in' the house as under it.

Particularly since men adopted by their maternal uncles also do not have *tobo* paid on their behalf when they die, *ana ghawe* (and *ana pendo*) might similarly be viewed as lacking 'trunks', and as not having properly 'descended' from a maternal line of origin. However, as the sole representatives of the estates of childless adopters, such adoptees in a more definite sense replace their wife-givers—their own 'trunks'—and so themselves become 'trunks' and points of origin from which others 'descend'. Something similar may, indeed, apply to men who, exceptionally, discharge their own mortuary payments (*logo sia*) and who, during their own lifetimes, thereby deliberately sever all ties with their maternal line of origin and other wife-givers.[19]

These several contrasts can be represented graphically (see Fig. 5). Incorporating the concept of 'true blood' (*ya tenge*) in reference to natural or agnatic heirs, the diagram depicts both *ana ndi'i* and illegitimates (*ana lora*) as marginal to the former without having attained a separate status implicitly

---

[19] This is an appropriate place to mention how the graves of such men, larger and more permanent than other graves (see Plate 13), serve as offering sites for deceased forebears in general—a practice that suggests a special identification with ancestors. In addition, only the survivors of *logo sia* are entitled to perform a special buffalo sacrifice at the conclusion of the mortuary period. Called *pébha gale yate*, 'slaughtering to trample the grave', the sacrifice might be interpreted as a method of negating or transcending death, resulting in a direct and unmediated promotion of these men to ancestorhood, a status obviously bound up, in Keo as elsewhere, with ideas about life sources or origins (*pu'u*).

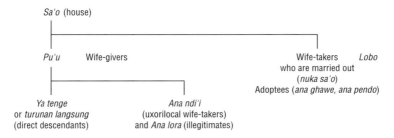

FIG. 5. Relations among categories participating in a house group

identified with the term *lobo* ('tip'), the opposite of *pu'u*. At the same time, the recursive nature of the opposition at the included level illuminates how Keo are able, contextually, to identify both *ana ndi'i* and *ana lora*, as well as wife-takers deriving from bridewealth marriages (those who have 'entered another house', *nuka sa'o*), as *ana weta*, 'children of sisters' or 'wife-takers'. By the same token, Keo also distinguish *ana ghawe* (or *ana pendo*) as 'indirect descendants', when they wish to contrast them with preferred natural heirs, the 'direct descendants' of agnatic forebears.

A review of social organization in this and preceding chapters has shown how Keo kinship and affinity depart from a classical model of asymmetric alliance wherein the affinal relation connects pre-existing groups defined by unilineal descent. As a local metaphor, 'descent' among Keo operates in a quite different way, complemented as a component of affinal alliance by the notion of 'blood' and the opposition of 'trunk' (or 'origin') and, implicitly, 'tip'. Articulating and co-ordinating these three major concepts is the category of 'house'. As remarked earlier, 'house' (*sa'o*) refers both to a physical structure and a social group. Yet institutions of alliance and incorporation indicate how the Keo concept involves even finer distinctions in its social application.

Varying social senses of 'house' are implicit in the circumstance that both children of uxorilocal marriages, who remain within the mother's group, and wife-takers (*ana weta*) incorporated into their father's group by virtue of bridewealth, are conceived as participating in a wife-giver's 'house'. Particularly for wife-takers born of bridewealth marriages, this house is an origin or source, or in the botanical idiom their 'trunk'. As implicit 'tips' or 'extremities', such wife-takers remain part of, and extend, this trunk; yet at the same time they are separate from and opposed to it. Conceived in other idioms, sister's children 'descend' from the house of the mother's brother, but since they descend *with* their mother—indeed only by virtue of the mother's 'descent'—they continue to be connected to this house in part by a flow of 'blood'. In one sense, blood flows between, and hence conjoins, separate houses. Yet in another respect, the flow of blood extends the house, expanding its notional periphery. By the same token, while both 'blood' and 'descent' for Keo imply a centrifugal movement of women, even females married with bridewealth—themselves classified as *ana weta* ('wife-takers')—do not depart absolutely from the house.

In so far as marriage alliance creates or recreates a duality that is nevertheless contextually conceived as a unity, the relationship recalls an aspect of Keo clan organization. As shown, in its most unitary representation, a clan (*suku*) is similarly conceived as a single house. Yet in another sense a clan minimally comprises two houses. Where such a group exclusively possesses a sacrificial instrument (*peo*), an arrangement Keo sometimes speak of as primordial, these two houses, coinciding with two estates, are associated with the two ceremonial offices distinguished, particularly in the case of a forked sacrificial post, as riders of the trunk and tip (*saka pu'u*, *saka lobo*). Although not necessarily coinciding with a relation of wife-giver and wife-taker, this duality thus formally replicates alliance—another articulation of encompassing trunk and encompassed tip—considered as both a connection between two houses and as a core and extension of a single house.

The main product of these first chapters has been the demonstration that various dualities existing within a more inclusive and similarly conceived and represented unity are consistently a function of whole–part relations, or encompassment. How far this same structure is discernible in more inclusive local groupings, both single villages and double settlements, is explored in Part II. Comprising a series of detailed ethnographic studies, this second part further addresses a closely related (but not identical) question, namely, to what extent binary relationships, including affinal alliance, provide the basis of instances of morphological dualism transcending individual clans, villages, and sacrificial associations.

PART II

Ethnographic Sketches

1

The Domain of Lape, Eldest of the Ga'e

As mentioned at the beginning of Part I, Lape Ga'e was the eldest of a group of male ancestors who divided the land of western Keo, and is therefore recognized as the principal Land Mother in the entire region. Although some Keo equate Lape Ga'e with an ancestor named Lape Mére, many specify the second figure as the son, SS, or SSS of Lape Ga'e.[1] Either way, Lape Mére, too, is designated as Land Mother (*ine tana*). Indeed, it is this name, more often than Lape Ga'e, that is given to the ancestor who first divided the territory of Lape Ga'e among several Defenders. At present, these Defenders comprise a number of independent clans, occupying several villages, whose male ancestors married sisters of Lape Mére, also surnamed Mére (for example, Wea Mére) or, in a few instances, other female relatives of the apical ancestor (see Fig. 6). These connections thus exemplify the common pattern whereby Defenders (*ana tuku*) were, originally at least, wife-takers (*ana weta*) of Land Mothers.

Descending exclusively in the male line from Lape Mére (or Lape Ga'e), the clan most closely associated with the senior ancestor is Céla (or in the local dialect Séla), resident in the village of Nua Nage. Since Céla is recognized as Land Mother within the domain of Lape, the group is alternatively identified as clan Lape or Lape Mére. Defenders of Lape include other clans in Nua Nage, as well as clans residing in the villages of Keo Ondo, Yoga (Kuyu Wulu), Suga Bhoja, Paga, and Lundu. The social organization of these settlements forms the subject of the present chapter. Other groups similarly related to Lape, and thus to Céla, are described later on.

1. Tamarind Village (Nua Nage)

Named after a geobotanical association, Nua Nage—or 'Tamarind Village'—has no particular connection with the Nage people to the north. In the stricter sense, Nua Nage denotes the single village (*nua*) which clan Céla shares with four other clans: Bajo, Bolo, Wulu, and Dhaga. In common usage, people further apply the name to the double settlement which Nua Nage forms with its immediate landward neighbour, the village of Keo Ondo.

The name Céla denotes an elevated site just below Mount Nata, as well as a former village (also called One Céla). Although Lape Ga'e is said to have resided in this place, in some genealogies the name also appears as the surname

---

[1] In accordance with a common repetition of names, mostly in alternate generations, the most complete genealogy of Lape Ga'e I recorded includes three men named Lape Mére.

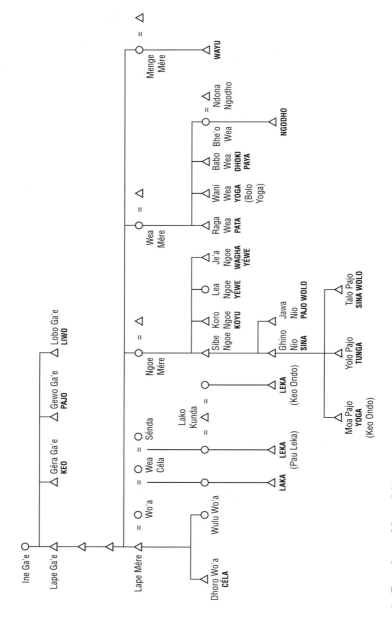

FIG. 6. Genealogy of Lape Mére

FIG. 6. *Notes*

The ancestor of Dhoki Paya is also given as Pe Ngoe, a son of Sibe Ngoe.

Ngoe Mére is reputed to have had seven children in all. The other three were named Kou (a female), Lipu, and Dhoi. Dhoi Ngoe is identified with the Bolo ancestor, Dhoi Léwa. Lea Ngoe is sometimes specified as a male.

While Ndona Ngodho is specified as the husband of Bhe'o Wea, the sister of Babo Wea and Raga Wea, in some accounts he is described as the brother of Raga.

Different accounts of the relationship between the ancestors of Koyu and Yéwe, and between those of the two segments of Yéwe (or Yéwe and Wagha Yéwe) are discussed in II: 1: v and II: 6: iii.

Ghino Nio is spoken of as having three sons, all surnamed Pajo. However, different traditions indicate a total of four: Moa, Yolo, Talo, and Babi. The fourth, Babi Pajo, was another ancestor of Yoga in Bolo Yoga (Kuyu Wulu).

Sibe Ngoe was assigned as heir to Wulu Wo'a (a daughter of Lape Mére) and her husband Bu'u Sei. Another genealogy of Pajo Wolo gives Jawa Nio (also called Jawa Milo) as a son's son rather than a son of Sibe Ngoe. (Yet other, decidedly less authorative, accounts specify him as either the father or a son of Lape Mére.)

A Céla woman named Wea Mére is also given as the wife of the Bindi ancestor, Ranga (the younger brother of Léwa, of clan Guyu Wolo), but this is not readily reconciled with other genealogical accounts. Also reputedly married to a woman named Wea Mére of Céla was Léna Dhuge of Pajo Kayo, father of the Pajo Kayo ancestor Késu Wea and his brother Céme Wea, the founder of Bale Wolo.

of a wife of this ancestor, Wea Céla. Lape Ga'e and Lape Mére similarly occur as place-names. Sometimes given as the name of a former village, Lape Ga'e specifically denotes the site of the reputed grave of this ancestor, which according to one source was never located inside a settlement. Local histories also mention Lépu, a site just below the hill called Céla, as another early residence of the Céla people, more particularly, the village they founded after moving from a place called Lape.

How many generations clan Céla has lived in Nua Nage is no longer clear. Occupying a magnificent location overlooking the Sawu Sea at the southern extremity of a ridge which also includes the hill named Céla and Mount Nata (the first settlement of the Ga'e siblings), Nua Nage now presents a somewhat desolate face. Only four houses remain, most of the population having moved during the twentieth century to lower-lying settlements near the coast. Among these is Ma'u Bajo, a hamlet which, as its name suggests, is principally occupied by members of clan Bajo, although Céla and Bolo people reside there as well. Over a rather longer period, clan Céla has suffered a comparable decline. Indeed, so overshadowed by allied groups has Céla become that many people are unaware of its existence. Nowadays, the Céla people, comprising just two adult brothers and their families and reduced to a single house, are more often than not identified as members of Bajo, as, indeed, are their illustrious ancestors Lape Ga'e and Lape Mére. Similarly, the sacrificial tree that they share with Bajo, and of which Céla is the senior owner, is regularly spoken of instead as the *peo* of Bajo.

Consistent with this nominal subordination of Céla to Bajo, older people related how, at some time in the distant past, the senior clan became virtually defunct and was displaced from a former position of prominence by other groups. Bajo may have been one of these; another may have been Pajo Wolo (II: 2: i). Whatever the precise cause, the decline of the Land Mother resulted in agricultural failure (I: 1: iii); so in order to return 'strength' to the land, the Bajo people, in particular, sought to restore Céla, securing their lands and inviting remaining members (who were then living in a hamlet called Ndegho Céla) to move to the old village of Bajo (Nua Bajo or One Bajo). Old Bajo was located not far from the village of Céla, in the seaward direction. When this settlement was later abandoned—following one account as a consequence of war—Céla and Bajo moved together to Nua Nage, which at the time was occupied by just two clans, Wulu and Dhaga.[2]

Although one can count five clans in Nua Nage, Keo usually represent the village as comprising just two groupings, themselves sometimes referred to as *suku*. Following the pervasive pattern of binary naming described earlier (I: 3: iii), these are designated as 'Céla Bajo' and 'Wulu Dhaga'. Members thus often give their clan name as, for example, Wulu Dhaga, whereas in fact it is more specifically Dhaga or Wulu to which they belong. This form of representation, of course, ignores the fifth clan, Bolo. Indeed, Keo sometimes describe members of Bolo as people of Céla Bajo. Bolo is a small group usually reckoned as a segment of the clan Bolo, now resident in the inland village of Muka. Distinguished from other Bolo people as 'Bolo Céla', the group was further described in one account as descendants of Bolo men who took wives from Céla and thereafter remained with their wife-givers, initially in a settlement named Lape. At this time, the Bajo people were still living in their original village of the same name. It thus appears that the clan of the Land Mother may once have been paired with Bolo rather than Bajo, and that Bajo later replaced Bolo.

However that may be, at present Bajo is recognized as principal Defender of Céla, with Bolo as the second Defender. Although Bolo is sometimes described as Defender of Bajo, this probably reflects the usage whereby 'Bajo' subsumes Céla as well. Further obscuring the relationship between Bolo, Céla, and Bajo

---

[2] According to one account, an ancestor of Munde (II: 4: iii) arranged for the 'Bajo' people to take up residence with Wulu Dhaga after they were expelled from Bajo village in a war. In view of the present confusion of Bajo and Céla, however, one cannot be sure that it is not the displacement and subsequent restoration of Céla that is referred to here. The account is also redolent of the part played by Munde in resolving conflict between clans Keo and Wayu (II: 4: ii).

are contradictory histories of the Bolo people in general, which I outline below in Section 4.

Suggesting a possible identity of their name with that of the nomadic sea people called 'Bajau', and consistent with their association with the most seaward part of the territory of Lape, the Bajo people are variously described as hailing from an overseas location far to the west named Bajo, from Lebuan Bajo ('Bajau anchorage') on the western tip of Flores, from Makassar, or from 'Bugis Bonerate'. At the same time, like other Defenders of Céla, Bajo claim descent from Lape by way of women provided in marriage by the Land Mother.

Within the grouping named Céla Bajo, the present order of precedence is quite clearly Céla (= Lape), Bajo, Bolo. While, as Land Mother, Céla is the oldest group within the entire domain of Lape, the area occupied by the present village of Nua Nage was, however, ceded long ago to another Defender, Wulu. More specifically a segment of the clan Pata (also called Ebu Pata) from the village of Wulu (II: 6: ii), the Wulu people founded and initially resided alone in Nua Nage. Later they were joined by clan Dhaga, hailing from the village of Mawo in eastern Ngadha. A Dhaga ancestor married a woman of Wulu and took up permanent residence in Nua Nage. Receiving rights to land, he and his offspring thus became Defenders of Wulu.

At present the two clans, named together as Wulu Dhaga, jointly possess a single sacrificial tree (*peo*). Céla, Bajo, and Bolo share another sacrificial tree, planted beside the *peo* of Wulu Dhaga. In accordance with its position as Land Mother, Céla was an early wife-giver of Wulu. Ultimately, this relation is traced to Lape Mére, whose sister, Wea Mére, gave birth to Raga Wea, the ancestor of Pata (the clan of which Wulu in Nua Nage is a branch). In accordance with this marriage alliance, the *peo* of Céla (or Céla Bajo) is a *kesi* tree (see Plate 5), while the sacrificial instrument of Wulu (or Wulu Dhaga), though no longer in evidence, was traditionally a *dheyo* tree (I: 2: iv). As one would expect, the earth breaker and excavator (*ta koe* and *ta kabhe*) for the first tree are respectively Céla and Bajo, while for the second, the statuses are assigned respectively to Wulu and Dhaga.

An elder of clan Yoga in the neighbouring village of Keo Ondo speculatively suggested that, as the first occupant of the site, it should be clan Wulu that acts as earth breaker in respect of the *peo* of Céla Bajo, and moreover that his own clan, as wife-giver of Wulu, should perform this function at the sacrificial tree of Wulu Dhaga. Although unsupported on both counts, these claims are of comparative interest, particularly in regard to the practice in some other villages, where Land Mothers act as earth breaker of sacrificial instruments belonging to separately established Defenders (II: 3, 4). Nevertheless, other evidence affirms that it is Céla (or Céla Bajo) that maintains precedence over Wulu (or Wulu Dhaga), even though Wulu and Dhaga were earlier established in the specific region of Nua Nage. Evidently the main factor is Céla's identification as principal Land Mother within the entire domain and Wulu's ultimate status as Defender of Lape (and hence Céla). Significant in this connection is the general claim that of all the clans in Nua Nage, Céla is the only one ever to have planted a ritual garden (*uma gua*; I: 1: iii). As constituted at present, Wulu in Nua Nage is barely distinct from another segment of Wulu resident in Wulu Wayu (II: 4: iv), largely because the single remaining adult male member of the group is an adoptee from Wulu Wayu.

Wulu's subordination to Céla is further reflected in the formal name of Nua Nage: Ulu Céla, Eko Bolo (Head that is Céla, Tail that is Bolo). Although generally in accord with the relative landward–seaward locations of the territories of the two named groups, the designation is curious in so far as it leaves out Bajo, whose lands are also located towards the coast. How far the disposition of houses of the three clans in Nua Nage accounts for this situation is unclear. While in some accounts Bolo is described as residing closest to the tail (*éko*) of the village, a Bajo elder claimed that Bolo people had never possessed a house in Nua Nage, residing always in the coastal settlement of Ma'u Bajo. It is just conceivable, then, that 'Ulu Céla, Eko Bolo' may reflect the possible earlier arrangement mentioned above, wherein Céla shared a village only with Bolo.

As indicated by the positions of their respective *peo*, relations between the groupings Céla Bajo and Wulu Dhaga find expression in the lateral division of the village. Though the pattern is no longer so apparent, the houses and sacrificial tree of Wulu and Dhaga are traditionally located on the right-hand (*mena*) side of the village, and those of the other three clans on the left (*rale*) side. Until the structures fell into disrepair, the two groupings each further possessed a pair of ceremonial buildings (*yenda* and *nde*). So far as it is now possible to determine, the two *yenda* were placed side by side, *mena* and *rale*, at the 'head' (*ulu*) of the village, while the two *nde* were similarly disposed at the tail. Although not a common arrangement, an identical positioning of paired sacrificial trees and other ceremonial structures is still encountered in the village of Paga, occupied by clans Laka and Nila (see Section 6 below). In the present case, such a marked dualism obviously reflects a merging of two villages into one. In most other instances of this process, however, the result has been a more complete amalgamation expressed in the sharing of a single sacrificial instrument. One reason this has not happened in Nua Nage may be the contradiction implicit in the precedence of Wulu as the oldest inhabitant of the immediate territory and the position of Céla as the senior Land Mother.

2. A Village called Keo (Keo Ondo)

Now located immediately landward of Nua Nage, the adjacent village of Keo Ondo (see Plate 2) moved around 1926 from a former site of the same name situated a short distance inland. The earliest site, even further landward, was located on a hill named Wolo Ondo ('Ondo Hill'; *ondo* is the edible tuber *Dioscorea hispida* and also a kind of tree), which lent the village part of its name. Contrary to what the other component might suggest, the connection between Keo Ondo and the clan and village named Keo (or Keo Bélo, in the territory of Géra Ga'e, II: 4: ii) is tenuous at best. I recorded two accounts of the name Keo Ondo. According to one, 'Keo' alludes to the original use of the site on Ondo Hill as a palm gin distillery (*loka tua*) by men from Keo Bélo. According to the other, the term refers to a cock's crow (*kako keo*) and commemorates an incident that occurred when Keo Ondo people were considering a move from their earlier village on Wolo Ondo. When they had taken the decision to do so, a cock crowed. In order to affirm the positive significance of such an event, construable as a sign of ancestral approval, as well as to disavow a possible negative interpretation (*keo* in the sense of 'to cut (short)' can connote a shortened lifespan, or early death), it was then decided to appropriate 'Keo' as part of the name of the new village. Thus designated as Keo Ondo, the village acquired the formal appellation Ulu Feo Bhaya, Eko Nunu Kono (see Appendix 2), referring to its location on a low hill named Wolo Feo Bhaya ('White Candlenut Hill'). This formal name was also transferred to the present village of Keo Ondo, built immediately landward of Nua Nage.

While only recently have the two villages come to occupy contiguous sites, relations between the component *nua* of the present double settlement nevertheless go back much further. As noted, Keo regularly refer to Keo Ondo simply as 'Nua Nage', thus suggesting a subsumption of the more recent village by its longer-established seaward neighbour. Yet in earlier times as well Keo Ondo fell within the orbit of Nua Nage in so far as its two component clans, Yoga and Leka, acquired land from clans Céla and Wulu.

Sometimes named together as 'Yoga Leka', the two clans of Keo Ondo, Leka and Yoga, are both junior branches of groups bearing the same names resident respectively in the villages of Pau Leka and Bolo Yoga (Kuyu Wulu). The first to arrive in the original village was Yoga. According to the headman of Yoga, this was specifically an ancestor named Moa Pajo, whose brothers, Babi Pajo and Talo Pajo, founded Yoga in Bolo Yoga and clan Sina Wolo in Wulu Wayu (Bo'a Ora) respectively. According to the headman of Yoga in Bolo Yoga, however, Yoga people removed to Wolo Ondo (Ondo Hill) when the entire clan dispersed following a famous war with Bolo and the breakup of Bolo Yoga (see Section 4 below). Further inconsistency arises from suggestions that an ancestral pair named Ule and Ranga were the first Yoga people to settle in Keo Ondo's earliest settlement. Whichever version is accepted, on founding the village Yoga people received land from Wulu, while continuing to exploit a section of Yoga land ceded to the clan as a whole by Lape.

Distinguished with the name of its co-resident clan as 'Leka Yoga', Leka in Keo Ondo derives from Soyo and Méko, two sons of a junior wife of Leka's apical male ancestor, Lako Kunda. His senior wife, a daughter of Lape Mére, also gave birth to two sons, who then gave rise to Leka in Pau Leka, the clan's original settlement. Following an argument between the two women, the junior wife, Bheku Ebu, described as the first ancestor (*ebu wunga*) of Leka in Keo Ondo, decided to return with her sons to Liwo, her natal village. But before she was able to do so, the family were 'detained' (*te'o tange*) by ancestors of clan Yoga in Keo Ondo—the pair of brothers named Ule and Ranga (together designated as Ranga Ule)—and were persuaded to join them. The Yoga ancestors also provided the Leka men with land. Either at the same time or subsequently they acquired further land from the Dhaga people in Nua Nage. Since Yoga obtained land from Wulu in Nua Nage, the territorial relation between the older clan in Keo Ondo and the longest established in Nua Nage thus parallels the relation between their more junior partners.

Despite the grant of land from Yoga, Leka in Keo Ondo do not consider themselves Defenders of Yoga. Nor is Yoga usually counted as a Defender of Wulu in Nua Nage, even though part of its territory similarly derives from clan Wulu. By contrast, Leka is described as a Defender of Dhaga. Judging partly from local explanations, a possible factor in this is the continuing dependence of Yoga in Keo Ondo on the senior segment of Yoga resident in Bolo Yoga (Kuyu Wulu) evidenced by their lack of separate ceremonial structures (*yenda* and *nde*). In the same regard, the headman of Yoga in Keo Ondo further referred to Wulu's status as a wife-taker of Yoga. It may also be relevant, then, that in the first recorded marriage between Leka and Yoga, the land grantor, Yoga, was similarly the wife-taker.[3] This of course runs contrary to what Keo regard as the more usual pattern, whereby land-givers are also wife-givers.

Yet another factor may be the status of the senior groups of both Leka and Yoga (and in a sense each clan as a whole) as both Defenders and, originally, wife-takers of the senior Land Mother, Céla. Accordingly, rather than Defenders of Wulu, Yoga people in Keo Ondo prefer to describe themselves— like their agnates in Bolo Yoga—as Defenders of Lape (*tuku Lape*). (As noted earlier, Wulu, more specifically the clan Pata, is another Defender and land grantee of Lape, which is to say, of Céla.) Consistent with this structural equality, though by no means determined by it, Yoga and Leka in Keo Ondo maintain separate *peo*.

Until recently, Leka possessed a forked Cassiawood post (*peo yebu*) erected to the right (*mena*) of the stone column (*peo watu*) that serves as the sacrificial instrument of Yoga. The two instruments replicate those found in their respective villages of origin. Standing next to one another in the centre of Keo Ondo, moreover, they are relatively disposed in the same way as the two *peo* of Nua Nage. Indeed, of all double settlements in western Keo, Keo Ondo and Nua Nage are the only pair containing all four kinds of sacrificial instruments.

---

[3] Otherwise, genealogies reveal no clear pattern of marriage alliance between the two Keo Ondo clans. Yoga has taken wives three times and given them twice.

While both Keo Ondo clans maintain *peo* of their own, however, Leka is ceremonially more complete, and in that respect seemingly more independent of
the senior division of Leka (in the village of Pau Leka), than is Yoga. Never
having possessed a *yenda* or *nde* of their own, Yoga people who slaughter
buffalo in Keo Ondo are obliged to deposit the skulls and horns in the *yenda* of
their original village, Bolo Yoga. By contrast, Leka maintains both *nde* and
yenda in Keo Ondo. As the headman of Yoga pointed out, moreover, until the
practice was locally discontinued in the 1950s, in Keo Ondo only Leka people
planted a ritual garden (*uma gua*). Yoga never did so, apparently because the
custom was observed, for the benefit of all Yoga, by the main body of the clan
resident in Kuyu Wulu (Bolo Yoga).

At the same time, Leka as well as Yoga expressly recognize ties of common
clanship (*ka'e ari*) with their agnates in other villages, reciprocally providing
clanmates elsewhere with heirs when estate holders die without male issue.
Although in most respects quite separate, the continuing unity of Leka in Keo
Ondo and Leka in Pau Leka is expressed in another way. In 1953, at the last
collective buffalo sacrifice (*pébha tua ae uta lebo*) in Keo Ondo, one of the six
animals slaughtered by Leka was provided by their kin in Pau Leka.
Accordingly, at sacrifices in Pau Leka, the Leka people in Keo Ondo jointly
contribute a single animal. Interestingly, the Yoga people do not engage in this
particular form of reciprocity; nor is quite the same practice encountered in
other villages.[4] Perhaps the most unusual feature of Keo Ondo, though, is the
fact that its two component clans are not related as Land Mother and
Defender. A similar situation is encountered in Upper Pajo Mala, although in
this village the two groups, Kate and Bale, have recently begun to share a single
sacrificial post (II: 2: ii).

3. *Wulu's Pasture (Kuyu Wulu) and the Old Settlement of Bolo Yoga*

Nowadays people mostly use 'Bolo Yoga' to refer to the village otherwise
known as Kuyu Wulu, located near the northern limit of the territory of Lape.
Conjoining two distinct names, the designation continues to reflect an older,
double settlement consisting of the villages of Yoga and Bolo, located a short
distance landward of the present Bolo Yoga (Kuyu Wulu). Like one half of the
older duality, the present, single, village of Kuyu Wulu is also known simply as
Yoga. Hence this settlement is known by three names: Yoga, Kuyu Wulu, and
Bolo Yoga. In a similar way, Keo often use 'Bolo' to refer to the present settlement of the Bolo people, a village otherwise named Muka, located a short
distance east of Kuyu Wulu.

---

[4] Yoga in Keo Ondo comprises four estates (*ngapi*) and Leka five. Altogether, therefore, ten buffalo were killed at
the *pébha* in 1953.

With due regard to varying uses of the term *suku* ('clan'), Kuyu Wulu can be described as comprising two principal clans: Yoga (whose name also applies to the entire village) and Sina. Clan Yoga ultimately traces descent to Wea Mére, a sister of Lape, and mother of the apical male ancestor of Yoga, Wani Wea (see Fig. 6). As long-standing Defenders of the northern boundary of Lape's domain, over the generations the Yoga people have occupied a number of settlements, about four or five (a total commonly remembered by Keo genealogists). Several sources specified Piga Sina (apparently 'Chinese plate') as the clan's original village. Connected with this, the present village of Kuyu Wulu, like all earlier settlements of clan Yoga, is formally designated as Ulu Piga Sina, Eko Nunu Toli ('Head that is Chinese Plate, Tail that is the Rebounding Banyan').[5]

Although no one could illuminate its derivation, the clan name Sina is probably drawn from Piga Sina. The first male ancestor of Sina, called Ghino Nio, was the son of Sibe Ngoe, who in turn was the son of Ngoe Mére, a sister of the Land Mother, Lape Mére. Following another account, Sibe was born to Wulu Wo'a, a daughter of Lape Mére, and a man named Bu'u Bunge or Bu'u Se'i, who also resided in Piga Sina and who was described as belonging to Yoga. Whether as a true or adopted son, Sibe Ngoe then inherited the estate of Wulu Wo'a and Bu'u.

Whatever the precise details, both Sina and Yoga therefore derive by way of females from Lape, the Land Mother. Wulu Wo'a, or Mother Wulu (Ine Wulu), according to clan Yoga, lent her name to the site of the present village of Kuyu Wulu ('Pasture land of Wulu'). More particularly, Yoga claims that the area was originally given by Lape Mére as *tana ka tuka* ('belly food land'; I: 3: i) at the marriage of his daughter. However, this account is disputed by people of Wulu, particulary the clan Pata in the village of Wulu, who argue that the name 'Pasture land of Wulu' specifies the territory as part of the domain of the Pata ancestor, Raga Wea (also known as Raga Kico). Competing interpretations of the name played a part in a dispute over land surrounding Kuyu Wulu which was recently resolved in favour of Yoga. (Here it should be noted that Raga Wea was a full brother of the apical ancestor of clan Yoga, Wani Wea, and hence another sister's son of Land Mother Lape Mére.)

While Kuyu Wulu (or Yoga) is generally described as comprising just two clans, Yoga and Sina, also discernible in the village are two other separately named groups: Doya (elsewhere pronounced as Ndoya and alternatively designated, after two ancestors, as Géle Mére) and Tunga. Yet people of clan Yoga, in particular, tend to dispute this representation, describing Doya as a part of Yoga, or as one

---

[5] The second phrase refers to a banyan tree that stood outside the seaward extremity of the village. The sense of *toli* ('sling, catapult') in this context is unclear, but local exegesis suggests 'rebounding' as a provisional gloss. As for Piga Sina, it is a point of some interest that, on the island of Savu, Piga Hina, a variant of the name with the same meaning, designates a large, flat stone located in the centre of the island that marks the common boundary of the three territories into which Savu is divided (Kana 1983: 120).

of Yoga's several estates (*ngapi*). Named after their original place of residence somewhere near the former double settlement of Bolo Yoga, Doya later removed with clan Yoga to Kuyu Wulu. At present, the Doya people mostly reside a short distance outside Kuyu Wulu in a hamlet called Koya. While their genealogical history is complex, Doya claim a relationship through both male and female ancestors to the Wulu clan Pata. Accordingly, they assert rights to land within the territory of the above-mentioned Pata ancestor, Raga Wea, the apical ancestor of clan Pata, and, moreover, claim the status of Defenders of Pata.

Living with Doya in the hamlet Koya is a segment of clan Yoga usually distinguished as Fele or Yoga Fele (after their ancestor Fele Yako). Formerly resident with the main body of Yoga, both Fele and Doya moved to Koya after siding with Wulu in the previously mentioned dispute with the majority of clan Yoga over ownership of the site of Kuyu Wulu village. Wulu lost the dispute, and it is only recently that the several parties have become sufficiently reconciled for Doya and Fele to begin relocating their houses in Kuyu Wulu. Although previously aligned with Wulu, Doya has a long association with Yoga, and at present operates in most respects as a division of clan Yoga. As accords with their residential and political associations, Doya may even be construed as a part of Fele, a formulation made explicit in the present Yoga headman's description of Doya as one of two *ngapi* composing Fele.

The group named Tunga is sometimes represented as a fourth clan in Kuyu Wulu. Yet just as Doya is subsumed by Yoga, so Tunga may be more exactly conceived as a part of Sina. Hailing from Taka Tunga in eastern Ngadha, Tunga is a later arrival in the domain of Lape, being among those drawn to the region by the spectacle of Jawa Pogo (I: 1: ii). Accepting an invitation to remain, the Tunga people founded a village, also called Tunga, not far from the old village of Doya. However, the original Tunga people soon died out, and their lands were then assigned to Yolo Pajo, the second of three sons of the Sina ancestor, Ghino Nio. If not its sole basis, this agnatic connection evidently underlies the local view of Tunga as part of clan Sina. Indeed, all four named groups in Yoga (or Kuyu Wulu) share putative genealogical connections, as can largely be seen from Figure 6.

Tunga's association with Sina is further borne out by local accounts of the former Bolo Yoga. Generally depicted as a double settlement, Bolo Yoga included just two sacrificial instruments, a *peo kesi* in the village of Bolo and a *peo dheyo* in the village of Yoga, a contrast that accords with Bolo's status as an early wife-giver of Yoga. At the same time, present descendants sometimes describe old Bolo Yoga as comprising three villages (*nua*). The furthest landward was Yoga and the furthest seaward Bolo, while between these two was a third *nua*, named Tunga.[6] The designation is curious since not only Tunga,

---

[6] This description is borne out by Le Roux's map of the Ngada subdivision (see *Schetskaart* 1916) compiled during the first decade of the colonial period.

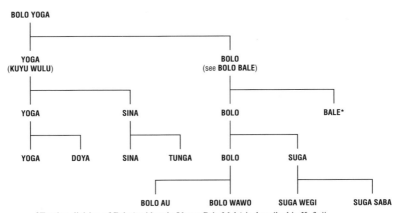

*Further division of Bale (resident in Upper Pajo Mala) is described in II: 2: ii.

FIG. 7. Encompassment of named groups in Bolo Yoga

but Sina also, is described as residing in Nua Tunga. Nevertheless, Sina's precedence over Tunga is confirmed by the usual order of sacrificing buffalo, now and formerly, as well as by the fact that Sina (but not Tunga) traditionally planted a ritual garden, a task expedited immediately after clan Yoga had planted a similar plot.

However one might account for Sina's inclusion in a residential unit named Tunga, in sacrificial matters all residents of this section of Bolo Yoga, lacking a *peo* of their own, were obliged to slaughter at the sacrificial *dheyo* tree of clan Yoga. Similarly, both Tunga and Sina now sacrifice at Yoga's *peo watu*, a stone column replacing the former *dheyo*. Normally identified as the *peo* of (clan) Yoga, the large vertical stone, erected in 1938 and surrounded by seven shorter stones, stands in the centre of the new village of Kuyu Wulu near the houses of the seniormost clan (see Plate 6).[7] As this would indicate, not only is Tunga encompassed by Sina, but both are encompassed by clan Yoga. Accordingly, 'Yoga' is still employed as an alternative name for Kuyu Wulu, the present residence of

---

[7] While it is generally recognized that the earth breaker (*ta koe*) and first to slaughter at this *peo* should belong to clan Yoga, which estate (*ngapi*) of Yoga should have precedence was subject to much dispute. Some people even claimed that this right belonged, or once belonged, to Sina. The last time the Kuyu Wulu people held a collective buffalo sacrifice was in 1964. On this occasion, according to the present Yoga headman, the second to slaughter was the group named Doya. The headman further claimed that Doya should have slaughtered first, and should thus be recognized as *ta koe*, having formerly acquired this status from another house of Yoga, identified with the ancestor Poso Gogo.

To some extent these claims may be bound up with Doya's identification with Pata, the Wulu clan that claims Kuyu Wulu as its own. The Yoga headman also described Doya as the *toya tana* in Yoga village, that is, the group which, after Yoga and Sina plant their ritual gardens (*uma gua*), was annually the first to clear, burn, and so create new fields. Although apparently corresponding to what Nage call *toa tana* (see Fontijne 1940), this term appears not to be widely known in western Keo.

both Sina and Tunga. Indeed, some people even described 'Yoga' as the true name (*ngara tenge*) of the village. In addition, Keo in other villages tend to identify Sina and Tunga people as Yoga, and even as people of clan (*suku*) Yoga. Relations among the four named components of Kuyu Wulu are shown in Figure 7 which, anticipating the next section, also shows relations among component groups of Bolo, Yoga's former partner.

4. Bolo: The Village of Dhoi Léwa

Once forming one half of the double settlement of Bolo Yoga, inhabitants of the former village of Bolo are usually represented as later arrivals in western Keo who were eventually invited by the Yoga ancestors to found a village adjacent to their own. Both historical precedence in the region as a whole as well as precedence in the locality that was to become Bolo Yoga thus accord with the continuing use of the compound name for Kuyu Wulu, the village now occupied by the Yoga group exclusively.

The breakup of old Bolo Yoga constitutes an important chapter in the history of western Keo, informing narratives accounting for the present composition of several settlements besides Kuyu Wulu (see Section 2 above regarding Yoga in Keo Ondo; also II: 6: i regarding the clan Wulu Wogo). Conflict erupted when goats belonging to the Bolo people ate the leaves of tubers (*sura*) planted by Yoga. On the urging of Raga Wea, the above-mentioned ancestor of the Wulu clan Pata, Yoga retaliated by placing lime on the leaves, causing seven female goats to die. Thus began what Keo call the 'war of the tuber-eating goats' (*lawa yongo sepa sura*).[8] Bolo prevailed, killing sixty-six Yoga people, while Yoga was able to kill only half as many members of Bolo. The Yoga group then fled in all directions. Following the intervention of the co-resident clans, Sina and Suga (the latter still residing with Bolo, in Muka), Yoga and Bolo concluded a peace but were unable to restore their former unity. Bolo then settled in a place called Nunu Mada, from where they later moved to the present village of Muka, while Yoga, after returning for a time to their old village, eventually established themselves in Kuyu Wulu. Nevertheless, a continuing bond between the two groups apparently finds expression in modern funerary practices, whereby men of Muka dig the grave and construct the coffin whenever a resident of Kuyu Wulu dies, and vice versa (I: 2: iii).

Throughout both Keo and Nage, the Bolo people are closely identified with Dhoi Léwa, a Bolo ancestor who, rather curiously, is more specifically named as the founder of the more junior of two Bolo clans, Bolo Au (Lower Bolo). In some Keo genealogies this ancestor is, moreover, equated with Dhoi Ngoe, a

---

[8] This involvement of goats may reflect a particular symbolism. As noted, Keo describe villages composing double settlements as 'like goats that can hear one another bleating' (see I: 2: iii).

son of Ngoe Mére and therefore a nephew of Lape Mére. A virtual culture hero whose exploits are no less remarkable than those of Lape and the Ga'e siblings, Dhoi Léwa was a famous warrior who allied himself with various groups in central Flores, including the Nage people of Bo'a Wae in their war against 'Goanese' (*ata goa*) invaders from the north.[9] Further associating this figure with a group of early ancestors, Keo legends also depict extraordinary encounters between Dhoi Léwa and either Géra Ga'e, a brother of the principal Land Mother, or Géra Lagha, a more recent forebear of the Keo people in Keo Bélo (II: 4: ii).

Casting Dhoi Léwa as a contemporary of original Land Mothers illustrates how Keo traditions tend anachronistically to associate persons who, according to other information, should belong to mutually distant generations. Another example is the reputed involvement in the war between Yoga and Bolo of Raga Wea (another nephew of Lape Mére) and Wulu Wo'a (specified as a daughter of Lape) who, according to one account, lent her name to Kuyu Wulu. Obviously contrary to the view of Bolo as descending from a nephew of Land Mother Lape, moreover, Keo historians usually describe Bolo as one of the several groups of later arrivals who came to witness foreigners (*ata jawa*) levelling the hilltop known as Jawa Pogo. Now represented in three separate villages, as an immigrant group Bolo exemplifies more recent arrivals who have gained prominence in western Keo. Indeed, it is precisely this achievement that may account for the partial depiction of their most famous ancestor as a contemporary of the original dividers of the land.

When described as immigrants, Bolo's origin is always given as the village of Ola Bolo ('place of Bolo'), well to the northwest, in what is now eastern Ngadha.[10] After discovering the fertility of the Keo region, the Bolo people decided to remain. Obtaining lands partly adjacent to those of Yoga within the territory of Land Mother Lape, Bolo are sometimes described as Defenders (*ana tuku*) of Lape; yet according to an equally authoritative view, this is formally speaking incorrect. Although they do support the Land Mother whenever requested, Bolo were never actually granted this status. Rather, they

---

[9] Dhoi Léwa is especially remembered by Nage as the owner of a cannon which proved decisive in the victory. Afterwards, he established a cult house (*sa'o waja*) in Bo Kodhi, a village near Bo'a Wae, and left descendants who are there known as 'clan Bolo Bale' (see II: 2: ii). Dhoi Léwa's association with Goanese is further revealed in the legend of Baca Bolo. A sister of Dhoi's with an extraordinarily light complexion, she married an *ata goa* from the Mbai region, on the north coast of Flores, where she introduced the sacrificial *kesi* tree. In Bo'a Wae, Dhoi Léwa—and 'Bolo Bale'— are still recognized as major wife-givers of Deu, the clan of the Nage rajas.

Accounts recorded in Keo locate Dhoi Léwa's grave in Bo'a Wae, as apparently did the Dutch administrator Beker (1913), who described the stone base of the *peo* in Bo'a Wae as the resting place of an early ancestor named 'Doy'. According to other accounts, Dhoi Léwa died and was buried in Togo (Tonggo) in eastern Keo, while Bo'a Wae people, who mostly associate his name with the Bale people (who they do not distinguish from Bolo), claim he was buried in Pajo Mala (II: 2).

[10] When I pointed out the inconsistency between this account and traditions linking Dhoi Léwa with Lape Mére, one local authority explained that, while Bolo originated in Kéli Nata (the home of Lape and the Ga'e siblings), they removed to Ola Bolo and from there later returned to western Keo to 'watch Jawa Pogo'. Only one informant, the headman of Kate in Pajo Mala (II: 2: ii), explicitly distinguished Dhoi Léwa from Dhoi Ngoe, Lape's nephew, identifying the former as a far more recent immigrant.

simply cleared virgin forest (*pogo kaju tébe, yota are una*; I: 3: i) in the northern part of the domain of Lape and have retained possession of this area to the present day. Since they received no land from the Yoga people, one of Lape's earliest Defenders, Bolo are by general agreement not Defenders of clan Yoga either. (Here we may also recall that Yoga, as accords with their former possession of a *dheyo* tree *peo*, are reckoned as wife-takers of Bolo, in spite of their earlier presence in the region.)

Keo history describes the Bolo people as arriving in waves. As in all earlier settlements of Bolo, their present village, alternatively named Bolo or Muka and founded early in the twentieth century, contains two groups: Bolo Wawo (Upper Bolo) and Bolo Au (Lower Bolo). Being designated with reference to the positions their houses traditionally occupied within the village, the two groups are mostly spoken of as separate clans (*suku*). Accordingly, the two are further described as having originally been linked by marriage alliance. Upper Bolo (Bolo Wawo) derives from a group named Bolo still found in their original village of Ola Bolo. They arrived somewhat in advance of Lower Bolo (Bolo Au), which derives from another group, sometimes specified as another 'clan' named Lére (or, in the Ola Bolo dialect, Léze). Hence Bolo Au is also known as Bolo Lére. Present leaders of Bolo Wawo further identified Upper Bolo with Bolo Céla (see Section 1 above), claiming that their ancestors first resided with clan Céla, the Land Mother.[11] Other accounts specify the original village of all Bolo people in western Keo as Bolo Ndata, though interestingly enough, various statements reveal a closer identification between this place and Lower Bolo (Bolo Au). Equating 'Ndata' with BI *datang* ('to come, arrive'), some Keo also identify Bolo Ndata with the spot from which the Bolo people viewed the construction at Jawa Pogo. Whichever particulars are accepted, some generations later Bolo Ndata was abandoned. Both Upper and Lower Bolo then moved to found a new village adjacent to the village of Yoga, in the double settlement of Bolo Yoga.

Apparently reflecting a third movement of people from Ola Bolo, ancestors of the group now named Bale, who, like Lower Bolo, originally belonged to the Ola Bolo clan Lére, also took up residence in Bolo Ndata. When Bolo Ndata disbanded and other Bolo removed to Bolo Yoga, the Bale people established a separate village named Nua Bale (or One Bale). There they eventually formed a double settlement with the clan Kate, with whom they still reside in the modern village of Upper Pajo Mala (II: 2: ii).

Replicating a former arrangement in Bolo Yoga, Upper and Lower Bolo share their present village of Muka with a third group, clan Suga. Suga's place of derivation is usually specified as the western Nage district of Solo, where another segment of the clan still resides. Having obtained land from Bolo, the

---

[11] 'Bolo Céla' also occurs as the name of the first wife provided by clan Upper Bolo to the clan Upper Bale, in the village of Upper Pajo Mala (II: 2). This is plausible in so far as both Bolo and Céla are female names.

Suga people are now recognized as the single Defender of the earlier arrival. As presently constituted, Suga—also specified as Bolo Suga—comprises two estates (*ngapi*), named after ancestors as Suga Saba and Suga Wegi. As noted above, in Bolo Yoga the Bolo group possessed a sacrificial *kesi* tree. As co-resident Defenders, Suga people also slaughtered at this tree. Reputedly reflecting renewed contact with Ola Bolo during the last century, after moving to Muka the Bolo people erected a forked *peo* of Cassiawood (*yebu*).[12] As might be expected, the senior and junior, or Upper and Lower, divisions of Bolo respectively provide the 'trunk rider' and 'tip rider' of the forked *peo*, while Suga Saba and Suga Wegi divide other functions connected with obtaining and installing a new sacrificial post (*yada yiwu* and *lado bépi*; see I: 2: iv, n. 9). Also in a ceremonial vein, the two estates of Suga are each responsible for one of the four posts of the *yenda* belonging to Bolo, the other two posts of the building being supplied by the two Bolo groups themselves (see Fig. 2).[13]

In these ways, a set of three clans is rendered as a quadripartite series more in accord with the formal dualism implied by the presence of just two group names, Bolo and Suga. Quadripartition is also discernible in quite another respect. While clan Suga is subordinate to all of Bolo, it is more specifically described as operating in association with, or under the auspices of, Bolo Au (*kapi ne'e Bolo Au*). In a similar vein, Upper Bolo (Bolo Wawo) subsumes yet another immigrant group, now known as Bolo Wae. Hailing from the village of Wae in the southwestern part of Nage, Bolo Wae descend agnatically from people of clan Je'a (II: 3: ii) who were driven from Wae by the neighbouring Dadho people. In this connection, an Upper Bolo leader described his clan as containing two *ngapi*: Bolo Wae and 'Bolo Céla' (that is, Bolo Wawo), two components alternatively named, after their ancestors, as Ngapi Ria (the first ancestor of Bolo Wae) and Ngapi Bapi.

Keo representations thus connect various groupings of Bolo people by way of a series of successive subsumptions (see Fig. 7). While Bolo Yoga, now at least more closely identified with Yoga, encompassed the whole of Bolo, so Bolo Wawo (Upper Bolo)—the first group to leave Ola Bolo, and the one bearing the same name as this village—encompasses later arrivals from clan Lére (or Bolo Lére), now called Bolo Au (Lower Bolo). In turn, all of Bolo, but more specifically Bolo Au, partly subsumes clan Suga. As we shall see in the next chapter, Bolo also subsumes the Bale people, resident in Pajo Mala. Similarly, Bolo Wawo specifically encompasses the group named Bolo Wae.

---

[12] The return of both Bolo and Bale people to Ola Bolo during the last one hundred years or so is said to have been encouraged, even initiated, by the Nage leader 'Oga Ngole, who later became the first Dutch-appointed raja of Nage.

[13] As is often the case, the order of precedence of Bolo over Suga finds expression in the reputed disposition of their houses in the former Bolo Yoga. Bolo Wawo (Upper Bolo) occupied the 'head' (landward) section, Bolo Au (Lower Bolo) was in the middle, while Suga resided in the tail section. After moving to the present village of Muka, this order was transformed when Lower Bolo and Suga changed places. Since Upper Bolo and Lower Bolo have thus come to be associated with the two named extremities of the settlement, the inversion might be understood as effecting or reflecting a further incorporation of Suga by Bolo.

On a further point of comparison, it should be noted how the formation Bolo Yoga parallels in an intriguing way the double settlement of Nua Nage–Keo Ondo. As shown, in each case one village of a pair includes houses of clan Bolo and the other clan Yoga. Moreover, in both cases Yoga is established in the landward village, and Bolo in the seaward. Finally, both Nua Nage and Yoga (Kuyu Wulu) are connected with Wulu, more specifically the Wulu clan Pata.

5. A Village with Two Double Names: Suga Bhoja and Koyu Yéwe

Located about three kilometres southeast of Kuyu Wulu (Yoga) and Muka (Bolo), the village of Suga Bhoja exemplifies a single settlement (*nua*) named after two component clans, Suga and Bhoja. The dualism is replicated in the village's formal name: Ulu Bhoja, Eko Suga ('Head that is Bhoja, Tail that is Suga'). Reflecting this designation is the disposition of groups within the village, whereby Bhoja, or more exactly clan Upper Bhoja (Bhoja Wawo), occupies the landward extremity, and Suga the seaward. Despite their nominal prominence, however, Suga and Upper Bhoja are recent arrivals in the village. The oldest members are clans Koyu (more completely called Ana Koyu) and Yéwe, in relation to whom Suga and Upper Bhoja are, with an interesting qualification to be detailed below, considered Defenders (*ana tuku*). Villagers therefore specify the true or original name (*ngara tenge*) of the village as Koyu Yéwe, a name still used alternatively to Suga Bhoja.[14] Somewhat complicating the picture, the village contains yet another group, named Bhoja Kisa, or 'Middle Bhoja', which, as will be shown, intervenes both spatially and temporally between the oldest and most recent pairs.

If not always as a single clan (*suku*), Suga Bhoja people frequently treat Koyu and Yéwe as a unity, an original grouping separate from more recent arrivals. Like members of agnatically related segments of clans resident in different villages, Koyu and Yéwe men can thus mutually replace one another as heirs, and some even claim rights to estates in both groups. At the same time, in regard to land possession and in other ways, the two are counted as separate clans. For example, only Yéwe people observe a prohibition on pork, a taboo they share with clan Yoga (in both Kuyu Wulu and Keo Ondo) and three clans in the village of Wulu (II: 6: ii).

Most evidence, including the testimony of the majority of Keo in other villages, points to Koyu as the senior member of the pair. For one thing, Koyu was the name of the original village jointly occupied by Koyu and Yéwe below

---

[14] Founded in 1968, the present Suga Bhoja is now mostly known as 'Suka Maju', an Indonesian name meaning 'wishing to advance, progress'. A pun on 'Suga Bhoja', the name reflects the current government-promoted value placed on economic development.

the eastern slope of Mount Nata (Kéli Nata). Recently, however, Koyu's precedence has been challenged by Yéwe, who have succeeded to the extent of
becoming the first to slaughter a buffalo at the last collective sacrifice
performed in the mid-1950s. Not surprisingly, the competing parties adduce
different versions of local genealogy in this connection. According to Koyu,
the ancestors of both Koyu and Yéwe were children of Ngoe Mére, the sister
of Lape Mére mentioned earlier as the mother of Dhoi Ngoe and Sibe Ngoe.
At the same time, Koyu people specify the Yéwe ancestor as an unmarried
woman named Lea Ngoe, who was the sister of the Koyu ancestor, Koro Ngoe
(see Fig. 6). As agnatic descendants of a male sibling, Koyu therefore claims a
superior position *vis à vis* Yéwe. In this context, Koyu further describe Yéwe
as *ana meta* ('children of sisters'), or 'wife-takers', subsumed affines who, while
composing a unity with Koyu, are nevertheless subordinate to the senior group
(see I: 4: iv; I: 5: iv). Koyu's seniority also finds support in an external account
according to which their original village (like the clan itself) was named after
Koyu Yengo, the common father of the Koyu and Yéwe ancestors.

In contrast, people of Yéwe claim as their apical ancestor, not a daughter of
Ngoe Mére but a son, named Je'a Ngoe. While the genealogy adduced in this
connection included another child named Lea, this person, too, was given as
male, and then further specified as the ancestor of a junior branch of Yéwe
established in the village of Wagha (II: 6: iii).[15] It should be stressed that most
people I questioned regarded Koyu's version of Yéwe's ancestry, and of the
relation between the two groups, as the more accurate. (Evidence given by the
main proponent of Yéwe's claim to precedence was moreover inconsistent, not
least of all because he initially gave Koro Ngoe, the Koyu ancestor, as the first
child of Ngoe Mére!) Despite the peculiarity of paired clans recognizing a
brother and a sister as their respective founders, the arrangement is not unique
to Koyu and Yéwe; it is also encountered in the western Keo village of Liwo
(II: 6: i) as well as in some neighbouring regions.

While inhabitants of the present village of Suga Bhoja, founded in 1968,
have yet to plant a *peo*, all previous settlements, including the original Koyu,
are described as possessing a single sacrificial *kesi* tree. As should be expected,
Koyu and Yéwe disagree as to which clan rightfully occupies the principal
status of earth breaker (*ta koe*). What is more generally conceded is that the
junior status of excavator (*ta kabhe*) was at some time in the past assigned to
the third clan, Bhoja Kisa ('Middle Bhoja'), which then replaced either Yéwe
or Koyu in this capacity. Also named Bhoja Au, or 'Lower Bhoja' (thus distinguishing it from Bhoja Wawo, or Upper Bhoja), Bhoja Kisa derives from the
village of Téya Bhoja well to the east near Sela Lejo. Having acquired land

---

15 This particular genealogy also included Dhoi Ngoe, equated with the Bolo ancestor Dhoi Léwa, as another son
of Ngoe Mére. In contrast, an elderly Koyu man described Dhoi Léwa as Ngoe's husband. Other accounts however
give Tande Bolo, a man of the eastern village of Léwa and perhaps identical with Tande Ga'e (another of the Ga'e
siblings), as the husband of Ngoe Mére.

from the older groups, Bhoja Kisa was described, following my initial enquiries, as their Defender (*ana tuku*), with Koyu informants specifying the clan as Defender of Koyu, considered as the local Land Mother (*ine tana*). According to later, and apparently more informed interpretations, however, Bhoja Kisa is more correctly regarded as a *ka'e ari* ('sibling') of Koyu and Yéwe, while only the most recently arrived clans, Suga and Bhoja Wawo, are properly classified as Defenders of the older pair. In view of the general characterization of Defenders as people occupying the margins of a Land Mother's domain (*ndi'i singi, mera sepu*, 'dwelling at the side, living at the end', I: 1: iii), it may be significant here that the name of the clan, 'Middle Bhoja', refers to its position in the mid-section (*kisa*, 'centre') of both previous settlements and the present village, where houses of Koyu and Yéwe are also located.

Occupying the seaward extremity of the village, Suga, the fourth clan to arrive, derives from Suga people who left former Bolo Yoga where, as has been noted, they resided with Bolo. Although some Suga men stated that their ancestors had proceeded directly from Solo, the contention is inconsistent with Suga's continuing dependence on Bolo, which I detail below. In their new residence, Suga obtained land mostly from Bhoja Kisa. As this was reputedly exchanged for a quantity of tubers (*sura*), the clan is distinguished from Suga people elsewhere (most notably in Bolo) as Suga Sura. Suga is further represented as a combination of two segments (or estates, *ngapi* or *sa'o pu'u*). The more senior of the pair, named after its ancestor as Raga Daga, was the first to settle in Suga Bhoja, and was granted two plots of land by Koyu. Later, the Raga Daga group invited other Suga people to join them, providing the later migrants with land secured from Bhoja Kisa. In regard to these territorial connections, villagers describe Suga as Defenders of both Bhoja Kisa and Koyu, although it is specifically Raga Daga that is recognized as Koyu's Defender.

Alternatively named as 'Bhoja at the end' (Bhoja Sepu), Bhoja Wawo, or Upper Bhoja, was the last to arrive in Suga Bhoja. Contrary to their name, they in fact descend from people of Bolo, more specifically a segment of the clan Lower Bolo (Bolo Au), who, like Suga, moved from old Bolo Yoga. Receiving rights to land from Bhoja Kisa, they changed their name to Bhoja while simultaneously becoming assigned as Defenders of the original Bhoja.

As remarked above, Suga and Upper Bhoja are the only two groups clearly recognized as Defenders (*ana tuku*) in Suga Bhoja. At the same time, neither group can claim complete independence from Bolo, their village of immediate origin. Both Upper Bhoja and Suga thus continue to recognize the sacrificial post in Bolo (or, nowadays, Muka) as their '*peo* of origin' (*peo pu'u*), and both are invited to join in Bolo sacrifices. While the two clans slaughter buffalo in Suga Bhoja as well, for the same reason they are obliged to take the horns and skulls to Bolo and place them in the *yenda* there. (As noted, Yoga people in Keo Ondo are similarly obliged with regard to the *yenda* of Yoga in Kuyu Wulu, although Yoga possess *peo* in both villages.) Also owing to their continuing dependence on Bolo, the tethers of buffalo belonging to neither Suga nor Bhoja Wawo may be inserted in the crotch of the *peo* in Suga Bhoja. After passing the ropes through the bamboo framework (*yaka*) erected seaward of the sacrificial tree, victims must be tethered directly to a bamboo stake (*madhu*) erected on the landward side (I: 2: iv). Encountered in no other village, this arrangement clearly underlines the marginal status of both Suga and Upper Bhoja—a status which, though concordant with the location of their houses at either extremity of Suga Bhoja, may seem ironic in view of the two clans' lending their names to the village as a whole.

Suga Bhoja displays a fairly pronounced pattern of affinal relations whereby older groups have generally given wives, as well as land, to younger groups. The genealogies of neither Yéwe nor Koyu—by most accounts the main Land Mother—reveal any wife-givers within the village. Koyu has given wives to Middle Bhoja (Bhoja Kisa) and once to Upper Bhoja, while Yéwe has given to Suga as well as to the two Bhoja groups. For its part, Middle Bhoja has given wives to Suga (including Raga Daga) but has also taken wives. Most marriages of Upper Bhoja women, too, have been with men of Suga.

Like several settlements described earlier, Suga Bhoja exemplifies a village basically constituted of a pair of clans which, through a historical process of augmentation, has come to include an additional pair. This, however, is a simplified view. Rather like clan Bolo in Nua Nage or Tunga in old Bolo Yoga, closer inspection reveals a fifth element deriving from the distinction of Middle Bhoja and Upper Bhoja. At the same time, this separation is somewhat offset by a local representation of Koyu and Yéwe as composing a single grouping, forming another dualism with Middle Bhoja largely with reference to the ceremonial distinction of earth breaker and excavator. By quite another means, quadripartition—or double dualism—is restored in a purely nominal view of Suga Bhoja as comprising just four named units: Koyu and Yéwe and Suga and Bhoja. Finally, it is noteworthy how the appearance of a third named group, Raga Daga, among the younger pair (Suga and Upper Bhoja) parallels, at least numerically, the implicit subsumption of Middle Bhoja by the older pair (Koyu and Yéwe).

6. *Paga*

Although now included administratively with Liwo and other villages linked with the ancestor Lobo Ga'e in the modern *desa* (administrative unit) of Wuli Walo, Paga is another village whose territory falls within the domain of Land Mother Lape. Located about two kilometres west of Nua Nage and not far from the south coast, this is a recent settlement replacing the village of Lopi, formerly situated a short distance landward. Paga is another village inhabited by just two clans: Laka and Nila. The older clan, Laka, was once settled in a village of the same name located atop a hill called Wolo Laka, not far inland from Lopi. Their original place of residence in western Keo was reputedly Tangi Dona, another site located somewhere landward of Paga.

Recognized as another Defender of Lape, clan Laka was founded by Teka Lébo, a man from Wére, in eastern Ngadha, who married Boku Wea, a daughter of the Céla ancestor Lape Mére and, according to one account, a woman named Wea Céla. Upon their marriage, Lape gave the couple an area of land called Tana Laka, whereupon Boku came to be known as 'Boku Laka'. Another, probably less reliable account, diverges from the foregoing in so far as it specifies Boku Wea as the daughter of Wea Mére, the sister of Lape Mére and the mother of Raga Wea (the ancestor of the Wulu clan Pata; II: 6: ii). Whichever details are accepted, one again encounters Lape Mére as a major source of both territory and wives to other groups, including later arrivals in the region. Also, according to Keo classification (I: 4: iv), people of Laka are counted as *ana weta* ('wife-takers') of Lape, whether descended from his D or his ZD.[16]

When still settled in the village of Laka, clan Laka was joined by the clan Nila, to which it ceded part of its territory. At present, Nila occupies the landward part of Paga while houses of Laka are located in the seaward section, a division the two groups say they have always maintained.[17] Hailing from a village named Bawa Nila (or Mbawa Nila) in the region of Ma'u Mbawa near Keo's extreme southwestern corner, Nila fled to Laka when their former village was invaded by swarms of black caterpillars (*ngota*), an event ultimately attributed to the marriage of a Nila man to a female *nitu* spirit (see Forth 1998: 75).[18] Receiving land from the older clan, Nila thus became the Defender of Laka, who at the same time provided the immigrant group with wives. Although relatively meagre genealogies suggest that this affinal connection has not been perpetuated, as originally a wife-taker of Laka, Nila erected a sacrificial *dheyo* tree next to Laka's *peo kesi* (I: 2: iv).[19] Since moving to Paga, both clans have planted *kesi* tree *peo*, side by side in the centre of the village (see Plate 11). Nevertheless, in accordance with Laka's position as the source of Nila's land, it is still a man of Laka who should act as earth breaker (*ta koe*) when Nila plants a *peo*, while Nila maintains the secondary position of excavator (*ta kabhe*).

---

[16] One genealogy of Laka lists an otherwise unidentified man named Léna as the husband of Wea Mére and the father of Boku. Following yet another, less elaborate version, Laka derives from 'Boku Ga'e', specified as a sister of Lape Ga'e. Here, then, Boku is represented not as a D or ZD of the senior Land Mother, but as a female sibling (*weta*).

[17] An additional four houses of Laka are now located in Koli Laja, a hamlet (*bo'a*) situated immediately below and seaward of Paga.

[18] The clan Nila is also found in several Nage villages close to Bo'a Wae. Interestingly, these other Nila people also have traditions describing how ancestors abandoned former villages owing to similar infestations linked with *nitu*. The theme is encountered in other parts of Keo and Nage as well, for example, among the Ngina people of Mala Laja (Sura Laja) in southwestern Nage, and in the myth of Bi Tua (I: 1: i; Forth 1998: 74–6).

[19] I was unable to obtain details of spouses for many Paga marriages. Where these were available, however, in the three or four unions involving Laka and Nila it was Nila who had given a wife to Laka. Nila men appear to obtain most of their wives from the clan Wulu Wogo in the village of Liwo (II: 6: i). A sample of 28 detailed marriages indicates that Laka has also taken two wives from Wulu Wogo, as well as four from the Liwo clans named Liwo and Jadho.

PLATE 11. Two sacrificial *kesi* trees (*peo kesi*) planted side by side in Paga

PLATE 12. The two structures called *nde* at the seaward end (or 'tail') of Paga

As well as two sacrificial trees, Paga now contains two pairs of ceremonial buildings (*yenda* and *nde*), one pair belonging to clan Laka and the other to Nila. Of the four buildings, only the *yenda* of Laka has posts decorated with carving, as does the wooden horse erected in front of this structure; the posts of the other three buildings are all undecorated. This pattern accords not only with the superiority of *yenda* to *nde* (I: 2: v) but also with clan Nila's subordination to Laka. Also distinguishing Paga from most other villages is the disposition of the two sets of ceremonial structures. While Laka and Nila respectively occupy the seaward and landward halves of the village, the two *yenda* stand side by side at the head (*ulu*) while the two *nde* are built at the tail (*éko*) of the settlement (see Plate 12). In this arrangement, moreover, the *nde* and *yenda* of the older clan, Laka, are placed towards the right (*mena*) side of the village, as is the clan's sacrificial *kesi* tree, while the identical *peo* and ceremonial buildings of Nila are all located to the left (*rale*) of these. Elsewhere more often distinguishing senior and junior houses of a single clan, in this case the opposition of *mena* and *rale* is associated with older and younger clans, and moreover with the contrast of Land Mother and Defender.

In respect of its double ritual structures, Paga is quite unusual. As shown earlier, until their recent disappearance, a comparable arrangement of sacrificial trees and ceremonial buildings was encountered in Nua Nage. In Nua Nage, however, each set was the possession of a pair of clans rather than a single clan.

7. Lundu (Upper Pau Lundu): One Half of a Pair

Also included in the domain of Land Mother Lape, Lundu largely resembles villages described above. Yet Lundu differs significantly from these in so far as it composes a double settlement with a village falling outside of Lape's domain. Located immediately seaward of Lundu, this is a village named Pau. Together the pair, which Keo nowadays often speak of as a single village, are known as Pau Lundu. In this context, Lundu is distinguished as Pau Lundu Nua Wawo (Upper Village of Pau Lundu), while Pau—not to be confused with other groups bearing the same name (see II: 3)—is specified as Pau Lundu Nua Au (Lower Village of Pau Lundu). The present sites of Lundu and Pau have been occupied since 1918. Previously, the two villages, similarly conjoined in a double settlement, were located on higher ground a short distance to the west.

Originally, Lundu was called Dhoki Paya. Referring to physical features of the site (see Appendix 3), the earlier name is retained as that of Lundu's oldest clan. Yet another sister's son of Lape Mére (see Fig. 6), the apical ancestor of clan Dhoki Paya appears in different genealogical accounts as Babo Wea (whose mother was Wea Mére) or Pe Ngoe (a son of Ngoe Mére). Initially, Dhoki Paya was the exclusive possessor of a forked sacrificial post (*peo yebu*). The statuses of trunk rider and tip rider were then divided between component estates (also described as *suku*), named after their ancestors as Ndutu Ndona and Légu Wawo. Later, when clan Loka Poma joined Dhoki Paya, the position of tip rider was transferred to the immigrant group, and the village name was eventually changed to Lundu.

Comprising a Lower and an Upper division—Loka Poma Au and Loka Poma Wawo—the people of Loka Poma ('Place of Poma') derive from the Poma region, far to the northwest.[20] Their ancestor, or more particularly, the ancestor of Loka Poma Au, was Koba Réja. An able warrior and reputedly a huge man with extraordinarily large ears, he was yet another migrant drawn to the region by the spectacle of Jawa Pogo. Soon after arriving, Koba Réja came into conflict with Nuga Raga (that is, Nuga and Raga), ancestors of the clan Pau in the village of Kota Pau (II: 3: i), and with people of clan Pajo in the village of Pajo Réja.[21] The war with Pajo erupted when the latter falsely accused the Loka Poma ancestor of stealing their buffalo. Proving victorious, Koba Réja then received as reparation a large area of land from Pajo, the clan of the Land Mother named Gewo Ga'e (II: 5: i). This land still makes up the largest part of the present territory of Loka Poma. A much smaller portion of land was given by Dhoki Paya, in connection with Loka Poma's taking up residence in Lundu and assuming the status of the older clan's Defender.

Although sometimes spoken of as two clans, the Upper and Lower divisions of Loka Poma operate for most purposes as a single *suku* and recognize a single headman. They are, therefore, sometimes described as *ngapi* (estates) of a single clan. The leader is always drawn from Lower Loka Poma. Contrary to what may be suggested by the names, which actually describe the relative spatial position of the two segments in the village, Lower Loka Poma is accordingly the superior member of the pair. This group, also, claims exclusive agnatic descent from Koba Réja, the legendary ancestor credited with obtaining territory currently shared by both divisions of the clan. In addition, it is specifically Lower Loka Poma that holds the status of tip rider of the *peo* in Lundu. Upper Loka Poma (Loka Poma Wawo) derives from Wodhu Lalo, an ancestor whom the clan's senior division describe as a servant or follower (*ana kapo*) of Koba Réja. In contrast, another genealogical account, provided by an elder of the clan Wolo Sabi in the village of Guyu Wolo (II: 3: ii), specifies Wodhu Lalo as a son of Koba Réja. The senior ancestor's other son, who also accompanied his father from Poma, is then given as Sapu Nai, the ancestor of Wolo Sabi.

Completing the population of Lundu is clan Bajo Léwa, an amalgamation of two formerly separate clans with distinct geographical origins. Even at present, different component houses and estates distinguish themselves as Léwa or Bajo, and the two divisions are occasionally designated as *suku* (thus

---

[20] This is also expressed as 'So'a Poma', a parallelism linking Poma with the So'a region, also to the northwest. As noted earlier, So'a is more generally recognized as the major homeland of both western Keo and Nage people.

[21] Questioning revealed no connection between Koba Réja's name and the village of Réja, or Pajo Réja (II: 5: i).

Suku Bajo and Suku Léwa). Yet, in most respects, the pair compose a unitary group. Recalling the organization of clan Loka Poma, both segments recognize a single headman, who is always drawn from a Léwa house. Nevertheless, Bajo and Léwa cannot straightforwardly be deemed *ngapi* (estates) of a single clan, since each itself comprises two estates. As I show presently, there is also a fifth estate, held by an extraneous group.

Léwa comes from the village of the same name located in eastern Keo. Recognizing a common ancestor named Lage Bajo, some Bajo people vaguely claimed to derive from Wolo Wea in eastern Nage. According to another account they hail from Lina (or Tiwu Lina), a village just to the west of the present study area. There is nothing to suggest that the group is in any way connected with the clan Bajo settled in Nua Nage, nor with a hamlet named Bajo located near Lédho Woru, several kilometres to the southeast. Indeed, in accordance with present personal naming conventions, 'Bajo' is sometimes interpreted as the name of a parent of the ancestor Lage Bajo. Léwa's ancestor was a man called Léna Mosa. Emphasizing their present combination, Léwa and Bajo people name their apical ancestors together with the compound designation Lage Léna, a formula usually reserved for full brothers or, less often, spouses. Similarly, the respective sons of these two men are named in tandem as Bobo Léba, thus conjoining Bobo Se'i (of Bajo) with Léba Pea (of Léwa).[22]

After arriving in their present location, Bajo and Léwa founded a village, also named Bajo Léwa, on what is now the present site of Lundu. In this former settlement Léwa people occupied the landward half, while Bajo resided in the seaward half. Whether the two groups initially maintained separate *peo* is no longer clear. However, when later they came to share a single sacrificial instrument, Léwa—as the first of the pair to arrive in the vicinity of Pau Lundu—was assigned the senior position, and Bajo the junior. Different local accounts describe this *peo* as either a forked Cassia post or a sacrificial *dheyo* tree. If it were the former, then erecting a forked *peo* would accord with the custom in the reputed place of origin of Léwa as well as in a possible homeland of Bajo, the Nage district of Wolo Wea. Their use of this sort of sacrificial instrument might further account for the circumstance that, for as long as anyone can remember, Dhoki Paya and Loka Poma have also employed a forked *peo*—whereas according to their inclusion within the domain of Lape, the older pair (and especially clan Dhoki Paya) should originally have planted a sacrificial *kesi* tree.

Since Léwa and Bajo acquired rights to land from Dhoki Paya, the amalgamated clan Bajo Léwa, like Loka Poma, is counted as a Defender of the oldest group. What is more, as the son of the Bajo ancestor, the above-mentioned Bobo Se'i, married a woman of Dhoki Paya, the group is recognized as an early wife-

---

[22] There is actually a further compounding here, since Pea is the name of the yB of Léba. Pea is said to have moved, and apparently to have lent his name, to Mala Pea, near Tiwu Lina, a village mentioned as a possible place of derivation of Bajo.

taker as well. In 1918, Dhoki Paya, indeed all the people of Lundu, abandoned their hilltop village to join Bajo Léwa in their lower-lying site. In this way, the original inhabitants of the latter effectively became incorporated in the new village of Lundu. Bajo Léwa thus no longer maintains a separate *peo*, but shares a single sacrificial post with Dhoki Paya and Loka Poma.

As indicated above, Bajo Léwa has for some time incorporated yet another group, named Boa Tébo, or, less often, Bo Boa or Boa Bajo (see Appendix 3). Deriving from immigrants belonging to the clan Boa in western Nage, the original Boa Tébo is now extinct. At present, its estate, which comprises territory originally belonging to Dhoki Paya, is contested by a man from Kota Pau (II: 3: i) now resident in the single house of Boa Tébo in Lundu, and the leader of Loka Nunu, one of the clans in Pau (the lower village of Pau Lundu). Whether Boa Tébo has ever operated as a separate clan is doubtful. Usually described as a *ngapi*, for all practical purposes it exists as a segment of Bajo Léwa, subordinated to the two groups that lend their names to that clan. It may be relevant, then, that *tébo*, the second part of the group's name, was explained to mean 'enveloped (in cloth)'.

As described thus far, Lundu's internal constitution appears generally comparable to that of other villages within the domain of Lape. An original group, and wife-taker of Lape Mére (Dhoki Paya), was joined by a later immigrant (Loka Poma) and both subsequently merged with another pair that have since amalgamated to form a single clan (Bajo Léwa). In recent decades, however, the position of Dhoki Paya and Loka Poma, as the two oldest groups, has become obscured. Reputedly with the support of some men of Dhoki Paya, in the 1960s Bajo Léwa took it upon themselves to replace a deteriorated Cassiawood post with a *peo* of the same forked form but constructed of a new material—concrete. In this endeavour, clan Bajo Léwa rationalized its usurpation of the premier status of trunk rider on the grounds that the object was erected on the site of its earlier settlement, the old village of Bajo Léwa, and thus on land it had occupied longer than Dhoki Paya or Loka Poma. Also involved in the undertaking was clan Ngodho (Pau Ngodho), the oldest of several groups currently composing the adjacent village of Pau (Lower Pau Lundu). Although the concrete *peo* has yet to be inaugurated in the proper sacrificial manner, Ngodho was moreover named as tip rider.

It should be stressed that this entire project has drawn much criticism, from outside Lundu as well as from within. A major objection focuses on the use of concrete, not only a modern but also a highly durable substance, which renders the object, unlike a post of Cassiawood or a living tree, permanent. The success of Bajo Léwa's venture and its attempted usurpation of Dhoki Paya therefore remain uncertain. Although the motives of collaborators within Dhoki Paya are unclear, the role of clan Ngodho deserves comment. In relation to *peo* planted by Dhoki Paya, Ngodho men claim the position of excavator (*ta kabhe*), if not explicitly that of tip rider (which would put them in contention with

Loka Poma). Rationalizing this, Ngodho referred to their status as wife-taker, deriving from the marriage of their founding ancestor, Ndona Ngodho, to a woman of Dhoki Paya, Bhe'o Wea (the sister of the Dhoki Paya ancestor Babo Wea). Although at this marriage they received a parcel of land as part of the wife-giver's prestation (*tana ka tuka*), in response to questioning Ngodho leaders denied they were Defenders (*ana tuku*) of the Lundu clan. In contrast, elders from co-resident clans in Lower Pau Lundu affirmed that Ngodho was indeed a Defender of Dhoki Paya. If this is accepted, then a relationship of Land Mother and Defender obtains between components of the two villages composing the double settlement of Pau Lundu, which moreover form part of the domains of two different major Land Mothers (see further II: 3: iii). It is similarly noteworthy that the division of senior and junior ritual positions between the oldest groups in Lundu and Pau respectively, though otherwise exceptional, is quite consistent with the fact that Lundu is the older (*ka'e*) and Pau the younger (*ari*) village.

8. *Summary and Prospect*

All tracing descent to Land Mother Lape, the several villages discussed above reveal common organizational themes. With one possible exception—the village of Bolo—settlements recognize the precedence of an original clan whose ancestor was related to Lape Mére (or Lape Ga'e) as sister's son or daughter's son (or alternatively ZDS in the case of clan Laka in Paga). Stressing this connection, sister's or daughter's husbands of Lape are often unknown or otherwise anonymous individuals. Thus, ignoring ultimate agnatic origins, emphasis is placed on connections through women, and the relationship of Land Mother and Defender is represented as one of whole and part in accordance with the principle, demonstrated in Part I, whereby wife-givers (*moi mame*) encompass wife-takers (*ana weta*). In all the villages described above, later immigrants, mostly deriving from outside western Keo, have joined original clans, while in some instances (Nua Nage, Lundu) combination has involved the merging of formerly separate villages. For the most part, this historical accretion has eventually resulted in a formal quadripartition. Yet all such four-part orders clearly reduce to a combination of two pairs. Also, where a grouping of four is not clearly present (as in the village of Yoga, or Kuyu Wulu, as presently constituted), the settlement comprises—or is locally conceived as comprising—a single pair (for example, Yoga and Sina in Yoga, or Bolo and Suga in Bolo). Alternatively, quadripartition is created for certain purposes by a process of division—as when the two estates (*ngapi*) of Suga, in Muka, are treated ceremonially as equivalent to the two clans of Bolo.

Seemingly challenging dualistic and derivative quadripartite representations is the appearance of third or fifth groups, generally the most recently arrived in their respective localities (for example, Tunga in Kuyu Wulu, or

Bolo Yoga; Bolo in Nua Nage; Bhoja Wawo in Suga Bhoja). In ways already illustrated, however, Keo tend to accommodate these 'odd' groups by treating them—practically as well as conceptually—as subsumed, and thus subordinated, parts of pre-existing wholes. Further instances of, and variations on, these several themes are explored in later chapters.

I began the present chapter by describing an instance of incipient inversion. Being the one group agnatically derived from Land Mother Lape, and thus 'directly descended' (as Keo now express it) from the eldest of the several Ga'e siblings, Céla is the paramount clan in the whole of western Keo. Yet, at present, Céla is all but subsumed by its principal Defender, clan Bajo. If not fully realized inversions, such contestations of precedence are similarly apparent in regard to clans Koyu and Yéwe in Suga Bhoja, and Dhoki Paya and Bajo Léwa in Lundu. The following chapter documents yet another instance, exploring the development of relations among clans occupying one half of the double settlement of Pajo Mala.

2

The Two Villages of Pajo Mala

About a kilometre seaward of Kuyu Wulu, one comes to another double settlement, just off the modern road that leads to the coast. In its entirety, the settlement is now known as Pajo Mala and, like Pau Lundu, described in the last chapter, is often spoken of as a single village. Originally, however, the name Pajo Mala designated only the older of the two components, the more seaward of the two villages currently distinguished as Pajo Mala Nua Au ('Lower Pajo Mala') or, more often, simply as Pajo Au ('Lower Pajo'). Accordingly, Keo call the landward village Pajo Wawo ('Upper Pajo'), or Pajo Mala Nua Wawo ('Upper Pajo Mala'). The two villages are immediately recognizable by their possession of different sacrificial instruments. Lower Pajo Mala employs a stone column (recently replacing an earlier *kesi* tree), while in the centre of Upper Pajo Mala one finds a forked Cassiawood *peo* (see Plate 4).

Despite the name, Pajo Mala is unrelated to the village of Pajo (or Pajo Réja) or its principal inhabitants, the clan Pajo, the direct descendants of the Land Mother named Gewo Ga'e (II: 5). Nor do Keo know of any connection between the village and clan of Pajo and the clan Pajo Wolo, one of the groups resident in Lower Pajo Mala. Even so, the name Pajo Wolo may very well explain the village name Pajo Mala, which translates as 'Pajo of the plain (*mala*)'. Denoting a central or intermediate location, *pajo* evidently names populations by reference to the physical setting of their villages, and as such was probably adopted independently by the people of Pajo Wolo and the descendants of Gewo Ga'e (clan Pajo). *Wolo*, on the other hand, means 'hill', and corresponds with the fact that before clan Pajo Wolo moved to their present settlement, their village of the same name was situated on higher ground at the foot of Mount Belu, a peak adjacent to Jawa Pogo. After the Pajo Wolo people moved to the lower-lying site of Pajo Mala, the village then came in effect to be named after them, with *mala* ('plain, flat, low-lying area') substituting for *wolo* ('hill').[1] Detracting from this interpretation is the circumstance that clan Pajo Wolo is not acknowledged as the first clan to settle in Lower Pajo Mala, and in fact appears to have been the last. As we shall see, however, Pajo Wolo was by all indications the dominant group in the village and surrounding region even before its arrival in Pajo Mala. In this regard, moreover, the name

---

[1] *Mala* and *wawo* occur elsewhere in central Flores as terms distinguishing lower- and higher-parts of single regions. After formulating my interpretation of the derivation of the name Pajo Mala, it was confirmed by spontaneous remarks from a Pajo Wolo leader in 1999.

provides a qualified instance of the more general pattern whereby entire villages are identified with a superordinate component.[2]

1. *Lower Pajo Mala (Pajo Mala Nua Au)*

Like surrounding lands held by component clans, the double settlement of Pajo Mala incorporates territory derived from two major landowners, Land Mother Lape and an ancestral couple named together as Boa Maga (Boa was the wife, and Maga the husband). Indeed, the present site of Lower Pajo Mala itself includes land belonging to both domains. Following the villagers' own enumeration, Lower Pajo Mala now comprises three clans: the previously mentioned Pajo Wolo, Bindi (or Bindi Wae), and Kayo, now usually named as Pajo Kayo. As their genealogies attest, the three groups also form a three-unit cycle, an arrangement first brought to my attention by participants themselves. Pajo Wolo have thus several times given wives to Bindi Wae, who several times have provided brides to Pajo Kayo, who are in turn long-standing wife-givers of Pajo Wolo.[3] As I presently show, Bindi Wae's connections with Pajo Wolo and Pajo Kayo respectively correspond to the order of precedence recognized among the three clans in respect of the sacrificial instrument they currently share.

Descending agnatically from the ancestor Jawa Nio, a grandson (variously specified as SS or DS) of Lape, clan Pajo Wolo claims the status of Defender of Lape and controls that part of Lower Pajo Mala territory falling within the original domain of the senior Land Mother. (As noted, Jawa Nio was a brother of Ghino Nio, the ancestor of clan Sina in Kuyu Wulu, or Yoga; see Fig. 6). The other part, the domain of Boa Maga, is claimed by Bindi, which traces direct (agnatic) descent to the ancestral pair. Bindi itself is thus acknowledged as Land Mother (*ine tana*) in respect of land held by other clans in Pajo Mala, and in this regard is recognized as the largest landowner in the region. Curiously, Bindi possesses no Defenders, a circumstance possibly connected with the group having been expelled from its original village, named Guyu Wula, and with the fact that it descends from the younger of two male heirs to the domain of Boa Maga. In this connection, it may also be relevant that, like several groups I describe in the next chapter, the Bindi ancestors are not known to be related in any definite way to the Ga'e siblings. Unlike other Keo clans, the Bindi people also do not claim to derive from So'a, nor indeed from

---

[2] Pajo Wolo is implicitly denoted simply as 'Pajo' in the name Poma Pajo ('Pajo's Pool'), a former bathing place, now disappeared, located just below the old village of Pajo Wolo. A curious prohibition once applied to Poma Pajo: it was forbidden for any group of Pajo Wolo women numbering seven to bathe there. Were they to do so a natural catastrophe (*wuya wando*) would occur; the earth would then collapse or water would gush from the ground. Apparently linked with this, the place was also supposed to be inhabited by a fantastic creature with the head of a cat and body of a serpent (Forth 1998: 89).

[3] Bindi Wae has also given wives to Pajo Wolo, but not in a way constituting direct exchange between houses, and evidently not affecting the villagers' own model of a three-group cycle.

anywhere else outside of western Keo. There is thus no certainty as to whether their ancestors preceded or came after Lape and the other Ga'e, although most local speculation favoured the second possibility.

Contrary to what the lengthy tenure of both Bindi and Pajo Wolo might suggest, neither clan was in fact the first to settle in Pajo Mala. Rather, this was Pajo Kayo, a group hailing from Kayo Wawo (*kayo*, 'thorny plant'; *wawo*, 'above, upper'), a village in the Wére region of eastern Ngadha. As the clan is more simply, and by some accounts more accurately, designated as Kayo, the element 'Pajo' in their name would appear to reflect their long association with clan Pajo Wolo. On removing to western Keo, the Pajo Kayo people first settled in a village, also named Kayo, just east of the present Pajo Mala.

Pajo Kayo is one of the few western Keo clans that observes a food prohibition. Applying only to natal women of the group, and not to Pajo Kayo men or their wives, the ban concerns the heads of any animal. Risking sores to the breasts and genitalia in the event of a breach, Pajo Kayo women continue to observe the taboo even after they marry out of the clan; but they do not pass it on to their daughters.

Although one account speaks of Pajo Kayo originally settling on land belonging to Pajo Wolo, the clan subsequently acquired rights to additional land within the territory of Bindi, the second group to settle in the region of Pajo Mala. As mentioned, Bindi's original settlement was Guyu Wula, a village located high up the slopes of the Ebu Lobo volcano, directly north of Pajo Mala. In Guyu Wula, the ancestors Boa (the woman) and Maga (her husband) had two sons, regularly named together as Léwa Ranga. Léwa was the elder, and Ranga the younger. Bindi derives from the younger brother. Once, the two brothers dug a water channel leading from a certain spring in order to flood a buffalo wallow. This, however, offended local water spirits (*nitu*); hence Guyu Wula became overrun with caterpillars (*ngota*; II: 1: vi), and everyone was forced to flee. Later, Léwa joined the ancestors of clan Pau in Kota Pau and founded the adjacent village of Guyu Wolo, whose name is partly taken from the original village of Guyu Wula. In contrast, after abandoning Guyu Wula, Ranga, the Bindi ancestor, established a hamlet called Pu'u Bindi ('Starfruit tree'), not far from the present Pajo Mala. It is from this place, named after a large starfruit tree (*bindi mére*, *Averrhoa carambola*) growing nearby, that the clan came to be known as Bindi.[4]

Unlike the Guyu Wolo people, who have since become Defenders of clan Pau in Kota Pau, Bindi retained possession of the domain of Boa Maga. After remaining for a time in Pu'u Bindi, the Bindi people joined clan Pajo Kayo in Pajo Mala. At this time, the village did not yet have a *peo*. The first sacrificial instrument was erected only after the third clan, Pajo Wolo, removed to Pajo Mala from their original settlement (also named Pajo Wolo), located a short

---

[4] One Bindi man stated that his ancestors had used this starfruit tree as a *peo*. Referring to the highly unconventional nature of such a usage in relation to current practices, other Pajo Mala villagers, belonging to other clans, dismissed the claim as ridiculous.

distance away at the foot of Mount Belu (Kéli Belu), near Mount Nata. This *peo* was a living *kesi* tree, the kind employed by Pajo Wolo in their original village and the sort maintained by villagers of Lower Pajo Mala until about three decades ago, when they replaced their sacrificial tree with a stone column (*peo watu*). Responding to an invitation from clan Pajo Kayo, who required their military assistance, Pajo Wolo was presented by Pajo Kayo with a single plot of land to serve as 'a place for discarding branches from a living *peo* and chips of wood carved from ceremonial objects' (*tana ndoi cawa kaju, tau guyu piye moke cake*). On such land, Keo people also plant bamboo exclusively for ritual use (*guyu piye*) and tap palm wine (*moke*) for festive consumption (*cake* is a bamboo ladder or climbing pole for ascending arenga and lontar palms). As this would suggest, the first *peo* planted in Pajo Mala was in effect a replacement for the sacrificial tree Pajo Wolo left behind in their own village, a tree first granted to the Pajo Wolo ancestor, Jawa Nio, in recognition of his status as Defender of Land Mother Lape. In accordance with this circumstance, Pajo Wolo, although the last of the three clans to arrive in Pajo Mala, claims the status of earth breaker (*ta koe*) in respect of the Pajo Mala *peo*. This status, however, is otherwise credited to clan Bindi, as I describe below.

Although the sequence of events is not entirely clear, some time after moving to Keo, clan Pajo Kayo acquired from Céla, the clan of Land Mother Lape, seven plots of land as part of a marriage prestation (*tana ka tuka*). The bride was a Céla woman named Tuwa, hence the area, a section of which coincides with part of the present site of Pajo Mala, is known as Tana Tuwa (Land of Tuwa). After the marriage, a Pajo Kayo ancestor named Céme Wea accused Tuwa of witchcraft, whereupon she returned to her parents in Céla. Céla then reclaimed Tana Tuwa. Although rights to the land remain in contention to the present day, according to clan Pajo Wolo, Céla transferred the entire area to them, as principal local Defenders of the Land Mother.[5]

How exactly Pajo Wolo's removal to Pajo Mala village might be connected with this event is uncertain. Nevertheless, it almost goes without saying that Pajo Wolo's acquisition of Tana Tuwa, augmenting their earlier grant of lands from Land Mother Lape (designated as Tana Jawa Nio, after their male ancestor), would have consolidated their position in Pajo Mala. As noted above, on removing to Pajo Mala, Pajo Wolo appears also to have lent its name to the village, thus replacing an earlier name that villagers no longer recall, but which may have been Kayo (or Nua Kayo, 'Kayo Village'). The history of Lower Pajo Mala, therefore, tends to suggest that, on joining Kayo and Bindi, the Pajo Wolo people may at least nominally have incorporated a pre-existing settlement comprised, like many others, of just two clans.

---

[5] After abandoning Tana Tuwa, some members of Pajo Kayo swore an oath never to return to the territory. However, Pajo Kayo people are also described as attempting to recover the land and to secure the return of the woman Tuwa. For this purpose, Céme Wea was required to make a payment of seven cow buffalo and seven winnows of gold; but this he was never able to provide.

Responses to enquiries indicated that, despite their affinal connection, clan Pajo Kayo was never a Defender of Lape; nor (unlike Pajo Wolo) did it acquire a *peo* from the Land Mother. Even so, it is possible that at one time Pajo Kayo did possess this status and that, following the dispute over Tana Tuwa, it was revoked. Noteworthy in this connection is the genealogy provided by Pajo Kayo, which shows Léna Dhuge (the ancestor of the clan as now established in both Pajo Mala and Bale Wolo; see Section 2 below) as married to Wea Mére of clan Céla, and thus either a sister of Lape Mére or a descendant with the same name. Similarly, the genealogy given by clan Bindi describes the wife of their ancestor, Ranga, as a woman from Céla named Wea. Whatever the value of these claims, at present neither Pajo Kayo nor Bindi is recognized as Defender of anyone. The only group maintaining this status, in relation to the senior Land Mother, is therefore Pajo Wolo.

Towards the end of the 1940s the village of Lower Pajo Mala was extended landwards. Before this it had been separated from Upper Pajo Mala (the higher-lying of the two villages composing the double settlement of Pajo Mala) by thick stone ramparts (*kota*) and a banyan tree. Then, on the instructions of the government headman (BI *kepala kampong*), a man of Pajo Kayo who wished to convert the settlement into a 'single village', the tree and stone wall were removed, so that Lower Pajo Mala came immediately to adjoin Upper Pajo Mala. In 1958 the location of the *peo* in Pajo Au was changed as well. Originally the sacrificial tree was planted further seaward, somewhere roughly adjacent to a large boulder named Watu Toyo ('red stone') situated on the 'right' (*mena*) side of the village and very close to its seaward extremity. As noted, Lower Pajo Mala combines land belonging to clans Bindi and Pajo Wolo. Significantly perhaps, the Watu Toyo marks the boundary between these two territories, with Bindi's land (the domain of Boa Maga) located landward and the land of Pajo Wolo (falling within the domain of Lape) located seaward of the large stone. By contrast, as currently disposed, by far the largest part of the village is situated on land belonging to Bindi.

Although local accounts diverge as to whether the site of the original sacrificial *kesi* tree fell within the territory of Bindi or Pajo Wolo, it seems more likely to have stood on Bindi land, as, indeed, does the present stone *peo*. Accordingly, villagers most often describe clan Bindi as the rightful occupant of the principal ritual status of earth breaker (*ta koe*). Bindi, moreover, appears to be the only group in Lower Pajo Mala which, in recent times at least, has planted a ritual garden (*uma gua*). Nevertheless, ritual experts commonly describe both Bindi and Pajo Wolo—and hence both Land Mothers—as receiving equal recognition as possessors of the *peo*, by way of a special procedure followed whenever a new sacrificial tree or a bamboo lattice (*yaka*) is erected. While Pajo Kayo occupies the secondary position as excavator (*ta kabhe*), the earth is initially broken by two men, one of Pajo Wolo and one of Bindi, who grasp the digging implement (*tuju*) together, thus in effect sharing the principal ritual task.

In respect of this arrangement, which group can claim sacrificial precedence is now equivocal. Inasmuch as Bindi is more widely recognized as earth breaker, it should, however, be the headman of this group who slaughters first. Though erected in the part of the village belonging to Bindi, the last *kesi* tree *peo* in Lower Pajo Mala was planted on the initiative of a Pajo Wolo leader, Jawa Co'o, who hoped that by installing a new sacrificial instrument he would recover from a serious illness. Sacrifices were to follow if the strategy proved successful; but Jawa Co'o died shortly afterwards, so the tree was never inaugurated (*reme peo*). Then, some time in the 1960s, the people of Lower Pajo Mala replaced the *kesi* tree with a *peo* of stone. But this, too, has yet to be inaugurated with a collective buffalo sacrifice, even though over thirty years have passed since it was erected.

As the territory of Bindi, the land of Boa Maga, has always adjoined land of Pajo Wolo, villagers describe the two clans as possessing 'lands that adhere to one another, stones that mingle together' (*tana papa dhaka, watu papa kabhu*), 'like two hands pressed together' (*bhia lima labu*). In the same spirit, fields belonging to Bindi should always bound fields cultivated by Pajo Wolo, and vice versa. Requiring that the two groups co-operate in a variety of undertakings, their possession of adjacent territories is also explicitly connected with their joint occupation of the status of earth breaker. In recognition of this special connection—sometimes classified as an instance of 'land siblingship' (*ka'e ari tana watu*; I: 4: i)—Bindi and Pajo Wolo further share ownership of a single plot, located just east of the present village, which they cultivate in turns (*tana kema papa pesi*). People of one clan clear and plant for four or five years before leaving the area to grow over; then the other clan does the same.[6]

Arguably, the net effect of these customs is to constitute clans Pajo Wolo and Bindi Wae as a partial unity, thus accommodating the dualism of the ritual offices of earth breaker and excavator (occupied by Pajo Kayo), and perhaps in some degree resolving the issue of sacrificial precedence. At the same time, Bindi is itself organized dualistically, as the clan incorporates an extraneous and separately named element. This is the group named Wae, a co-resident wife-taker of Bindi's named after their village of origin in southwestern Nage. At present, therefore, clan Bindi is usually designated as 'Bindi Wae', a designation which, as we shall see, serves to distinguish it from branches of Bindi now established in other villages. Although originating in a uxorilocal marriage without bridewealth, Wae was later provided by Bindi with separate ceremonial accommodation, including a flat stone altar (*nabe*), a special granary (*bo buti*), and a 'ladder house' (*sa'o tangi*, see I: 3: iv). All these things, which allowed Wae to conduct its own first-fruits rituals (*ka pae muri*), were

---

[6] This custom, described as unique to Bindi and Pajo Wolo, is no longer observed; and a Bindi man has (illegitimately) planted the area with clove trees.

given in an attempt to alleviate illness among women married to Wae men. Bindi also provided its Wae affines with four plots of land, but without initially ceding full rights, and with the original specification that Wae should only plant cultigens with a short growing period (such as turmeric, ginger, green vegetables, and tubers; *toni kune lea, tau tura uta ne'e lege téte*). Nevertheless, owing in part to their ceremonial separation, Wae subsequently gained recognition as a distinct estate (*ngapi*) within clan Bindi (or Bindi Wae), with full rights to this land.

Although Wae no longer takes wives from Bindi, the two groups are still sometimes described as wife-giver (*moi ga'e* or *ana naya*) and wife-taker (*ana weta*). Either as parts of the same clan or as hereditary affines, Wae is obliged to support Bindi in all undertakings, an obligation enshrined in the standard expression *Bindi taku tenda, Wae yape* (roughly 'if Bindi fears the level, then Wae is on the terrace below'). The phrases are a play on words. As a segment of Bindi, Wae is more completely known as 'Yape Wae' ('Wae level, terrace'), while in respect of their unity the two groups are named together as 'Tenda Bindi, Yape Wae' (*tenda*, 'level' is roughly synonymous with *yape* in this context). At present, Wae possesses just one house in Pajo Mala, but formerly there were more. In this regard, Bindi Wae people say that wherever one group (Wae or Bindi) erected a house, the other was obliged to construct another next to it.

In a way broadly comparable to what one encounters in other villages, the present Lower Pajo Mala is the product of a series of amalgamations. Unlike previously described instances, however, the settlement is unique in so far as its lands, and even the present village site, conjoin territories identified with two ancient landlords, Boa Maga and Lape Ga'e. At the same time, all clans in Lower Pajo Mala maintain binary connections with groups resident outside the village. Not only is Bindi linked by common agnatic descent with Guyu Wolo, but the same relation of 'siblingship' (*ka'e ari*) connects Pajo Wolo and Sina in Bolo Yoga (Kuyu Wulu), in respect of the ancestors Jawa Nio and Ghino Nio. Similarly, clan Kayo (or Pajo Kayo) continues to recognize an agnatic connection with the people of Bale Wolo (see Section 3 below).

As I describe later (II: 5), both Bindi Wae and Pajo Wolo are further linked by special ties of 'siblingship' with clans Se and Late in the village of Nua Muri, whose territory also bounds on the domain of Boa Maga, while as I explain in the next section, people of Pajo Wolo recognize as 'house siblings' (*ka'e ari sa'o ténda*) the senior segment of clan Kate in Upper Pajo Mala. The several dyadic relationships in which clan Pajo Wolo participates with external groups appear further to consolidate this clan's position in relation to the other two clans resident in Lower Pajo Mala. As demonstrated in the following section, a more diffuse relationship of *ka'e ari* connects clans resident in the adjacent village of Upper Pajo Mala with the village of Bolo (Muka).

PLATE 13. Two men of Bale beside a large grave in Upper Pajo Mala

2. Upper Pajo Mala (Pajo Mala Nua Wawo) or Kate Bale

Although still recognizable as two *nua*, the recent conjoining of the Lower and Upper villages of Pajo Mala is consistent with the adoption of a single formal designation for the entire settlement. Nowadays, all of Pajo Mala is known as Ulu Rala Oto, Eko Rita Léwa, 'Head that is the Motor Road, Tail that is the Tall Alstonia Tree'. The first phrase refers to the modern, Dutch-built road that runs above the village. The second is drawn from the formal name of Lower Pajo Mala: Ulu Kota Papa, Eko Rita Léwa. Kota Papa, 'dividing stone wall' denotes a structure that once separated the two villages of Pajo Mala. Accordingly, Upper Pajo Mala is distinguished as Ulu Rala Oto, Eko Kota Papa.[7]

---

[7] An earlier compound name for Lower Pajo Mala may have been Ulu Nunu, Eko Rita, referring to the large banyan tree (*nunu*) that once grew at the head of the village and thus just below the tail of Upper Pajo Mala. Interestingly, the same designation is now applied to the derivative village of Bale Wolo (see Section 3 below). Referring to the same banyan, an alternative name recorded for Upper Pajo Mala is Ulu Kota, Eko Nunu, which is almost identical to a formal name given for the old settlement of Kate Bale: Ulu Kota, Eko Nunu Kawi (see Appendix 2).

Founded in the 1920s, Upper Pajo Mala (Pajo Mala Nua Wawo, or Pajo Wawo) is by far the more recent of the paired villages. Incorporating the clans Upper Bale (Bale Yape Wawo, or 'Bale of the Upper Level'), Lower Bale (Bale Yape Au), and Kate, the village replaces an older double settlement. Located a short distance to the west of Upper Pajo Mala, this was called Kate Bale, a name still occasionally applied to the present village. Old Kate Bale comprised two villages (*nua*), Nua Bale (or One Bale), and Nua Kate, the names of which are obviously retained for the clans resettled in Pajo Mala. Nua Kate, or Kate Village, was located seaward of Bale, and separated by a distance of just 20 or 30 metres. The division of Bale into two clans (*suku*) reflects a similar disposition. Thus Upper Bale had their houses in the landward section of Nua Bale, while Lower Bale occupied the seaward part. In certain contexts, Pajo Mala people describe the Upper and Lower clans of Bale as a unity, even characterizing them as a single *suku*.[8] This usage, then, reduces the three clans of Upper Pajo Mala to a duality isomorphic with the two *nua* composing old Kate Bale.

As mentioned in the preceding chapter, the Bale people are one of several waves of migrants who came to western Keo from Ola Bolo, following the people still known as Bolo, now resident in the village of Muka (II: 1: iv). Initially, the Bale ancestors lived for a time with Bolo in the village of Bolo Ndata. (As also noted previously, like the clan Lower Bolo, Bale are described as a segment of the clan Lére in Ola Bolo.) Later, after abandoning Bolo Ndata, the Bolo people removed to Bolo Yoga while Bale founded the separate village of Bale (or One Bale), the immediate predecessor of Upper Pajo Mala. Owing to their common geographical origins, however, Bale remains subordinate to Bolo. Indeed, Keo alternatively designate Bale in Upper Pajo Mala as 'Bolo Bale'. This is also the name by which the Bale people announce themselves when they participate in buffalo sacrifices in Muka (Bolo).[9] In this context at least, 'Bolo Bale' does not distinguish Bale so much as designate the two groups together and affirm their continuing unity. On the other hand, the headman of the Muka clan Upper Bolo argued that 'Bolo Bale' should be understood as referring to Bale as 'people who became Bolo' (see *bale*, 'to change (into), transform') upon their incorporation into the old village of Bolo Ndata. The name was then later shortened to Bale.[10]

The link between Bolo and Bale, and more particularly Bale's continuing subordination to Bolo, is expressed in several other ways. Identifying themselves as *ka'e ari* ('siblings'), Bale and Bolo men can inherit one another's

---

[8] Bale genealogies show two marriages between men of Upper Bale and women of Lower Bale. Although some people said such marriages ought not to occur, in other cases Keo allow marriage within one and the same clan, so long as these involve different houses.

[9] Although no known genealogical connection exists between Bolo and Bale, the two are sometimes described as having originally been estates (*ngapi*) of a single clan. The same speculation is offered in regard to the two Bale clans, which, similarly, no longer recognize a single agnatic origin.

[10] Bale occurs as a clan name in eastern Ngadha, but this has no bearing on its appearance in western Keo, or at least none that Keo people recognize.

estates (*ngapi*) when natural heirs are lacking, as genealogical records reveal has occurred in several instances. In the same vein, a reciprocal relationship (*ka'e tuku wutu, ari wina lima*; see I: 4: i) initiated by the ancestors of Bolo and clan Keo is interpreted to include the Bale people as well (II: 4: i). Genealogies also reveal that the clan Upper Bale was an early wife-taker of Bolo, particularly of clan Upper Bolo. One thus encounters another example of how relations classified as *ka'e ari* do not preclude affinity, while in the present instance the subordination of Bale to Bolo in regard to the *ka'e ari* relationship accords with their respective alliance statuses.

Further consistent with their close association, Bolo and Bale are obliged to attend buffalo sacrifices at one another's *peo*. A recent acquisition, the *peo* of Bale is, moreover, considered a 'branch' or 'derivative' (*taya so, kamu lana*, 'extended branch, spreading root') of Bolo's sacrificial post. In their former village of Bale, the Bale people lacked a *peo* altogether; hence when sacrificing buffalo they employed only a bamboo lattice (*yaka*) and a stake (*ia*). Associated with parts of the village occupied by Upper and Lower Bale respectively, these instruments are still referred to in names alternatively applied to the two Bale clans. Occupying the landward section of Bale—indeed the most landward part of the present Upper Pajo Mala—Upper Bale is thus known as Bale Yape Ia (Bale of the *ia* level), while Lower Bale is called Bale Yape Yaka (Bale of the *yaka* level). Also in accordance with their subordination to Bolo, Bale—and hence the village of Upper Pajo Mala—has never possessed a *yenda*. Thus whenever they kill buffalo, even at their own *peo*, the Bale people have always been obliged to take the trophy horns to the *yenda* of Bolo (now in the village of Muka). Signalling their continuing dependence on the senior group in sacrificial matters, Bale's position is thus comparable to that of clans Suga and Bhoja Wawo in Suga Bhoja, as well as that of Yoga in Keo Ondo in respect of Kuyu Wulu (II: 1: ii, v).

After removing from Bolo Ndata and establishing the village of Bale (One Bale), Bale acquired lands from Land Mother Lape (clan Céla) in exchange for gunpowder and other goods. Following one account, this land was actually part of the territory already ceded by Lape to clan Pajo Wolo in Lower Pajo Mala. Also through purchase, Bale later obtained an additional seven plots from Bindi, the other major landowner in Lower Pajo Mala.[11] The present status of these lands is subject to conflicting local interpretations. Neither transaction, however, conferred on Bale the status of Defender, in respect of either Lape or Bindi, nor, indeed, the right to erect a *peo*.

Several generations after founding Bale Village, the Bale people invited ancestors of clan Kate to build a village just seaward of their own. Known

---

[11] As noted earlier (I: 1), seven, a generally valued total among Keo, is a commonly specified number in mythical or historical contexts. The land Bale acquired from clan Bindi is known as *tana ulu manu*, 'chicken head land', referring to the report that Bale (specifically Upper Bale) obtained it in exchange for the heads of seven fowls and seven containers of palm wine.

simply as Nua Kate (Kate Village), this village and Bale thus came to form the double settlement known as Kate Bale.[12] Originally from the village of Kate Kela (*kate*, 'wild cucumber'; *kela*, 'giant reed') just south of Wolo Wea in eastern Nage, the Kate people were driven westward after a major military defeat by the people of Kéli Mado (see Map 1).[13] In western Keo, Kate first settled at a place called Watu Wula (also known as Jawa Wawo), on land belonging to clan Bindi in Lower Pajo Mala. Their later removal to Nua Kate was led by Mepe Lape, the SS of Kawi Léwa, the Kate ancestor who was killed in the war with Kéli Mado. Following the Kate genealogy, Léwa Dhéma, the son of Kawi and the first to arrive in western Keo, lived eight generations before the present Kate leader, a man in his sixties. If the genealogy is historically accurate, and a generation is estimated at 25–30 years, then the removal of the Kate people from the Wolo Wea region would appear to have taken place some time during the early or mid-eighteenth century.

Kate people still retain rights to the lands obtained from Bindi, acquired in exchange for a large buffalo and seven containers of palm wine. Later, after founding Kate Village and with the mediation of their Bale neighbours, Kate obtained further territory from the domain of Lape, for which they reputedly paid just a winnowful of gunpowder. Some accounts suggest that this land was drawn from Tana Tuwa, the area originally given to clan Pajo Kayo in Lower Pajo Mala and then later reassigned to clan Pajo Wolo. However that may be, land of Kate falling within the domain of Lape appears to have been ceded by Pajo Wolo, rather than granted directly by the Land Mother. Some time later, Kate people further augmented their territory with four plots provided by Bale.[14] At present, therefore, the land of Bale bounds land of Kate on the west, and pasture land of Pajo Wolo on the east, north, and south. In fact the present territory of both Kate and Bale—and thus the village of Upper Pajo Mala—is virtually surrounded by land belonging to clan Pajo Wolo, resident in Lower Pajo Mala.

It is important to emphasize that none of the foregoing land transfers, usually described as purchases (*beta*), made Kate the Defender (*ana tuku*) of any other clan; nor by this means did they acquire an independent sacrificial instrument. In Nua Kate, the Kate people did, indeed, erect a *peo*; but as I explain below, this act is rationalized in another way. As noted earlier, Bale are similarly unable to claim the status of Defender in relation to groups from which they obtained land. Employing a standard expression, both Kate and Bale are thus characterized as 'breaking (earth) themselves, excavating alone'

---

[12] The village actually lay somewhat to the west (*rale*) of Bale. For topographical reasons, the two villages were, therefore, not placed in a completely straight line.

[13] An account of Kéli Mado's defeat of the Kate people is also found in Fontijne's history of Kéli Mado (1940). While broadly similar, Fontijne's account and the one I recorded in Pajo Mala reveal a number of interesting differences. These, however, cannot be examined here.

[14] Two of these plots were given by Bale as *tana ka tuka* (land given as a marriage prestation; I: 3: i) at the first marriage of a Kate man (Léwa Wea) to a Bale woman.

(*koe beki, kabhe dhato*; both modifiers gloss as 'own', 'alone'), phrases which imply that, in so far as they possess sacrificial instruments, these are not derived from any local Land Mother.

By the same token, Kate appears not to be in any strict sense a Defender (*ana tuku*) of Bale. Nevertheless, the clan is sometimes described as such. In regard to temporal precedence and the older group's sponsorship of the later arrival, Kate people, furthermore, describe themselves as 'the child' (*ta ana*) and Bale as 'the mother' (*ta ine*). Perhaps also relevant in this connection, not long after establishing Nua Kate, men of Kate began taking wives from Bale, in particular the clan Upper Bale. The first to do so was Léwa Wea, the son of Mepe Lape, the Kate leader who founded Nua Kate and thus in effect inaugurated the double settlement of Kate Bale. Although apparently less reliable than other sources, one version of Kate's genealogy similarly indicates a marriage between the apical ancestor in western Keo, Léwa Dhéma, and another woman of Upper Bale. Genealogies further reveal that, over five generations, Kate men have contracted seven marriages with Bale women, different houses (*sa'o*) of Kate taking wives from either the Upper or Lower clan of Bale. In this way, even though Bale cannot claim the title of Land Mother (*ine tana*), the group's precedence in old Kate Bale and its role in providing Kate with lands constitute one of numerous examples where wife-givers in Keo are simultaneously land-givers. In regard to Kate's possession of land ultimately derived from Lape, it is interesting, moreover, that Mepe Lape himself is reputed to have taken a wife from Céla, the clan of the Land Mother.

As indicated above, the two halves of Kate Bale differed in so far as only Nua Kate incorporated a *peo*. This was a forked post of *yebu* wood, the same sort of sacrificial instrument as Kate had employed in Kate Kela, their village of origin. Indeed, it is solely with reference to their possession of a *peo* in Kate Kela that clan Kate expressly rationalize their former erecting of a similar sacrificial instrument in western Keo, describing this as a 'branch' (*taya so, kamu lana*, 'extended branch, spreading root') of the post erected in their homeland near Wolo Wea. It is important to stress that Bale people had no rights in this *peo* and never slaughtered buffalo there. When the first forked post was planted in Nua Kate, therefore, the positions of trunk rider and tip rider (*saka pu'u* and *saka lobo*) were both assigned to men of Kate, two ancestors associated with the first binary division of clan Kate into estates (*ngapi*). These were sons by different wives of the above-mentioned Léwa Wea and a woman of Bale.

Early in the twentieth century, Kate's *peo* was in effect appropriated by Bale. This occurred after Kate and Bale abandoned the double settlement that bore their names and the two groups together established a new, single village, the present Upper Pajo Mala. Located on slightly lower ground close to the Dutch-built road, the site had previously been a hamlet occupied by people of clans Pajo Wolo and Pajo Kayo from Lower Pajo Mala, and was ceded to Bale and Kate by Pajo Wolo.[15] Bale initiated the move after Nua Bale, their earlier residence, had suffered serious damage in a landslide, some time between 1910 and 1920. Kate followed later. By about 1927, therefore, old Kate Bale was abandoned completely, and what had formerly been two adjacent villages became one. In accordance with their relative positions in the earlier double settlement, Bale built their houses in the landward section of Upper Pajo Mala, with clan Upper Bale occupying the most landward part, while Kate established themselves towards the seaward extremity.

The removal of Kate and Bale to Upper Pajo Mala was encouraged by local officials appointed by the colonial government, and particularly by Lowa Bule, a government appointed 'foreman' (*mando mére*, or 'major *mandur*') from clan Bo Bana in Pau Lundu.[16] The same man, the husband of a woman of Lower Bale, was reputedly instrumental in the erecting of a *peo* in Upper Pajo Mala in 1929. Eventually, both Kate and Bale co-operated in this endeavour. The *peo*, it was decided, would be a forked post of Cassiawood, the same kind that had formerly stood in Nua Kate. Both clans of Bale, as well as Kate, contributed to the 'bridewealth' owed to the landowner from whose territory a *yebu* tree was obtained (I: 2: iv): the Bale people provided a buffalo while Kate gave golden ornaments. However, the two groups disagreed over who should appear as trunk rider and tip rider. Citing their previous possession of a forked *peo*, and conceiving the new one as its replacement, the Kate people argued that both positions should be filled by men of Kate. As noted, the two functions had been associated with different houses or estates of Kate since the early years of their occupation of Nua Kate. Although Bale was the older group both in Kate Bale and in western Keo, Bale's claim to these positions suffered from the fact that Bale had never possessed a *peo* of its own. What is more, especially in sacrificial matters, Bale was subordinate to Bolo (in Muka), and remains so to the present day.

Nevertheless, owing partly to the machinations of the above-mentioned Lowa Bule, it was Bale who were finally assigned as both trunk rider and tip rider, the first position going to the senior clan, Upper Bale, and the second to Lower Bale. Although the details remain unclear, the fact that Bale's senior associates, the Bolo people, had themselves already erected a forked *peo* in Muka (replacing their earlier sacrificial *kesi* tree, which had grown in Bolo Yoga) may well have been invoked in support of this development. As Kate was thus excluded from this dualism altogether, in their own view at least, what had originally been Kate's *peo* hereby became the *peo* of Bale. The history of the

---

[15] At some earlier time, Bindi and Pajo Wolo were in dispute over ownership of the site. This was settled by way of a procedure called *pa'a kaba*, involving the slaughter of a single buffalo. As the person able to dispatch the animal was a man of Pajo Wolo, this clan was declared the winner. The procedure thus manifests the more general equation of ability to slaughter and possession of rights to land.

[16] A 'major *mandur*' was a functionary assigned to execute the decisions of a *kepala haminte* (or *kepala mere*; in this case of the district of Sawu) and to organize and supervise public activities, such as corvée. Ordinary *mandur* did the same for appointed 'village' heads (*kepala kampong*; see Introduction).

forked post was revisited in 1991, when the *peo* planted in 1929—by this time much deteriorated—had to be replaced. Owing in some measure to the personal standing of their headman, by 1991 Kate had so to speak regained ground lost in 1929.[17] Although still harbouring claims to the premier position in respect of the forked *peo*, in the end they were willing to compromise. Thus when the replacement post was cut and carried to Upper Pajo Mala in September 1991, a man of Kate (specifically, the younger brother of the head-man, acting as his substitute) rode on the tip while a man of Upper Bale sat astride the trunk.

By virtue of this most recent arrangement, the consolidation of Kate Bale, as co-residents of a single village (*nua*) and common possessors of a single *peo* (*peo a toko, nabe a li'e*, 'a single peo, a single altar stone'), has become more complete. At the same time, particularly in the view of the Bolo people of Muka, the *peo* in Upper Pajo Mala specifically belongs to Bale. Indeed, Bolo regards the post as a 'branch' of their own, just as they tend to consider the entire village as subordinate to Bolo, or a subsumed part of the larger whole identified as 'Bolo Bale'. In this representation, then, Kate remains a margin-alized, if not a totally extraneous, element.[18] The incomplete integration of Bale and Kate is evident in another way. As described earlier, clans sharing a single *peo* also share ceremonial buildings, *yenda* and *nde*. Yet, as noted, the Bale people have never possessed a *yenda*, and so are obliged to store trophy horns of buffalo in the building belonging to Bolo. Kate, too, has never owned a building of this sort, either in the former Nua Kate or in their present resi-dence. In Nua Kate, however, some time after planting their forked *peo* Kate erected a simpler storage structure of the sort called *bhaga* or *joto bhaga* (I: 2: v) near the seaward extremity of the village. Since moving to Upper Pajo Mala, they have, moreover, replaced this building with a more elaborate *nde*, deco-rated with anthropomorphous statues (*ana ndeo*), which is also erected at the seaward end, near to Kate's houses. Although Keo normally employ *nde* for other purposes, it is nevertheless in this building, and earlier in the simpler *bhaga*, that Kate have always placed their own trophy horns.

In regard to its ceremonial incompleteness, Upper Pajo Mala contrasts with the older, adjacent village of Lower Pajo Mala. Complementing their stone *peo*, here one finds a *yenda* and a *nde*, both of which are shared by all three resident clans.[19] In so far as most lands occupied by Bale and Kate, including the site of

[17] A relatively wealthy man and former civil servant, this man, as I describe below, is able to claim membership not only of Kate but also of Pajo Wolo, the leading clan in Lower Pajo Mala.

[18] Bolo and Bale are not alone in this view. For example, the highly influential headman of clan Pau Padhi Mena in Lower Pau Lundu characterized the Kate people as 'outsiders'—an apparent reference to their derivation from Kate Kela—and argued that they therefore had no right whatsoever to mount the *peo* (*saka peo*) in Pajo Mala.

[19] The *yenda* is located in Bindi's part of the village site, and the *nde* in Pajo Wolo's. In 1995, villagers in Lower Pajo Mala replaced the wooden horse that stood in front of their *yenda* with a new statue. A relatively large sum of money received from the sale of the old statue, reputedly to a Chinese trader, was partly used to cover costs of installing the new statue. The remainder was then divided equally among the three clans. In 1996, I learned from the staff of a major American museum that they had been offered the old statue but had decided not to acquire it.

their present village, are drawn from the territories of clans Bindi and Pajo Wolo, Upper Pajo Mala can further be characterized as derived from, and even encompassed by Lower Pajo Mala. Consistent with this is the present application of the name Pajo Mala, formerly designating only the older village, to the entire double settlement. Although none of the clans in the newer village is designated as a Defender (*ana tuku*) of a Lower Pajo Mala clan, affinal relations as well tend to accord with the generally superordinate position of the older settlement. Since early times, Lower Bale and Upper Bale men have contracted numerous marriages with women of clans Pajo Wolo and Pajo Kayo—just as, in the context of Kate Bale the younger Kate was a regular wife-taker of Bale. Kate, also, has taken wives from Pajo Kayo and Pajo Wolo. On the other hand, Kate and, to a lesser, extent Bale—which is to say, particular houses belonging to these groups—have given women to groups in Lower Pajo Mala, especially in recent years. In addition, while clan Bindi has more often than not contracted marriages with groups outside Pajo Mala, in several instances Bindi men have taken wives from Upper Bale. Hence, there is by no means a complete concordance in this respect.

When describing the organization of their recently formed double settlement, Pajo Mala people appear to stress the symmetry of the two component villages, usually describing each as comprising three clans. Yet local histories indicate how each trio has developed from more fundamental binary relations still evident in a variety of particulars. Not the least of these is the development of the three clans of Upper Pajo Mala from the enduring dualism of Kate Bale. While Pajo Mala illustrates organizational themes revealed in the previous chapter, it also exemplifies further variations. One is the incorporation, within a single village territory and, indeed, within the single village site of Lower Pajo Mala, of parts of the domains of two ancient Land Mothers—Lape (represented primarily by clan Pajo Wolo) and Boa Maga (represented by clan Bindi). Of at least equal interest, however, is the way in which Upper Pajo Mala, while in one sense subsumed by its older partner, is further encompassed by a larger social whole which does not coincide with a single village or even a double settlement. I refer of course to Bale's subordination to Bolo, now resident in Muka.

The relatively short history of Upper Pajo Mala, or Kate Bale, provides an especially instructive case of how a common process, whereby two villages merge to form one, has entailed the negotiation of a hierarchy focused in sacrificing and the notionally unifying instrument of sacrifice, the *peo*. As demonstrated, deciding which of two or more parties should occupy the senior ceremonial position can invoke conflicting criteria. At the same time, it can involve manipulation reflecting shifting power relations, some of which are quite extraneous to a local, traditional order.

As shown in the preceding chapter, not just Bale but also clans Bhoja Wawo and Suga resident in the village of Suga Bhoja are subsumed by Bolo (or more exactly, by Bolo and Suga resident in Muka). In this connection it is worth noting how not just the two Bale groups, but clan Kate as well, maintain close links with the village of Bolo (Muka). The seniormost house and estate (*ngapi*) of Kate and one of the two estates of clan Suga in Bolo thus regard one another as 'house siblings' (*ka'e ari sa'o ténda*; I: 4: i). Although reputedly initiated four generations ago by Mite Bule, the ancestor after whom Kate's senior estate is named, the leaders of neither group could explain its basis. Nevertheless, as *ka'e ari*, each group can provide the other with heirs (*ghawe*), and each may work land belonging to the other without providing material compensation. They further lend one another general assistance in all customary matters (*kura kesa, bora penu*, 'adding to what is insufficient, making up what is lacking'), while in the context of affinal exchange, members expressly treat one another as brothers—*ana weta* of one group then being obligated to the other as though they were their own wife-takers.

A 'house sibling' relationship also connects Kate's leading house and the senior estate of clan Pajo Wolo in Lower Pajo Mala. In fact, the present Kate headman is the natural son of an adoptee from Pajo Wolo, Gawe Co'o, who came to succeed the Kate leader Jago Uko, whose name the present leader (Gallus Jago Uko) has also inherited. Following from the relationship between the two groups, the first Jago Uko inherited the widowed mother of Gawe Co'o (the wife of Lako Boti of Pajo Mala). Partly for this reason, the present Jago Uko claims membership of both Kate and Pajo Mala. When discussing Kate's similar connection with Suga in Bolo, moreover, he noted how Suga could be reckoned as his 'third clan'.

Even though it concerns specific houses or estates of the two clans, the relationship between Suga and Kate formally parallels that of Bolo and Bale. As noted, the latter, too, is classified as a relationship of *ka'e ari* ('siblingship'). The difference, of course, is that the dualism designated as 'Bolo Bale' is asymmetrical, whereas the 'house siblingship' linking Kate and Suga is completely symmetrical. A comparable asymmetry, albeit one internal to each of the two villages (Muka and Upper Pajo Mala), recurs in the subordination of Suga and Kate to Bolo and Bale respectively. Kate and Suga are also, as it were, outnumbered by their superordinate co-residents, since Bale and Bolo are identically divided into Upper and Lower clans. At the same time, Kate is no longer subordinated to (or subsumed by) Bale to the same degree as Suga is to Bolo; for one division of Kate, as the new tip rider in Upper Pajo Mala, has recently gained precedence over Lower Bale. Nevertheless, internal and external relationships combine to produce an implicit quadripartite order encompassing Bolo (Muka) and Upper Pajo Mala (Kate Bale), which in turn formally replicates instances of quadripartition encountered within each of the two villages (Upper Bale, Lower Bale, plus two divisions of Kate; and Upper Bolo, Lower Bolo, plus the two estates of Suga). Consistent with this isomorphism of whole and part is Bolo's subsumption of Bale (in the entity called Bolo Bale), and hence the superiority Bolo claims in respect of the whole of Upper Pajo Mala. The former relationship was illustrated in Figure 7, where it was shown in a more inclusive, regional context.

Internal quadripartition in Bolo (Muka) and Upper Pajo Mala finds expression in particular ritual settings. Whenever a new *yenda* is constructed in Bolo, Upper Bolo (the trunk rider) and Lower Bolo (the tip rider) contribute the right front and left front posts respectively. The two other posts are then provided by the two *ngapi* of Suga, with the senior estate contributing the left back post in accordance with a general rule of 'proceeding to the right' (or 'anti-clockwise', *gili kago molo*; see Fig. 2). Similarly, when the people of Upper Pajo Mala erected a new *peo* in 1991, four upright stones (*watu ngapi*; I: 2: iv) were set in the surrounding foundation (see Plate 4). Planted landward and to the right of the forked post—thus in a position corresponding to the (heraldic) right front corner of a building—the first stone to be set in place belonged to Upper Bale (the trunk rider). Proceeding anti-clockwise, stones were then erected by Lower Bale, the senior estate of clan Kate (the group recognized in 1991 as tip rider), and finally, a junior estate of Kate. Formerly, when the two clans of Bale were assigned as trunk rider and tip rider, just three stones encircled the old *peo*, representing these two clans plus Kate. Thus, in addition to acquiring the status of tip rider, Kate has gained a sort of numerical parity with Bale.

The social order reflected in the arrangement of the four new stones obviously parallels that observed in regard to the four posts of Bolo's *yenda*. At the same time, the 'house siblingship' connecting Kate and clan Pajo Wolo provides another link between the Upper and Lower villages of Pajo Mala, now conjoined as a double settlement. Initiated generations ago, before the founding of Upper Pajo Mala, it does so, moreover, in a way that arguably lends support to Kate's position *vis-à-vis* Bale.

3. Bale Wolo: A Derivative Settlement

Located about one and a half kilometres southeast of Pajo Mala, the village of Bale Wolo reveals further variation on the themes of derivation, separation, and clan fission. At the same time, it displays a greater independence from its local origin than does Upper Pajo Mala (or, more specifically, Bale) in relation to Bolo. Comprising a junior agnatic segment of clan Pajo Kayo centred in Lower Pajo Mala, the Bale Wolo people possess not only a *peo* of their own but also a *yenda* and a *nde*, or at least they did so before the latter two structures fell into disrepair.

Paradoxically, 'Bale Wolo' bears no connection to 'Bale' as the name of two clans resident in Upper Pajo Mala. Following the general opinion, the village name refers to a geographical feature of the site and might be glossed as 'becoming a hill'. All Bale Wolo people derive from a single ancestor, Céme

Wea, who was the younger brother of Késu Wea, the apical ancestor of clan Pajo Kayo in Pajo Mala. Clan history attributes the fission to conflict between the two brothers, and ultimately to actions of the elder brother which the younger interpreted as tantamount to an accusation of witchcraft. As noted earlier, Céme Wea is also reputed to have accused Tuwa, a clanmate's wife from Céla, of being a witch, an accusation that lead to a demand for the return of land given by the woman's parents. Whether or not the land dispute was in any way connected with the conflict between the two brothers is not known. In either case, Céme Wea left Pajo Mala, taking with him part of the heirlooms of clan Pajo Kayo, a large golden object the size of a maize grinder.[20]

The site of Bale Wolo village comprises land obtained partly from clan Pau Padhi Mena in Pau Lundu and partly from Koyu Yéwe (Suga Bhoja). Since this was acquired through purchase, and because Bale Wolo continued to exploit agricultural land within the territory of Pajo Kayo, the Bale Wolo people did not thereby become Defenders of either of these two groups. Accordingly, the *peo* erected in Bale Wolo was not granted by any Land Mother, but is considered a derivative (an 'extended branch, spreading root', *taya so, kamu lana*) of the sacrificial instrument in Pajo Mala. Originally, the Bale Wolo *peo* was a *kesi* tree, the same sort as employed by Pajo Kayo and other clans in Pajo Mala. The last tree was replaced with a stone column in the 1960s, thus, interestingly enough, about the same time as the Pajo Mala people replaced their last *kesi* with a *peo* of stone.[21]

Although Bale Wolo comprises a single clan (sometimes called clan Céme Wea, but more often known as clan Pajo Kayo), it nevertheless manifests the same ceremonial dualism as do all Keo villages. Céme Wea, the single ancestor, had two wives. Named Boa, the senior wife bore five sons, while the junior, who was called Pénu, had two, thus producing the generally valued total of seven (*lima rua* = 'five (plus) two') male offspring.[22] Bale Wolo people continue to recognize the seven sons as the founders of the seven estates (*ngapi*) into which the village, or clan, is divided. Descending agnatically from the first son of the first wife, the seniormost *ngapi* (Léna Boa) holds the premier position of earth breaker (*ta koe*), while the junior status of excavator (*ta kabhe*) belongs to the estate descending from the elder of the two sons of the second wife (Léna Pénu). With regard to the occurrence of the number seven, it may be significant

---

[20] The relatively detailed genealogies in this case suggest that Céme Wea's removal to Bale Wolo may have occurred as recently as six or seven generations ago. One Pajo Kayo genealogy suggests that the brothers may have resided in Kayo's original village (Nua Kayo) before clan Pajo Wolo moved to Pajo Mala, but this may well not be reliable. Nevertheless, it is possible that the breakup of Pajo Kayo, and the departure of one part of the clan, was the reason the remaining, senior segment of Pajo Kayo invited Pajo Wolo to join them.

[21] How coincidental this was is not clear. Bale Wolo people told me that they erected a stone *peo* because their sacrificial *kesi* tree was blown down just as they were planning to sacrifice in order to inaugurate new *nde* and *yenda*. As this was taken as a negative portent, they did not complete the buildings; hence at present Bale Wolo lacks both *yenda* and *nde*.

[22] Actually, the first wife is herself claimed to have had seven sons. Of the additional two, one died childless while the other removed to the Nage village of Pago Nage, where his descendants now include people of the clan Mude.

that, while the estate of the first son of the junior wife is, of course, the second to slaughter at collective sacrifices, the estate of the second son (Lagho Pénu) is specified as the fifth.

In sacrificial matters, Bale Wolo thus functions quite independently of Pajo Kayo in Pajo Mala. Yet their *peo* is still considered a 'branch *peo*' (*peo taya*) of the one in Lower Pajo Mala.[23] Accordingly, in major ceremonial matters, the Bale Wolo people are obliged to consult the senior division of their clan. The two groups continue to recognize a common clanship (or 'siblingship', *ka'e ari*) in other ways as well, including the transfer of members between estates in Pajo Mala and Bale Wolo respectively. Bale Wolo provides an especially clear case of hierarchical connection with another village following from a genealogically documented agnatic segmentation. In the same vein, the settlement also provides a useful illustration of how, historically or conceptually, a group recognizing a single ancestor and composing a single clan (*suku*) has developed in a way conforming to a pattern of dual organization found throughout western Keo.

---

[23] Consistent with Bale Wolo's derivation from Lower Pajo Mala is the appearance of the phrase 'Eko Rita' in Bale Wolo's formal name: Ulu Nunu, Eko Rita (Head that is a Banyan Tree, Tail that is an Alstonia Tree). In fact, according to one account, exactly the same name was once applied to Lower Pajo Mala.

3

Unaffiliated Ancestors: The Pau Enclave

In this chapter I describe several villages whose territories are surrounded by the domains of Land Mother Lape and other Ga'e siblings. Deriving from ancestors not related in any known way to the Ga'e siblings, these groups remain something of a curiosity; they are unequivocally depicted as neither an aboriginal population, nor as descendants of immigrants more recent than the Ga'e. After lengthy discussions with group members and other Keo, I can only characterize them as independent Land Mothers (*ine tana*) who in no instance are simultaneously the Defenders (*ana tuku*) of other, earlier populations. Not being territorially subordinated to others, the groups are thus equal to direct (agnatic) descendants of the several Ga'e siblings but are not unambiguously connected with any of them. It is just possible that one or more of these populations derive from intruders who wrested control of parts of Ga'e territories and, more particularly, sections of the domain of Lape, and for this reason recognize the precedence of no other group. This, however, is pure conjecture, and I never encountered the representation in any clan or village history.

One unaffiliated group of this sort was introduced in the previous chapter, namely the clan Bindi, now in Lower Pajo Mala, which traces agnatic descent from the ancestral pair Boa and Maga. Others are clans, or in one case a pair of clans, that bear the name 'Pau' ('mango tree'). No reason for this common naming is explicated by Keo, nor does it in any obvious way illuminate their present standing.

1. Kota Pau

Located nearly five kilometres seaward of Pajo Mala, another double settlement comprises the adjacent villages of Kota Pau and Guyu Wolo. Both sites provide a commanding view of the Sawu sea, while almost directly to the north, the massive form of the volcano Ebu Lobo dominates the view from the head (*ulu*) of Guyu Wolo. Kota Pau, the more seaward village, is recognized as the centre of the domain of Nuga Raga, the conjoined names of an ancestral sibling pair. Conforming to a common representation accompanying this form of nomenclature, Nuga, the elder brother, died childless, while his younger brother, Raga, became the apical ancestor of the clan Pau. Pau (hereafter labelled 'Pau (KP)' to distinguish it from other groups named Pau) is thus recognized as Land Mother of all other clans in both Kota Pau and Guyu Wolo, as well as of groups resident in the village of Lower Pau Lundu (see Section 3 below).

PLATE 14. Bamboo lattice (*yaka*) erected before the forked sacrificial post in Kota Pau

Named after its principal clan and clan Kota, the oldest of Pau's several Defenders, Kota Pau contains four clans altogether. As the senior pair, clans Pau (KP) and Kota respectively occupy the positions of trunk rider and tip rider in relation to the forked *peo* that stands before the seniormost house of Pau (see Plate 14). Also included in the present village are the clans Lina and Wuwu, more junior Defenders of the Land Mother. At one time, Lina and Wuwu each inhabited villages of their own located not far from the present Kota Pau, as did clan Kota. Lina's old village was located somewhere seaward of Kota Pau, while Wuwu occupied a site near the landward extremity of the present village. Referring to these spatial associations, and recalling a pattern found elsewhere (for example in Suga Bhoja, II: 1: v), the junior Defenders lend their names to the formal designation of the entire settlement: Ulu Nunu Wuwu, Eko Lina Olo (Head that is Wuwu's Banyan Tree, Tail that is Old Lina).

Nowadays, Keo people mostly speak of Nuga Raga, the two Pau ancestors, in connection with their struggle against Koba Réja, the intruder who gave rise to the clan Loka Poma in the village of Lundu (II: 1: vii). While their derivation is as obscure as that of the ancestors of other unaffiliated groups, Nuga Raga are vaguely linked with Géra Ga'e, a younger brother of Lape and Land

Mother in the adjoining territory to the southwest, centred in the village of Keo (Keo Bélo). Although generally regarded as an unreliable source, the present headman of clan Pau (KP) even claimed that Nuga and Raga were sons of Géra. Other historical accounts cite Géra Ga'e as one of several ancestors whose assistance Nuga Raga requested in their war against Koba Réja.[1] A connection between Géra Ga'e and the Kota Pau people is further suggested in a myth identifying part of the present settlement with a place where Géra once emerged from an underground passage (II: 4: i). Other local statements, however, link Nuga Raga with Lape Ga'e (or Lape Mére), while one man suggested a connection with Gewo Ga'e (II: 5).

In the earliest of remembered times, the ancestors of Pau (KP) occupied a site just south of Pau Lundu and close to the lands of Lape. Local references to the territory of Nuga Raga as being subsumed by the wider domain of Lape may reflect no more than the general idea that all lands within the area of the present study in some sense belong to Lape, as the eldest of the Ga'e siblings. What is more certain is that Nuga Raga are usually regarded as temporally and genealogically subordinate to the several Ga'e, even while, in respect of present territorial relations, the ancestral pair are treated as structurally equivalent to the latter.

Local histories further connect Nuga Raga with Léwa Ranga, another sibling pair now recognized as the apical ancestors respectively of clan Bindi (Ranga) and clan Guyu Wolo (Léwa). In the war with Koba Réja, Nuga fell victim to the intruder, whereupon Raga (his younger brother) fled eastward, either to Téya Bhoja or Kela. In the absence of the Land Mother, the land bore only plants that were bitter tasting and were ravaged by pests (I: 1: iii). Thus Léwa Ranga, or more particularly Léwa, the Guyu Wolo ancestor and elder of the pair, undertook to secure Raga's return and to reinstate him as Land Mother and planter of the ritual garden (*uma gua*). For his assistance in defeating Koba Réja, Léwa was given land by Raga. He thus established the village of Guyu Wolo, just seaward of the present Kota Pau, thereby founding the clan of the same name. Clan Guyu Wolo continues to be numbered among the several Defenders (*ana tuku*) of Land Mother Nuga Raga or, otherwise stated, of clan Pau (KP).

The present village of Kota Pau occupies a site somewhat landward of its earlier location. Several decades ago an extension containing nine houses (mostly occupied by members of clans Pau and Kota) was built just seaward of the main village, thus below the *nde* located at the tail (*éko*) of the settlement. Some accounts describe this area as part of an earlier site of Kota Pau. Following others, it was once a separate village belonging to clan Kota. The second interpretation seems inconsistent with the location, in the present Kota

---

[1] In so far as this entails that Nuga Raga and Géra Ga'e were contemporaries, these accounts are contradicted by others.

Pau, of the all houses of Kota at the landward extremity, and of all dwellings of Pau (KP) towards the seaward end. As noted, moreover, other evidence associates clan Lina with the modern village's seaward extremity. Whichever account is accepted, Kota is described as joining Pau, in a single settlement, early in the twentieth century.

The oldest Defender of Pau, clan Kota comprises two segments (*ngapi*) recognizing separate origins.[2] The more senior of the pair derives agnatically from Riti Kota, an ancestor who lent his name to the entire clan, which villagers thus sometimes designate more completely as *suku* Riti Kota. Riti Kota was a man of clan Dhoki Paya in Lundu (II: 1: vii) who left in search of new land. Although this man, or more likely his descendants, eventually founded a settlement named Kota (or Kota Olo, 'Old Kota') within the domain of Nuga Raga, local accounts differ as to whether the Kota people ever possessed a sacrificial instrument (*peo*) of their own. Clan elders claimed that they have never done so, and that in sacrificial matters they have always been conjoined with Pau (KP). Other reports suggest that Kota may once have separately employed a sacrificial *kesi* tree or used only a stake or short stone column (*ia*) when slaughtering buffalo (rather like the Bale people before their removal to Upper Pajo Mala). Whichever version might be historically correct, since coming to share a forked *peo* with Pau (KP) clan Kota has acquired the secondary ceremonial position of tip rider, a status more specifically held by the senior *ngapi*, the direct descendants of Riti Kota. Following their own claim at least, Kota people may actually have preceded clan Pau (KP) in the specific part of Nuga Raga's territory occupied by the present village of Kota Pau. (As evidence of this, they cited the fact that the name Kota precedes Pau in Kota Pau—an argument which, as it turns out, is unsupported by any general principle.) However, since Pau (KP) is recognized as Land Mother of the entire territory, it is this group that is recognized as the principal owner of the *peo* and which always sacrifices first.

In so far as Kota is named after the ancestor of the senior estate, Riti Kota, this segment, being identified with the entire clan, nominally subsumes its junior partner much as do the paired clans, Kota and Pau, in respect of the entire village. Named Kou Tei, after its ancestor, the more junior of Kota's two segments claims to derive from So'a, and like many other groups, to have come to western Keo to 'watch Jawa Pogo'. Initially settling in Lundu, where he resided with the clan Loka Poma, the ancestor Kou Tei later moved to the old village of Kota (Kota Olo), where he joined the descendants of Riti Kota and was granted land by Sanda Molo, apparently a man of Kota but also described as a descendant of Nuga Raga. At present, the senior and junior divisions of clan Kota are further distinguished as Kota Bhisu Rale and Kota Bhisu Mena, referring to the location of their houses respectively on the left (*rale*) and right

---

[2] Although called *ngapi*, according to a particular account, one member of the pair may itself comprise two estates.

(*mena*) sides of the village plaza (*bhisu* is 'corner', 'side'). In this regard, Kota provides a striking example of what I earlier described as the modular form of Keo clans (*suku*). In this case, moreover, a spatially articulated duality of estates (*ngapi*) suggests a possible former ceremonial division analogous, for example, to that which once obtained between the two groups composing clan Bajo Léwa in the village of Lundu. If the Kota people ever did possess a sacrificial instrument of their own, therefore, the two ritual functions (earth breaker and excavator, had this been a living *peo*) would most likely have been assigned respectively to the two estates.

Following Kota in the ceremonial order of Kota Pau is clan Lina. Also initially established in a village of its own (located perhaps 100 metres seaward of the present settlement), Lina is described in different accounts as hailing either from Liwo (II: 6: i) or Tiwa, two villages well to the west (*rale*). Possibly reflecting the clan's western derivation, their single house in Kota Pau is found on the *rale* ('left') side of the village plaza. Following one report, in their former settlement the Lina people once independently maintained a *dheyo* tree *peo*, a claim consistent with their possible derivation from Liwo, where a single sacrificial tree of this sort is also encountered. Kota Pau history describes Léwa (or Léwa Ranga), the ancestor of Guyu Wolo, as having requested the Lina people to lend assistance in the war against Koba Réja. After Koba's defeat, Lina had planned to return home but were invited to remain as Defenders in the domain of Nuga Raga and were provided with land.

The most junior of the four clans of Kota Pau, clan Wuwu once maintained an independent settlement on a site that is now the landward part of Kota Pau. In the present village, Wuwu occupies two houses on the *mena* (or 'right') side of the plaza, immediately opposite the houses of Lina, as well as a third house located in the village's recently founded seaward extension. The group's name, however, attests to their longer association with the landward end of the village. Denoting a vent or hole in the ground, *wuwu* refers to a cavity, once located within the bounds of Wuwu's independent settlement, which formed the beginning of an underground passage leading to the sea.[3] Although no longer in evidence, the vent was reputedly once visible near the landward end of modern Kota Pau, about where the *yenda* now stands. Formerly, people say, one could see crabs emerging from this hole at high tide. That some remnant of the vent might still exist is suggested by the local report that rainwater never collects beneath the *yenda*, but quickly disappears into the earth. The spot is now covered by a flat stone (*nabe*). As I explain later, this particular vent retains a significant place in local history, in the previously mentioned tale connecting Kota Pau with the ancestor Géra Ga'e (II: 4: i). It is, therefore, more completely known as Géra's Vent (Wuwu Ema Géra).

---

[3] More completely known as *wuwu mesi*, 'sea cavity', such vents are reported from several parts of Keo and Nage (see also Barnes 1974: 34–5, s.v. *wowon*). *Wuwu* also means 'fontanelle' and further designates a kind of tree.

Although local tradition thus suggests that Wuwu may have been present in this place for some considerable time, the clan is the least of the several Defenders of the domain of Nuga Raga and, therefore, always the last to slaughter in Kota Pau. Connected with this is the claim that, while other Defenders of Pau (KP), notably Lina and Guyu Wolo, came to assist the ancestral pair Nuga Raga in their struggle with Koba Réja, the Wuwu folk appeared rather later. According to the only genealogy I could obtain, the earliest known Wuwu ancestor (named Goa Keo) arrived just four generations ago from a place called Koli Wuwu (*koli* is 'lontar palm'), somewhere near Ma'u Nori (see Map 1). If the name of this place is linked with the clan's name, it would appear to contradict the attribution of the latter to the vent once visible in Kota Pau.[4] Whether the Wuwu people ever had a *peo* of their own is doubtful, though such an assertion was made by the group's present leader, who stated that traces of the object, either a *kesi* tree or a stone column, were once visible near the present forked post. Whichever account is accepted, in Kota Pau one clearly encounters one of several instances where groups claiming greater precedence in respect of a wider territory come eventually to found villages on sites once occupied by hamlets or villages of subordinate groups. Similar examples were described in previous chapters, in regard to clan Céla (or Lape) in Nua Nage, clans Kayo and Pajo Wolo in Lower Pajo Mala, and clans Dhoki Paya and Loka Poma in Lundu. Another illustration is given below in Section 3, in regard to Lower Pau Lundu.

Even more straightforwardly than other villages described so far, the four clans of Kota Pau provide an instance of local quadripartition. In this case the quartet is less obviously reducible to two pairs. Nevertheless, Pau (KP) and Kota are manifestly separate from the younger two by virtue of their special association with the forked sacrificial post, of which they serve as trunk and tip rider respectively. What is more, it is of course just these two clans that lend their names to the village, and hence to the entire quartet, even though the more junior pair are mentioned in the settlements formal, *ulu éko* name. Lina and Wuwu's connection to the *peo* of Kota Pau is marked with two upright stones (*ia*) placed left and right (*rale* and *mena*) of the forked post, thus in accordance with the location of their houses. In other villages possessing forked *peo*, ceremonial functions subordinate to the two riders, designated as *yanda yiwu* and *lando bépi*, are assigned to junior groups, usually junior houses of the rider clans (II: 1: iv; I: 2, n. 9); but no evidence suggests that Wuwu or Lina have ever occupied such positions in Kota Pau.

In regard to its dual composition, clan Kota is comparable to clans Bajo Léwa and Loka Poma in Lundu (II: 1: vii). Yet Kota differs from these in so far as the two divisions of Loka Poma are often described as separate clans, while Bajo and

---

[4] A village simply called Wuwu and located far to the northeast, close to the village of Sule, appears to have no connection with Wuwu in Kota Pau.

Léwa, though no longer independent clans, are themselves further divided into estates (*ngapi*). Once again, therefore, general structural similarities are accompanied by minor variations in manifest form. Other features linking Kota Pau with other settlements named Pau are reviewed later. First, though, we need to explore the organization of Guyu Wolo, the adjacent village located immediately landward, with which Kota Pau forms a double settlement.

2. *Guyu Wolo*

Referred to in ritual contexts as Ulu Nunu Bera, Eko Loka Ra'u (see Appendix 2), Guyu Wolo is yet another village named identically to its principal component. As noted, this is the clan agnatically linked, through the ancestral siblings Léwa Ranga, to Bindi in Lower Pajo Mala. Since establishing the village of Guyu Wolo, clan Guyu Wolo has been joined by two others: Je'a and Wolo Sabi. (For the sake of clarity and simplicity, I shall sometimes call the oldest group clan Guyu, an abbreviation often employed by villagers themselves.)

As described in the last chapter, Guyu Wolo ('Hill Bamboo'), traces its origin to the similarly named settlement of Guyu Wula ('Moon Bamboo'). The name of the present village and clan obviously reflects the name of this former village. After fleeing from Guyu Wula, the Guyu ancestor, Léwa (or, to follow the most common nomenclature, Léwa Ranga), resided for a time in Wolo Kinde, a hamlet near Pau Leka. There he was called upon by the ancestors of Pau (KP) for assistance in their war against Koba Réja, and in reciprocation was granted land and a *peo*, invited to found the present village of Guyu Wolo, and promoted to the status of Defender of Pau. Sometime later, clan Guyu divided the sizeable territory it had been granted and thus acquired Defenders (*ana tuku*) of its own. Although recognized as (minor) Land Mother within its own village, according to their own testimony, the Guyu people have never planted a ritual garden (*uma gua*)—a task which, in the domain of Nuga Raga, has only ever been performed by clan Pau (KP).

The first of Guyu's Defenders, clan Je'a also derives from the old settlement of Guyu Wula. There, the Je'a people occupied a site just seaward of the residence of the Guyu Wolo ancestors—a disposition suggesting that Guyu Wula was a double settlement, with the name of the landward component further designating the whole. The same arrangement was later replicated when Je'a eventually joined Guyu Wolo. Initially, the newcomer founded a village (*nua*) immediately seaward of Guyu Wolo's, and each maintained a separate *kesi* tree *peo*. Then, during the first half of the twentieth century (about 1942 following one account), the two *nua* amalgamated, forming the present Guyu Wolo and coming to share a single *peo kesi*. Like clan Guyu, Je'a is also related agnatically to a group resident in another village, indeed in the domain of another Land Mother. After leaving Guyu Wula, the Je'a ancestors first took refuge in Wae (in southern Nage), from where they were eventually expelled by the Dadho people. As noted previously (II: 1: iv), one Je'a ancestor (Ria Muja) joined the clan Upper Bolo, then resident in Bolo Yoga, while the remainder eventually rejoined Guyu Wolo, their former neighbours in the old village of Guyu Wula. People of clan Je'a are still found in Wae, a village refounded several generations after the dispersal of its members resulting from the war with Dadho.

The third and most junior clan in Guyu Wolo, Wolo Sabi (or 'Ironwood Hill') was formerly settled in a village of the same name located on an elevated site immediately northwest of the present Guyu Wolo. Affording a magnificent view of the volcano Ebu Lobo on one side and the Sawu Sea on the other, the place has since 1936 been occupied by the Catholic church which forms the centre of the Parish of Wolo Sambi (Wolosambi).[5] In this case, too, an agnatic connection links a clan with a group in another village. As noted earlier, the ancestor of the Wolo Sabi people, Sapu Nai, was a son of Koba Réja, the ancestor of the Lundu clan Loka Poma. At the same time, genealogies specify the wife of Sapu Nai as a woman of Loka Poma (specifically Lower Loka Poma); hence the two groups recognize an affinal connection as well.

In their former village of Wolo Sabi, the descendants of Sapu Nai maintained a sacrificial *kesi* tree. Following a military defeat at the hands of the people of Sawu (II: 5: iii), possibly about one hundred years ago, the Wolo Sabi people abandoned their village on Ironwood Hill and sought refuge with clan Je'a, a previous wife-giver. Later of course, Je'a, already incorporating Wolo Sabi, merged with Guyu Wolo. In this instance, then, a village of three clans derives from a double settlement, one component village of which itself comprised a duality resulting from a similar merging. By the same token, what were once three separate *peo* have now become one.

In the 1950s, the single sacrificial *kesi* tree of Guyu Wolo (apparently the first to be planted in the consolidated village) was destroyed, according to different accounts either by fire or high winds. The tree was replaced in 1995. On this occasion the Pau people in Kota Pau, acting as Land Mother of the territory granted to Guyu Wolo, provided the new *kesi*. (Although the arrangement is customary in this instance, it is not observed by other groups employing living *peo*, who provide their own trees.) In respect of this performance, and according to information collected earlier as well, members of clan Guyu further specified Pau (KP) as the earth breaker (*ta koe*). While not unique, the Guyu Wolo usage suggests an elaboration of the basic binary division found elsewhere. Men representing two estates of Guyu, designated as the right branch and left branch (*nda'a mena* and *nda'a rale*), are also specified respectively as earth breaker (*ta koe*) and excavator (*ta kabhe*). However, before they enact these roles, a man (formally the headman) of clan Pau marks the place where the hole is to be dug, using a parang he receives from Guyu in exchange

---

[5] The name refers specifically to an Ironwood tree (*sabi, Schleichera oleosa*) that once stood at the head (*ulu*) of the old village. The substitution of /mb/ for /b/ follows a common pattern among local place-names that acquired an official status during the colonial period.

for the *kesi* tree. In this capacity, Pau is designated as *ta koe* (earth breaker), but also more specifically as *ta toke* (the indicator) or *ta toke koe*, a phrase explained as a more elaborate form of *ta koe* (I: 2, n. 13).

Although they also sacrifice there, the other two Guyu Wolo clans, Je'a and Wolo Sabi, play no particular part in planting the *kesi* tree. Nevertheless, their association with the *peo* is signified by erecting vertical stones, called *ia* or *ngusu* (I: 2: iv), at the base of the trunk, together with a third stone representing the senior clan Guyu. When the stones of Je'a and Wolo Sabi are planted (*toni*), a man of Pau, the senior Land Mother, should act as earth breaker. The part of excavator is then jointly assigned to Guyu and the clan associated with the stone; a man from the first group begins scooping earth from the hole, while the task is finished by a member of the second. Once this is done, the headman of clan Guyu Wolo formally presents the stone to the headman of the junior clan (Je'a or Wolo Sabi), who then plants it in the ground. The procedure obviously expresses the subordination of the two junior clans of the village to both the senior clan and the ultimate Land Mother of all Guyu Wolo.

As villagers pointed out, the *ia* of Wolo Sabi and Je'a replace the former *peo* possessed independently by these two clans.[6] The third stone, belonging to clan Guyu, is always erected on the *mena* ('right') side of the *kesi* tree, while those of the junior clans are placed *rale* (or to the 'left'), with the *ia* of Je'a planted closer to the trunk. Since all three clans now have houses on both sides of the village plaza, this disposition does not reflect residential arrangements. That Je'a's stone stands closer to the Guyu Wolo *peo*, however, accords with the group's precedence over Wolo Sabi as well as their association with clan Guyu in the ancestral village of Guyu Wula. It is tempting to attribute a similar distinction to the contrast of *mena* and *rale*. Yet as previous examples have shown, this lateral contrast does not consistently distinguish superior from subordinate social units.

Not only is Guyu the leading clan in Guyu Wolo; it is by far the largest as well. Reputedly a man of great wealth, the ancestor, Léwa, had no fewer than seven wives. From these women derive the seven *ngapi* (estates) into which clan Guyu is divided.[7] Reminiscent of the seven estates of Bale Wolo—which, however, are traced to just two wives of the apical male ancestor—the internal organization of clan Guyu provides a further instance of the symbolically valued total of seven (or 'five plus two' in the Keo idiom). The clan genealogy moreover reveals several endogamous unions, contracted by members of different estates, or different houses, as this is more commonly expressed. Yet

---

[6] In regard to this sacrificial tree, it was thought that the roles of earth breaker and excavator were assigned to Je'a and Wolo Sabi respectively.

[7] The seven are now effectively reduced to six, as one estate has detached itself from Guyu. Perhaps about one hundred years ago, two brothers occupying this estate transferred to the clan Bo Bana in Lower Pau Lundu, one as an adoptee (*ana ghawe*), the other simply following his brother, but similarly acquiring rights in Bo Bana as well as in clan Guyu. Of the seven ancestresses, not all details are known; nor, indeed, are their exact genealogical connections with present members of the seven *ngapi*, or of these with one another.

in all instances where details are clear, a single group (*ngapi* Betu Beda) figures as wife-taker. This circumstance thus suggests a binary division within the group of seven.

The topic of marriage also bears upon the relation between clan Guyu, as the superordinate group in Guyu Wolo village, and Kota Pau, the older half of the double settlement. Within the domain of Lape, the coincidence of affinal connections with the relation of Land Mother and Defender is widely attested, as is shown by the cases reviewed in previous chapters. In contrast, the pattern is far less pronounced in the domain of Nuga Raga. For one thing, the senior wife of the Guyu ancestor Léwa, the only one whose origin is still known, came from clan Sawu and not as one might expect from the Land Mother, clan Pau (KP). Two Guyu houses have, indeed, taken wives from Pau, in four marriages, but all of these have occurred in recent generations. On the other hand, there is no record of clan Guyu having given brides to Pau, nor to Kota, from which it has taken wives in three marriages. In a similar way, affinal relations are not especially evident between Pau and its co-resident Defenders (Kota, Lina, and Wuwu) or between Guyu and Je'a and Wolo Sabi.

In fact, rather than wife-giving coinciding with land-giving, the history of the domain of Nuga Raga reveals that the granting of territory to later arrivals is mostly ascribed to military assistance or the provision of refuge in times of strife. Certainly, original land grants are not linked with specific ancestral marriages, or with wives related in some particular way to male Land Mothers, as in the domain of Lape and, albeit in a less pronounced way, in the domains of other Ga'e siblings. Noteworthy here is Guyu's characterization of the sacrificial tree granted by Pau (KP) in return for support in the war against Koba Réja, as a *peo wuli lando* or *peo bani*, a 'war peo'.[8] How far the same characterization might apply to the relation of Pau (KP) to groups in the village of Lower Pau Lundu, located at the boundary of the domain of Nuga Raga, is considered presently.

Not only has Guyu Wolo evolved from a gradual merging of three villages, and three *peo*, resulting in a single settlement with a single sacrificial instrument, but at successive stages a village (*nua*) encompassing more than one clan has been named identically to its senior component, so that the clan claiming temporal precedence has in each instance lent its name to the entire settlement. Some evidence suggests a similar encompassment governing the present double settlement of Kota Pau and Guyu Wolo. Interestingly, however, at this level it is the younger component, Guyu Wolo, which Keo identify with a local whole that subsumes Kota Pau as well. As, for example, in a recent dispute with outsiders held responsible for the destruction of Guyu Wolo's *yenda* and wooden horse statue, sometimes Guyu Wolo is represented as a settlement

---

[8] The last phrase glosses the partly BI expression '*peo pahlawan*'. The local language terms translate as '*peo* of sea shells and head-dresses', referring to the costume of warriors, and '*peo* of bravery, aggression'.

comprising seven clans, a total that also includes the four clans of Kota Pau. In a similar vein, the two villages are described as forming a single 'head and tail' (*ulu éko*), a notion consistent with the fact that this is one of the few double settlements designated with a single formal name: Ulu Guyu, Eko Lina (see Appendix 2).

Recalling the recent history of Bale and Kate in Upper Pajo Mala, the use of the name Guyu Wolo when referring to the entire double settlement may partly be attributed to the political prominence of Guyu Wolo (and especially clan Guyu), at least since the beginning of the colonial period. In the creation of units of colonial administration, Guyu Wolo and Kota Pau were joined to form a single *kampong* ('administrative village', BI) called 'Guyu Wolo' and led by a headman (*kepala kampong*) from the village of Guyu Wolo. What is more, it was a prominent man of clan Guyu who served as the last 'district head' (*kepala haminte*) of the colonial district of Sawu, a position never occupied by anyone from Kota Pau. Possibly also relevant is the location of the Dutch-built road that runs past the landward entrance to Guyu Wolo, thus giving immediate access to that village rather than its traditionally superordinate seaward neighbour. As I describe below, colonial prominence may similarly have benefited the clan Pau Padhi Mena in consolidating its position *vis-à-vis* older groups in the village of Lower Pau Lundu, to which we now turn.

3. The Lower Village of Pau Lundu (Pau Lundu Nua Au)

Closely associated with Kota Pau and located less than three kilometres to the northwest, another village, named simply as Pau, abuts the seaward extremity of the village of Lundu (II: 1: vii). As noted, the two parts of this double settlement, designated together as Pau Lundu (see Plate 1), are often distinguished as Upper and Lower Pau Lundu. In order to avoid confusion with other social entities named Pau, hereafter I refer to the village of Pau which adjoins Lundu as Lower Pau Lundu (Pau Lundu Nua Au).

Lower Pau Lundu forms one limit of the domain of Nuga Raga. The adjacent village of Lundu, on the other hand, falls within the domain of Lape. Thus, in a way comparable to what one encounters in Pajo Maja, the double settlement combines territories associated with two Land Mothers. Until 1918, the entire settlement, comprising both Lundu and Pau, was situated a short distance to the west of the present location, on a more elevated site that had become overpopulated. In its form, the present double settlement replicates the earlier one. As regards content, it has increased in size through the incorporation of previously separate Defenders.

In the 1940s local officials instructed villagers to consolidate the Lower and Upper villages of Pau Lundu (that is Pau and Lundu), much in the same way as did their counterparts in Pajo Mala. A stone wall separating the two *nua* was disassembled and replaced with an earthen ramp (*ngi'i kojo*). In addition, the *yenda* that stood at the landward end of Lower Pau Lundu was moved to the head of Lundu, while Lundu's *nde*, at the seaward end of Upper Pau Lundu, was relocated to the seaward extremity of Lower Pau Lundu. The arrangement, whereby a pair of *yenda* and a pair of *nde* stand side by side at either end of a continuous plaza, thus resembled what is now found in the single villages of Nua Nage and Paga (II: 1: i,vi). The ritual buildings of Pau Lundu are no longer in evidence, having fallen into disrepair some years ago. However, the duality of the Pau and Lundu (or Lower and Upper Pau Lundu) remains clearly evident from their separate possession of two forked *peo*, erected in the centre of each village.

According to the most common local reckoning, Lower Pau Lundu comprises five clans (*suku*). These however divide into two groupings. The first includes the triad of Pau Padhi Mena ('Right Side Pau'), Pau Padhi Rale ('Left Side Pau'), and Pau Ngodho. The names of the first two clans refer of course to the location of their houses, respectively on the *mena* ('right') and *rale* ('left') sides of the village.[9] Completing the five clans are the pair Bo Bana and Loka Nunu. Both villagers and other Keo often represent the three clans that include 'Pau' in their names as a unity, more specifically as a single collection of 'siblings' (*ka'e ari*). These are the groups most closely associated with the forked *peo*, maintaining the positions of both trunk rider and tip rider. Sometimes, moreover, all three Pau clans are described together, or without distinction, as the 'mother' (*ta ine*), and even the Land Mother, in Lower Pau Lundu. As this may suggest, the other pair, Bo Bana and Loka Nunu, are considered Defenders (*ana tuku*) of the other three. Yet in a more exact sense it is clan Pau Padhi Mena that occupies the former status. Accordingly, Pau Padhi Mena also holds the position of trunk rider of the forked *peo*, and is described as the only group ever to have planted a ritual garden (*uma gua*). The second ceremonial position of tip rider is then claimed by Pau Padhi Rale, while in the context of collective sacrificing, Pau Ngodho is the third in order of precedence. Pau's Defender clans then slaughter after Ngodho.

Whereas Pau Padhi Mena, in particular, is Land Mother in relation to its two Defenders, this clan (and in an extended sense, the entire trio of Pau clans) is in turn considered a Defender of Nuga Raga, that is, clan Pau in Kota Pau. Despite being identically named as Pau, the two clans—Pau Padhi Mena and Pau in Kota Pau—are not known to be agnatically connected in any way, nor (with the exception of a single union contracted in the twentieth century) are they related by marriage. Indeed, in spite of their present association and a tendency to consider them as a single grouping, all three Pau clans in Pau Lundu recognize quite separate genealogical and geographical origins.

Although currently the third among the clans of Lower Pau Lundu, by

---

[9] Like the two divisions (*ngapi*) of clan Kota in Kota Pau, the two groups are alternatively called Pau Bhisu Mena and Pau Bhisu Rale.

general agreement clan Pau Ngodho is actually the oldest group and was originally trunk rider in respect of the *peo* to which the present forked post is heir.
As the clan's original, and more correct, name is simply Ngodho, the inclusion
of 'Pau' in the group's present designation reflects its long association with,
and indeed subordination to, the other two Pau clans. This development thus
parallels one discernible in Lower Pajo Mala, where clan Kayo (incidently also
the earliest to settle at that particular site) later became known as Pajo Kayo (II:
2: i). The ancestor of Ngodho, a man named Ndona or, more completely,
Ndona Ngodho, was reputedly a sibling of Raga Wea, the previously
mentioned ancestor of the Wulu clan Pata (II: 1). Raga Wea, it may be recalled,
was a sister's son of Lape Mére. Hence in so far as Ndona is sometimes
described as a full sibling of Raga, the clan Ngodho is another of the many that
can trace their origins to a sister of the senior Land Mother.

By the same token, people outside of Pau Lundu recognize clan Ngodho as
one of the numerous Defenders of Lape. Local historians describe Ndona and
Raga as originally resident together in a village named Rea, within the domain
of Lape, in reference to which they are also known as Ndona Rea and Raga
Rea.[10] One generally knowledgeable source, an elder of clan Pata in Wulu,
claimed that this Raga was not the original Raga Wea, but rather a son or
descendant of the latter. Either way, Raga and Ndona separated after a quarrel
over the ownership of edible rodents caught in traps (*gate dhéke*). Ndona
moved out of Rea to a hamlet named Ngodho, or Wolo Ngodho (see Appendix
3), located just landward of the old village of Lundu, originally known as
Dhoki Paya. Thus Ndona Rea came to be known as Ndona Ngodho. For
reasons explained below, the hamlet of Ngodho eventually changed its name to
Pau.

Connected with his move to Ngodho was Ndona's status as wife-taker of
clan Dhoki Paya, from whom he received an affinal land grant (*tana ka tuka*; II:
1: vii). As noted previously, the link between Ngodho and Dhoki Paya—
another Defender of Lape Mére and the oldest clan in Lundu (or Upper Pau
Lundu)—finds particular expression whenever the Lundu people erect a *peo*.
For it should then be a man of Ngodho who acts as excavator (*ta kabhe*), after
a man of Dhoki Paya, the clan of the trunk rider, first breaks the earth (*koe*)
where the post is to be planted. Once settled in Ngodho, the Ngodho people
erected a *peo* of their own. But, some time later, they found themselves threat-
ened by powerful enemies. They then sought assistance from ancestors of clan
Pau Padhi Mena, who promised their support only on condition that, if they
were able to secure a victory, the premier position in the village should become
theirs. Thus it was that Pau Padhi Mena became trunk rider of Ngodho's *peo*,
a status it retains in Lower Pau Lundu to the present day.

The origins of clan Pau Padhi Mena are not much clearer than those of

---

[10] Rea was located just above Nua Céla, an earlier settlement of Céla, the clan of Lape Mére.

groups named Pau in Kota Pau or Pau Leka (Section 4 below). The only specific account, which seems not to be widely known or recognized, describes the group's male ancestor as a man named Riwu who came from a place called Wolo Riu (Riu Hill), just seaward of the present Pau Lundu. According to the local interpretation, the place-name attests to an ultimate derivation of Pau Padhi Mena from the Riung district, locally pronounced as 'Riu', far to the northwest.[11] As noted, the territory of Pau Padhi Mena falls within the domain of Nuga Raga, or, otherwise stated, of the clan called Pau in Kota Pau. In what circumstances the land was ceded is no longer known. The transfer seems not to be connected with Nuga Raga's war with Koba Réja, the event used to explain the acquisition by Land Mother Pau (KP) of its several other Defender clans. Nevertheless, it is a point of some interest that Loka Poma, the clan founded by Koba Réja, became established in Lundu, the village that forms a double settlement with Pau, where Pau Padhi Mena is at present recognized as the principal group.

What is more certain is that Pau Padhi Mena is closely associated, even identified, with Nuga Raga or Pau in Kota Pau, even in the absence of genealogical knowledge that could substantiate a particular connection. In so far as lands held by clan Ngodho (or Pau Ngodho) may still be counted as part of the domain of Lape, their present subordination to Pau Padhi Mena might be interpreted as an expansion of the domain of Nuga Raga at the expense of the ancestral territory of the most senior of the Ga'e siblings. On this issue, direct questioning usually evoked contrary, if not contradictory, responses from people of Ngodho and Pau Padhi Mena respectively. Yet it is undeniable that the village of Lower Pau Lundu lies at the margin of the territory of Nuga Raga, and that Ngodho, while formerly a Defender of Lape and while still maintaining a long-standing ritual association with another Defender of Lape—clan Dhoki Paya in the adjacent village of Lundu—is now thoroughly incorporated within Lower Pau Lundu. Indeed, Ngodho is effectively subordinated to both Pau Padhi Mena and Pau Padhi Rale.

During the colonial period, Ngodho unsuccessfully endeavoured to reclaim the status of trunk rider in Lower Pau Lundu. Their failure is attributed to the power of a famous leader of Pau Padhi Mena named Jago Kunda who, partly by exploiting his authority as a colonially appointed local administrator (*kepala mere* or *kepala haminte*), was able to suppress Ngodho's claims. Including a resort to physical violence, Jago Kunda's reputed actions against the Ngodho people provide a further example of how positions assigned within the colonial order were used to consolidate, if not create, local relations of political subordination. At the same time, although Ngodho's historical precedence is widely recognized in Pau Lundu and neighbouring villages, there is a general consensus that they

---

[11] Interestingly, the headman of Pau Padhi Mena once informed me that Nuga Raga, actually the ancestors of Pau in Kota Pau but also closely associated with his own clan, hailed ultimately from Riung.

have no grounds for reclaiming the position of trunk rider in Lower Pau Lundu. As third parties pointed out, their former precedence was freely surrendered to a more recent arrival in exchange for military support and therefore cannot be regained.

Clan Pau Padhi Rale ('Left Side Pau') settled in western Keo after both Ngodho and Pau Padhi Mena ('Right Side Pau') were established in Pau. Their apical ancestor, named Ndona Wea, was born in Pau Tola (dialectal, Pau Toda), actually a double settlement originally comprising the villages of Tola and Pau, in the eastern part of Keo. The clan's founding myth describes how Ndona Wea fled from Pau Tola owing to poverty and a failure to reciprocate in village feasts—a theme repeated in the history of the clan Loka Nunu which I describe below.[12] People of Ngodho told me that it was specifically their fore-bears who took in Ndona Wea and gave him a place in Old Pau (the settlement that preceded the present Pau, or Lower Pau Lundu). Contradicting this claim is other evidence indicating that Pau Padhi Mena had assumed leadership of the village before the incorporation of Pau Padhi Rale. Whichever version is accepted, Pau Padhi Rale, though the third to arrive, is now tip rider in Lower Pau Lundu. Noteworthy here is the fact that 'Left Side Pau' is not considered a Defender of 'Right Side Pau'. In relation to the major Land Mother (Nuga Raga, or Pau in Kota Pau), the two groups are represented as equivalent and, indeed, are sometimes even spoken of—especially in contrast to Ngodho—as two parts of a single clan.

It is probably in this context that one is to understand the frequent, although evidently incorrect, assertion that Pau Padhi Mena, like Padhi Rale, derives from Pau Tola. Most interestingly, when I first began to investigate the village, a group of informants dominated by men of Pau Padhi Mena stated that it was Ngodho who, together with Pau Padhi Rale, derived from Pau Tola. 'Right Side Pau' was then described as being 'original' or 'native' (*tenge*; BI *asli*) to Pau Lundu. This contention, which was later controverted even by the 'Right Side' people, was obviously motivated by the present pre-eminence of Pau Padhi Mena in Lower Pau Lundu. At the same time, it does accord with a regularly expressed identification of Pau Padhi Mena with Pau in Kota Pau, the direct descendants of the Land Mother, Nuga Raga.

A wider context for these ideas will be explored presently, in regard to connections between Lower Pau Lundu and other villages partly named Pau. For the moment it may be sufficient to note that, if Pau Padhi Rale and Pau Padhi Mena were considered a single clan in opposition to the older Ngodho, then together with clans Bo Bana and Loka Nunu, the village would provide another instance of quadripartite constitution. As noted, Bo Bana and Loka

---

[12]   That both this ancestor and the founder of clan Ngodho bear the same name, Ndona, is probably a coincidence, as this is a common men's name. It is nevertheless interesting that if the Ngodho ancestor had been a son of Lape's sister, Wea Mére, as some evidence would imply, then one version of his name would be Ndona Wea, precisely the same name as that of the ancestor of Pau Padhi Rale.

Nunu became assigned as Defenders of Pau Padhi Mena once the latter clan had become dominant in the region of Pau Lundu. Clan Bo Bana is a relatively large group, while Loka Nunu is the smallest of clans, described by its current headman as having always possessed but a single 'house'.

Before the present village was founded, Loka Nunu and Bo Bana resided separately from the three Pau clans, inhabiting a double settlement consisting of adjacent villages each with its own *peo*.[13] The site of the old village of Bo Bana largely coincides with the location of the present village of Lower Pau Lundu (established in 1918), and for this reason people still sometimes refer to the village as 'Bo Bana'. Bounding on one extremity of Bo Bana's old settlement was the village of Loka Nunu.[14] Consistent with a putative marriage alliance, Bo Bana, as wife-giver, planted a sacrificial *kesi* tree while Loka Nunu planted a *dheyo* tree. Although the two groups thus represent themselves as affines, their limited genealogies do not reveal a single marriage between them; hence in this case an ancient affinal relationship apparently continues to be recognized in the absence of recent unions replicating the original tie.

At present, the former *peo* of Bo Bana is commemorated with a short stone *ia*, erected next to the forked *peo* in Lower Pau Lundu, of which Pau Padhi Mena is the trunk rider. Now that the two Defenders share the village with the three Pau clans, they also sacrifice at this post. Nevertheless, with reference to the location of the new village on land of Bo Bana, villagers represent the present consolidation as involving an incorporation of a 'mother' (*ta ine*) by 'children' (*ta ana*). Though somewhat unusual, this is not unique. As should be recalled, a virtually identical arrangement is found in the adjacent village of Lundu, where the senior clans Dhoki Paya and Loka Poma now occupy a site partly coinciding with a former settlement occupied solely by Dhoki Paya's Defenders, clan Bajo Léwa. In view of their earlier occupation of the present site of Pau village, Bo Bana and Loka Nunu still maintain what might be called a residual claim to ceremonial precedence. In 1992 Bo Bana, with assistance from Loka Nunu, erected miniature ritual buildings called *wondi* and *bhaga*, respectively at the landward and seaward extremities of Lower Pau Lundu (I: 2: v; see Plate 15). Serving as places to mount trophy horns and make offerings to beneficent spirits—in this instance specifically in connection with a series of illnesses that had overtaken the clan—the buildings in effect replace the former *yenda* and *nde* belonging principally to the three Pau groups. At the same time, men of Bo Bana and Loka Nunu described the structures as replacing similar

---

[13] This contradicts the claim that Loka Nunu has always comprised a single house. Ownership of a *peo*, of course, entails a minimum of two houses, or two estates.

[14] Information concerning the relative disposition of these two old villages is inconsistent. According to one account, Bo Bana's village was landward of Loka Nunu's. However, according to another source, rather than having their 'heads' (*ulu*) pointing landward, as is usual, both pointed *rale*, that is, to the left as one faces the Ebu Lobo volcano. Other reports describe the name Watu Mutu ('Stone Cluster'), now applied to the 'tail' of the Lower Pau Lundu (see Appendix 2), as formerly designating both the 'tail' of the old village of Bo Bana and the 'head' of the village of Loka Nunu.

PLATE 15. Men of clans Loka Nunu and Bo Bana before the *bhaga* at the seaward end of Pau (Lower Pau Lundu)

PLATE 16. A *joto* with a single post and ladder in Pau (Lower Pau Lundu)

buildings they possessed in their former settlements, before amalgamating with the Pau clans.[15]

The longer-established of Pau's two Defenders, the Bo Bana people recognize no geographical origin other than their present location. By contrast, external sources described them as once residing at a higher elevation, according to one account in a place called Sela, located somewhere above the old village of Ngodho (or Pau). Loka Nunu, on the other hand, hails from Téya Bhoja, to the east, from where its founder came, together with the ancestor of the clan Bhoja Kisa, now in the village of Suga Bhoja (II: 1: v). With regard to this common origin, Loka Nunu people consider themselves *ka'e ari* ('siblings') of Bhoja Kisa—or rather did so until a serious dispute, concerning the molestation of a wife of a Loka Nunu forebear, effectively ended their former relationship of mutual assistance.

According to their own genealogy, the apical ancestor of clan Loka Nunu, Ebu Ngadha, married a sister of Nuga (or Nuga Raga) of clan Pau in Kota Pau. Although evidently anachronistic (in so far as Nuga was the brother of the apical ancestor of the major Land Mother), the union nevertheless corresponds to the pattern of early marital connection reported for Land Mothers and Defenders within the domains of the Ga'e siblings. By the same token, however, the marriage is unusual within the domain of Nuga Raga. Not only is the pattern not evident with regard to the several Defenders of Nuga Raga resident in Kota Pau and Guyu Wolo, but genealogies for the three Pau clans in Lower Pau Lundu reveal not a single marriage where a wife was taken from Pau in Kota Pau.[16] Bo Bana, also, appears never to have taken a wife from the last clan, although in once instance it has given one.

Be that as it may, Loka Nunu's status as wife-taker of the Land Mother in Kota Pau accords with their occasional claim, echoed by Bo Bana, to be Defenders of Nuga Raga and not, or not simply, Defenders of Pau Padhi Mena, or the three Pau clans in Lower Pau Lundu. Consistent with this, the pair are usually described as having acquired rights to land directly from Nuga Raga, even while they were designated as Defenders of Pau in Lower Pau Lundu. The assertion also corresponds to another phenomenon noted earlier, namely the tendency to identify Nuga Raga as the ancestor of Pau Padhi Mena. Accordingly, the Loka Nunu headman once stated that clan Pau—by which he referred to 'Right Side' Pau in Lower Pau Lundu—was Defender (*ana tuku*) of no one, but was itself the Land Mother (*ine tana*). Bearing as well on the connection between groups named Pau in several villages unaffiliated with the Ga'e siblings, this matter will be taken up again later on.

Despite its somewhat complex history, the structure of Lower Pau Lundu

---

[15] Prior to 1992, Bo Bana men had also told me that the former *nde* and *yenda*, too, were rightfully theirs and not Pau's.

[16] The genealogy provided by Pau in Kota Pau indicates that Pau Padhi Mena has, on the contrary, given a wife to the former, in a marriage that occurred in the mid-twentieth century.

is fundamentally similar to what is encountered in other Pau villages. Itself one half of a long-standing double settlement, the present village comprises two parts that became residentially conjoined in relatively recent times. These are the three Pau clans on the one hand, and the pair Bo Bana and Loka Nunu on the other. As noted earlier, viewing 'Right Side' and 'Left Side' Pau as a unity opposed to Ngodho (or Pau Ngodho) reveals an instance of the quadripartite order common elsewhere, including the adjacent village of Lundu. Yet contextually valid alternative perspectives produce totals of three or five clans (*suku*). Certainly, if one were to count as separate clans groups claiming different geographical origins—a principle that is not always observed—then the total would be five (or more exactly a grouping of two and another of three).

Before leaving Pau Lundu, some further remarks about affinal connections are in order. Even if the three Pau clans were counted as a single clan, this would not, of course, rule out marriage among them. Initial enquiries in Lower Pau Lundu evoked the claim that, since the three groups were all 'siblings' (or 'kin', *ka'e ari*), they should not intermarry. Yet subsequently recorded genealogies reveal six unions, including three in which Pau Padhi Mena had taken women from Pau Padhi Rale (thus contrary to the order of precedence entailed in their relation as trunk rider and tip rider). In the other three, Ngodho, the oldest of the trio, appears as wife-giver to Pau Padhi Mena in two instances, and to Pau Padhi Rale in one instance. Although all groups have contracted many more marriages with clans outside Lower Pau Lundu, here one can nevertheless discern the pattern, already mentioned in reference to other villages, whereby the oldest of several groups provides wives, as well as land, to later arrivals. The pattern is even clearer with regard to affinal connections between Pau (that is, Lower Pau Lundu) and the senior, adjacent village of Lundu. Genealogies thus show the three Pau clans taking wives quite regularly, in at least eleven cases, from the oldest clan in Lundu, Dhoki Paya. Just as significantly, in no instance has any of these groups given wives to Dhoki Paya. (Loka Nunu has also taken two brides from Dhoki Paya; one house of Bo Bana has taken one while a different house has given a wife to the Lundu clan.)

At the same time it should be recalled that, with the possible exception of Ngodho (see II: 1: vii), none of the three Pau clans is a Defender or land grantee of Dhoki Paya. Conversely, while the major Land Mother of nearly all Lower Pau Lundu groups is Pau in Kota Pau (the clan of Nuga Raga), the latter appears never to have been a wife-giver of any of the former.

4. Pau Leka

Not much more than a kilometre southwest of Pau Lundu one encounters the village of Pau Leka. In several respects, Pau Leka is remarkably similar to Lower Pau Lundu. The present village, founded in the 1930s, combines the former village of Béngi with a previous double settlement comprising the villages of Leka and Pau (thus a village named identically to the seaward half of Pau Lundu). In their present single settlement, the three names are mostly construed as the names of three component clans (*suku*). In the three former villages (*nua*), each group possessed its own *peo*. Both Leka and Pau employed forked Cassiawood posts (*peo yebu*), while Béngi maintained a sacrificial *kesi* tree. In the present Pau Leka—which, like numerous other settlements, obviously takes its name from its two leading clans—all three groups share a single forked *peo*. The sacrificial post is, however, more specifically conceived as the *peo* of Leka, recognized as the oldest of the three and occupant of the position of trunk rider. Clan Pau—which in accordance with a local usage I hereafter distinguish as Pau Kolo Ndinga (incorporating the name of its major ancestor)—is the tip rider. Following the common practice of distinguishing identically named localized groups with reference to co-resident groups, people sometimes distinguish Pau Kolo Ndinga as 'Pau Leka'. As this is not the group's regular name, however, the village (or former double settlement) does not unequivocally bear the same name as any single component.

In the present Pau Leka, houses of the three clans are disposed in a way corresponding to the relative locations of their respective former villages, located on higher ground a short way to the west. Leka thus occupies the landward section of the village, while houses of Pau Kolo Ndinga are built just seaward of those of Leka. Since its former village was located less than a kilometre seaward of the old double settlement of Pau Leka, clan Béngi inhabits the most seaward part, or 'tail', of the present settlement. Principally associated with Leka and Pau Kolo Ndinga, the present *peo* is erected on the boundary of the two sections inhabited by these two clans.

Possibly hailing from somewhere near Lejo (in the direction of eastern Keo), the apical ancestor of Leka, Lako Kunda, married a daughter of Lape Mére, named Molo Sénda. The couple then produced two sons, Uwa Molo and Moa Molo, usually named together as Uwa Moa (see Fig. 6).[17] In accordance with this affinal relation, Leka acquired land from Lape and so is counted among the many Defenders of the major Land Mother. As indicated previously (II: 1: ii), Leka people resident in Pau Leka (and formerly in the old village of Leka) represent the senior segment of the clan, while a junior segment, maintaining its own forked *peo*, has long resided in the village of Keo Ondo together with a segment of clan Yoga. With reference to their co-resident clans, Keo distinguish the two groups as 'Leka Pau' and 'Leka Yoga'.

If Leka's history and present status is reasonably straightforward, it contrasts sharply with that of Pau Kolo Ndinga. Not recognizing any external geographical origin, this is the third of the groups called Pau which are unaffiliated with Ga'e siblings. Like the domain of Nuga Raga shared by Pau in

---

[17] Another version of the genealogy, probably less authoritative, distinguishes Uwa and Moa as the male ancestors of Leka in Pau Leka and Keo Ondo (II: 1: ii) respectively.

Kota Pau and Pau in Lower Pau Lundu, territory claimed by Pau Kolo Ndinga is, moreover, quite separate from the domains of Lape and the other Ga'e. At the same time, neither genealogically nor territorially is Pau Kolo Ndinga linked with Pau in Kota Pau or the ancestors Nuga Raga. The history of Kota Pau depicts the ancestor Kolo Ndinga, as well as the Leka ancestors jointly named Uwa Moa, as parties from whom Nuga Raga, unsuccessfully as it happened, requested military assistance against Koba Réja. But this is the only indication of any connection between these groups.

Keo commonly describe Pau Kolo Ndinga as the original (*tenge*) group. Although not particularly reliable, one source—people of clan Lui, whose status I discuss below—even claimed that the ancestor Kolo Ndinga arrived, or was present, in western Keo before Land Mother Lape. Yet the designation of Pau as 'original' seems to mean no more than that the descendants of Kolo Ndinga, so far as is known, have always been where they are now and that their territory is not known to have been previously occupied by any other extant population. In accordance with its status as Land Mother within its own domain, Pau Kolo Ndinga possesses a single Defender, the clan Béngi, with which it now shares a single settlement and single sacrificial instrument. As regards Pau's relation with Leka, local representations do not unequivocally ascribe precedence to one group or the other, even though Leka recognizes an external origin somewhere to the east. What is clear is that, like the two villages of Pau Lundu, the present Pau Leka, as well as the identically named former double settlement, conjoin the domains of two Land Mothers: Lape and Kolo Ndinga. At the same time, the site of the present village of Pau Leka—also known as Bo'a Sepu—belongs to the territory of Leka.[18] Hence it is clan Leka that claims the status of trunk rider in respect of the single, shared *peo*.

Although usually spoken of as a single clan, Pau Kolo Ndinga is actually an amalgam of two distinct groups. In this respect it resembles clan Kota and, in a qualified sense, even 'Right Side' and 'Left Side' Pau in Lower Pau Lundu. While Keo tend to identify Kolo Ndinga as the ancestor of the entire group, it is specifically the senior segment, often distinguished as Pau Tenge ('Original, True Pau'), that traces agnatic descent to Kolo Ndinga. Accordingly, the head-man for the entire clan is drawn from Pau Tenge. Distinguished as Pau Ndi'i Ipi ('Pau Standing by the Side'), the junior part of the clan is actually a branch of Pau Padhi Mena ('Right Side Pau') that left Pau Lundu several generations ago. This agnatic connection is the only genealogical tie linking Pau Leka with Lower Pau Lundu or Kota Pau. The relationship continues to be recognized in so far as men of Pau Ndi'i Ipi and Pau Padhi Mena can provide one another with heirs when holders of estates die without issue, as in one recent case

---

[18] Meaning 'hamlet at the end', Bo'a Sepu was the name of a former hamlet located at one extremity of Leka's territory.

where a man of Pau Padhi Mena (in fact a younger brother of the present head-man) had succeeded a Pau Leka man.

Although I never heard it expressly mentioned, in Pau Kolo Ndinga's former separate village, the senior group, Pau Tenge, would almost certainly have occupied the position of trunk rider, while Pau Ndi'i Ipi, as the later arrival, probably provided the tip rider. Later, when the entire clan (or village) joined with Leka, Pau—and more specifically, Pau Tenge—then became tip rider in respect of the single shared *peo* of which Leka is the principal owner. As noted, prior to the 1930s the third clan, Béngi, the sole Defender of Pau Kolo Ndinga, also occupied its own village, located some distance seaward of Leka and Pau.

Occupying the 'tail' section (*éko*) of the present settlement, the Béngi people are an offshoot of clan Bindi Loga from the village of Pajo (now Pajo Réja) in the domain of Gewo Ga'e (II: 5: i). Recognizing this connection, the present Pau Leka is formally designated as Ulu Réta Leka, Eko Bindi Loga, an expression that also acknowledges Leka's occupation of the most landward (*réta*) part of the village. In respect of their former sacrificial *kesi* tree, Béngi comprises two estates (*ngapi*) bearing the ancestral names Kuku Gini and Ebu Toyo. Identified with the landward end of the village, Kuku Gini occupied the status of earth breaker (*ta koe*) while Ebu Toyo, located in the seaward part, served as excavator (*ta kabhe*). In formal speech Béngi village was thus named Ulu Kuku Gini, Eko Ebu Toyo. Actually the paired names of two brothers (Kuku Liu, the elder, and Gini Liu, the younger), Kuku Gini refers to fore-bears considered apical ancestors of the clan as a whole, whose genealogy thus subsumes Ebu Toyo as the ancestor of a more recently derived segment. The dualistic constitution of Béngi is however qualified by the recent incorpora-tion, several generations ago, of a later wave of immigrants from Bindi Loga. Since these were originally wife-givers of the main body of Béngi, their assim-ilation exemplifies the inverse of what one encounters in Lower Pajo Mala, where clan Bindi (also related to Bindi Loga in Pajo Réja), or Bindi Wae, subsumes former wife-takers, Wae, as a component estate.

The present Pau Leka thus further exemplifies an apparently tripartite grouping of clans derived from several earlier dualisms. In addition, the village and the earlier double settlement from which it has developed provide another example of social unities that subsume parts of the territories of different Land Mothers. Also conforming to a more widespread pattern, all three clans in Pau Leka recognize agnatic connections with groups resident in other villages and maintaining separate sacrificial instruments. In this way the composition of the settlement attests to the general principle whereby sacrifi-cial unities, indicated by the common possession of a shared *peo*, have their basis in present territorial association or contiguity rather than common genealogy or shared geographical origins. Connections of the latter kinds do, however, link Pau Leka with another settlement: the village of Lui.

5. Lui (or Pau Lui)

Situated about half a kilometre seaward of Kota Pau, and just 200 metres or so northeast of Munde (II: 4: iii), the village of Lui and its surrounding lands intervene between the domain of Nuga Raga, to the north, and the domain of Géra Ga'e—one of the Ga'e siblings—to the south. At the same time, Lui territory forms a whole with the territory of Pau Kolo Ndinga, extending from a place just to the east of Lui village called Gopo Gewo (which, as the name may suggest, bounds the domain of Gewo Ga'e) westward in the direction of Pau Leka.

The present Lui comprises just two clans, an older group named Lui and another, rather peculiarly called Nua Muri ('new village', not to be confused with the village of Nua Muri in the domain of Gewo). Although reputedly from So'a, the ancestor of clan Nua Muri resided in Léndo and other places to the east before arriving in the vicinity of Lui. Clan Lui traces agnatic descent to an ancestor named Wénde, or Bhaya Wénde. Paralleling the designation of the ancestors of Bindi in Lower Pajo Mala (Boa Maga), Bhaya is actually the name of the male ancestor's wife, Bhaya Ndue, from Munde (clan Béle Jawa). By most accounts, Wénde was the younger brother of the Pau ancestor Kolo Ndinga; thus, following the common pattern, his name also appears in the compound Kolo Wénde. By the same token, clan Lui is further known as Pau Lui, a name alternatively construed as designating Lui and Pau Kolo Ndinga together. As this might suggest, lands occupied by the two groups were once a single territory which was divided when Lui founded its own settlement near the eastern boundary. Accordingly, Lui possesses its own *peo*, a *kesi* tree—now destroyed and in need of replacement—which it shares with the co-resident clan Nua Muri. Even so, Lui still recognizes its common agnatic origin with Pau Kolo Ndinga. Indeed, contrary to the general opinion, some men of Lui even claim that their ancestor was the elder of the pair named Kolo Wénde, and further that, as Kolo was replaced by an adopted sister's son, only they descend directly (that is, exclusively through males) from the ancestral sibling pair. Invoking these arguments, Lui men have recently claimed precedence not only in their own village but also in Pau Leka. Regarded by most people as an extravagant position, not least because the *peo* in the present Pau Leka principally belongs to Leka rather than Pau, their stance appears to be a major factor delaying the replacement of Pau Leka's forked *peo*, which was dug up and removed about 1990.[19]

Currently, relations are also strained between Lui and its co-resident clan, Nua Muri. Lui claims clan Nua Muri as a recipient of land, and hence as its

---

[19] There was still no sign of a new post being erected during my last visit in 1999. In line with Lui's claims, members of that clan first reported the name of their ancestor as Wénde Kolo, thus inverting the components of Kolo Wénde. Even so, Lui people acknowledge that it was Wénde who moved from Pau Leka to found the village of Lui, while Kolo remained in the original settlement.

Defender, but Nua Muri disputes this. Earlier, the two groups occupied separate villages, a short distance from the present Lui. Composing a double settlement, Nua Muri's village was then just seaward of old Lui. As in other instances, this spatial contrast is reflected in the present single village, where Lui's houses are located towards the head (*ulu*) and Nua Muri's towards the tail (*éko*).[20] While they are connected mainly by virtue of common residence, the history of the two clans reveals an agnatic link of sorts. In order to combat a common enemy—the people of Sawu (II: 5: iii)—Lui and Nua Muri requested assistance from Aja Laya, a sibling pair (Aja Toyo and Laya Toyo) from the former village of Loka Sina, to the east. After defeating the enemy, Aja was granted land and membership of clan Nua Muri, while his brother, Laya, was similarly inducted into clan Lui. As Laya was childless, however, his line did not continue.

6. The Three Pau Villages

Regularly describing them as 'siblings' (*ka'e ari*), Keo commonly represent clans called Pau resident in Kota Pau, Lower Pau Lundu, and Pau Leka as components of a single social whole. Co-ordinate with this, of course, are descriptions of the three Pau clans in Lower Pau Lundu as a single group, even a single *suku* ('clan'). Closer inspection, however, seriously qualifies or contradicts this view.

On several occasions, otherwise well-informed Keo, including both villagers themselves and knowledgeable outsiders, rationalized interpretations of 'Pau' as a single group represented in all three villages by claiming that 'all Pau' derived geographically from the eastern village of Pau Tola. Yet the bulk of evidence, including the later testimony of persons advancing this generalization, indicates that it is only the clan Pau Padhi Rale ('Left Side Pau') in Lower Pau Lundu that has its geographical origin in Pau Tola. In one instance, a widely recognized local authority advanced the hypothesis of a general derivation from this eastern region expressly in explanation of the circumstance that the groups all bear the name 'Pau'. Indeed, the common designation, appearing both in the names of clans and villages (in so far as these can be distinguished) would appear to be the main basis for the notion that groups in all three villages share a common geographical or genealogical source. Yet given the fact that 'Pau' evidently does not designate a single place of derivation, the name provides no obvious clue to the character and origin of the imputation of unity. The most common sense of *pau* ('mango tree') also does not illuminate the issue, other than to suggest the possibility of a botanically derived toponym coincidentally shared by distinct residential locations.

---

[20] In formal speech, Lui is thus known as Ulu Lui, Eko Nua Muri. According to another report, the village should be called Ulu Lui, Eko Bonga. Bonga refers to a location where lands of Géra Ga'e bound on the territory of Sawu (II: 4; II: 5: iii).

But there is no indication why the three villages in question should all have been named in this way. What is more, some people I asked wanted to deny that the sense of 'mango' was in any way relevant in this context.

A comparable generalization is found in the idea that, because Pau groups in all three villages are 'siblings' (*ka'e ari*), they should provide one another with mutual assistance in provisioning feasts, contributing to funerals, and the like, and that they can obtain heirs from other Pau groups when estate holders die childless. To be sure, there are instances where these obligations have in recent times been honoured. Yet, again, they clearly pertain only to specific pairs of clans, particularly clan Pau Padhi Mena in Lower Pau Lundu and Pau in Kota Pau, or the former group and its agnatic derivative, a segment of clan Pau (called Pau Ndi'i Ipi) in Pau Leka. Although also described as *ka'e ari*, the first relationship would seem to be partly predicated on the connection of Land Mother and Defender that obtains between these two clans. Indeed, not being genealogically linked in any known way, this is the only formal relationship that the two groups plainly share.

Clearly, Pau Padhi Mena is pivotal in this regard, being the only clan definitely linked with groups in the two other villages. On the other hand, clan Pau in Pau Leka (Pau Kolo Ndinga) appears not to be related at all to Pau in Kota Pau (the descendants of Nuga Raga), nor to the other two Pau clans (Ngodho and Pau Padhi Rale) in Lower Pau Lundu. Here I refer not just to recognized agnatic connections, but also to affinity. The absence of marriage ties between Pau in Kota Pau and Lower Pau Lundu has already been noted. Affinal connections are also not particularly pronounced between Lower Pau Lundu and Pau in Pau Leka. Pau Leka genealogies reveal just four marriages, two of which involve Pau Padhi Rale ('Left Side Pau') and Pau Ndi'i Ipi (the segment of Pau in Pau Leka deriving agnatically from 'Right Side Pau' in Pau Lundu). In the other two marriages, Pau Padhi Mena had given wives to Pau Tenge, the senior or original segment of Pau in Pau Leka (Pau Kolo Ndinga).

In conceiving groups named Pau in different villages as reciprocally obligated components of a single social entity, Keo therefore appear to employ what may be called a polythetic reasoning, whereby particular binary links between groups comprised in the three villages are over-generalized and attributed to a single undifferentiated whole. The attribution of a shared geographical origin—the only local explication of the shared name—indirectly reflects the same process, either as a hypothetical explanation of the only partially attested 'sibling' relationship, or as a further inference from it. Yet, as other instances reveal, even common clanship does not always require recognition of a single agnatic or geographical source among Keo.

As much as anything, the three villages that form the 'Pau enclave' are defined by negative features. Occupying more or less contiguous territories, their ancestors are equally represented as unrelated to Lape and the other Ga'e siblings whose domains surround their own lands. Yet in addition to the common name, there is one positive feature of the Pau clans that seems to underline their collective distinctiveness: the fact that all employ forked Cassiawood *peo* (*peo yebu*). As noted, it is generally held that land grantees in the domains of the Ga'e siblings, by contrast, should erect living sacrificial trees (*peo kesi* or *peo dheyo*). Of course, the three Pau villages are not the only settlements to possess forked sacrificial posts. Clans Dhoki Paya (in Lundu) and Leka (in Pau Leka and Keo Ondo), both Defenders of Lape, also plant such *peo*, as, nowadays, do Bale and Bolo people. As described in previous chapters, however, the latter pair came to acquire forked *peo* in specific historical circumstances. What is more, it may be relevant that Dhoki Paya and Leka, the first of which was an early wife-taker of the second, are both clans that have long been associated, territorially and in other ways, with Pau groups.

Another intriguing resemblance among the three Pau groups concerns the circumstance that, while all maintain forked *peo*, all of their Defenders who possess, or once possessed, separate *peo* actually plant sacrificial *kesi* trees. While there is less consensus as to whether the three Defender clans resident with Pau in Kota Pau ever independently possessed *peo*, evidence to this effect describes these, too, either as living *peo* (*kesi* or *dheyo* trees) or as *ia* or *peo* of stone. Certainly, none is reported ever to have separately possessed a forked Cassiawood post. That this contrast may reflect a deliberate practice, specific to the Pau enclave, is indicated by local representations of the distinction between the two sorts of *peo*—described also as 'dead' or 'dry' (*mata* or *tu'u*) and 'living' (*muri*) *peo*—as signifying respectively the statuses of Land Mother and Defender, or 'mothers' (*ine*) and 'children' (*ana*).[21]

After investigating the matter at length, it seems unlikely that further field research could illuminate, much less resolve, the several questions surrounding the status of the Pau groups. There is also probably little more to be learned about their relation with clans associated with the Ga'e siblings, particularly whether their ancestors arrived earlier or later than the Ga'e. Apart from the partial contrast of *peo*, it is a point of some interest that Defenders, and thus land grantees, of Pau Land Mothers (Nuga Raga in Kota Pau and Kolo Ndinga in Pau Leka) are represented simply as military supporters rather than as wife-takers, in contrast to Defenders of Land Mother clans tracing direct descent to Ga'e siblings. Pau Leka conforms to this pattern in so far as genealogies record Béngi taking just one wife from its Land Mother, Pau Kolo Ndinga (specifically the senior segment, Pau Tenge), in a union contracted within the last few decades. At the same time, Béngi has given wives to the junior segment, Pau Ndi'i Ipi, in three instances and taken a bride in just one. Similarly, there is no

---

[21] Of further interest in this connection are remarks by Lui people regarding their sacrificial *kesi* tree, destroyed in a fire several decades ago. Claiming also to be the principal owners of the forked *peo* in Pau Leka, Lui men explained that they could not erect another *peo* of this sort in Lui because it was not possible to possess two forked posts. This, then, suggests a representation of the *kesi* tree *peo* as a replacement employed in derivative settlements.

pronounced pattern of alliance between Pau Padhi Mena, the Land Mother in Lower Pau Lundu, and the Defender clans Bo Bana and Loka Nunu.[22]

Also worth remarking is the way in which two of the three double settlements described in this chapter, Pau Lundu and the former Pau Leka, conjoin, in precisely the same way, villages led by unaffiliated groups (that is, clans called Pau) and Defenders of Land Mother Lape Ga'e (Dhoki Paya in Lundu and Leka in Pau Leka). Another combination of this sort was encountered in Pajo Mala, and particularly in Lower Pajo Mala, a settlement comprising a Defender of Lape (clan Pajo Wolo) and the heirs to the domain of Boa Maga (clan Bindi, or Bindi Wae), another unaffiliated group which, though not identified nominally or otherwise with the several populations named Pau, is nevertheless generally comparable to them. In the following chapter we encounter a more inclusive dual combination wherein the territory of a Defender of Lape, the clan Wayu in the village Wulu Wayu, forms a seamless whole with the domain of a younger brother of Lape, Géra Ga'e.

---

[22] Among 32 marriages recorded in the clan's genealogy, Bo Bana has taken five women from Pau Padhi Rale, to which group it has also, in recent generations, given two. Only in one case has a wife been taken from Pau Padhi Mena. The 13 detailed marriages included in Loka Nunu's brief genealogy reveal no unions at all with Pau clans in Lower Pau Lundu.

4

Keo Wayu and the Domain of Géra Ga'e

Compared to the domain of Lape, which comprises villages occupied by more than ten Defenders, the Pau territories described in the previous chapter may seem small. Yet equally small is the domain of the Ga'e sibling Géra, which at present includes just two extant villages: Keo (or Keo Bélo) and Munde. At the same time, lands of Géra form one half of a larger territorial whole designated binomially as Keo Wayu, and more completely as Tana Keo, Watu Wayu (Land of Keo, Stones of Wayu).

A possible source of the name 'Keo' as applied to the entire region, the village of Keo (not to be confused with Keo Ondo, the village adjoining Nua Nage) forms the centre of the domain of Géra Ga'e and the residence of a clan of the same name tracing an unbroken line of agnatic descent to this ancestor. Clan Wayu, on the other hand, is one of the numerous Defenders of Land Mother Lape, resident in the village of Wulu Wayu. The territory of Géra Ga'e lies immediately east of the land of Wayu (and thus the original domain of Lape). Although no longer marked or formally recognized, their former boundary was located somewhere between the coastal settlements of Ma'u Wayu and Ma'u Keo (see Map 2).

How the territories of the two populations came to be conjoined is described in a tradition known throughout western Keo. Long ago, clans Keo and Wayu were at enmity. Conflict broke out when Keo people poisoned Wayu's main water source at Ae Po'o. This resulted in the deaths of all the women of Wayu, so that only men remained. Wayu retaliated by poisoning Keo's water source, thus killing all of their men. Following these disasters, both groups fled the area. The Wayu men went to Wayu Pea to the north, not far from Wae in the southern part of Nage, while the female survivors of Keo removed to Nanga Keo ('Estuary, Bay of Keo'), a coastal settlement to which they reputedly lent their name, located far to the east, in the vicinity of Ende.

A man named Béle Jawa from Ndetu Ko'u in the Ende region would often sail westward to fish and obtain salt. One day he was fishing off the coast near Nanga Keo. Seeing there were so many women in this place, he decided to take a wife from the Keo people. Later, Béle Jawa moved to the original territory of Keo, where he became the founding ancestor of the clan that bears his name, settled at present in the village of Munde (Section 3 below). At this time, the sole occupant of the territory of Wayu was Mosa Ruja, a man from clan Wulu in Nua Nage. Together, Mosa Ruja and Béle Jawa began cultivating the land of Wayu and Keo. But while the harvests were plentiful, the men found that the crops tasted bitter (I: 1: iii). They then realized that the original landowners, Keo and Wayu, must make peace and return to their homelands. Once this was accomplished, the rice and maize resumed their normal flavours.[1]

In recognition of their part in securing the peaceful return of the two original groups, and to ensure that the peace would endure, clan Wulu, or a part thereof, was assigned as Defender of Wayu, while Béle Jawa (Munde) came to occupy the same status in relation to clan Keo, the descendants of Géra Ga'e. The arrangement provides a particularly clear instance of how Defenders may be created specifically in order to secure a peace following the cessation of hostilities. In addition, as Béle Jawa himself took a wife from Keo, this Defender (*ana tuku*) simultaneously became a wife-taker (*ana weta*) of the land grantor, thus replicating the general pattern in the domain of the elder Land Mother, Lape.

Also as part of the reconciliation, Keo and Wayu formally dissolved the boundaries between their adjacent territories, thereby creating the entity called Keo Wayu. As groups sharing a common domain, members of Keo and Wayu should not publicly acknowledge or speak openly of their former boundary (*nono bhondo, gae lange*, 'reveal borders, search for boundaries'). Sometimes classified as 'land siblings' (*ka'e ari tana watu*, I: 4: i), Wayu and Keo cultivators are thus free to use unassigned land anywhere within the combined territory, planting fields without permanent bounds which, in the conventional phrases, are described as being 'bordered (only) by stems of rice, bounded by stalks of maize' (*lange wai ku pae, bhondo wai toko yolo*).[2]

1. Tales of Géra

Besides Géra Ga'e, Keo villagers recognize an ancestor named Géra Lagha. Some say these are one and the same, others that the second name denotes a grandson or later descendant of the Ga'e sibling. The ambiguity of this relation thus parallels what was described earlier for Lape Ga'e and Lape Mére, while as will be shown later on, a similar situation obtains in regard to the Ga'e siblings Gewo and Lobo.

Partial distinctions between personages surnamed Ga'e and later ancestors partly identified with these invite a general observation. As sons of a common mother, 'Ga'e' identifies the original land dividers as a group of male siblings and hence as instances of the relational category of *ka'e ari* (I: 4: i). In contrast, other names, particularly other surnames, connect identically named male ancestors with one or more female siblings, whose children became principal Defenders of the male 'Land Mothers' and, at the same time, their *ana weta*

---

[1] Consistent with its status as a myth, the story does not explain how Keo and Wayu were returned to their homelands as viable groups if all the men of one and all the women of the other had been killed.

[2] Common rights are also expressed with the phrases *topo teka, taka le'e*, '(whoever has) a sharp parang and an efficient hoe (may simply begin clearing and planting)'.

('wife-takers'). The second series of names, denoting the starting point of several maternal lines of origin (I: 4: iv), thus situates apical male ancestors within a relationship of *meta naya*, or opposite sex siblings, so that Lape Mére, for example, is linked with sisters named Wea Mére, Ngoe Mére, and so on. Recalling the earlier analysis of *meta naya* and the derived relationship of affinal alliance as forms of social connection subsumed by *ka'e ari* in its most inclusive sense, the common conflation of Lape Ga'e and Lape Mére, or Géra Ga'e and Géra Lagha, may therefore be understood as a function of encompassment whereby the former term in each case is associated with a relational whole subsuming distinct parts. Expressing this another way, one might say that while the contrast is locally articulated with reference to different generations agnatically connected, it nevertheless bears on the hierarchical opposition of two fundamental forms of relationship.

Consistent with the foregoing, the same traditions concerning Géra sometimes specify the Keo ancestor's surname as Lagha and sometimes as Ga'e. In what follows, therefore, I refer to this personage simply as Géra. Earlier, reference was made to a myth connecting the Keo ancestor with a vent emerging in the present site of Kota Pau (II: 3: i). The myth describes how Géra entered a cave called Lia Opo ('Bat Cave'), on the coast near Ma'u Wo'o. His purpose was to catch small bats (*opo*) to consume as part of a ritual performed to relieve a lengthy dry season. Once he had entered the cave, however, the sea rose and he found himself unable to escape—a condition Keo describe as 'entrapped by spirits' (*nitu le'u*). Encountering a porcupine inside the cave, Géra managed to survive by following the animal's example of eating roots. After being trapped for two or three months, one day the porcupine began to ascend a vertical tunnel. Géra then followed the animal until he saw daylight and eventually emerged from the vent at Wuwu, now part of Kota Pau.

As noted, this spot lies some way north of the domain of the Keo ancestor, in the territory of Nuga Raga. Available evidence does not confirm the hypothesis that this might once have formed part, or a boundary, of Géra's domain. Nevertheless, that the myth may once have enshrined territorial limits is suggested by the location of Ma'u Wo'o (not a settlement but a location on the coast where torches, *wo'o*, were prepared for hunting bats) at the eastern limit of the territory of clan Keo, where it bounds on land claimed by clan Sawu, originally part of the domain of Gewo Ga'e.[3]

Further preserving the Keo ancestor's memory is Ena Géra ('Géra's Beach'), the name of a picturesque strand directly west of Ma'u Wo'o. Either at this place, or at a seaside location named Wuwu Lesu, near Ma'u Keo, Géra once contested with Dhoi Léwa, the notorious ancestor of the Bolo people (II:

---

[3] The precise boundary, established or affirmed following the resolution of a dispute between Sawu and Keo in the 1930s, is found at a spot named Sabi Saka, a short distance inland from Ma'u Wo'o and Lia Opo. Formerly marked with stones and now with a concrete pillar, Sabi Saka also forms the boundary of the modern administrative units (BI *desa*) of Sawu and Wolo Telu (which includes Keo, Munde, and Lui).

1: iv). Accepting Dhoi's challenge, Géra, a man used to the heat of the coast, attempted to spend the night in Bolo, up in the cooler highlands, sleeping outside in a livestock corral. But this test he failed utterly and, shivering in the night, he managed to survive only by warming himself by a fire. Responding to Géra's counter-challenge, Dhoi Léwa then endeavoured to withstand the heat of a shadeless day on the beach in Keo territory. This he managed to do by covering his head with coconut oil and a kind of plant (*tuka wayo*, unidentified).[4] Following one version of the myth, Géra's failure to provide a material reward for Dhoi's success eventuated in his temporary removal to Nanga Keo—a detail that evidently owes something to the tradition relating to Keo and Wayu as recounted above. The same source describes how, in order to resolve their disagreement, Géra gave Dhoi Léwa a piece of land near what is at present the coastal settlement of Ma'u Keo, as a place to produce salt and lime.

Other stories describe further strife between Géra and Dhoi Léwa. Owing to the treachery of Ua Leo, an ancestor of clan Suga in Suga Bhoja (II: 1: v), a protracted war broke out between the Keo and Bolo ancestors. In one encounter, Dhoi's forces wrapped themselves in palm fibre to gain protection from imaginary wasps controlled by Géra, but were decimated when Géra's troops, having learnt of this from Ua Leo, fired flaming arrows which stuck in the fibre causing severe burns. Later, Géra's side in turn suffered defeat. In order to restore good relations once and for all, Géra and Dhoi then agreed that they should become 'land siblings' (*ka'e tana, ari watu*) and military allies. By virtue of this relationship, people of Keo and Bolo (or Bolo Bale) may freely help themselves to garden produce, fruit, or coconuts if they become hungry or thirsty when travelling through one another's territories.[5] While not actually merging their territories, in regard to rights to products of the land this arrangement thus entails a dualistic reciprocity comparable to that obtaining between Keo and Wayu. What is more, in this instance the domain of Géra Ga'e, and the group claiming direct (agnatic) descent from that ancestor, are similarly linked with a population—Bolo (or Bolo Bale)—occupying part of the domain of Land Mother Lape.

2. The Other Village called Keo (Keo Bélo)

At present the name Keo Bélo serves to distinguish Géra's village from Keo Ondo, a settlement also simply called Keo. Bélo itself refers to a former village

---

[4] According to another version, related to me by a son of the last raja of Nage whose mother was from the clan of Géra Ga'e, it was Géra who was the victor. In this version, both men endeavoured to withstand the heat of the beach, Dhoi Léwa sitting for seven days and seven nights in the sand and Géra spending the same length of time without proper clothing at the top of a palm tree. Only Géra was able to endure, by covering himself with coconut oil from a container he had craftily hidden in his long hair.

[5] The relevant phrases are *la'a ka, lora inu; boko tolo poso, wonga tolo sowa*, 'to go eating, to travel drinking; plucking even young coconuts, picking even blossoms'.

located just landward of Keo, once occupied by an identically named group of Defenders. Some evidence, including the compounding of their names, suggests that the two villages may once have formed a double settlement. Their connection is further indicated by the formal designation of Keo Village: Ulu Bélo, Eko Tola, 'Head that is Bélo, Tail that is Tola'. Tola was the initial settlement of clan Béle Jawa, another Defender of clan Keo, now resident in Munde.

Having abandoned their village in the early part of the twentieth century, the Bélo people, now a remnant group, occupy just one house in the village of Keo. As indicated, 'Keo' also denotes a clan (*suku*), the principal inhabitants of Keo village comprising all agnatic descendants of Géra. Alternatively designated as clan Géra (Suku Géra), this grouping is in turn divided into two parts which are themselves classified as *suku*. Named after their apical ancestors, a pair of brothers born to a woman named Wale (reputedly from So'a), the segments are distinguished as Meo Wale and Wawo Wale, or alternatively as Suku Meo and Suku Wawo. Following different accounts, the brothers Meo and Wawo were born either five or nine generations after Géra. Houses agnatically derived from Meo Wale, the elder brother, are located in the tail section of Keo, thus seaward of the clan's sacrificial *kesi* tree, while houses descending from the younger brother, Wawo Wale, occupy the landward half. The pair are thus related in a way generally comparable to the two sections of clan Loka Poma in Lundu, as well as the two clans of Bolo in Muka and the two clans of Bale in Upper Pajo Mala. The two sections, or moieties, of 'clan' Keo are moreover allowed to intermarry, and have done so in several instances.[6]

In accordance with their derivation from elder and younger siblings, whenever a new *peo* is erected Meo Wale supplies the earth breaker (*ta koe*), and Wawo Wale the excavator (*ta kabhe*). While occasionally referred to as *ngapi* ('estates') as well as *suku* ('clans'), the two groups themselves each comprise three *ngapi*. As might be expected, it is the senior clan, Meo Wale, that is more closely associated with the apical ancestor. This is shown, for example, by the naming of the senior estate (*ngapi pu'u*) of Meo Wale—always the first to slaughter at collective sacrifices—as the *ngapi* of Géra (or more specifically, of Géra Lagha). Similarly, Keo people identify Meo Wale as the principal 'owner of the land' (*ngaya tana*) in Géra's domain, a status which is, of course, also accorded to the common ancestor of Meo and Wawo.

As the foregoing should suggest, the division of Keo into clans Meo Wale and Wawo Wale defines the dualistic order of the village. Although physically present in Keo, the single remaining house of the Bélo group holds no right to slaughter at Keo's *peo kesi*, nor does it possess a sacrificial instrument of its own. Describing themselves as no more than temporary residents in Keo, the Bélo people are as it were structurally invisible, being to all intents and

---

[6] I recorded five marriages where Wawo Wale, the junior group, had taken wives from Meo Wale. There were also two endogamous marriages within Wawo Wale, both involving members of different houses or estates.

purposes subsumed by the clan of Géra. Nominally at least, Bélo still holds the title of Defender (*ana tuku*) of Keo and retains rights to land granted by Keo ancestors, including the site of Bélo village, which they occupied until the 1930s. However, despite their Defender status, Bélo and Keo clansmen alike confirmed that, even in their own settlement, Bélo never possessed a *peo*, but sacrificed only with an upright stone (*ia*)—evidently in the manner of the Bale people in the former Kate Bale, and possibly clan Kota before their removal to Kota Pau.

The ancestors of Bélo were immigrants from the Boba region of eastern Ngadha. The first to come was Meo Pati, who is now mostly remembered as the owner of a cannon named Meo Bélo ('Cat of Bélo') which can still be seen, along with several others, at the abandoned site of Bélo's old village. As its form may suggest, 'Meo Bélo' also refers to the ancestor himself, who is said to have obtained the cannon, over a metre in length, from the Portuguese in exchange for seven slaves (three female and four male). Later, Meo Pati was joined by another man, also from Boba, named Laba Riwu. The clan therefore comprises two parts, sometimes specified as 'houses' (*sa'o*), which in their former, independent settlement probably coincided with two estates.

Apart from indications that Keo and Bélo once constituted a double settlement, evidence also suggests that Bélo may have been established earlier as a Defender of Keo than the Land Mother's other Defender, clan Béle Jawa in Munde. For one thing, although the Munde ancestor, too, was married to a woman of Keo, genealogies show Béle Jawa taking wives from Bélo in the earliest recorded marriages, but from Keo mostly in recent generations. Keo genealogies similarly list Bélo as the first remembered wife-taker of the Keo clan Wawo Wale.[7] Bélo's precedence is also implicit in the local characterization of Munde (Béle Jawa) not just as the Defender of Keo (or Géra), but also of Bélo.

In addition to Bélo, the village of Keo at present includes members of another remnant population, named Wio. Similarly lacking sacrificial status, and occupying a single dwelling in the landward part of the settlement near houses of clan Wawo Wale, the Wio people are fully subsumed by the Keo clan. How long they have been present in Keo Bélo I was unable to establish. In the distant past, Wio people are described as having occupied a village somewhere to the east of Munde. More completely designated as Ulu Wio ('Wio Head'), the settlement was destroyed long ago by Pogo Raga, sibling ancestors of clan Pajo (now in Pajo Réja; II: 5: i), which claims originally to have provided Wio with land and wives. Following their defeat, Wio people dispersed to various locations, but mostly to the region of Maja Mére

---

[7] Bélo has also given wives to Wawo Wale, but evidence suggests that it may only have been the group of Laba Riwu that has done so, while Wawo Wale has given wives only to descendants of Meo Pati. The Keo clan Meo Wale has also taken wives from Bélo. Genealogical information for both of these groups is, however, limited, especially by contrast to that for Wawo Wale.

(formerly Wolo Mogo), where they still claim rights to land and from where they may originally have come. Another Wio house is found in the village of Dhawe (II: 5: iv), where the father of the present leader of Wio in Keo Bélo was in fact born. Referring to the use of 'Wio' in various central Flores languages (Nage, Endenese, Ngadha) to name the island of Sumba, Keo often describe the Wio folk as ultimately having a Sumbanese origin. However, a more likely explanation of the designation is found in the former village name, Ulu Wio, which alludes to this place as an elevated site from where, gazing southward across the Sawu sea, it was sometimes possible to see the outline of Sumba, or fires burning on that island in the evening. In a similar vein, according to villagers in Lower Pau Lundu the seaward extremity of their earlier settlement (that is, 'Old Pau', II: 3: iii) was formally known as Eko Tei Wio, or 'Tail (where one can) see Wio (Sumba)'.[8]

Like Bélo, the small Wio group has no formal part in the constitution of the village of Keo (or Keo Bélo), in which respect it is significant that even their physical presence in Keo is sometimes denied. Formally, Keo village is thus dualistically composed of two agnatically related clans, the descendants of two brothers sharing a single male ancestor, Géra. At the same time, the village appears once to have participated in a more inclusive dualism, with the then extant village of Bélo. Comparable instances, where dualistic organization similarly confronts the *de facto* existence of third, fourth, and fifth groups, have already been described for Yoga and Bolo (II: 1: iii, iv). Further examples are reviewed later (II: 5).

Nowadays, many Keo people, including a Bélo family as well as people of clans Meo Wale and Wawo Wale, reside in the subsidiary settlement of Ma'u Keo. Located just a kilometre seaward of the main village, Ma'u Keo—now a rather dispersed collection of dwellings mostly disposed along the motor road running east to west along the coast—is clearly visible from the 'tail' end of Keo Bélo. Also in the vicinity are a few residences belonging to Munde and Lui people, as well as a number of Endenese and Buginese. In regard to its relatively large concentration of Muslims (who include members of the two Keo clans) and proximity to wet rice fields, Ma'u Keo resembles other coastal hamlets (*ma'u*), including Ma'u Bajo and Ma'u Wayu, a coastal extension of Wulu Wayu (see Section 4 below). Worth mentioning in this connection are genealogies indicating that the Keo people have for a long time maintained fairly extensive affinal connections with coastal populations to the east. In particular, genealogies show that clan Wawo Wale has taken wives in at least seven instances from Ma'u Ara in eastern Keo, beginning two generations after

---

[8] 'Wio' further occurs in other central Flores place-names, including Wio Wolo Ndoa, a village near Ngera and Léwa in eastern Keo, and Wolo Wio, located near Bajawa in the Ngadha region (see I: 1: i, ii). Various Nage uses of 'Wio' (for example, the mythological female epithet Bu'e Wio, as well as *sada wio* and *tuba wio*, referring to kinds of textiles and spears), expand the comparative context in interesting ways, but owing to lack of space cannot be discussed here.

the ancestor named Wawo Wale and about six generations before adults living at present.

3. Munde

Situated about 150 metres landward of Keo, the village of Munde is yet another settlement comprising just two clans. The older is the previously mentioned Béle Jawa. The younger clan is Welu, named after its village of origin to the east (in the present *desa* of Kéli).

On becoming established in the domain of Géra, clan Béle Jawa was first settled at a site named Tola, a short distance seaward of Keo Bélo. For this reason the clan is also known as clan Tola and their sacrificial instrument (*peo*), erected in the village of Munde, is called Peo Tola.[9] Munde people described their former village as lacking a *peo*; but this seems odd in relation to the naming of the present sacrificial instrument. Although in the stricter sense, Munde ('Citrus Tree', thus a botanical toponym) designates their present village, outsiders especially often refer to clan Béle Jawa as clan Munde (*suku* Munde), thus providing another instance of the identification of an older (or oldest) resident group with an entire settlement.

Also noteworthy in this connection is a food taboo observed by natal women of clan Béle Jawa and by wives of male members, a breach of which can result in ulcers on the tongue and breasts. Describing the prohibition as applying generally to 'round things', my initial informant, a recognized expert in local culture from outside Munde, claimed that the ban included eggs, aubergines, coconut flesh, and citrus fruits (*munde*).[10] The obvious inference, that the prohibition derives from the name of Béle Jawa's present village and the clan's especial association with this name, was, however, later contradicted by Munde people who claimed that the taboo did not apply to citrus fruits. On the other hand, I was unable to discover a myth or other rationalization for the prohibition.

Reflecting a theme encountered in histories of other clans, the Béle Jawa people are described as fleeing their initial settlement of Tola owing to an infestation of caterpillars (*ngota*). They then moved to a site named Wolo Pau Bhaya ('Pale Mango Hill') just landward—above the head (*ulu*)—of their present village. Alluding to this relative disposition, in formal speech the present Munde is accordingly designated as Ulu Pau Bhaya, Eko Bélo, the second phrase referring of course to the location of old Bélo a short way seaward. Once established in Munde, clan Béle Jawa was joined by the second clan,

---

[9] In the same vein, a valuable golden chain that once belonged to the Béle Jawa people was called Gala Tola (*gala* is the snake *Dendrelaphis pictus*).

[10] Keo further assert that if a woman from another clan suddenly stops eating these foods, she may be suspected of having an affair with a man of Béle Jawa. Béle Jawa men, as well as women, are also forbidden to consume areca nuts (*yeu*), although individuals can avoid this restriction by performing a rite. I do not know whether the same can be done with regard to the foods mentioned above.

Welu. The Welu people had suffered defeat at the hands of mercenaries (*ata aku*) led by a female warrior known as Bongo Bu'e Keo (Bongo, young woman of Keo), a kinswoman, possibly a sister or daughter, of Géra Ga'e. After abandoning their homes in the easterly village of Welu and its coastal subsidiary, Ma'u Welu, the Welu people first moved to Bélo. Later, Béle Jawa invited them to take up residence in the village of Munde, where the older clan arranged a grant of land—comprising a stereotypical set of seven plots—from the Land Mother, clan Géra or Keo. Until quite recently, Welu people in Munde recognized a relation of reciprocal kinship (*ka'e ari*) with clanmates who remained in, or perhaps returned to, Ma'u Welu. This, however, was discontinued in 1965, after the latter failed to invite the Welu people in Munde to a buffalo sacrifice.

In accordance with Welu's initial reception by the Bélo people, members of both Welu and Béle Jawa claimed that, originally, the clan was assigned as Defender of Bélo, even though Welu obtained no permanent right to land from Bélo. Later, when the Welu people moved to Munde, they were redesignated as Defenders of Béle Jawa, or as this is also expressed 'Defenders of Munde' (*tuku Munde*). Apparently referring to the source of their lands, people in Keo Bélo also describe them as Defenders of Keo (or Géra). Marriage patterns, however, are arguably more in accord with the first designation. Only in one recent instance has Welu taken a wife from Keo, while in another marriage between these two, Keo was the wife-taker. In contrast, Welu men have regularly married women of Béle Jawa, from their arrival in Munde until the present day.

Since coming together in Munde, clans Béle Jawa and Welu have always maintained separate *peo*. The instruments have always taken the form of stone columns (*peo watu*). Although such columns are sometimes erected to replace sacrificial trees (as, for example, in Yoga, Lower Pajo Mala, and Bale Wolo), Munde villagers assured me they have never employed 'living *peo*' (*peo muri*). Like the paired sacrificial instruments encountered in Nua Nage and Keo Ondo, the stone *peo* of Béle Jawa and Welu stand side by side in the centre of the village plaza, atop a single pedestal of stones. The sacrificial instrument of the older clan is placed towards the 'right' (*mena*) while Welu's *peo* is on the 'left' (*rale*). This relative disposition does not, however, accord with the arrangement of the two clans' houses. Houses of Béle Jawa are all located in the landward part of the village, whereas those of Welu occupy the seaward end.

Consistent with the status of Keo (clan Géra) as grantor of territory to both clans, Béle Jawa people describe their stone *peo* as having been planted by Géra, that is, by the Keo ancestor himself. The apparent anachronism in all probability reflects an identification of the apical ancestor with the derivative clan, also named Géra. In the same vein, Munde people described Keo as earth breaker (*ta koe*) in respect of the *peo* of both Béle Jawa and Welu, in consideration of which the Land Mother was reputedly provided with a parang (*topo*). The complementary function of excavator (*ta kabhe*) was then carried out by the owner of the *peo*, clan Béle Jawa or Welu, as the case might be. Although these arrangements evidently refer to a fairly distant past—for what they are worth, the genealogies show Béle Jawa arriving six or seven generations ago, and Welu's apical ancestor (Raga Mogi) some four generations ago—they nevertheless recall the procedure described earlier, with regard to clan Guyu Wolo's planting a sacrificial *kesi* tree provided by its Land Mother, clan Pau in Kota Pau (II: 3: i).

While there is reason to believe that Keo and Bélo formed a double settlement prior to Bélo's decline and informal incorporation in modern Keo Bélo, it is less certain whether Keo and Munde can be construed as constituting a pairing of this sort at present. Although villagers' statements were equivocal in this regard, one indication that they might be so considered is the simultaneous occurrence of 'Bélo' in the formal names of the two villages (see Appendix 2). Thus designating the 'head' of Keo (or Keo Bélo) and the 'tail' of Munde, the shared name suggests a conceptual contiguity of the two villages. One also encounters the expression 'Munde Keo'; but this seems to be merely a disambiguating term, distinguishing Munde from several other places in central Flores with this botanical toponym. Other instances of this pattern are 'Munde Lui', which alludes to Munde's location just 200 metres or so seaward (more precisely southwest) of Lui, and indeed 'Keo Bélo', which at present functions mainly to distinguish Keo, the village of Géra Ga'e, from the village of Keo Ondo. Somewhat more difficult to define is the designation 'Keo Tola'. Since Tola is still used to refer to Munde (though more particularly the senior Munde clan, Béle Jawa), the expression again suggests a pairing of Munde with Keo, as some informants confirmed. Yet 'Keo Tola' is also used to specify clan Keo in Keo Bélo, or indeed the latter village itself. Regardless of how this expression and 'Munde Keo' are to be understood, the fact that Munde is some 150 metres landward of Keo, with Bélo moreover intervening, rather stretches the definition of a double settlement. On the other hand, since the former Tola was actually located just seaward of Keo, the usage just possibly reflects an earlier pairing of adjacent villages that is no longer evident.

Both Keo and Munde exemplify single villages (*nua*) displaying a relatively simple form of binary order. Keo comprises two divisions deriving respectively from an elder and a younger brother. Munde consists of an older group later joined by a more recent arrival that became its Defender and wife-taker. In its former independence, Bélo too was dually constituted, being composed of segments deriving from the same geographical, if not agnatic, source, the region of Boba.

4. Wulu Wayu (or Bo'a Ora)

Since some time between 1910 and 1920, the Wulu Wayu people have inhabited a village named Bo'a Ora ('Middle Hamlet'), a site named after its central location in relation to the former villages of Wulu Wayu, Watu Wae, and Sina Wolo. Old Wulu Wayu occupied a more elevated site just southwest of Bo'a Ora. As its binomial designation should suggest, the settlement mainly comprised two clans, Wayu and Wulu. Further included was a third group, Loga Wena Wayu ('Loga Beneath Wayu'), a long-time associate of Wayu. After moving to Bo'a Ora, Wulu and Wayu were joined by people of Sina Wolo and Watu Wae, who then abandoned their earlier settlements bearing the same names.

The precedence of Wulu Wayu, and more specifically clan Wayu, extends to the entire territory occupied by all five groups. Accordingly, the present Bo'a Ora is still alternatively designated as Wulu Wayu, and in formal speech is named Ulu Wulu, Eko Wayu ('Head that is Wulu, Tail that is Wayu'). As in other instances, the last expression describes the location of houses of Wulu and Wayu respectively in their earlier village, and to a lesser extent in the present one as well.[11]

Tracing descent to a sister of Lape Mére named Menge Mére (see Fig. 6), clan Wayu is a Defender and early wife-taker of the senior Land Mother. As noted, clan Wulu was assigned as Defender of Wayu following the resolution of Wayu's dispute with the Keo people. A segment of clan Wulu in Nua Nage, itself originally a branch of the clan Pata centred in the village of Wulu (II: 6: ii), the Wulu people then came to share a village and a *peo* with Wayu. At present, the immigrant group is distinguished from Wulu in Nua Nage—also specified as Wulu Wawo ('Wulu Above', referring to its higher, more landward location) and Wulu Dhaga (from its association with clan Dhaga)—as Wulu Wayu, the name that also denotes the social and territorial unity principally comprising clans Wayu and Wulu.[12] The usage is of particular interest as it is actually Wayu, regularly described as the 'original' (*tenge*) group, which is the more closely identified with the settlement as a whole. In the latter context, 'Wulu Wayu' is of course comparable to 'Wulu Dhaga', 'Céla Bajo', and other names by which separable groups, or pairs of clans, are designated as local unities.

An unspecified number of generations after Wayu was joined by Wulu, Watu Wae, and Sina Wolo were named as additional Defenders of Wayu, occupying separate, satellite villages in the vicinity of Wulu Wayu. Although the circumstances in which this occurred remain unclear, one version of the local history describes how Sina Wolo and Watu Wae were appointed Defenders of Wayu following the reconciliation with Keo, at which time clan Wulu was already Wayu's Defender. Yet several factors (including the part attributed to

[11] Of four Wulu houses, two are at the landward extremity. All Wayu houses, of which there are nine, are seaward of these, and mostly in the seaward half. The most landward house belongs to Sina Wolo, while another house of this clan occupies a middle position in the *rale* ('left') row. At present, Watu Wae has no houses in Bo'a Ora.

[12] In accordance with its agnatic derivation, one also encounters affinal genealogies where Wulu in Wulu Wayu is specified as 'clan Wulu Dhaga' (II: 1: i). At present, Wulu in Nua Nage—that is, Wulu Dhaga—is represented by a single adult man who is an adoptee from Wulu in Wulu Wayu.

the Wulu ancestor, Mosa Ruja, in the affair) cast doubt on this variant of the tradition.

The *peo* found in the present village of Bo'a Ora is a stone column, a replacement of a similar sacrificial instrument that formerly stood in old Wulu Wayu. Unlike some other villages where a major or minor Land Mother shares a *peo* with one or more Defenders, in Bo'a Ora, as in the previous Wulu Wayu, both the positions of earth breaker and excavator (*ta koe* and *ta kabhe*) are held by the oldest clan, Wayu. Wulu is then the next to sacrifice, followed by Watu Wae, Sina Wolo and, finally, Loga Wena Wayu. All accounts agree that in their former, identically named settlements, neither Watu Wae nor Sina Wolo possessed *peo* of their own. In this respect, then, they were comparable to clan Bélo, the Defender of Keo in Keo Bélo, which similarly lacked a *peo*. Whereas the Bélo people sacrificed independently by employing a single stone *ia*, however, in the present instance local commentators suggested that before joining Wayu and Wulu in Bo'a Ora, Watu Wae and Sina Wolo may have continued to slaughter in their places of origin—respectively the villages of Wae and Bolo Yoga. Since the two sets of migrants were granted land rights within the domain of Wayu independently of their senior segments, however, this reconstruction may be doubted. Suggestive in this regard is the presence in Bo'a Ora of an upright stone *ia* belonging to Watu Wae, reputedly brought to the new settlement from their earlier village.

The former site of Watu Wae was located about 500 metres to the north of Bo'a Ora, near Ae Kéla, a hamlet mostly occupied by people from Keo Ondo. Hailing from the village of Wae in southwestern Nage, the Watu Wae people were originally called Katu or Katu Wae. Katu ('to enclose, envelop' but also the tree *Albizia procera*) was the name of the main body of the clan that remained in Wae. The history of Wayu might suggest that Watu Wae's move to Wulu Wayu, which was led by two men named Lu'u and Poso, was somehow connected with clan Wayu's temporary removal to Wayu Pea, near the village of Wae, following their hostilities with Keo. But this I was unable to confirm.

Formerly inhabiting a village to the west of Bo'a Ora, Sina Wolo is named after clan Sina in Bolo Yoga (now Kuyu Wulu), from where its founders derive. The element 'Wolo' ('Hill') evidently describes the hilltop location of the settlement. Yoga people described Sina Wolo as descending from an ancestor named Talo Pajo, a brother of the Yoga ancestors Babi and Moa, following the breakup of Bolo Yoga caused by the war between the principal clans Yoga and Bolo (II: 1: iii; see also Fig. 6). How closely this interpretation might accord with other village histories is, however, now difficult to determine, owing to a paucity of genealogical particulars partly attributable to the present extinction of Sina Wolo people tracing descent in an unbroken male line to any founding ancestor.

The combination of Wayu and Wulu, later augmented by two other Defenders of Wayu, Watu Wae and Sina Wolo, has resulted in a quadripartite order comprising two pairs of clans comparable to what is encountered in other villages. Yet, qualifying this configuration is the presence of a fifth group, the previously mentioned Loga Wena Wayu. Now virtually extinct, this group of Loga appears to have been present in old Wulu Wayu well before the removal to Bo'a Ora and the amalgamation with Watu Wae and Sina Wolo.[13] Agnatic ties link Loga Wena Wayu with the clan Loga (also called Bindi Loga), established in the village of Pajo (now Pajo Réja, II: 5: i). The most detailed accounts specify the group as deriving from ancestral siblings named together as Laba Riwu. As is typical of Keo genealogical representations, Laba, the younger of the pair, was childless, so that Loga Wena Wayu traces agnatic descent exclusively from the elder brother, Riwu. Genealogies further record the ancestors as taking up residence with the Wayu people just two generations after the time of the Ga'e siblings.

Whether it is merely coincidental that 'Laba Riwu' also occurs as the name of an ancestor of the clan Bélo, now in Keo Bélo, I was unable to clarify. Like the Bélo people, who hail from Boba, Loga Wena Wayu also recognizes a westerly derivation in the Ngadha region.[14] One of my most knowledgeable genealogical sources describes Laba and Riwu as the sons of a man called Jaja Rau, also the forebear of Loga people in Pajo Réja, who resided in Weso in the Ae Mére region. Local historians further describe the group as descendants of seamen from a place called Weso, who washed ashore near Ma'u Wayu, the coastal settlement belonging to Wayu. Whatever the details, Loga eventually came to occupy a single house, appropriately located in the seaward section of Wulu Wayu next to houses of clan Wayu.

In accordance with its apparently lengthy residence in western Keo, Loga Wena Wayu is spoken of as the first Defender of Wayu. From this, one must infer that the group preceded even clan Wulu. Yet, significantly perhaps, Loga receives no mention in the historical tradition that explains clan Wulu's assumption of the status of Defender of Wayu. Since Loga Wena Wayu is now specified as the last to slaughter in Wulu Wayu (or Bo'a Ora), the group was evidently replaced long ago by Wulu as Wayu's principal Defender. What is more, Loga has become virtually subsumed as an estate (*ngapi*) within Wayu, and in fact is sometimes described as such. Supporting this is the group's complete name: 'Loga Beneath Wayu'.

The present Wulu Wayu may, therefore, be construed as a recent amalgamation of two pairs of clans—or an initial pair plus two formerly separate groups—thus resulting in a four-part composition. Probably representing a remnant of a former duality, a fifth group is subsumed by the oldest clan and

[13] The patrimony of Loga Wena Wayu is now held by a man of Ma'u Keo who traces descent from Loga entirely through females.

[14] Accounts differ as to whether the homeland was Weso near Ae Mére in western Ngadha, a settlement of the same name in eastern Ngadha, or a location called Lia Loga—which might account for the name—also in the vicinity of Ae Mére. Arndt (1954: 360–1) mentions a Ngadha clan named 'Veso' (Weso) deriving from Ae Mére and resident in Boba during the early twentieth century.

so does not formally count as an additional component. Nevertheless, villagers usually describe Bo'a Ora (or Wulu Wayu) as comprising five named clans, thus recalling what one sometimes encounters for example in Lundu and Pau (Lower Pau Lundu). There is nothing to indicate that Wulu Wayu has ever formed half of a double settlement, or that Wayu has ever shared a village with one or more other groups possessing a separate *peo*. At the same time, the ancient territorial connection between Wayu and Keo, of course, exemplifies a dualistic relation of a far more inclusive kind.

For the sake of comparison, mention should finally be made of affinal connections between Wayu and its four Defenders. Although this is partly attributable to a paucity of detailed genealogies, the evidence does not indicate a pronounced pattern of asymmetric alliance coinciding with the relation of Land Mother and Defender in this territory. Mostly recent marriages reveal that Wayu has, indeed, given wives to Wulu, Watu Wae, and Sina Wolo; yet only a single marriage is recorded in each instance. Moreover, while Wulu has taken one wife from Wayu, it has actually given women in a further five marriages. Wulu has also provided Watu Wae with two wives, and taken one from Sina Wolo (whose genealogy only provides details of two unions within Bo'a Ora). Owing to the extinction of the original agnatic group, no genealogical information could be obtained for Loga Wena Wayu.

5

The Domain of Gewo and the Land of Pogo Raga

Although larger than the ancestral territory of Géra Ga'e, the original domain of Gewo Ga'e does not approach in size that of Lape, the eldest of the Ga'e siblings. Gewo's domain lies mostly inland, to the north of lands claimed by Géra. Originally, the territory extended to the sea, as far as Cape Loya (Ngalu Loya) near Ma'u Ponggo. Referring also to its northern limit, a stream called Lowo Koto, the entire domain is thus formally designated as Ulu Lowo Koto, Eko Ngalu Loya. Over the years, parts of this domain, including much of the coastal section, have been lost in wars. Although some were eventually returned as a reconciliatory gesture, several areas currently held by Gewo's agnatic descendants are bordered by lands retained by the victors, among them inhabitants of Pau Lundu and Suga Bhoja.

Among the several villages included in the original domain, the most prominent are Pajo Réja, Sawu (or Sawu Obo), Nua Muri, and Dhawe. Deriving exclusively in the male line from Gewo Ga'e, the Land Mother and principal clan in this region is Pajo. Until the 1930s, clan Pajo resided in a village of the same name together with a second clan, Bindi Loga. Later, Pajo villagers removed to a new site, a short distance to the west, where they were joined by the inhabitants of two other villages, Réja and Sopi Sabe. The move was encouraged by the Dutch colonial administration. There had been much sickness and many deaths in Old Pajo, which the authorities attributed to the narrow, restricted site bounded by steep cliffs that allowed little possibility for expansion. In a process culminating early in the twentieth century, therefore, what at one time had been three independent groups occupying separate, though neighbouring, settlements, Pajo, Réja, and Sopi Sabe, eventually merged to form a single village, Pajo Réja. Whereas the three had once maintained separate *peo*, all living *kesi* trees, in this consolidation they further came to share a single sacrificial instrument, albeit one in regard to which Pajo has retained the predominant position.

1. Pajo Réja

Like the earlier village of Pajo, the present Pajo Réja is situated about two kilometres to the east of Pajo Mala (II: 2), at a rather higher elevation. Old Pajo was located landward of the old village of Réja. As Sopi Sabe was situated between Réja and Pajo, the three villages occupied a single, almost continuously inhabited, ridge of hills. The arrangement thus recalls what was described earlier for the former settlements of Yoga, Tunga, and Bolo, now realigned in Yoga (Kuyu Wulu) and Bolo (Muka). The relative disposition of the three groups is largely maintained in the present settlement. Still known as *nua* Pajo (Pajo 'village', or 'village section'), the landward half of Pajo Réja contains houses of both Pajo and the co-resident clan Bindi Loga, while in the seaward part one finds the houses of clans Réja and Sopi Sabe. Although sometimes referred to as 'Sabe Réja' ('Sabe' being a contraction of 'Sopi Sabe'), the precedence of clan Réja in this half of Pajo Réja is indicated by the more common designation of the site as *nua* Réja. In formal speech, moreover, villagers refer to the entire settlement as Ulu Pajo, Eko Réja ('Head that is Pajo, Tail that is Réja), a designation which, like the common name Pajo Réja, leaves Sopi Sabe as it were submerged. In this respect, then, the present Pajo Réja is represented as comprising two parts, the more junior of which, Réja, is itself composed dualistically.

1.1 Pajo

Underlining its present status as a single village, Pajo Réja possesses a single *peo kesi*. Until its destruction some years ago, the sacrificial tree stood in Pajo's section of the village. In addition, the two principal ceremonial positions belong exclusively to groups resident in Pajo's half of the settlement, with clan Pajo claiming the status of earth breaker (*ta koe*), and Bindi Loga that of excavator (*ta kabhe*). Réja and Sopi Sabe also possess the right to sacrifice at this *peo*. Yet, as in similar cases elsewhere, by virtue of their amalgamation with Pajo these groups have forfeited an earlier ceremonial and therefore political independence. The overall superordination of clan Pajo—and *nua* Pajo—in this total configuration is further reflected in the common practice of referring, in affinal genealogies and elsewhere, to the whole of Pajo Réja simply as Pajo.

Although Pajo is recognized as Land Mother over the entire domain of Gewo, the clan's original territory is commonly designated as the Land of Pogo (and) Raga (Tana Pogo Raga), referring to a more recent ancestral pair. Specified as great-great grandsons (SSSS) of the Ga'e sibling, Pogo Raga's relation to Gewo Ga'e is thus comparable to that of Lape Mére and Lape Ga'e, and Géra Lagha and Géra Ga'e. At the same time, perhaps because it explicitly denotes a pair, the compound name Pogo Raga seems never to be conflated with Gewo, in contrast to what sometimes obtains in the other two cases. As offspring of different mothers married to a polygynous father, Pogo and Raga were actually half-brothers. Providing yet another instance of the pervasive representation, the younger half-brother, whose full name was Raga Séko, left no descendants; hence clan Pajo more exactly descends from the elder of the pair, Pogo Poi. Having become transformed in colonial times to 'Ponggo', it is Pogo's name that designates the coastal settlement of Ma'u Ponggo, now the administrative centre of the district that subsumes all of the area of the present study.

Residing with Pajo in the landward half of Pajo Réja, the second clan, Bindi Loga, represents a merging of two formerly independent Defender clans.

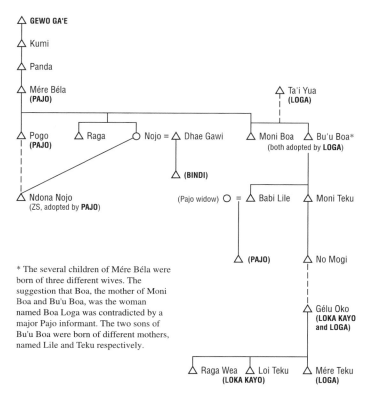

* The several children of Mére Béla were
born of three different wives. The
suggestion that Boa, the mother of Moni
Boa and Bu'u Boa, was the woman
named Boa Loga was contradicted by a
major Pajo informant. The two sons of
Bu'u Boa were born of different mothers,
named Lile and Teku respectively.

FIG. 8. Genealogy of Gewo Ga'e

Sometimes Loga and Bindi are described as two *ngapi* of a single clan; but this is to be understood in the sense of 'co-resident clan segments' rather than 'estates' or sacrificial units. Indeed, according to different methods of reckoning, Loga itself comprises two or four estates, also specified as 'trunk houses' (*sa'o pu'u*). At present comprising just a single house (*sa'o*) and estate, Bindi derives from a man named Dhae Gawi of clan Bindi (or Bindi Wae) in Lower Pajo Mala who married a Pajo woman named Nojo Séko, the full sister of the Pajo ancestor Raga. A son of this couple then perpetuated an heirless Pajo. Having only daughters, the above-mentioned Pogo Poi adopted (*ghawe*) his half-sister's son, Ndona Nojo, as his legitimate son and successor (see Fig. 8). As an early wife-taker, the segment of Bindi deriving from Dhae Gawi was granted an area of land and assigned as Defender of Pajo. Taking up residence with clan Pajo, in recognition of their affinal alliance Bindi was then also given a *dheyo* tree *peo*, complementing Pajo's *peo kesi*.

Some evidence suggests that clan Bindi—or their predecessors in their original village of Guyu Wula (II: 2: i)—may have begun taking wives from clan
Pajo at a rather earlier time. The headman of Pajo identified Boa, the wife of
the Bindi ancestor Maga, as a woman of Pajo whose full name was Boa Loga,
a claim not denied by people of Bindi Wae in Lower Pajo Mala. This identification, however, contradicts other information specifying Boa Loga as a wife of
the Pajo ancestor Mére Béla (see Fig. 8), and, furthermore, as a natal member
of Loga.[1] Whatever the details of their possible earlier alliance, at some point
Bindi ceased to maintain their sacrificial *dheyo* tree and began to share a *kesi*
tree *peo* with Pajo. Although it was never exactly stated, this may have occurred
when Bindi merged with Loga, a group established before Bindi in the territory of Pajo. As noted in the preceding chapter, Loga is agnatically related to
Loga Wena Wayu, the virtually extinct group established until recently in Bo'a
Ora (Wulu Wayu). Genealogies recorded in Pajo give the first ancestor of Loga
in Pajo Réja as Lako Sigho, a brother of the Loga Wena Wayu ancestors, Laba
and Riwu, who arrived in the vicinity of Pajo two generations after the time of
Gewo Ga'e.

Upon their arrival, the Loga people were granted land just above the 'head'
(*ulu*) of Pajo's original village, in an area which then came to be known as Ulu
Loga ('Head that is Loga', 'Loga Head'). Whether Loga initially founded a
separate village, perhaps thereby forming a double settlement with Pajo, is
doubtful. Pajo statements suggest that Loga has long shared a single village
with the Land Mother clan. According to a specific description, which implicitly referred to a time before Loga's amalgamation with Bindi, in Pajo's
former village Loga houses always stood on the left (*rale*) side of the settlement
facing houses of clan Pajo on the right (*mena*).[2] Referring to the name Ulu
Loga, and alluding to the sense of *ulu* ('head') as 'earlier, first (in time)', Loga
people, on the other hand, told me that Loga preceded not only Bindi but also
Pajo. Invoked in this context was the selection of Ulu Loga as the name of the
desa (administrative unit) which includes Pajo Réja. This choice largely reflects
the recent economic and political prominence of certain Loga men, one of
whom was appointed administrative headman of what was to become *desa* Ulu
Loga when the name was selected. People of clan Pajo agreed to the name, but
explain its temporal implication as a reference to Loga's status as an early
Defender of their own clan.

As direct agnatic descendants of the Ga'e sibling Gewo, the precedence of
clan Pajo is, however, scarcely in dispute. What is more, the present Loga

---

[1] Since Loga is a common female name, as the surname of Boa Loga, it is not a definite indication of clan affiliation. I also recorded Ine Loga, 'Mother Loga', as the name of an ancestress of clan Loga; but I was unable to confirm
whether this referred to the same woman as Boa Loga.

[2] This arrangement is still discernible in the present village, in regard to the present dualism of Pajo and Bindi
Loga. Eight of ten Pajo houses are thus located on the right (*mena*) side, while the same number of Bindi Loga houses
are found on the left (*rale*). Loga's association with the *rale* direction is consistent with the location of Ulu Loga, not
just landward of Pajo's old village, but also to the west (here identified as *rale*) of the stream Lowo Koto.

people trace descent partly from an adoptee from Pajo, and, indeed, have been without male issue and thus in need of external replacement more than once in their history. Two generations after the first Loga ancestor, a childless Loga man named Ta'i Yua was succeeded by two Pajo brothers named Moni Boa and Bu'u Boa. According to one account, Ta'i Yua did not formally adopt an heir, a representation which implies that Loga simply died out and that its estate was taken over by the two Pajo men. Only the younger of these, Bu'u Boa, produced a son. The son, No Mogi, was, however, abnormal and incapable of marrying, and so was in turn replaced as the Loga heir by a man from the village of Loka Kayo (see Section 5 below). Named Gélu Oko, this man continued to be recognized as an heir within his natal group. Bu'u Boa's first son, Babi Lile, moreover had children only by the widow of a Pajo man, who were thus reckoned as members of Pajo. Hence Loga was in effect continued by a junior line of the Land Mother clan (see Fig. 8). In addition, the present holders of the Loga estate are agnatically related to men claiming membership of Loka Kayo. Thus Loga barely exists any longer as a distinct group; and to the extent that it does it is plainly subordinate, through recognized agnatic ties and in other ways, to clan Pajo.[3]

Apart from providing a useful illustration of a fairly regular non-agnatic perpetuation and hence constitution of Keo clans, the foregoing genealogical excursion reveals an original connection among all components of the old village of Pajo, in the common ancestor Mére Béla of clan Pajo. According to the most detailed genealogical texts, this ancestor, the SSS of Gewo Ga'e, married at least three women. Relations of precedence follow the seniority of these wives and the birth order of their children. Thus, the Land Mother and principal clan, Pajo, descends from Pogo, the son of the first wife; Bindi descends from Nojo, a daughter of the second wife; while Loga partly derives from a later wife (the mother of Bu'u Boa). These relations further illuminate a simplistic yet popular representation whereby Pogo (the elder half-brother) and Raga (the childless younger half-brother) are described as the ancestors of Pajo and Bindi Loga respectively. Probably of relevance here is Raga's status as full brother of Nojo, the wife of Dhae Gawi, and hence as wife-giver of the Bindi ancestor. At the same time, of course, as a wife-taker Bindi is encompassed by Pajo, just as Loga is subsumed by the senior clan as both a derivative group and (contrary to some of their own claims) a later arrival in Land Mother Pajo's domain.

1.2 Réja

Resembling the internal constitution of Pajo, the seaward half of Pajo Réja—the part distinguished as *nua* Réja or Sabe Réja—includes two clans: Réja and

---

[3] This refers mainly to Loga's principal house and estate. Other people identified as Loga descend from an outsider of unknown derivation who joined the group three generations ago.

Sopi Sabe. Each represents an amalgamation of two formerly separate groups. Much like clans Kota, Bolo, and others encountered in previous chapters, clan Réja combines two agnatically unrelated segments (*ngapi*), themselves sometimes referred to as 'clans' (*suku*). Named after their apical ancestors, the two groups are called Sa'e Bapu and Koju Ko'u. Bapu (alternatively pronounced as Bapi) and Ko'u denote their respective villages of origin, both located in the vicinity of Ende. Ko'u actually refers to Ndetu Ko'u, also the homeland of the Munde ancestor, Béle Jawa (II: 4: ii; iii); and it is from this place in particular that the two Réja ancestors are said to have begun their journey by sea to western Keo.

Owing to their association with the sea, upon their arrival the Pajo ancestor Pogo (or Pogo Raga) assigned Réja as Defenders of the southernmost, coastal part of Pajo's territory. Settling initially at Nanga Réja (*nanga*, 'estuary, bay'), just east of the present coastal settlement of Ma'u Ponggo, the Réja people gradually moved inland, successively occupying at least two later sites named Réja before their merger with Pajo in the 1930s. Historical circumstances suggest that Réja's movement from the coast may have been occasioned by the arrival of the Sawu people (see Section 3 below). The original association of the Réja ancestors with the sea finds further expression in a folk etymology of the group name. Recalling the dual composition of the clan itself, the name is locally analysed as a fusion of two words, *re* and *ja*, denoting two varieties of ocean waves.[4] Whatever its linguistic validity, the interpretation attests to the pervasive dualism of Keo representations, and particularly to the common conception of binary social forms as combinations of similar, yet distinct parts.

While residing separately, the Réja people formally designated their village as Ulu Ko'u, Eko Réja. Planting a sacrificial *kesi* tree, the two segments divided ritual positions, with Sa'e Bapu taking the part of earth breaker, and Koju Ko'u that of excavator. As accords with these assignments, the headman for all of Réja is normally derived from the Sa'e group, an arrangement that further agrees with the implicit identification of this segment with the name Réja suggested by one half of the settlement's formal name (Eko Réja). From this it might also be inferred that descendants of Koju Ko'u once resided in the landward part, or 'head', of the village (named Ko'u Head), while the senior segment, Sa'e Bapu, had their houses in the 'tail' section ('Réja Tail'). The arrangement would further agree with the association of the entirety of Réja with the sea and the seaward part of the domain of Pogo Raga. Descriptions of older settlements of Réja, however, provide no clear support for this spatial contrast; for these locate houses of Sa'e Bapu on the right (*mena*) side of the village, and those of Koju Ko'u on the left (*rale*). In the present Pajo Réja, by

---

[4] The first term refers to a wave as it rolls gradually and swells upwards, and the second to a wave that breaks, thus a white head (cf. the BI distinctions *ombak tolak* and *ombak tarik*, and *gelombang* and *ombak yang pecah*).

contrast, Réja houses are all located on the *rale* side, the *mena* side then being occupied entirely by houses of the clan Sopi Sabe.[5]

1.3 Sopi Sabe

Whether Réja or Sopi Sabe were earlier established as Defenders of Land Mother Pajo is equivocal. Genealogies show Sopi Sabe as one of Pajo's earliest wife-givers; thus a daughter-in-law of Céme Poi, a brother of Pogo Poi, was a woman of Sopi Sabe. But while this suggests that the clan has been associated with Pajo for a long time, the affinal tie is, of course, contrary to what Keo otherwise describe as characterizing the relation of Land Mother and Defender. In contrast, clan Réja is by far the most regular of Pajo's wife-takers. Réja men appear as husbands in nearly a quarter of women's marriages recorded in Pajo genealogies, including early unions such as that of the BD of the ancestor Pogo. Similarly, the genealogy of Koju Ko'u, one of the two *ngapi* of Réja, lists Pajo as wife-giver in five of fifteen men's marriages.[6]

As a combination of two estates (*ngapi*) distinguished as Sopi and Sabi, also sometimes described as 'clans' (*suku*), Sopi Sabe is organized identically to clan Réja. In this case, too, the segments are named after male ancestors, a pair more completely remembered as Riwu Sopi and Sabe Ugha.[7] As noted, before joining Réja the Sopi Sabe people resided in a village of their own, located between the older settlements of Pajo and Réja. In this village, Sabe, recognized as the senior (*ka'e*) of the pair, is described as having occupied the landward part, while Sopi, the junior (*ari*), was resident in the seaward section. In accordance with their seniority, Sabe people served as earth breaker in respect of their former *peo kesi*. Sopi then took the part of excavator. But while these distinctions recall the relation of clans Meo Wale and Wawo Wale in Keo, genealogical information reveals no recognized agnatic connection between the two groups. In recent times, Sopi has in a couple of instances taken wives from Sabe; but this affinal tie, also, sheds no light on their apparently long-standing residential combination. Information on former settlements of the Sopi Sabe people is similarly minimal. Before establishing the village of Sopi Sabe (near the old villages of Pajo and Réja), they are described as residing in Wolo Pau Bhaya, apparently the same elevated site once occupied by the Munde clan Béle Jawa, and once specified as Sopi Sabe's 'original village' (*nua tenge*). No one I asked knew where their ancestors might have been before then.

Following one version of their history, Sopi Sabe gave up their earlier

---

[5] In 1991 there were five Réja houses within the settlement, four belonging to Sa'e and one to Koju. The last stands between houses of Sa'e. In addition to those on the *mena* side, two houses of Sopi Sabe were built landward of the Réja houses, thus also on the *rale* side of the village.

[6] The figure drawn from the Pajo genealogy relates particularly to two lines, where five out of 22 and two out of seven women's marriages were with Réja. Another two Pajo lines for which information was available show no marriages with Réja, nor, indeed, any obvious pattern of affinal consistency. The foregoing mostly refers to the estate of Koju Ko'u. Genealogical particulars for the other Réja estate are very scarce.

[7] I was never able to determine why it was the first ancestor's surname that came to designate the derivative group.

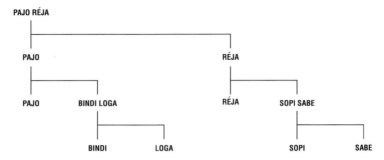

F IG . 9. Relations of encompassment among named groups in Pajo Réja

village of this name and joined Réja in the former settlement named Réja (or Nua Réja, 'Réja Village'), some time, perhaps not long, before Réja merged with Pajo early in the twentieth century. In contrast, other accounts describe three independent villages, Pajo, Réja, and Sopi Sabe, merging simultaneously to produce the present Pajo Réja. Whichever is correct, Sopi Sabe nowadays figures as one half of a dualistic unity, the *nua* (in the sense of 'section' of a village) called Réja or Sabe Réja, which in turn constitutes one half of a more inclusive binary whole, the modern settlement of Pajo Réja.

In addition to the identical dual composition of clans Réja and Sopi Sabe, the Réja half of Pajo Réja reveals an intriguing symmetry with the older, Pajo half. Pajo comprises clan Pajo and clan Bindi Loga, further divisible as Loga and Bindi, while Réja consists of clan Réja plus clan Sopi Sabe, an amalgamation of formerly separate groups still distinguishable as Sabe and Sopi (see Fig. 9). A single disparity lies in the fact that, like Sopi Sabe and Bindi Loga, clan Réja is also composed of genealogically unrelated parts—the segments named Sa'e Bapu and Koju Ko'u—whereas Pajo, the Land Mother, presents itself as a genealogical whole. Interestingly enough, the resulting asymmetry of four plus three would seem to allow an interpretation of the entire present configuration as an instance of the symbolically important total of seven, a figure also glimpsed in the constitution of Kota Pau and Guyu Wolo (II: 3: i; ii), and Nata Nage and Keo Ondo (II: 1: i; ii). Whatever the value of this observation, in Pajo Réja one clearly discerns the same process that has produced a variety of other Keo settlements whereby, over time, binary combinations have further consolidated, forming new unities, most tangibly signalled by the sharing of single sacrificial instruments (*peo*), which in turn have become further paired with similar amalgams. Perhaps the most notable feature of Pajo Réja is that, in regard to its two sections—still called *nua* (otherwise 'villages'), yet sharing a single *peo* squarely located in the senior section—it suggests a formation intermediate between a double settlement (with two *peo*) and a dually constituted single village.

2. Nua Muri: The New Village of Late

About a kilometre above Pajo Réja one encounters the village of Nua Muri ('New Village'). At an elevation of some 850 metres, Nua Muri is the highest village in western Keo and the furthest inland of all settlements falling within the original domain of Gewo. Occupying a steep site neatly divided into nine levels (*tenda*) with just two opposite facing houses built on each level, the present village comprises three clans: Late, Se, and Sina. For the most part, however, the settlement is locally construed as a dualistic formation composed of the oldest group, Late, on the one hand, and Se and Sina, on the other.

One reflection of this binary order is the formal name of the village, Ulu Se, Eko Late ('Head of Se, Tail of Late'). The phrases describe both the relative disposition of houses of the two clans in the present Nua Muri, founded in the 1920s, and a former arrangement where Se, together with Sina, occupied a separate village a short distance landward of Late. In effect then, the present Nua Muri developed from a double settlement, in which the older of the two villages was located seaward of the younger. As accords with its lack of recognition in the formal designation, Sina is associated with neither the landward nor seaward extremity. Sina houses are dispersed throughout the village.

Late and Se also exclusively divide the statuses attaching to the *peo kesi* which stood in the present village until the 1950s, when it twice sustained damage from heavy winds. In this connection, Late, as senior member of the pair, was recognized as earth breaker. The precedence of Late is also reflected in the location of the *peo*. The tree stood in a central position, on the fourth level from the head of the village and somewhat to the right (*mena*) side, in front of Late's seniormost house. Before merging to form a single village with Se and Sina, Late of course maintained both ceremonial positions in the village it occupied separately. Yet Late men also claim to have carried out the task of earth breaker (*ta koe*) in respect of the *kesi* tree maintained in the separate village occupied by Se and Sina. At this second *peo*, Se then filled the junior position of excavator. In so far as Late recognizes Se as its sole Defender (an assignment challenged by some outsiders), here we encounter an arrangement paralleling that of the Guyu Wolo people in relation to Land Mother Pau (Nuga Raga, II: 3: i), and the clans of Munde in relation to the clan of Géra Ga'e in Keo (or Keo Bélo; II: 4: ii). Also relevant in the present instance, however, is Late's claim never to have surrendered full land rights to Se, for reasons recounted below.

By all accounts, inhabitants of Nua Muri are relatively recent immigrants who settled in the region long after the time of the Ga'e siblings. Late, the first to arrive, hails from a former village of the same name located in the south-western Nage region coinciding with the modern administrative district (*desa*) of Légu Déru. Also applied to settlements preceding the present one, the village name Nua Muri, or 'new village', is consistent with Late's seniority in its present location in so far as it describes settlements founded by Late after leaving southwestern Nage. In other words, Nua Muri is specifically the *nua muri* ('new village') of clan Late, a circumstance providing another, albeit implicit, instance of a proper name identifying an entire village with its leading clan.

The main branch of the Late people is now established in the modern Nage village of Nunu Kae, while another is found in Maja Mére, to the northeast of Nua Muri, where the group is known as clan Ada (from *'ada 'iwu*, a ceremonial position Late still occupies in Nunu Kae). Agnatic connections (*ka'e ari*) among these groups continue to be honoured at major sacrificial feasts, when Late in Nua Muri contributes buffalo for slaughter in Nunu Kae and Maja Mére.[8] Conversely, I was told, members of these other local segments of Late should always be invited to sacrifice in Nua Muri. On the other hand, such reciprocation may pertain specifically to Ada in Maja Mére, since the Nua Muri branch of Late recognizes only this group as 'land siblings' (*ka'e ari tana watu*), or heirs to a common patrimony.

Settling in the northernmost part of the territory of Gewo Ga'e, Late's ancestors, a male sibling pair jointly named Ua Ae (that is, Ua and Ae), first established a village alternatively designated as Late or Nua Muri. Late people claim this area was completely empty and covered in thick forest when their ancestors arrived, so that the land in effect lacked an owner. In contrast, Pajo people in Pajo Réja argue that the territory had indeed been exploited by Gewo, but owing to a scarcity of water—making it unsuitable for raising buffalo—and the presence of numerous leeches and wild pigs, Gewo (or more probably, his direct descendants) later abandoned the area. As proof of a tacit acknowledgement by Late of Gewo's—or Pajo's—prior claim, the Pajo headman pointed to the fact that Late had always planted a *peo kesi* in all the settlements they occupied in this region, noting, correctly, that in their earliest village, in southwestern Nage, Late, like Nage folk in general, employed a forked post of Cassiawood (*peo yebu*). The upshot of this disagreement is that, according to Pajo, Late cannot legitimately claim the position of Land Mother in Nua Muri, nor, for that reason, can it correctly designate Se, or any other group, as its Defender.[9] At the same time, Pajo does not recognize Late as a Defender; nor does Late claim to be such. As noted earlier, a similar situation pertains to the Bolo people, also relative latecomers to northerly parts of western Keo, within the domain of Land Mother Lape.

Later arrivals still, Se clansmen identify their geographical origin as a village named Mabha Séle, to the east, near Sela Lejo. One of several groups

---

[8] As in comparable instances, agnation does not prevent intermarriage, and at least one union, involving a Late woman and a man of Maja Mére, has taken place in living memory.

[9] Connected with Late's claim to the status of Land Mother within its present territory, their leader told me that, before the custom fell into disuse, only Late planted a ritual garden (*uma gua*), and if others commenced planting before this was done, Late could demand that they kill a pig as reparation.

that reputedly travelled to western Keo in order to witness the construction at Jawa Pogo (*moni jawa pogo*), the Se people lodged temporarily at a place named Ndoya where, impressed by the fertility of the soil, they decided to remain. In response to their request, Late then provided Se with land, including a site on which to build a permanent village and plant a *peo*. Called Ndéna (or, locally, Déna), the former settlement is now also designated as Nua Se Olo, 'Old Se Village'.[10]

A popular phrase characterizes the people of Se as 'having large bellies' (or, more literally, as 'defecating a lot') and as being inclined 'to eat and drink everywhere they go' (*Se ta'i mére, la'a tolo ka, lora tolo inu*). Wishing only to gain a living from the land, their ancestors, it is said, did not require full rights to any particular territory but only a permanent right of usufruct. In consultation with Late, Se people may, therefore, cultivate anywhere within the earlier clan's territory; and for the same reason, the two groups describe themselves as *ka'e ari tana pinda watu faya* ('siblings of shared land and common stone').

While resident in Ndéna, or Old Se, clan Se were joined by the Sina ancestor, Wanda Teku, who married a Se woman and took up residence in the village. It is generally supposed that this Sina man was of clan Sina in Bolo Yoga (Kuyu Wulu), though a precise connection is no longer possible to establish. In accordance with Se's sharing of land rights with Late, Sina similarly did not acquire separate title from their wife-giver, and people I asked were at best equivocal as to whether Sina could be considered a Defender of Se. Nevertheless, Sina retains some identity as a separate group. In this respect, as in regard to its status as co-resident wife-taker, Sina's position in relation to Se is generally comparable to that of Wae (or *ngapi* Wae) in relation to Bindi in Lower Pajo Mala (II: 2: i).[11]

At present, Se is almost a remnant clan, virtually extinct and occupying just three houses. Although numerically stronger, Sina is in a similar state of decline, comprising a noticeably impoverished cluster of families without much knowledge of their history. In this connection it is also relevant that in recent decades a number of people from the village of Dhawe (or Dhawe Mére; Section 4 below) have moved to Nua Muri and have in effect become incorporated into Sina.[12] It would not be inaccurate, therefore, to characterize Sina as a miscellaneous grouping of later arrivals who, over the years, have taken up residence with Se and Late. Other Dhawe people regularly cultivate lands within the territory of Nua Muri, yet remain resident in their home village. As possessors of an indefinite usufruct, their rights appear indistinguishable from

---

[10] This is possibly the village given on Le Roux's map (*Schetskaart* 1916) as 'Seeh', located two to three kilometres directly east of the present Nua Muri.

[11] I seem not to have heard Sina described as a *ngapi* within Se—as Wae commonly is with regard to Bindi Wae. This, however, may be explained by villagers' claims that Late and Se are no longer divided into estates, or at least that these are not clearly determinable because it has been so long since buffalo were slaughtered in Nua Muri.

[12] In a count made in 1994, ten of 18 houses were specified as Sina, but many of the ten are in fact inhabited by Dhawe people.

those of Dhawe families subsumed by Sina, and differ but little from those of
Sina in relation to Se, or Se in relation to Late. At the same time, clan Se and,
in so far as it is distinguishable, clan Sina sacrifice buffalo at the *peo* in Nua
Muri as a matter of right, while Se was even once in possession of a sacrificial
tree of its own.

Dhawe cultivators resident with Sina, on the other hand, are normally
invited to participate in collective sacrifices but, as Late people in particular
explained, have no actual right to do so. They do not slaughter in their own
names or proclaim formal rights to the land (*bhea tana watu*) but simply
provide victims in order to 'wash (with blood)' (*basa*) the land whose ultimate
owners are the ancestors of Late. Residents of the village of Dhawe who cultivate Nua Muri territory are not required to make a formal payment (*fedho*) in
return for land use. Nevertheless, they are generally obliged to honour requests
for material assistance (small animals, palm gin, rice) and labour in connection
with rituals performed by Nua Muri clans, including funerals of Late, Se, and
Sina, which they always attend.

Broadly speaking, Nua Muri is organized identically to other settlements
comprising three or more named groups, which are nevertheless formally
construed as a dual organization or a quadripartite order of two pairs of clans.
It is even arguable that Nua Muri consists of just two clans, inasmuch as Sina,
the last group to arrive, may be considered as an encompassed segment of Se.
In this connection it is relevant that in neighbouring villages, even people affinally related to Nua Muri and possessing an impressive knowledge of local society and history were aware of only two Nua Muri clans—namely, Late and
Se—and so consistently represented the village dualistically.

All the same, Nua Muri reveals noteworthy variations on other themes.
Among these is the extent to which component clans rely on uxorilocal
marriage (*ndi'i dhato*) to ensure continuity. About 20 per cent (or eight out of
forty-one) of the marriages I recorded were of this sort. While the figure may
not appear particularly striking, instances are concentrated in the early generations of relatively shallow genealogies. Thus three generations of Late
women, for example, connect the father of that clan's current headman with
Late's earliest known male ancestor. Similarly, my main genealogical informant
in clan Se revealed that both his mother and mother's mother were natal Se
women married to uxorilocal husbands who had not paid bridewealth. The
present headman of Sina is the grandson of a natal Sina woman who was
married in the same way. The only local rationalization I encountered for this
marriage practice was the demographic argument that the village had usually
produced more females than males. But how far Nua Muri differs from others
in this respect is difficult to substantiate. So long as their male relatives
contract marriage with bridewealth, marrying Nua Muri women without
bridewealth to men of other villages could, of course, serve as way of increasing membership. It may be relevant, then, that Nua Muri is described as a

formerly small village that has recently expanded. In 1994, there were twenty-eight houses in all, of which ten formed an extension to the village proper.

It is consistent with the foregoing that only in one case did a uxorilocally married male, a man of clan Se married into Late, belong to one of the Nua Muri clans. Marriages of this sort, therefore, have little bearing on patterns of affinal connection between the three groups. Although Late claims Se as its sole Defender, the only instance in which Se had taken a wife from the older clan was the above-mentioned union contracted without bridewealth. There were also two marriages where Late had taken women from Se. In contrast, Sina people have maintained their position as Se's wife-taker. In addition to the marriage which involved the initial Sina ancestor settling with clan Se, of fifteen unions of Se women I recorded, five (thus one-third) were with men of Sina. More recently, Se has also taken wives from Sina.

Apart from the normal inter-village relations of affinity, and agnatic ties linking Late with groups in southwestern Nage (Nunu Kae) and Maja Mére, Nua Muri clans recognize special relations of 'kinship' (*ka'e ari*) with people of Lower Pajo Mala. As noted earlier, connected with the fact that their lands bound on the territory of Boa Maga, Nua Muri cultivators and members of the Pajo Mala clan Bindi (Bindi Wae) enjoy reciprocal rights of usufruct in much the same way as do the populations of Wayu and Keo Bélo. At the same time, Pajo Mala people describe the relationship as applying not to the whole of Nua Muri, but specifically to the clan Se. Paralleling this connection, the other major clan in Lower Pajo Mala, Pajo Wolo, was once engaged with clan Late in a special military alliance (*ka'e ari tuku wutu, wina lima, bani papa kapi, tego papa geu*; I: 4: i) which allowed each to call freely upon the other for support in disputes. Reputedly initiated after the cessation of strife between Nua Muri and Pajo Mala people, the partnership was formalized with an exchange of land, so that each group owns a plot within the territory of the other.[13] Like the relationship with Bindi Wae, therefore, this reciprocal arrangement also possesses a territorial aspect.

It will be recalled that while Bindi Wae is owner of the land of Boa Maga, clan Pajo Wolo is a Defender of the domain of Lape Ga'e. Since Nua Muri clans occupy territory originally claimed by Gewo Ga'e, in the foregoing arrangements we once again encounter territorial unities whose components are groups associated with different Land Mothers. Although Nua Muri and their Pajo Mala counterparts do not sacrifice at one another's *peo*, they do provide reciprocal assistance in ritual undertakings and are particularly obliged to attend and contribute to one another's funerals, firing 'bamboo cannon' (I: 5: iv, n. 16) whenever a death occurs in the partner's village. Nua Muri is one of several examples of villages in which a discernible three (or more) groups

---

[13] Though Pajo Wolo considers the relationship still to exist in principle, Late no longer acknowledges Pajo Wolo as *ka'e ari* owing to subsequent conflict that remains unresolved.

formally reduce to two. Alternatively, one might speak of a dualistic order in which a third group is, as it were, submerged. Yet of as much interest is the way the village exemplifies various sorts of binary connections with groups outside, linking the original domains of three different Land Mothers.

Recent ceremonial history provides a telling illustration of the characteristic form of relations among Nua Muri clans. Attending the major buffalo sacrifice performed in the Nage centre of Bo'a Wae in August 1988, Late was actually invited by the senior branch of Late in Nunu Kae, who in turn were invited by Déru in that village, who were obliged to attend as clanmates of Deu (a dialectal form of Déru), the Bo'a Wae leaders and hosts. Late in Nua Muri then invited Se (as their co-resident wife-takers), who in turn invited Sina. Hence men from all three groups in Nua Muri attended the great Nage festival. For the most part these several binary connections turn on relations of *ka'e ari* ('siblingship' or agnatic kinship), although in regard to the Nua Muri clans they also involve relations of affinity, wife-takers then assuming an identical role to junior agnates.

3. Sawu (or Sawu Obo)

Founded in 1953, the village of Sawu—more completely known as Sawu Obo—is a recent merging of two villages, Sawu and Obo, whose names further designate two clans. Both present and former villages are located about three kilometres south of Pajo Réja. The present Sawu Obo contains a single sacrificial *kesi* tree, planted in the centre of the village between the halves occupied by Obo and Sawu respectively. By contrast, the two old villages (Sawu Olo and Obo Olo), built on more elevated sites just to the east, each possessed *peo kesi* of their own.

Obo and Sawu are both relatively large clans, the former comprising six and the latter eight estates (*ngapi*). As indicated by one formal name of their present village—Ulu Obo, Eko Sawu ('Head that is Obo, Tail that is Sawu')—clan Obo occupies the landward section, and Sawu the seaward. As occupants of the lower (*au*) part of the settlement, Sawu people are sometimes distinguished as 'clan Sawu Au' ('Sawu Below' or 'Lower Sawu'). The two groups were spatially distinguished in the same way in their separate former villages where, according to local estimates, the 'tail' of Obo was located some 30 or 40 metres from the 'head' of Sawu. At that time, the name Sawu Obo referred to the two villages as a pair. Hence we encounter another instance of a former double settlement that has recently evolved into a single village still known by the same name.[14]

[14] In formal contexts, both the present village and the former double settlement are alternatively designated as Ulu Bélo, Eko Sawu ('Head of Bélo, Tail of Sawu'). Ulu Bélo—not to be confused with the Bélo situated just above Keo (or Keo Bélo)—refers to a hamlet located a short distance landward of Old Sawu (clan Sawu's former separate village) which was once inhabited by people of clan Obo. Some people specified Ulu Bélo, Eko Sawu as an exclusive reference to Old Sawu (Sawu Olo); yet the epithet is still applied to the present, amalgamated settlement.

The older of the two groups, Obo derives from two brothers jointly named as Ngoba Ndona. Obo in Sawu (regularly distinguished as Obo Sawu) traces agnatic descent from the younger brother, Ndona, more completely named Ndona Lo'a. The elder brother, Ngoba, or Ngoba Lo'a, is the apical ancestor of Obo Dhawe, a segment of the clan established in the village of Dhawe (Section 4 below), where Obo is similarly recognized as the longest resident group. Otherwise, little is known about this ancestral pair. Following one account, both were born in western Keo, in a hamlet named Bo'a Bare, located just east of the present village of Dhawe Yoja (see Section 5 below). Later, as adults, they founded respectively Old Obo and the village now called Dhawe.[15]

Both acquiring rights to lands within the original domain of Gewo Ga'e, the two branches of Obo are recognized as Defenders of clan Pajo in Pajo Réja. In fact, apart from the co-resident group Bindi Loga, Pajo reckons the Obo people as its oldest, and most loyal, Defenders. Both localized segments of Obo are, moreover, wife-takers of Pajo, their genealogies each showing three marriages with Pajo women (amounting to 13 and 27 per cent for segments in the villages of Sawu and Dhawe respectively). Noteworthy in this regard is a special, and evidently unique, dispensation applying exclusively to Obo men who marry women of Pajo. Although the former provide Pajo with buffalo and metal valuables when contracting marriages, these goods are not spoken of as 'bridewealth' (*ngawu*) and, though reciprocated with textiles, their amounts are not negotiated or specified by the wife-giver.

While Obo is the principal Defender of Pajo, the more recently arrived group, Sawu, is in turn recognized as Defender of Obo, but more specifically of the junior branch now resident in Sawu Obo. With regard to earlier remarks concerning affinal relations between groups thus connected, it may be noted that Obo generally takes wives from Sawu, thereby inverting what is elsewhere represented as the more usual relation between Land Mother and Defender. In fact, this pattern is quite pronounced: among twenty-one men's marriages recorded in the Obo genealogy eleven, or over one half, were with women of clan Sawu.[16]

Consistent with the relative seaward position of its earlier and present settlements, clan Sawu occupies territory formerly held by clans Obo and Réja, mostly in the southern part of the domain of Gewo Ga'e. Included in this territory is an extensive area of wet-rice fields (estimated at 80 hectares), known as Mala Sawu ('Sawu Plain') and stretching to the sea. While these

---

[15] Possible meanings of 'Obo' are discussed in Appendix 3. There is a hamlet in the Nage district of Kéli Mado named Obo, but I found no evidence that this is connected with the Obo people in Dhawe and Sawu. Owing perhaps to the proximity of Obo's original village to the village of Dhawe, people sometimes describe Obo Sawu as deriving from Obo Dhawe (a name that, strictly speaking, refers to that part of the clan settled at present in Dhawe). The representation may alternatively reflect the seniority of Obo Dhawe, as the descendants of the elder of the two brothers.

[16] The Obo genealogy provides details of only five women's marriages, and none of these involve Sawu. The genealogy of clan Sawu, however, lists different Sawu houses as wife-giver of Obo in four or five instances and as wife-taker in six or seven.

lands were ceded to clan Sawu by Obo, the area, including the coastal site of Ma'u Pogo (or Ma'u Ponggo), had earlier been occupied by the Réja people who, indeed, seem generally to have been displaced from their seaward territory following the arrival of the Sawu folk. According to a major Sawu informant, the area about Ma'u Ponggo was formally granted to Obo by Land Mother Pajo; but even if this is correct, the transfer may merely have rationalized an accomplished expansion of Obo and Sawu. The same man stated that Sawu recognizes only Obo as Land Mother, and as the original *moi tana* ('owner of the land') in this coastal region, adding without further explanation that this was partly because Pajo had been defeated in war. Possibly connected with this is the further report that, before the custom began to disappear, it was Obo who, both in Sawu Obo and Dhawe, planted a ritual garden (*uma gua*, I: 1: iii).

As explained earlier (I: 1: ii), clan Sawu regards the island of Savu as its place of origin. Variously specified as the son or son's son of the apical ancestor, Jara Waju, the first Sawu ancestor to settle permanently in western Keo was Koke Sae. Once established, he and his followers immediately became a major political force in the region, participating in numerous military exploits. In order to control the activities of the Sawu people and prevent their further expansion, the local Land Mother, Obo, invited them to leave their earlier settlement, a village called Wudhi (or, in formal speech, Ulu Futa Wula, Eko Tonga Nanga) located near Wolo Sabi, and to found a new settlement just seaward of Old Obo. This was the old village of Sawu (Sawu Olo), one half of the double settlement of Sawu Obo which eventually developed into the present village of the same name.

The fact that Keo usually refer to the village of Sawu Obo simply as Sawu evidently reflects the enduring prominence of clan Sawu. During the colonial period, the former double settlement of Sawu Obo was treated as a single administrative village (BI *kampong*), also named 'Sawu'. In addition, Sawu formed the centre of, and lent its name to, one of the ten colonial 'subdistricts' (BI *haminte*) into which the Dutch divided the Keo region. In fact, subsumed in the colonial subdistrict named Sawu was most of the area I describe as western Keo, including villages now belonging to the administrative divisions (*desa*) of Jawa Pogo, Loka Laba, Wolo Telu, Ulu Loga, Loda Olo, Wolo Ede, and Woe Wolo (Hamilton 1918). Nevertheless, of the six men who successively served as native administrators (BI *kepala mere*) of the Sawu subdistrict, the first three were from clan Obo, while none belonged to clan Sawu. At present, 'Sawu' survives administratively as the name of the *desa* (administrative unit), which, besides Sawu Obo, includes the villages of Guyu Wolo, Kota Pau, and Lédho Ngule, as well as Ma'u Ponggo, the capital of the modern subdistrict (BI *kecamatan*) of the same name.

In a way comparable to what one encounters in Nua Muri and other Keo villages, the formal dualism of Sawu and Obo barely disguises the presence of a third clan, Wani Wona. Deriving from a place called Au Wani in the Ende region, the group once occupied a separate village named Guyu Wani not far from Lédho Ngule, a settlement located just northeast of the present Sawu Obo, where they maintained their own *peo kesi*. In return for military assistance, the Wani Wona people obtained land from Sanda Bi'a, a group resident in Lédho Ngule, whose Defenders they thus became. Later, however, Wani Wona abandoned their village and, seeking protection in a time of strife, founded a new settlement close to Old Obo. This evidently occurred before the arrival of the Sawu people, as the group is described as erecting houses on the site of what subsequently became the old village of Sawu (Sawu Olo) and as later being joined there by the Sawu ancestors. A small group occupying just three dwellings, Wani Wona nowadays still resides with clan Sawu, in the seaward half of Sawu Obo. Regarding this residential connection, it should be mentioned that, at some stage and in return for military assistance, clan Sawu, too, obtained land from Lédho Ngule. Sawu people are thus recognized as 'Defenders of Ngule' (*tuku Ngule*) as well as of Obo.[17]

In the present Sawu Obo, Wani Wona's position is somewhat anomalous. The group consists of a single *ngapi* or, as this is also expressed, a single 'house' (*sa'o*), which local commentators described as subsumed in Sawu, referring ambiguously to the clan or to the seaward section of Sawu Obo. At the same time, the group never acquired territory from Obo or Sawu and continues to work land given by Lédho Ngule. Thus, they are Defenders of neither of the larger co-resident clans. By virtue of their residential situation, however, Wani Wona sacrifices at the *peo* in Sawu Obo and not in Lédho. Furthermore, while Obo, as the oldest group, holds the position of earth breaker in respect of the present sacrificial tree, as even men of clan Sawu affirmed, the position of excavator rightfully belongs to Wani Wona. Evidently, this is in recognition of the group having arrived in the region before the people of clan Sawu. The present order of buffalo slaughter in the village of Sawu was thus given as: the seniormost estate (*ngapi pu'u*) of Obo, Wani Wona, the seniormost estate of Sawu, the other five estates of Obo, and finally, the other seven estates of Sawu.

Similarly associated with clan Sawu is a group named Joka. Deriving from an ancestor from the Ende region whose vessel capsized off the south coast and who was rescued by men of Sawu, Joka has never consisted of more than a single house. Formerly, the group resided in Old Sawu (Sawu Olo) but have since moved to a nearby hamlet named Nai Wali. In remembrance of their ancestor's maritime origin, Joka reputedly once kept a model of a sailing vessel in their house. Like Wani Wona, Joka received land from the people of Lédho Ngule, and though they are said at one time to have sacrificed in Old Sawu, they now do so only in Lédho. As former military allies (but not Defenders) of

---

[17] As a 'child' of two 'mothers' (that is, Land Mothers), Sawu people are described as *tuku Obo roga nodho, tuku Ngule roga nu'e*, 'Defenders of Obo—men of fortitude, Defenders of (Lédho) Ngule—men who do not retreat'—(*roga* is a dialectal variant of *yoga*, 'man, person').

Sawu, the relation between the two groups is expressed in the aphorism *Sawu Joka tana mona, bholo ola wika ola*. Translating as 'Sawu and Joka have no land, (and are) only conquerors of other villages', the first phrase somewhat hyperbolically characterizes Sawu as well as Joka as a group whose territorial rights are derivative. In view of its contrasting military and political prominence, clan Sawu indeed provides a good illustration of a group which, though powerful in temporal terms, is ritually subordinate. This subordination is especially manifest in the assignment of the small clan Wani Wona as excavator in Sawu Obo. Although construable as a segment of (clan) Sawu, the presence of this group moreover qualifies the formal dualism of the settlement, as, in the past at least, the tiny Joka group might also have done.

4. Dhawe (Dhawe Mére)

Located some three kilometres north of Sawu, and a shorter distance southeast of Pajo Réja, is the village of Dhawe. Although usually known simply as Dhawe, the settlement is also called Dhawe Mére, or 'Major Dhawe', a usage that distinguishes it from the smaller village of Dhawe Yoja (II: 5: v).[18] In several respects, Dhawe closely resembles the modern village of Sawu, or Sawu Obo. Although now described as a single village (*nua*), the settlement comprises a landward and a seaward section; these, too, are referred to as *nua*, thus replicating the pattern found in Pajo Réja. As in Sawu, a segment of the clan Obo (indeed the senior branch), occupies the landward part, distinguished as Nua Obo, while the seaward section, called Nua Dhawe, is occupied by the clan mostly known as Dhawe. Like clan Sawu, Dhawe lends its name to the settlement as a whole. Interestingly, the view of the settlement as consisting of two *nua* (Obo and Dhawe) appears to have greater currency among people of clan Obo than among their neighbours in the larger, and generally more prominent, clan Dhawe. In recent years, Dhawe has expanded while Obo has declined in numbers; hence some houses of Dhawe are now found in Obo's part of the village. Formerly, however, the two groups more consistently divided the two sections.

While thus displaying a generally dualistic form, the Dhawe group incorporates a third clan named Ndoi which, somewhat like Wani Wona in Sawu, formerly enjoyed a greater autonomy. On the other hand, the village as a whole contrasts with Sawu in so far as, within the present formation, each of the two major components, Dhawe and Obo, still claims the right to erect a *peo* of its own. Although neither is visible at present, the last one having died around 1969, within living memory both clans maintained sacrificial *kesi* trees as well

---

[18] Together with several other villages described below, Dhawe is now included in the modern *desa* (administrative unit) of Loda Olo. Though interpretable as 'old (gold) chain', the *desa* name is locally explained as an amalgam of parts of the place-names Loka Kayo, Dhawe, Oja, and Loka Sua. Denoting a site rather than a village, the last name was chosen for reasons I was unable to establish.

as separate ceremonial buildings (*nde* and *yenda*), thus providing a far clearer physical division of the village than is now apparent. Indeed, until quite recently Dhawe and Obo evidently composed a double settlement, the outlines of which are just barely discernible in the present village. To the extent that they now constitute a single settlement, however, it is remarkable that this is named identically to the younger component, Dhawe, just as is Sawu, the modern village incorporating the other branch of clan Obo.

Arriving later in the region, clan Dhawe is recognized as Defender of Obo, more particularly of the senior part of the clan. As its name attests, clan Dhawe derives from the Nage village of Dhawe, located far to the northeast (see Map 1). The ancestors of the group were a husband and wife named Gore and Oe. Gore had his hair cut by an elder brother, who (perhaps owing simply to incompetence) sheared only the right side of his head, thus conferring on him the nickname Bapi (meaning '(on, to) one side'). This caused Gore such embarrassment that, as is typical of this mythological genre, he decided to flee with his wife to a distant land. Local commentators link Gore's removal to western Keo with the derivation of Dhawe people in northeastern Nage from the ancestress named Pénu Ga'e. A sister of Lape and the other Ga'e siblings, according to a mythical tradition known throughout Nage and Keo, this woman was taken in marriage by the famous Dhawe ancestor known as Wégu the Orphan (Wégu Ana Ralo; see Forth 1998).[19] As a Pajo man remarked, by settling on land falling within the ancestral domain of Gewo Ga'e (his own apical ancestor), the Dhawe people now resident in western Keo were actually returning to a point of origin (*pu'u*). The interpretation of course reflects the general representation of wife-givers as a wife-taker's place of origin (I: 4, 5).

On arriving in Keo, the Dhawe people initially settled in Loka Léna, a former hamlet just north of the present village of Dhawe, which was already inhabited by the previously mentioned clan Ndoi. Divided into upper and lower sections named Ndoi Wawo and Ndoi Au, the Ndoi people apparently maintained some form of dual organization before the arrival of the Dhawe ancestors. All the same, present reports describe them as lacking a *peo* in this earlier settlement. Neither the place of origin of Ndoi nor the circumstances of their settling within the domain of Gewo Ga'e is any longer known. As prior inhabitants, Ndoi shared their lands with the Dhawe newcomers. Yet it is not clear whether Dhawe were ever recognized as their Defenders; and, indeed, some time after the two clans joined in Loka Léna, Ndoi became merged with Dhawe as a subordinate segment.[20]

After their merging, the two groups together removed to the present village of Dhawe, where they planted a single *peo kesi*. Later still, they were joined by

---

[19] This relationship of wife-giver and wife-taker, connecting the male Ga'e and the descendants of Pénu Ga'e, is also acknowledged in the mythology of the northeastern Nage district of Dhawe.

[20] Ndoi has given at least two wives to Dhawe and, more recently, has taken one. Genealogical information, however, is not so complete as to shed further light on their relationship.

the Obo people, who founded a separate village, with a separate *peo*, immediately landward of Dhawe. Prior to this, Obo—that is, the senior branch now resident with Dhawe—had been residing with the junior segment of the same clan. After abandoning their previous settlement, therefore, clan Obo bifurcated, with the senior and junior halves removing to Sawu Obo (or what eventually became named as such) and Dhawe (Dhawe Mére) respectively. Thus, while Obo was longer established in the general vicinity, it was in fact Dhawe which, together with Ndoi, arrived earlier at the site presently shared by Dhawe and Obo. This sequence of events would explain why the settlement as a whole is now known as Dhawe, and not as Obo or Dhawe Obo.[21] Nevertheless, Dhawe recognizes Obo as the source of both this residential site and other territory they occupy; hence Dhawe are considered Defenders of Obo. Consistent with this, Dhawe men claimed that when planting their *peo*— something they last did in the early twentieth century—a man of Obo, as the Land Mother, should take the part of earth breaker (*ta koe*). In recognition of their earlier occupation, the group named Lower Ndoi (Ndoi Au), though now reduced to a segment (*ngapi*) of clan Dhawe, should then serve as excavator (*ta kabhe*), while Dhawe, that is, descendants of Gore and Oe, would actually plant (*toni*) the sacrificial tree. Even so, the first to slaughter (*pébha wunga*) should be the principal estate (*ngapi pu'u*) of clan Dhawe.[22]

In accordance with Ndoi's inclusion within clan Dhawe, houses occupied by Ndoi people are interspersed among Dhawe houses on the left (*rale*) side of the present village. The right side (*padhi mena*) is then occupied exclusively by dwellings of original Dhawe people, the descendants of Gore and Oe. In the same vein, particularly in sacrificial contexts Ndoi comprises three estates within Dhawe, with Upper Ndoi (Ndoi Wawo) counting as one *ngapi* and Lower Ndoi (Ndoi Au), the more senior group, as two. Original Dhawe people, on the other hand, are divided into five estates, each identified with a son of the apical ancestral pair. Completing this somewhat heterogeneous unity are the owners of a single house located on the right (*mena*) side and towards the seaward end of Nua Dhawe. Deriving from refugees driven from their former village of Ulu Wio in a war with Pajo, these are a small group of Wio people now incorporated in clan Dhawe as a separate *ngapi*. As noted in the previous chapter, the Wio house in Dhawe is agnatically related to the Wio house in Keo Bélo. Yet only in Dhawe do Wio people possess a separate sacrificial status.

Coinciding with Nua Dhawe, that is, the seaward half of the entire village named Dhawe, clan Dhawe thus provides another, particularly clear example of the modular structure of Keo clans. At the same time, the group reveals a peculiarity in its internal order in so far as its most senior segment (*ngapi*), descending from the eldest son of the apical ancestral couple, is nominally

[21] Only once did I record 'Dhawe Obo' used to refer to the present village.
[22] With regard to affinal implications of the relationship of Land Mother and Defender elsewhere, it is noteworthy that just one of 23 Dhawe men's marriages involves a woman from Obo.

distinguished as Ki'a, and sometimes even as clan (*suku*) Ki'a. The only instance I encountered where an estate is not named after its founding ancestor (who in this case was called Iko), 'Ki'a' refers to the location of the group's house at the seaward extremity of the village (see *ki'a*, 'end', 'edge'). How this senior segment came to acquire a separate name is no longer known. A reasonable surmise is that the name may once have applied to clan Dhawe as a whole, perhaps in regard to their location in the earlier settlement they shared with Ndoi, and has since become restricted to the clan's principal estate (*ngapi pu'u*). Suggestive in this regard are usages, some encountered while recording affinal genealogies, which tend to identify Ki'a with Dhawe in its entirety. Affines of Dhawe in Loka Kayo (see Section 5) also described Ki'a people as being 'original' to western Keo in contrast to other Dhawe people who hail from Dhawe in northeastern Nage. In subsequent questioning in the village of Dhawe, however, this representation (which may conflate different senses, or connotations, of the term *pu'u*; see I: 5: i) was strongly denied, and it was affirmed that Ki'a as well trace their origins to the Nage district of Dhawe.

Whether or not it was once used as a formal name for the entire Dhawe clan, Ki'a now serves as a term distinguishing the agnatically most senior segment of Dhawe, which, in accordance with the identification of principal segments (or 'trunks', *pu'u*) with entire clans (I: 3: iii), is further employed synecdochally, in a way formally similar to the use of the clan name Dhawe for the entire settlement (Dhawe Mére), which also incorporates Obo. Interestingly, in both instances, the part that stands for the whole (Ki'a or clan Dhawe) is located relatively seaward of the remainder of the whole. Both spatially and socially, moreover, Ki'a's position is reminiscent of that of the estate named Raga Daga (after its ancestor) within clan Suga in Suga Bhoja (II: 1: v), a segment which similarly claims precedence within the larger clan and which also occupies the seaward extremity of the village.

Like the village of Sawu (Sawu Obo), with which in several formal respects it bears an especially close resemblance, Dhawe provides yet another example of dualistic organization accommodating additional groups besides the principal two. At the same time, Dhawe differs from Sawu in so far as it retains the form of a discernibly double settlement, manifest particularly in the circumstance that clans Obo and Dhawe continue to maintain separate *peo*. It is also noteworthy that the subordination of Ndoi, as a group existing within clan Dhawe, appears on the whole to be more complete than what one finds in Sawu in regard to the group named Wani Wona. The seniormost of the Ndoi estates, however, occupies the secondary ceremonial position of excavator (*ta kabhe*) in Dhawe, just as does Wani Wona in the modern village of Sawu (Sawu Obo). Indicating a continuing recognition of the temporal precedence of these earlier, yet now subordinated groups, this isomorphism reveals yet another striking parallel between Sawu and Dhawe, two settlements within the domain of Gewo Ga'e dominated by clans of the same names, both of which are Defenders of Obo.

Before concluding this section, attention should be given to the formal designation of the present village of Dhawe: Ulu Sua Sina, Eko Watu Mite ('Head that is Sua Sina, Tail that is Black Stone'). Referring to a place somewhere near the landward end of the settlement, Dhawe men described Sua Sina (a phrase translatable as 'Chinese, or foreign, iron') as a site once inhabited by the Ndoi people. Despite the common name, Ndoi seems not to be related to groups named Sina now resident in Yoga, Wulu Wayu, and Nua Muri. Watu Mite, on the other hand, was explained as a reference to a large dark stone that formerly served as an obstacle to enemies approaching from the seaward direction. Similarly, people in Wajo (see Section 5 below), gave Watu Mite as the name of a place close to Dhawe that was once inhabited by some of their ancestors. At least in part, therefore, both Sua Sina and Watu Mite appear to designate former habitations. Nevertheless, with regard to their combination in the formal designation of Dhawe, it is curious that the same paired phrases—*sua sina, watu mite*—appear in a generic expression, first recorded in Nage, which describes a place fortified against both human and spiritual intrusion (Forth 1998: 131).

5. Other Villages in the Domain of Gewo

Several smaller villages within the domain of Gewo Ga'e can be sketched more briefly than those described above. Although included mostly for the sake of completeness, in one or two respects their analysis reveals organizational variations not encountered previously. Brevity is mainly justified by the fact that, owing partly to their location towards one geographical limit of the study area, I am less familiar with some of these villages than with others described in this chapter.

5.1 Dhawe Yoja

Less than a kilometre to the north of Dhawe (Dhawe Mére) one encounters the village of Dhawe Yoja. Now virtually abandoned by residents who have constructed houses along a main pathway, the village belongs to a single group tracing agnatic descent from a man named Séwa Wae, who was born in the coastal settlement of Ma'u Mbawa. Like the ancestor of clan Sawu in Sawu Obo, the Dhawe Yoja founder was originally an immigrant from the island of Savu. After landing on the south coast of Flores, his father (named Paja Wae) settled in Ma'u Mbawa, where he was given land by a clan named Keka, and where siblings of Séwa Wae remained. According to their genealogy, the ancestor of Dhawe Yoja lived just four or five generations ago—thus about the same time as the forebears of clan Sawu are supposed to have taken up permanent residence in western Keo (I: 1: ii).

Séwa Wae's removal to the vicinity of Dhawe was occasioned by his marriage to Lako Nage, a woman of clan Dhawe (more specifically, the segment named Ki'a). Because his wife would not return with him to Ma'u Mbawa, Séwa was granted land by his wife-giver and allowed to found a village and to plant a forked Cassiawood *peo*. Later, however, he returned to Ma'u Mbawa, where he died. As villagers explained, the first part of the name Dhawe Yoja reflects their status as both wife-taker and land grantee of Dhawe. The second part—a palatalized variant of Oja—refers to the neighbouring village of Oja, located a short distance to the east, and was described as acknowledging the derivation of Séwa Wae's mother-in-law from Oja. In this way, then, the village name combines the name of the founder's wife-giver with that of his wife-giver's wife-giver.

Despite what this designation and the proximity of Dhawe Yoja might suggest, the village does not compose a double settlement with either Dhawe Mére or Oja. Generally represented as comprising a single clan sometimes called *suku* Bawa (Mbawa) or *suku* Sawu (not to be confused with the clan so named in the village of Sawu, or Sawu Obo), dualistic order within Dhawe Yoja is mostly manifest in the statuses of trunk rider and tip rider connected with the forked *peo*. As Land Mother, clan Dhawe should appear as earth breaker whenever the Dhawe Yoja people erect a new post. In the same context, Oja was described as the rightful holder of the complementary position of excavator, though the basis of this assignment is rather less obvious.

5.2 *Oja*

Located about a half kilometre east of Dhawe Yoja and about the same distance northeast of Dhawe Mére, the village of Oja forms a double settlement with the adjacent village of Wajo. Both named after trees (see Appendix 3), Oja is the seaward settlement while Wajo is the landward.

Oja is one of several western Keo villages inhabited by a single clan bearing the same name. The clan is divided into two estates, each named after one of a pair of male siblings. Ta'i Owa, the senior group (*ngapi pu'u*), occupies the position of earth breaker in respect of the village's *peo kesi*, while the junior segment, Céme Owa, is designated as excavator. Both functions were exercised in 1992 when the Oja people erected a new sacrificial *kesi* tree (see Plate 17) and new ceremonial buildings (*yenda* and *nde*). Descending from an elder and a younger brother, the segments are further associated respectively with the landward and seaward sections of the village. Although actual residential arrangements no longer fully accord with this division, it nevertheless finds ritual expression in the recent erecting of two upright stones representing the two estates (I: 2: iv), one immediately above the central *peo* and belonging to the senior group, and the other placed below and belonging to the junior.

Although the Oja people remember settling in five prior villages, all appear to have been located in the vicinity of their present settlement. Describing themselves as Defenders of Pajo (the senior Land Mother), people of Oja occupy and maintain territory near the eastern limit of the domain of Gewo

PLATE 17. Newly planted
peo kesi in Oja

Ga'e. Pajo, however, considers Oja as a Defender of Obo, one of Pajo's older
Defenders.

5.3 Wajo

Despite the location of their village immediately landward of Oja, the Wajo
people, sometimes called 'Wajo Oja' to distinguish them from other central
Flores populations bearing the same name, do not regard themselves as
Defenders of Oja, nor indeed of any other clan. While Oja was granted land by
Obo, Wajo obtained territory from clan Dhawe in exchange for slaves and
textiles. Nevertheless, Wajo claim always to have resided jointly with Oja,
having accompanied them in a series of moves and being bound by oath never
to separate. They also recognize Oja as the senior member of the pair.

Wajo comprises three segments, named after their respective ancestors.
Although these might be construed as estates (*ngapi*) of a single clan, the three
ancestors are described as having different geographical origins and as entering

Wajo at different times, a circumstance tending to support one local assessment of them as three separate clans (*suku*). In spite of this apparent tripartite division, dualistic order is nevertheless manifest in respect of the single sacrificial *kesi* tree which, until its recent destruction, stood in the centre of Wajo. Reputedly the oldest, the group named Noe Raga, whose houses occupy the landward part of the village, claims the position of earth breaker. The status of excavator is then attributed not to the second but to the last group to join Wajo. Named Lua Toyo, this segment occupies the seaward part of the village. The division thus seemingly excludes the second group, Céme Wea, whose houses are centrally located between those of the other two.

Whether Céme Wea is somehow more closely associated with the first or third group in Wajo, thus lending the village a more binary cast, I am unable to confirm. Possibly relevant in this connection is the report that the original settlement of the Lua Toyo people was Watu Mite, the site named in the formal *ulu éko* designation of Dhawe and situated near Dhawe's seaward extremity. The most junior component thus previously resided very close to the present Wajo, whereas the two older divisions claim derivation from far more distant locations. This circumstance suggests that only the older pair of Wajo clans (or estates) has long been residentially linked with Oja, and that they were joined by Lua Toyo only after arriving in their present location. It might then be surmised that the latter group's longer residence in the vicinity accounts for its recognition as excavator. Interestingly, in this regard Lua Toyo's position in Wajo would exactly parallel those of Ndoi and Wani Wona, the 'third groups' recognized as excavator (*ta kabhe*) in Dhawe Mére and Sawu Obo respectively.

5.4 Loka Kayo

Located directly east of Dhawe, the head (*ulu*) of the village of Loka Kayo ('Thorny Place') lies a short distance to the right (*mena*) side of Dhawe's tail (*éko*). Despite the similar name, Loka Kayo is not related to clan Kayo, or Pajo Kayo, in Pajo Mala. Sometimes represented as a single clan (Suku Loka Kayo) comprising three estates, especially in respect of ancestral origins the village reveals a binary order. Descending agnatically from a common ancestor hailing from the Nage district of Wolo Wea named Goyu or Kou (the original form of the name in eastern Nage), the senior grouping includes two estates named after the two eldest sons of Goyu: Taka Noe, the elder brother, and Meo Noe, the younger.[23] Much later, indeed just two generations before present adults, these two estates were joined by another group. Also named after an ancestor, these later arrivals are called Ebu Pae. Reflecting another binary view of the village, Ebu Pae is sometimes described as a clan separate from 'clan Loka Kayo', which is then alternatively specified as 'clan Wolo Wea'.

---

[23] Another son of Goyu, Wago Noe, settled in Lédho Ngule. Some of his descendants are now found in the eastern Nage district of Raja, near Wolo Wea.

After leaving the southeastern Nage district of Wolo Wea five generations ago, and after a sojourn in the village of Gélu (to the northeast), the Loka Kayo ancestor, Goyu, was taken in by the ancestors of clan Dhawe and given two plots of land. Partly because most land of Taka Noe and Meo Noe has been obtained through purchase from other sources, these two groups do not, however, consider themselves Defenders of Dhawe.[24] The group named Ebu Pae holds no title to land in the vicinity of Dhawe. Coming from the village of Sule, near Gélu, they cultivate land belonging to the people of Lédho Ngule. As noted earlier, members of the Loga group in Pajo (Pajo Réja) are agnatically related to the main body of Loka Kayo people, descending from Gélu Oko, the SS of Taka Noe, who acquired rights to the land of heirless Loga ancestors. While Gélu is described as belonging both to Loga and to Loka Kayo, his Loga estate was inherited specifically by his second son, Mére Teku. For this reason the present leaders of Loga in Pajo Réja are first parallel cousins (FyBS) of the leaders of *ngapi* Taka Noe in Loka Kayo.

By far the most peculiar feature of the Loka Kayo people —specifically the more senior pair of estates, or clan Loka Kayo in the stricter sense—is their continuing connection with Wolo Wea, their ancestral homeland. As accords with their not being recognized as Defenders of Dhawe, or for that matter any other group in western Keo, the Loka Kayo people possess no *peo* of their own. Although they have on at least one occasion slaughtered buffalo in their own village employing a temporary bamboo stake (*madhu*), they still speak of one of two forked posts in Wolo Wea as being their real *peo*.[25] By the same token, and further consistent with their not having been granted a *peo* by Dhawe (their original land donors), the village of Loka Kayo, though generally spoken of as a *nua* (i.e., a permanent settlement), does not have a formal *ulu éko* name. In more than one respect, then, Loka Kayo is peripheral to the domain of Gewo Ga'e, and, indeed, scarcely exists as an independent community.

6. Comparisons

As shown in previous chapters, villages in the territory of Géra Ga'e are quite straightforwardly binary in their formal composition, while settlements in the domains of Lape and Nuga Raga exemplify varieties of quadripartite order. To a quite remarkable degree, nearly all of the villages in the domain of Gewo Ga'e can, in one way or another, alternatively be construed as combinations of

---

[24] With regard to marriage, however, Dhawe has apparently taken wives from Loka Kayo for some considerable time, as indicated by five of 23 Dhawe men's marriages. Loka Kayo is also relatively prominent among more recent wife-givers of Land Mother Pajo, a circumstance that illustrates yet again how a group's status in regard to land need have nothing to do with present affinal status.

[25] Villagers claimed that, in 1945, they sacrificed buffalo in Loka Kayo employing the *paya* or *sése* method (I: 2: iv), enclosing the village plaza and tying the animals with a long cable to a stout length of planted bamboo. Two victims were sacrificed on this occasion, one provided by Loka Kayo proper (the descendants of Taka Noe and Meo Noe) and the other by Ebu Pae. While killing buffalo in this way accords with the practice in Wolo Wea, doing so without a *peo*, and particularly without a forked Cassiawood post, is to say the least highly unusual.

either two or three named groups. In Pajo and Réja, dualism involves two of the three in each case being recognized as a single unit (Bindi and Loga, Sopi and Sabe). Somewhat in contrast, in Sawu (Sawu Obo) and Dhawe, third groups (Wani Wona, Ndoi) are subsumed by one of the two others, indeed by a group which in both cases is more recently arrived in the present village territory. In Loka Kayo, on the other hand, a dual division of two agnatic segments, identifiable as a single clan, has recently been joined by what can alternatively be construed as either a second or a third group (Ebu Pae). Wajo looks like the inverse of this, in so far as here an incoming pair may have joined a third, earlier, group now recognized as second in order of sacrificial precedence. Only Dhawe Yoja and Oja appear straightforwardly binary in their composition. Further variations on the generally dualistic order of Keo settlements are demonstrated in the following chapter.

6

The Land of Lobo, the Youngest Ga'e

The furthest west of the original ancestral territories, the domain of Lobo Ga'e, the youngest of the Ga'e siblings, is also the smallest. The area is further distinguished dialectally and culturally from the other territories, most obviously in regard to the naming and disposition of ceremonial buildings. With qualifications explained later, the domain includes lands belonging to three villages: Liwo, Wulu, and Wagha. Agnatically related to Wagha is the former village of Béna which, together with the paired settlement of Ki and the subsidiary Ma'u Béna, I describe towards the end of the chapter.

1. Liwo

Central to the domain of Lobo Ga'e is the village of Liwo, where two clans (*suku* or *woe*)—Liwo and Jadho—claim direct agnatic descent from this ancestor. By contrast, a third clan, Wulu Wogo, traces descent to an immigrant named Wogo from Kuyu Wulu (Bolo Yoga). Situated on a steep and irregular site oriented towards Mount Nata, the present Liwo, founded over sixty years ago, replaces two earlier villages located just 100 metres or so inland. Specified as Liwo Loka Lére, or Liwo Lére, the more seaward of the pair is described as the residence of Aga Reti, the son of Lobo Ga'e and the common ancestor of clans Liwo and Jadho. The village of Wulu Wogo, inhabited by the clan of that name, was then located a short distance landward of Old Liwo.

Although members of clan Liwo described Wulu Wogo and Liwo as always sharing a single 'village' (*nua*), other evidence thus suggests that the modern Liwo village descends from a double settlement, with the older village situated just below, or seaward, of the younger. While still discernible in the present site, this dualism has become greatly obscured by a recent relocation of clan houses. Broadly speaking, the present village comprises two physical halves, Lower Liwo (Liwo Loka Au) and Upper Liwo (Liwo Loka Wawo), located seaward and landward respectively. All houses of clan Liwo are found in the Lower section, as is their *peo*, a sacrificial *dheyo* tree (see Plate 18). Liwo shares this *peo* with clan Jadho. Yet in spite of this connection all Jadho houses are located in Upper Liwo, the site of a separate stone *peo* (*peo watu*) belonging to clan Wulu Wogo. Moreover, houses of Wulu Wogo are divided between the Upper and Lower sections of Liwo, with the majority (eight of the present ten) located in Lower Liwo. It is thus rather as though a formerly separate settlement of Wulu Wogo had been superimposed upon Liwo village, and then

PLATE 18. Sacrificial *dheyo* tree in Liwo

mostly on its landward half (see Fig. 10). Although nowadays spoken of as a single village (*nua*), especially in regard to the two sacrificial instruments erected in parts of the village nominally distinguished as 'upper' and 'lower', the present Liwo otherwise resembles Dhawe (Dhawe Mére), described in the previous chapter.

Apart from the two *peo*, the landward–seaward (or upper–lower) contrast that once more clearly articulated the opposition of Wulu Wogo, on the one hand, and Liwo and Jadho, on the other, is physically manifest in the disposition of two trees, serving as places of offering, which are planted just beyond the landward boundary (or 'head') of the present settlement. Located further landward, a banyan tree (*nunu*) with a stone altar beneath is where people of Wulu Wogo offer rice, meat, and tobacco to beneficent spirits in times of affliction (*tu mara*, I: 3: iv; see Plate 19). A few metres seaward of the banyan one finds a *sayo* tree (also called *sayo kayo*, 'thorny sayo'; unidentified) that is similarly employed. This belongs to clan Liwo but is used as well by Jadho.

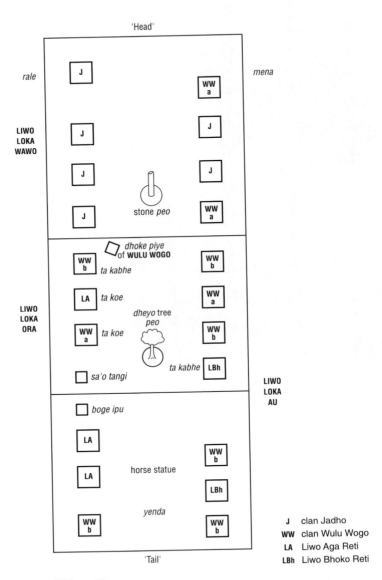

FIG. 10. Plan of Liwo village

PLATE 19. Place of offering of clan Wulu Wogo beneath the banyan tree at the land-ward end of Liwo

Clans Liwo and Jadho claim a single agnatic origin in a male ancestor named Paya Léba, the son of the above-mentioned Aga Reti. Paya had two wives. Clan Liwo descends from Paya's first wife, while clan Jadho stems from the second (see Fig. 11). Liwo is thus senior to Jadho. At a higher genealogical level, however, another bifurcation of Liwo confers separate ancestral status on the sister of Aga Reti. Named Bhoko Reti, this sister is recognized as the forebear of the junior half of clan Liwo, usually distinguished simply as 'Liwo Bhoko Reti'. Thus, whereas the socially more inclusive contrast—between the separately named clans Liwo and Jadho—is founded on the relation of *ka'e ari* (elder and younger same-sex sibling), a division within Liwo, the senior clan, is grounded in the relation of opposite-sex siblings (*weta naya*). At the same time, common descent within clan Liwo is traced to a woman—Reti, the mother of both Aga Reti and Bhoko Reti. Of course, Jadho, too, can in principle trace its derivation to this woman. Yet Jadho is separated from, and subordinated to, clan Liwo by virtue of their specific male ancestor's birth to a

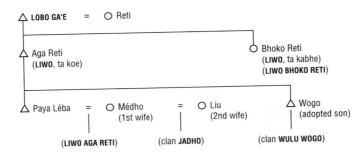

FIG. 11. Genealogical relations among named groups in Liwo

different mother, the junior wife of Paya Léba (the son of Aga Reti). As already shown, deriving paired groups from a brother and a sister is not unique to Liwo; it is also encountered in the village of Suga Bhoja, in regard to clans Koyu and Yéwe (II: 1: v).

Liwo village provides yet another instance of a settlement nominally identified with its major, and in this case oldest clan. The two segments of clan Liwo divide the main ritual positions connected with their common *peo dheyo*; the descendants of Aga Reti, the male sibling, claim the position of earth breaker (*ta koe*) while the descendants of Bhoko Reti, the female sibling, claim that of excavator (*ta kabhe*). Clan Jadho is thus left out of this ceremonial division, although Jadho people, too, rightfully slaughter at the sacrificial *dheyo* tree.

Since the two segments of clan Liwo, descending respectively from a brother and sister, could be construed as related originally as wife-giver and wife-taker, it might be supposed that the *dheyo* tree *peo* is a remnant of that relationship (I: 2: iv). However, Liwo claim that they have always possessed a sacrificial tree of this sort, and that it has never been paired with a *kesi* tree as is done elsewhere. With one possible exception, members of the segment of Liwo descending from Bhoko Reti appear not to have taken further wives from the group descending from Aga Reti since the initial marriage of their anonymous male ancestor. Apart from one other union involving a wife from clan Jadho, I recorded no other marriages between these three groups.

Sometimes Liwo villagers equate the division of the entire present settlement into Lower and Upper sections with the division of the two clans Liwo and Jadho. More particularly, Upper Liwo is identified with Jadho, and vice versa. Possibly relevant here is the local gloss of 'Jadho' as 'elevated place'.[1] Occasionally, one also hears the name Liwo Loka Ora, or 'Central Liwo'. Referring to that part of Liwo village occupied by the leader of the senior segment of clan Liwo (or 'Liwo Aga Reti')—the group recognized as earth

---

[1] Despite repeated enquiries, I was never able to discover any separate meaning for the name 'Liwo'.

breaker (*ta koe*)—'Central Liwo' in fact denotes the landward part of Lower Liwo, lying above the *peo dheyo*. Interestingly, when explaining this association of the headman of clan Liwo with this notionally central area, informants described the leader as belonging to both Upper and Lower Liwo, an idea that might be understood in regard to his group's agnatic seniority in relation to Jadho (sometimes identified as 'Upper Liwo') as well as its genealogical connection with Liwo Bhoko Reti, clan Liwo's junior segment. Some villagers initially identified clans Liwo and Jadho respectively with the male and female ancestors Aga Reti and Bhoko Reti. Although later information showed this to be incorrect, in regard to the generally dualistic tendency of Keo representations it is nevertheless interesting how these associations involve identifying the junior of a pair of clans with the junior segment—the one deriving from a female ancestor—of the senior clan.

The foregoing distinctions all subtend the more inclusive dualism comprising an original grouping (clans Liwo and Jadho) and an immigrant clan, Wulu Wogo. Named partly after its apical ancestor, clan Wulu Wogo derives from Wogo, a man of clan Yoga in Kuyu Wulu who, as an infant, was abandoned during the civil strife that resulted in the breakup of the double settlement of Bolo Yoga (II: 1: iii). According to one account, Wogo was rescued and brought to Liwo by Wulu Wo'a, the wife of a Yoga ancestor. Other versions give the Liwo ancestor Aga Reti as Wogo's rescuer. Either way, the infant was raised to maturity by Aga Reti, who provided him with land located in the vicinity of the present village of Wulu. Clan Wulu Wogo is thus counted as Defender (*ana tuku*) of Liwo, more particularly of the senior segment of the clan (Liwo Aga Reti). Some time later, Wulu Wogo people acquired further land from the Wagha people; hence the group is also considered a Defender of Wagha. Owning land close to Wulu village, Wogo eventually took up residence in Wulu, from where his clan derived the other part of its name. There, Wogo's agnatic descendants remained for some considerable time until, perhaps about six generations ago, they rejoined Liwo, settling just landward of the descendants of Aga Reti and erecting a stone *peo*.

Retaining rights to land in the region of Wulu, a few Wulu Wogo people continue to cultivate fields there, residing in field huts in the nearby hamlet of Wolo Poma. Although they no longer reside within Wulu village, an elder of the Wulu clan Pata claimed that Wulu Wogo could rightfully erect houses in Wulu, more specifically in the old village of Wulu Olo, if they wished to do so. Indeed, until recently, Wulu Wogo maintained a *bhaga*, a small ceremonial building, within the bounds of the old village, and on the stone altar (*nabe*) that still marks its former site they still place food offerings when one of their number suffers illness or other affliction. This continuing connection with Wulu village also finds expression in the context of buffalo sacrifice in Liwo, when the horns of animals slaughtered by Wulu Wogo at their stone *peo* in Upper Liwo are taken to the *yenda* in which the four clans of Wulu, also, place their trophy horns. Similar relations of subordination in sacrificial contexts have, of course, been noted in earlier chapters. Accordingly, in relation to the *peo* that stands in the old village of Wulu (Wulu Olo), Wulu Wogo's sacrificial instrument in Liwo is conceived as a 'branch *peo*' (*taya so, kamu lana*, 'extended branch, spreading root').

Owing to their ancestor's ultimate derivation from clan Yoga, Wulu Wogo people are also recognized as possessing rights to land within the territory of Kuyu Wulu (Bolo Yoga). The clan thus participates simultaneously in the internal order of two separate villages (*nua*) as well as three distinct village territories. Similarly, within Liwo the clan at present occupies both the Upper and Lower sections of the village. As noted, its sacrificial pillar (*peo watu*) is located in Upper Liwo (Liwo Loka Wawo), where it is mostly flanked by houses of Jadho. On the other hand, the two principal houses of Wulu Wogo, those holding the ritual positions of earth breaker (*ta koe*) and excavator (*ta kabhe*) in respect of the stone *peo*, are both situated in Lower Liwo (Liwo Loka Au), in proximity to houses belonging to the *ta koe* and *ta kabhe* of the sacrificial *dheyo* tree, also located in this part of the settlement and most closed identified with clan Liwo. By virtue of this arrangement, then, the paired ritual statuses associated with both *peo* are localized in the central area of the present village sometimes distinguished as Liwo Loka Ora ('Central Liwo').

While forming one half of an inclusive social dualism still partly manifest in the spatial order of Liwo village, clan Wulu Wogo is itself constituted dualistically, comprising two segments associated respectively with the two ceremonial positions attaching to the clan's *peo*. Sometimes described as separate *suku* (clans), the two groups are nowadays usually distinguished with the first two letters of the Roman alphabet as 'Wulu Wogo A' and 'Wulu Wogo B'.[2] The senior group (A), the one recognized as earth breaker, traces a direct line of descent from an ancestor named Koro Géto. Following the typical pattern, the name actually refers to a pair of brothers, the sons of Wogo and a Liwo woman, of whom one, Géto, was childless. In contrast, the junior division of Wulu Wogo (group B), which occupies the position of excavator, descends from a later descendant of Wogo named Ese. In the present settlement, there are two houses of Wulu Wogo located in Upper Liwo, and both belong to the senior segment (A). The remaining eight are all located in Lower Liwo, and with two exceptions (one being the house of the earth breaker), these belong to the junior segment (Wulu Wogo B). Even though the division of the clan does not, therefore, exactly articulate with the two physical sections of the village, houses of the senior group are still mostly placed landward of those belonging to the junior—a pattern which, it may be noted, is contrary to the relative

---

[2] These are alternatively called Wulu A and Wulu B, or simply Suku A and Suku B. I seem not to have heard the two groups referred to as *ngapi*. In any case, each comprises more than one *ngapi* (estate): the A group has four, and the B group two. The group of three incorporating the two segments of Liwo plus Jadho also do not coincide with single estates; each of the former includes two *ngapi* while Jadho comprises three.

PLATE 20. *Yenda* on two posts with horse statue at the seaward end of Liwo

disposition of Liwo and Wulu Wogo as a whole, as well as that of clan Liwo and clan Jadho.

Like Wagha, Wulu, and other villages in the far-western part of the study area, Liwo displays an arrangement of ritual structures that reverses the pattern found elsewhere in western Keo (I: 2: v). Owing largely to the greater deterioration of traditional buildings elsewhere, Liwo in fact provides the clearest instance of this inverted order (see Fig. 10). Whereas in other western Keo villages, buildings called *yenda* are placed at the head, or landward extremity, of a village, the present *yenda* (locally pronounced *yeda*) belonging to clans Liwo and Jadho is placed at the seaward extremity, or tail, of Lower Liwo (see Plate 20). What is more, the wooden horse statue erected in front of the building faces *rale* (the left side of the village site), rather than *mena* as in other Keo settlements. By the same token, the *nde*, the ritual building complementing the *yenda* which elsewhere is found at the seaward extremity of a village, is replaced in Lower Liwo by a building, designated as *sa'o de*, or *joto*, which stands on just two posts some distance landward of the *yenda*. This building does not, however, occupy the actual head (*ulu*) of Lower Liwo, but rather is placed on one side, to the left (*rale*) of the sacrificial *dheyo* tree. Also supported by two posts, just seaward of Liwo's *nde* (*sa'o de*) one further encounters a special building known as *boge ipu*, a structure not employed in any of the villages previously described.[3] The Wulu Wogo people, too, claim once to have maintained a structure of this sort in Upper Liwo, supported by a single post and equipped with a small ladder of seven rungs. Although I have no record of Wulu Wogo possessing a *nde*, until recently the clan maintained a building called *joto dhoke piye* (or simply *dhoke piye*) at the landward extremity of Lower Liwo, which appears partly to have served a similar function.[4]

No one I questioned could explain why in Liwo and neighbouring villages ritual structures are arranged contrary to their disposition elsewhere in the region. Indeed, some people, including one elderly traditionalist who had often visited other Keo villages, appeared unaware of the difference, describing the opposite orientation of wooden horses, for example, as simply wrong and likely to result in social disorder.[5] It would seem too fanciful to suggest that the inversions somehow reflect the association of Liwo and other villages with Lobo Ga'e, the youngest of the Ga'e siblings, even though his name (Lobo is 'tip, top extremity' of a plant or length of wood) partially sets him off from older members of a group considered collectively as a source or origin (*pu'u*, the stem or trunk end of a plant or tree). For one thing, the village of Loka Mude, located to the west of Liwo, also has *yenda* and *nde* placed respectively at its seaward and landward extremities, but this community is not clearly connected with Lobo Ga'e. Since Liwo and neighbouring villages are vaguely described as historically associated with the Nage region, it is interesting that in Nage as well, *yenda* (there called *heda*) are located at a village's seaward end. In Nage, however, wooden horse statues erected in front of such buildings face towards the *mena* side of the village, as they do in most of western Keo, rather than towards the *rale* side, as in Liwo, Wulu, and Wagha. The wooden horse in Loka Mude, also, faces *mena*.[6]

In spite of the foregoing physical differences, the village of Liwo reveals variants of social arrangements widely encountered in other parts of Keo. Particularly noteworthy is the subsumption of junior by senior components as signalled by several applications of the name Liwo. In its most general application, Liwo denotes the entire village, including Liwo in a stricter

---

[3] Although apparently connected with the fish fry (*ipu*) which appear in river mouths three times a year, the function of this building is obscure. Liwo elders described the structure only as a place to store a container (*tuku*) filled with fish fry. The term *boge* otherwise refers to preserved meat. The account I was given of a similarly named building in Wagha, however, suggests a different usage, and perhaps one involving a metaphorical association of fish fry and rice seed (see n. 21).

[4] *Dhoke* denotes a large bamboo container, while *piye* means 'restricted, prohibited'. Elsewhere kept inside a *nde* or in a special granary (*bo*), containers thus named are used to store 'old rice' (*pae olo*) before this is ritually consumed and replaced with rice from the new harvest. *Dhoke piye* should always be kept full of rice, in order to ensure continuous harvests. (As noted earlier, Wulu Wogo has never possessed a *yenda* in Liwo, being still bound to the structure of this kind in the village of Wulu.)

[5] Wooden horses pointing *mena*, or towards the sunrise (the disposition observed in most western Keo villages) were thus claimed to cause children to 'turn their backs on', or disobey, their mothers (*logo du ine*).

[6] The local notion of a historical connection with Nage possibly derives mainly, or even entirely, from the colonial decision to make the former Maukeli region, including Liwo and neighbouring villages, part of the Nage district. This may in turn have been based on apparent linguistic and cultural similarities, such as the location of ritual buildings, which the Dutch deemed significant in their efforts to identify indigenous political units.

sense coinciding with the descendants of Lobo Ga'e, plus the immigrant group Wulu Wogo. Conceived separately from Wulu Wogo, Liwo then comprises clan Liwo and clan Jadho, while in the most exclusive contrast the name is more closely associated with the descendants of Aga Reti, the principal owners of the *dheyo* tree *peo* in Lower Liwo, as opposed to the group derived from Aga's sister, Bhoko Reti. Worth noting here is the way in which distinctions within the older half of Liwo are conceived identically to the division of Wulu Wogo. Perhaps influenced by the use of the letters A and B to articulate the latter, one nowadays encounters the names 'Liwo A' and 'Liwo B', sometimes used to distinguish the groups derived from Aga Reti and Bhoko Reti respectively, but also employed to distinguish clan Liwo from clan Jadho. In this respect, we might further recall the local confusion between Liwo Bhoko Reti and Jadho mentioned above.

Liwo displays several peculiarities that distinguish it from other villages. Prominent among these is the spatial 'overlap', whereby the principals (*ta koe* and *ta kabhe*) of the two *peo*, erected in the landward and seaward parts of the village respectively, are all resident in a central section coinciding with the landward half of Lower Liwo. Expressed another way, this involves the formerly separate landward settlement (*nua*) of Wulu Wogo overlapping the area now occupied by Liwo (that is, clans Liwo and Jadho, occupants of the former village of Liwo Lére), and in this way spatially conflating, as it were, two parts of an earlier dualism. It is as though one were looking at a merging of two villages that has stopped half-way.

By virtue of a continuing formal presence of clan Wulu Wogo in Wulu, Liwo as a whole displays a similar overlap with the village of Wulu, thus suggesting another sort of incomplete transition. In so far as Liwo can be said to comprise three clans (Liwo, Jadho, and Wulu Wogo), this has plainly resulted from merging the formerly more separate immigrant group, Wulu Wogo, with a pre-existing pair. How far one can identify a more exclusive triad, by considering the two divisions of Liwo—Aga Reti and Bhoko Reti—as structurally equivalent to clan Jadho is a moot point. It is, however, a matter of some interest and, indeed, a further peculiarity of Liwo that, whereas Jadho and Liwo Aga Reti are genealogically closer than either is to Liwo Bhoko Reti (see Fig. 11), socially—that is, in regard to their membership of clan Liwo as distinct from Jadho, as well as in respect of their occupying the paired statuses of *ta koe* and *ta kabhe*—it is the descendants of the brother and sister pair (Aga and Bhoko) who are more closely bound together. Here the crucial factor would appear to be the birth of the ancestors Aga and Bhoko from the same woman (Reti), and thus derivation from the same wife-giving house (I: 4, 5). In contrast, the Jadho ancestor and Aga Reti's senior heir were born of different women; thus the two groups derive from different wife-giving sources.

For purposes of comparison with previously described villages, we may conclude this section with a brief review of affinal relations within Liwo.

Although Wulu Wogo has sometimes given wives to Liwo and Jadho, it has more often been a wife-taker, a status that accords with the clan's position as Defender of Liwo. The wife of the ancestor Wogo was a woman of Liwo; also, men in the three most recent generations of Wogo's descendants have married women of Liwo Aga Reti. Although the distinction of the two divisions of clan Liwo does not consistently figure in these patterns, it is noteworthy that the senior segment of Wulu Wogo (Wulu Wogo A) has also taken wives over several generations from clan Jadho, whereas the junior segment (Wulu Wogo B) has during the last three generations given wives to Jadho, although in a couple of other instances, including the earliest recorded marriage, it has taken women from Jadho. Whether or not one includes Jadho with clan Liwo as a member of the older moiety (also called Liwo), in these patterns one discerns a general correspondence between territorial precedence and alliance status, as is in varying degrees exemplified in the other Ga'e domains, where older groups provide both land and wives to latter arrivals. Also noteworthy in this context is a relatively early marriage between a forebear of the senior segment of Wulu Wogo and a woman of Wagha (specifically, clan Wagha), Wulu Wogo's other land grantor.

2. *Wulu*

As shown above, part of the territory associated with the village of Wulu is included within the original domain of Lobo Ga'e and his son, Aga Reti. Another part belongs to the domain of Lape Ga'e (or Lape Mére). This territorial combination coincides with a division of Wulu into two pairs of clans: Pata and Poma, and Tongo and Néso. The eldest and the youngest clans, Tongo and Néso, share land derived from Aga Reti, while Pata and Poma occupy territory inherited from the most senior Land Mother, Lape. This quadripartite representation does not, of course, take into account the residual presence of Wulu Wogo; but for the time being, it may be noted that clan Néso, the most recent arrival, appears in effect to have taken the place of Wulu Wogo.

The four clans of Wulu display a distinctive pattern of nomenclature in so far as the name of each is optionally prefixed with 'Ebu'. One thus hears, for example, Ebu Pata as well as Pata (or Suku Pata). Also the term for 'grandparent, ancestor' and 'grandchild, descendant' (as well as a personal name), Wulu people interpreted *ebu* in this context as equivalent to *suku* (clan), further glossing the term as 'descendants of'.[7] However that may be, it is almost certain that Néso, named after a former hamlet, was never called Ebu Néso before its recent incorporation into Wulu. Contrary to what the kinship or vocative usage of *ebu*

---

[7] Following this interpretation, Ebu Pata, for example, could be translated as 'descendants of Pata'. 'Ebu' similarly occurs in clan names in the village Loka Mude, to the west of the study area. The term is not, however, employed to refer to clans in the abstract; thus if one wants to ask 'how many clans' there are in a village, one must say *suku pira*, not **ebu pira*.

might suggest, none of the other three names appears to refer to an ancestor either. Although all three are employed as personal names, the application of Pata and Poma to clans more straightforwardly reflects their status as place-names (as I show below). The case of Tongo, the oldest of the four clans, is less clear. Although this group does not descend from anyone called Ebu Tongo, it is nevertheless possible that this name may have provided a model for the naming of the three later arrivals.

Somewhat consistent with the unity suggested by the common nomen-clature, Keo sometimes speak of Wulu as a whole as a single 'Suku Wulu'. In a more specific sense, however, this name refers to the three older groups, Tongo, Pata, and Poma, and thus excludes the youngest clan, Néso. Reflecting this distinction, only the three older groups observe a prohibition on pork.[8] As I describe later, still other evidence reveals a special, if not exclusive, association of 'Wulu' with clan Pata. At the same time, according to the only account I was able to record of the derivation of the village name, Wulu was the name of an ancestress of the oldest clan, Tongo, whose natal clan was possibly Liwo. Consistent with this, while the territory of Wulu encompasses parts of the domains of two major Land Mothers, the site of the actual village is on land belonging to Tongo.

As the first clan to occupy Wulu village, clan Tongo was granted land by the Liwo ancestor, Aga Reti. Thus, Tongo is recognized as a Defender of Liwo (or, as this is more often expressed, 'Defender of Aga'). Hailing from a place no longer known, the founder of Tongo, and hence the village of Wulu, was either Jata Rike or his son, Godhi Raga. Following one version of the charter myth, Jata Rike acquired land from Aga Reti by way of a wager, which he won by shooting and killing an Imperial pigeon (*rawa*; *Ducula aenea*). Jata then estab-lished himself in a hamlet called Sa'o Jata ('House of Jata'), before he or his son founded Wulu. According to one report, Jata Rike's son, Godhi Raga, was born illegitimately to a sister of Aga Reti (who, however, was not explicitly identified as the previously mentioned Bhoko Reti). If this is accepted, then informally at least, the Tongo ancestor was a wife-taker (*ana weta*) of Aga as well as Liwo's Defender.

According to another version of the myth, it was Godhi Raga who killed the pigeon and won the bet with Aga Reti. With reference to the second

---

[8] Some accounts describe the Wulu people, or more specifically the Pata ancestor Raga Wea, as having adopted the pork prohibition from clan Céla in Nua Nage, or from the Céla ancestor Lape Mére. According to others, Wulu derived the taboo, indeed took it over, from the Boba people of eastern Ngadha, while an elder of clan Yoga in Keo Ondo claimed that it was his clan that assumed the Boba prohibition. Interestingly, accounts referring both to Wulu and Yoga—links between which were outlined earlier (II: 1, and see Fig. 6)—associate the prohibition with a skin condition called *una*, which disappeared when members of the Keo clans ceased eating pork but, by the same token, became prevalent among the Boba people. Several narratives also link the taboo with *sudu*, an annual pugilistic compe-tition now held only in the village of Wulu. According to one, Wulu people adopted the prohibition as a reparation following a *sudu* in which one of their number struck and killed a Céla man. Apparently relevant to this account, as to other mythical explanations of the pork taboo, is Céla's status as wife-giver of Wulu and several other groups, includ-ing Yoga. Here it should be recalled that pork is the meat wife-givers generally serve to wife-takers.

component of his name, one account of the history of clan Pata links Godhi with the previously mentioned Pata ancestor Raga Wea, also known as Raga Kico (*kico*, 'harelip', is a nickname). Following this version, the pigeon killers were Godhi and Raga, or an unspecified one of the pair. After consuming the bird, apparently in or near Wulu, Raga was about to take his leave when Godhi invited him to stay and share his village. However this story might be reconciled with the other, apparently better known variant, it is generally agreed that clan Pata was the second group to move to Wulu. Prior to this, the group, or their widely known ancestor, had been resident in a village named Rea which in turn was the successor of an even earlier residential site in the vicinity of Mount Nata, bearing the same name as the Pata ancestor, Raga Kico.

As noted earlier (II: 1: iii), Raga Wea (Raga Kico) was the son of Wea Mére, the sister of Lape Mére, and thus was related to the founders of several other clans and villages (see Fig. 6). Land granted to clan Pata accordingly forms part of the domain of Lape, and the clan is recognized as a Defender of this Land Mother. The father of Raga Wea was a man named Léko Ana, but little is known about him. As in similar cases, what is stressed is clan Pata's connection, through Raga and his mother, with Lape Mére. Because Raga Wea had no children of his own, he appointed an outsider as heir. This man, named Tawa Owa, belonged to a family originating on Pata Island, located in Riung Bay off the north coast of Flores. From there they brought to the Keo region a miraculously powerful goat (named Buju Réno), which they sold to Raga Wea. It is, of course, from the reputed place of derivation of Raga's heir that his clan has since come to be named Pata, or Ebu Pata.

As Tongo was the first group to arrive in Wulu, it naturally holds the premier ritual position of earth breaker in respect of the *peo*—formerly a sacrificial *dheyo* tree, as in Liwo, but nowadays a vertical stone column (*peo watu*).[9] By the same token, Tongo is also the first to slaughter at collective sacrifices held in Wulu. As the second arrival, Pata is then recognized as excavator (*ta kabhe*). Nevertheless, in several respects clan Pata is more closely associated with the whole, or at least with the name 'Wulu', than is Tongo, a circumstance that may be ascribed to Pata's association with the seniormost Land Mother (Lape Mére). As noted previously, clans now known simply as Wulu in Nua Nage and Bo'a Ora (Wulu Wayu) are more precisely agnatic branches of clan Pata. By reference to the name, moreover, the area of the village of Kuyu Wulu ('Wulu's Pasture') is claimed specifically by Pata (II: 1: iii).[10]

Also relevant in this connection is the report that, because the gongs and

---

[9] During the first half of the twentieth century, the *dheyo* was replaced because it had become too large and, rather than pollard the tree (a procedure requiring a particular ritual), it was decided to remove it altogether. Pata people claimed that their clan had also possessed a stone *peo* in their original village of Rea.

[10] Although the usage cannot be fully discussed here, it might also be mentioned that a sort of ritual functionary, *teke mére*, apparently found only in Wulu, is most closely linked with clan Pata. Such functionaries were described as *ana ta gua* ('ritualist, performer, leader of ceremonies'; cf. *uma gua*), a term that recalls *ana susu* elsewhere (see I: 2: v).

drums played at buffalo sacrifices were first provided by Raga Wea, there was no sacrificing in Wulu before the Pata ancestor arrived. This, of course, is tantamount to claiming that Wulu was not a proper village (*nua*) prior to Pata's arrival. The parity between Tongo and Pata which this implies is further revealed by the fact that the two clans each plant separate ritual gardens (*uma gua*). Located about one metre apart and each consisting of four tiny terraced sections, these contrast with the miniature fields found elsewhere, which comprise seven sections. That both clans maintain this practice is evidently bound up with the inclusion of their territories within the domains of different Ga'e siblings. It is, however, the Tongo people who have precedence in this, Pata planting their garden on the day after the older clan.

Although Wulu originally comprised just Tongo and Pata, clan Pata also forms a pair with the present third clan, Poma (or Ebu Poma). Sharing land with the older clan, Poma is described as Pata's Defender, though at least one Pata elder wished to deny this attribution; and their relationship is more often classified as *ka'e ari* ('siblingship'). Poma's origin is somewhat obscure. Contrary to expectation, the group does not claim derivation from the Poma district, nor any relationship with clan Loka Poma in Pau Lundu. Following one account, Pata and Poma originally resided together in the village named after the Pata ancestor, Raga Kico. From there, Pata removed to Rea—located atop one of several hills surrounding Mount Nata and at one time also inhabited by the ancestor of clan Ngodho in Pau Lundu (II: 3: iii)—while Poma went to Wolo Poma ('Poma Hill'), the place from which the clan evidently took its name (*poma* means 'pool, wallow'). The two groups were then reunited after both moved to join Tongo in Wulu. According to another report, Pata as well as Poma once resided in Wolo Poma; but this is not easily reconciled with other histories of clan Pata. Although circumstances suggest that, before leaving Rea, Poma may have formed a single clan with Pata, no genealogical connection is any longer known or recognized.

How the arrival in Wulu village of the ancestor Wogo, and the establishment of his clan, Wulu Wogo, fit with the above is no longer certain. Since Pata is generally recognized as the second clan in Wulu, however, Wulu Wogo evidently came later than Pata, if not after Poma. What is more certain is that the very last of the present four groups to appear was clan Néso, and that Néso arrived after the Wulu Wogo people had removed to Liwo.

Before exploring the history of Néso, attention should be given to one of Wulu's more notable features. This is another aspect of internal social relations that sets apart the trio of Tongo, Pata, and Poma. As villagers themselves recognize, the oldest clans compose a regular three-unit alliance cycle, whereby Tongo gives wives to Pata, Pata to Poma, and then Poma to Tongo (see Fig. 12). As will immediately be clear, the first two relationships involve older groups standing as wife-givers to younger groups, while in the case of Pata and Poma asymmetric affinity coincides with the relation of land grantor and grantee (or

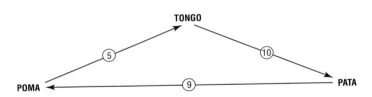

The figures in circles were computed by adding the number of marriages found in the genealogical record for each clan and then subtracting the number of unions recorded in both. For example Tongo's genealogy shows 8 women's marriages where the husband was a Pata man, while the genealogy of Pata reveals 7 men's marriages where the wife was from Tongo. Since 5 specific unions are recorded in both genealogies, this figure is subtracted from 15 (8+7) to give a total of 10. The size of the samples is indicated in note 12.

FIG. 12. Alliance cycle in Wulu

Land Mother and Defender).[11] The value Wulu people place on maintaining this cyclical relation is indicated by their insistence that Pata 'must' take wives from Tongo, Poma from Pata, and Tongo from Poma. Of course, all groups have other wife-givers and wife-takers; yet the genealogical record shows that each clan is the major wife-giver or wife-taker of another member of the triad rather than of any group outside Wulu.[12]

Most of the men's marriages recorded for clan Néso—seven of ten— involve one of the three older clans in Wulu. Wives were given by Pata in three unions, by Poma in another three, and by Tongo in just one. In another case, Tongo had taken a wife from Néso. While the record is incomplete (I was able to obtain detailed information from only one of Néso's two estates), the pattern is noteworthy because Néso's major wife-givers are Poma and Pata, rather than Tongo, the clan that granted Néso rights to land in Wulu territory.

Just as Wulu Wogo retains a residual presence in the village, so Néso contrariwise has never become fully incorporated into Wulu. Néso derives from people of clan Late who left Nua Muri (II: 5: ii), perhaps as recently as four or five generations ago. Tapping palms at a spot called Loka Néso or Wolo Néso ('Néso Hill'), these Late people were invited by the landowner, clan Tongo, to remain and begin cultivating near the site. Thus acquiring rights to this land, the Néso people, now named after their initial place of abode, estab- lished a permanent settlement that came to be known as Bo'a Néso (Néso

---

[11] Only one marriage I recorded, in which Poma took a woman from Tongo, appears contrary to the pattern. This is not considered incorrect as it concerns houses of the two clans that do not normally participate in the regular exchange.

[12] Tongo is wife-giver in seven of 22 Pata men's marriages, while Poma is wife-taker in three of 17 Pata women's marriages. Of 34 Poma men's marriages, Pata is wife-giver in eight instances, while Tongo is wife-taker in four of 25 women's marriages. The Tongo genealogy shows Poma as wife-giver in four of 25 men's marriages, and Pata as wife- taker in eight of 30 women's marriages.

Hamlet). Becoming recognized as Defenders of Tongo, moreover, they were eventually granted a *peo* of their own by the older clan. Like the present exemplar, this was a forked post of *yebu* (Cassia) wood. Although no one could clarify why Néso adopted a sacrificial instrument of this kind, the choice possibly reflects Late's ultimate derivation from the southern part of Nage, where forked posts are universal. As the source of Néso's land, clan Tongo is designated as earth breaker in respect of this *peo*, while the position of excavator remains with Néso.[13] But since this is a forked post, it also has trunk and tip riders (*saka pu'u* and *saka lobo*), positions that are assigned to the two *ngapi* (deriving from an elder and a younger brother, Mite Fedo and Ao Fedo) into which the clan is divided.

Although nowadays they are counted as one of the four clans of Wulu, most evidence suggests that Néso people have never resided in Wulu village. One account describes Néso as possessing just one house, located somewhere near the seaward end of Wulu. According to another report, this was not a house but a ceremonial structure (*bhaga*; I: 2: v) symbolizing their possession of land within Tongo's original territory. However, this, too, was later contradicted: the *bhaga* was not erected in Wulu, but in a village separately inhabited by the Néso people. Even before acquiring their own sacrificial instrument, Néso never slaughtered buffalo in Wulu, but continued to do so in their original village of Nua Muri. Following what seemed to be the most reliable information, under the auspices of Tongo, clan Néso erected their first *peo* after moving from 'Néso Hamlet' (Bo'a Néso) to Eko Nila, a place located just a short distance from Wulu village, early in the twentieth century.

Further clarifying social and spatial relations between Néso and the other three clans of Wulu is the more recent history of Wulu village. Sometimes distinguished as Wulu Olo ('Old Wulu'), Wulu nowadays includes just two houses, one belonging to Tongo (more particularly its senior estate, or *ngapi pu'u*), and the other to Poma. Both houses were built in the last few years, as part of a restoration following the abandonment of the settlement after a major landslide in the 1930s. At that time, people began moving to Déna (*déna*, 'flat area'), a slightly lower-lying site a short distance to the northwest. By the late 1960s, therefore, Old Wulu had become completely deserted, and Déna—or 'Wulu Déna', a compound that further designates Wulu and Déna together— had effectively replaced Old Wulu. As evidenced by the two recently built houses, villagers are, however, returning to Wulu Olo and their intention is eventually to renew the entire settlement.

Located a short distance inland from Old Wulu, Déna now merges with a settled area called Eko Nila. Whether this is the village where clan Néso first erected a *peo* or a different site not far away from the first and called by the

---

[13] A Pata elder contradicted this, arguing that Pata, not Néso, should act as excavator.

same name, is no longer certain.[14] Whichever it was, the present Eko Nila is equally associated with Néso, being the site of its present forked post (erected about 1950) as well as two of its three houses. Nowadays, villagers apply the name Déna to this site as well, so that Déna in effect comprises two parts: one closer to Old Wulu and also named Déna, and Eko Nila. This present duality, superficially resembling a double settlement, does not, however, quite coincide with a division of clans. In addition to the Néso houses, Eko Nila thus contains most of clan Poma's houses and one of Tongo's. Also, while Déna in the exclusive sense incorporates other houses of Tongo as well as all houses of clan Pata, it also contains the third Néso house. What the development of this new settlement appears to have effected, then, is a spatial dualism largely coinciding with the opposition of, on the one hand, the two oldest clans (Tongo and Pata, the Defenders of Aga Reti and Lape respectively) and, on the other, the two newest (Néso and Poma, the respective Defenders of the former pair).

Yet the contrast between the two parts of the present settlement is stronger than this characterization might suggest. Incorporating the *peo* of Néso, only Eko Nila can properly be called a village (*nua*), even though, for reasons I was unable to discover, it lacks a formal *ulu éko* name. In contrast, Déna, the area now mostly occupied by Pata and Tongo, has never possessed a sacrificial structure, nor, like Eko Nila, a ceremonial designation. In regard to Déna's lack of an *ulu éko* name, people pointed out that, because the two ends of Déna are disposed *mena* and *rale* (or 'right' and 'left') rather than landward and seaward, the settlement in effect lacks a 'head' (*ulu*) and a 'tail' (*éko*). At the same time, the area now distinguished as Eko Nila, as its name would suggest, is spoken of as constituting the 'tail' of Déna, a circumstance perhaps connected with Eko Nila's similar lack of a ceremonial designation. In effect, Déna lies below and perpendicular to Old Wulu, the 'head' of the rectangular settled area roughly pointing towards the *rale* ('left') side of the old village which, being oriented to the Ebu Lobo volcano, lies along the landward–seaward axis.

Even after leaving their old village, clans Tongo, Pata, and Poma continued to employ the stone *peo* that still stands in the centre of Old Wulu—as in the last large-scale sacrifice, performed in 1954, when fourteen buffalo were killed in Old Wulu while a further three were simultaneously slaughtered at Néso's *peo* in Eko Nila. Déna is thus most accurately understood as a hamlet (*bo'a*) serving as a temporary place of habitation for groups formally still resident in Old Wulu (Wulu Olo). Probably for practical reasons, Néso's present *peo* stands, not in the centre of Eko Nila, a rather constricted site, but rather at its 'head', the extremity that adjoins Déna. Superficially, the post might thus

---

[14] That it may be the latter is suggested by local statements to the effect that Eko Nila does not properly name the present settled area, but a spot outside, and beyond its 'tail' (*éko*). I was never able to discover any significance for 'Nila' as a component of the name. The location evidently has no connection with groups elsewhere named Nila (for example, in Paga, II: 1: vi). Although some people wished to deny it, in this context *nila* most likely refers to a kind of tree (*Grewia* sp.).

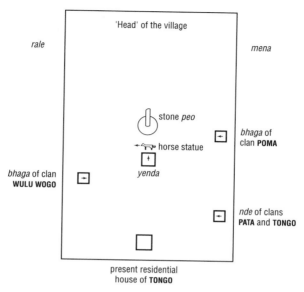

FIG. 13. Ritual structures in Old Wulu

appear to occupy a central location within Déna, understood in the more inclusive sense. But this is deceptive, since the sacrificial instrument belongs exclusively to clan Néso.

For comparative purposes, attention should be given to the arrangement of ritual structures in Old Wulu (see Fig. 13). Though now largely disappeared, their spatial order is still remembered by villagers. As in Liwo (and by contrast to what is found elsewhere in western Keo), the *yenda* in Wulu was situated seaward of the stone *peo*. Also, the wooden horse statue placed in front of the building faced the *rale* ('left') side of the village. Instead of occupying the seaward extremity, or the tail of Wulu, this *yenda* was, however, located about five metres away from the stone column, while the complementary structure called *nde* was erected seaward of the *yenda* and furthermore on the *mena* side of the village facing opposite, towards the *rale* side. This arrangement, then, contrasts with what is encountered in Liwo, where buildings corresponding to *nde* are actually located landward of the *yenda*. While the *yenda* is described as the common possession of all Wulu clans, the *nde*, a building said to have included four posts (as elsewhere in western Keo), was owned exclusively by the two oldest clans, Tongo and Pata. The third clan, Poma, possessed a separate, simpler structure, a *bhaga* supported by just two posts. Standing on the *mena* side of the village plaza, roughly in line with, and facing towards, the stone *peo*, Poma's *bhaga* was thus somewhat landward of the *yenda*. Opposite the *nde*, and therefore on the left (*rale*) side of Wulu, one can also see traces of the previously mentioned *bhaga* of clan Wulu Wogo. As indicated earlier, it is doubtful whether structures belonging to clan Néso were ever present in Wulu. In their own village as well, the Néso people have never possessed a *yenda* or *nde*, but at most a *bhaga*, even though they maintain a separate *peo*.[15]

As the foregoing arrangements should suggest, the landward half of Wulu, the part located above the stone *peo*, only ever contained residential houses (including, at one time, houses of Wulu Wogo). In this and other respects, the pattern can be construed as intermediate or transitional in relation to what is found in most of western Keo and what one encounters in Liwo—a circumstance that arguably accords with the combination in Wulu of groups associated respectively with Lobo and Lape Ga'e. As regards residential houses in Wulu, some evidence indicates that clan Tongo—the oldest clan, whose present house occupies the 'tail' of Old Wulu—was settled seaward of Poma and Pata, thus instancing a pattern found in several other villages. (As shown above, the relative locations of the *bhaga* of Poma and the *nde* shared by Pata and Tongo reflect the same arrangement.) As in the present village of Liwo, however, things are likely to have been more complex than this simple opposition might suggest, and I would therefore avoid a definite conclusion.

Conceived partly as a village and partly as a territory shared by four clans, Wulu reveals two distinct forms of dual combination. On the one hand, an older triad of clans linked in an enduring alliance cycle (Tongo, Pata, and Poma) stands opposed to a recently arrived group (Néso). As shown, this contrast coincides with a division of Wulu territory between two villages each with its own *peo*: Wulu (or Wulu Olo, 'Old Wulu'), now largely overlapping with Déna, and Eko Nila (a relatively recent replacement of Bo'a Néso). In view of connections between the two villages, including Néso's status as Defender of the oldest of the Wulu clans, this duality might just be construed as an instance of a double settlement, even though the distance between the two villages obscures such a configuration, as, of course, does the recent spatial intervention of Déna. While in several respects quite separate, Wulu and Néso (or Wulu and Eko Nila) are nevertheless regularly treated as a unity—including a ritual or sacrificial unity, since their buffalo sacrifices are co-ordinated. Not only is their connection quite comparable to what obtains in more palpable double settlements but the two, indeed, appear to be more unitary than do the components of many such settlements.[16]

Distinct from the foregoing, Wulu reveals a territorial contrast of another kind, with reference to which the four Wulu clans comprise two pairs. One pair

---

[15] Other small buildings serving particular ritual functions which cannot be described here, were formerly located outside the village. These included a structure called *sa'o ga'e* or *sa'o piye* which once housed a special drum used in an annual rite called *piye uyu*.

[16] The Néso people, I was told, participate in all festivities of Wulu village in the same way as do people of Tongo, Pata, and Poma, who in this context were described as the 'original Wulu people'.

(Pata, Poma) is thus linked with Land Mother Lape, the eldest of the Ga'e siblings, while the other (Tongo, Néso) is connected in the same way to Aga Reti (or Liwo) and thus ultimately to Lobo Ga'e, the youngest of the original land dividers. In regard to the suggestion that Néso, standing apart from the older three clans, has in effect replaced the virtually departed Wulu Wogo, it should be recalled that Wulu Wogo as well is subordinate to the Liwo ancestors Aga Reti and Lobo Ga'e. Thus this apparent substitution has not affected the particular combination of ancestral domains which is distinctive of Wulu territory. It may appear curious that while Tongo and Néso, both associated with the original domain of Lobo, have separate *peo*, Tongo shares a single sacrificial instrument with Pata, a Defender of Lape, and Poma, Pata's own Defender. This arrangement, however, is not entirely unique; a similar combination is evidenced in Lower Pajo Mala, with regard to groups descended from Lape Ga'e and Boa Maga (II: 2: i).

3. *Wagha*

Located on a steep incline about 250 metres seaward of Liwo, Wagha resembles Wulu in so far as this village, too, combines groups associated respectively with Lape and Lobo Ga'e. Wagha is a small settlement of just seven houses divided between two clans. The oldest clan, also named Wagha, traces descent to Géto Mite, an immigrant from the island of Savu. Described as a trader, this man landed at a place called Nage Rona on the coast near Ma'u Béna. According to the clan myth, Géto was always accompanied by his faithful dog. Upon disembarking, the dog caught scent of a wild pig and began to chase it. Pursuing the dog and the pig, Géto Mite cut down a large area of forest, thus establishing the boundaries of Wagha's territory and the site of his original village. Near the village of Loka Mude, the Wagha ancestor encountered two women named Ngura and Bhara, who suffered from a skin disease (*neka ya*, 'bleeding sores'). By washing their wounds, Géto cured both women and later took them as wives.[17] Since he could not afford the large bridewealth demanded by the Loka Mude people, however, he gave them instead an area of land named called Kuyu Kata.

Owing to the close bond between Géto Mite and his dog, people of clan Wagha may not eat dog flesh, lest their bodies become covered in sores. Although this is one of the few clan food taboos encountered in western Keo, the other clan resident in Wagha village, Yéwe, is coincidentally forbidden to eat pork, a prohibition it shares with clans in Wulu and clan Yoga (in Kuyu Wulu and Keo Ondo). Transgressing the pork taboo can similarly result in sores, with mental impairment as an additional possibility. While all Wagha

---

[17] One account gives Géto Mite as the paired names of two brothers. Although this accords with a pervasive pattern in Keo genealogical representations, others described Géto Mite as a single person.

people must avoid dog, their women are also forbidden to eat *yobo are*, a kind of bean.

Whereas the clan myth depicts Géto Mite as mapping out his own territory, falling within the domain of Aga Reti and Lobo Ga'e, this land was actually granted to Wagha by clan Liwo. Hence Wagha is counted as a Defender of Liwo. This territorial connection coincides with an affinal relation perpetuated over several generations. Although Géto himself married women of Loka Mude, his son was married to a woman of the Liwo clan Jadho. The genealogical record shows a further five marriages where Liwo clans have given wives to Wagha men. Other groups in Liwo have taken wives from Wagha, although the most consistent wife-takers are the two segments of Wulu Wogo, a clan that is a Defender of Wagha as well as of clan Liwo.

As Wagha villagers stressed, since their ancestor arrived on Flores, Wagha and Liwo have always lived and worked together; thus the two are often referred to jointly as 'Liwo Wagha'. Reputedly until the time of a Wagha ancestor named Koju Waja, Wagha village occupied the present site of Liwo. This was when the Liwo people resided at a higher elevation, just below the former separate village of Wulu Wogo. Evidently, then, there was once a string of three villages whose relative disposition is still maintained in the present two villages, Wagha and Liwo.[18]

Residing with clan Wagha in the village of Wagha is Yéwe, also called Wagha Yéwe, a junior branch of Yéwe established in Suga Bhoja (II: 1: v), in the domain of Land Mother Lape. Local history describes how an ancestor of Yéwe fled Suga Bhoja following an accusation of witchcraft levelled by his elder brother whose child had become ill. Arriving in the vicinity of Wagha, the Yéwe refugee was given land; thus Yéwe became co-resident Defender of the older clan. Yéwe's limited genealogy reveals no marriages at all with clan Wagha, even while the group maintains quite extensive affinal ties (in five of eleven men's and six of fourteen women's marriages) with clans in Liwo. Different versions of Yéwe's history specify the name of the ancestor who first settled in Wagha as Je'a Lea, Je'a Ngoe, or Lea Ngoe. The last two names refer to children of Ngoe Mére, a sister of Lape Mére (II: 1; see Fig. 6), while Je'a Lea is mostly interpreted as a compounding of the other two names. It was then either the younger of the two siblings or a son of the latter who founded Yéwe in Wagha.[19]

---

[18] Above the landward end of Wagha village, thus not far seaward of Liwo, is an uninhabited site named Ulu Wagha ('Head of Wagha'). Claiming that this place was already named as such before the arrival of the Wagha ancestors, villagers suggested that the name of the village and clan could derive from this place name. I was never able to discover any meaning of *wagha* that might illuminate either application.

[19] Yéwe people in Suga Bhoja gave their ancestor as Je'a Ngoe, and the ancestor of the branch in Wagha as Lea Ngoe, whereas Wagha people inverted this. Clan Koyu in Suga Bhoja favour yet another version, claiming that Lea Ngoe was actually a woman and thus the sister of their male ancestor, Koro Ngoe. Lea then had two sons, the elder of whom continued Yéwe in Suga Bhoja, while the younger founded the clan in Wagha. In view of the common practice of surnaming after the mother, the Koyu version accords with interpretations of the name Je'a Lea (including, interestingly enough, one advanced by a Yéwe elder) as belonging to a son of Lea. As indicated earlier (II: 1: v), disagreement between people of Yéwe and Koyu is largely a function of an ongoing dispute over precedence in Suga Bhoja.

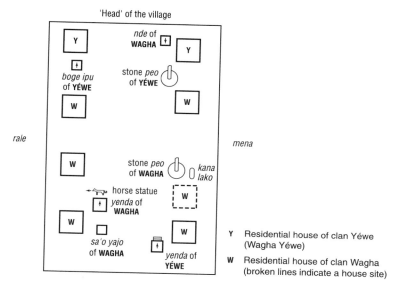

Fig. 14. Ritual structures in Wagha

Whichever version is accepted, the two branches of Yéwe still regard one another as *ka'e ari* ('elder and younger siblings'), even to the extent that each group can provide the other with heirs when component estates fall vacant.

Like several other villages comprising just two clans, Wagha also contains two *peo*, one belonging to clan Wagha and the other to Yéwe. Both consist of rather short stone columns. Wagha's is little more than half a metre in height while Yéwe's is about a metre. Numbering just two at present, Yéwe's houses, as well as their *peo*, are found at the landward extremity of the village. Accordingly, clan Wagha's houses and sacrificial instrument are all erected seaward of these. Qualifying this contrast, however, is the location of the stone *peo* of clan Wagha in a more or less central position within the village. While this may befit the older group's identification with the settlement as a whole, it should be noted that both stone columns are erected not in the middle of the village plaza but well towards the right (*mena*) side, very close to one row of houses. With regard to the relative disposition of its two *peo* along the land-ward–seaward axis, Wagha recalls the village of Dhawe (or Dhawe Mére; II: 5: iv). Yet in other respects, it resembles Liwo and Wulu, particularly as regards the disposition of ceremonial structures that distinguishes settlements associated with the domain of Lobo Ga'e from other parts of western Keo (see Fig. 14).

Although none of the buildings is clearly visible at present, formerly clan

Wagha and clan Yéwe both possessed *yenda*, but only Wagha maintained a *nde*. As in Liwo and Wulu, Wagha's *yenda* (mounted on just two posts, like the one in Liwo) was located seaward of the clan's *nde* and on the *rale* ('left') side of the village, while the wooden horse statue erected in front of the *yenda* also faced *rale*. Reminiscent of the overlap described for the Upper and Lower sections of Liwo, the *nde* belonging to clan Wagha was, however, erected in the section occupied by clan Yéwe, at the head (*ulu*) of the village, and moreover landward of Yéwe's stone *peo* on the *mena* side. Apparently reciprocating this location, the *yenda* of clan Yéwe (also on two posts) stood at the seaward end, or tail, of the village, also on the *mena* side, and below the *peo* of Wagha (see Fig. 14).[20] Although Yéwe never had a *nde*, a building with anthropomorphous *ana ndeo* statues, the clan nevertheless once possessed a small structure, consisting of a single post with a thatched roof and a ladder of three rungs and complementing Yéwe's *yenda*. Called *boge ipu* (like a similar structure in Liwo), this was located just seaward of a Yéwe house in the landward part of the village.[21] What one finds in respect of both clans, therefore, is a contrast of *mena* and *rale*, or 'right' and 'left' sides of the settlement, distinguishing complementary ritual structures (e.g. *yenda* and *nde*), as well as an unusual arrangement whereby each clan has one of a pair of ceremonial buildings in the section of the village occupied by the other clan.

Another curiosity of Wagha village is clan Wagha's possession of two objects not found anywhere else, both of which commemorate aspects of the arrival of the Wagha ancestor. Located just to the 'right' (*mena*) of the clan's stone *peo* there is a carved stone trough called *kana lako* ('dog trough'), described as a replica of one that Géto Mite brought to Flores in order to feed his dog. On the other (*rale*) side of the village, just seaward of Wagha's *yenda* and thus close to this extremity of the settlement, there is another large stone. Also associated with Géto Mite, this marks the former location of a small building with four posts called *sa'o yajo* ('boat house'), which used to house a model vessel representing the one in which the Wagha ancestor sailed from Savu.

4. Béna and Ma'u Béna

A further peculiarity of Wagha concerns its connection with Ma'u Béna ('Coastal Settlement of Béna'), a village distinguished from all other coastal

---

[20] An unusual feature of this *yenda* was the absence of a horse statue. Substituting for the statue was what villagers described as two posts surmounted by a plain wooden plank which, lacking a head and a tail, was not oriented either *rale* or *mena*. Whether the contrast of 'trunk' and 'tip' (*pu'u* and *lobo*) may have been relevant in this connection, I neglected to enquire.
[21] Wagha villagers described this *boge ipu* as a place where a portion of 'old rice' (*pae olo*) was stored, and furthermore as a structure connected in a particular way with rain. While it was otherwise forbidden to place ginger in the *boge ipu*, this was deliberately done about October in order to cause thunderstorms and hence rain. In the former respect, the structure is functionally comparable to a *nde* (I: 2: v).

hamlets (*ma'u*) by its possession of a *peo*. Ma'u Béna lies on the south coast, over two kilometres seaward of Wagha, west of the hamlet of Ma'u Bajo (linked with Nua Nage, in the territory of Land Mother Lape) and just east of Ma'u Kéli. Residents of Wagha and Ma'u Béna speak of themselves as *ka'e ari* ('siblings'), and even as composing a single 'clan' (*suku*) called 'Béna Wagha'. The two settlements are further described as forming a territorial unity (*ulu éko*, 'head (and) tail'). Designated as Ulu Siu Toyo, Eko Nage Rona (see Appendix 2), this area extends as far landward as a place called Siu Toyo located just landward of Wagha village. Nage Rona, on the other hand, is the spot where the Wagha ancestor Géto Mite landed on the south coast.

As the village name might suggest, Ma'u Béna is the present residence of a clan called Béna. The link between this group and clan Wagha ultimately reflects their common agnatic derivation from Géto Mite. The Béna people trace descent to the brothers Léba Ludu and Léki Ludu, grandsons (SS) of Géto and sons of a brother of Wagha's specific ancestor. Founding a village named Béna ('flat, level area', a synonym of *déna*), not far inland from Ma'u Béna and less than a kilometre seaward of Paga (II: 1: vi), the two brothers planted a sacrificial *kesi* tree, the elder then taking the part of earth breaker and the younger that of excavator. From this sibling pair thus developed the two principal estates (*ngapi*) into which the Béna people are now divided.[22]

Some time after the founding of Béna—nowadays distinguished as Béna Olo ('Old Béna')—a group of immigrants, probably from the east, established a village named Ki ('Imperata grass') just landward of Béna. Thus was founded a former double settlement Keo still refer to as Ki Béna. Since the Ki people erected a *dheyo* tree *peo* in their new village, they may then also have become wife-takers of Béna. What is more certain is that Ki has never been recognized as Béna's Defender. Just two or three generations ago, Ki acquired Defenders of its own: immigrants from clan Jadho in Liwo and from Tiwa, a village to the west of the present study area. Nevertheless, the ritual statuses of earth breaker and excavator connected with their sacrificial *dheyo* tree are both retained by two of the four estates of Ki.

Generally characterized as a warlike group who obtained land mostly through military aggression, Ki is unable to claim Béna, or any other group for that matter, as Land Mother. Some land they won from the Laka people of Paga, located not far landward of Ki village. Later, a Ki ancestor named Pori Moni, assisted by Ua Leo of Suga in Suga Bhoja (II: 4: i), murdered a man of clan Wayu (in Wulu Wayu) named Bapi Raga. As part of their subsequent reconciliation, Ki and Wayu agreed to share lands in a compact comparable to

---

[22] Owing to lacunae in the Wagha genealogy, the precise connection between the two Béna ancestors and clan Wagha is not clear. The genealogies for both groups give Koju Waja as the combined names of two sons of Géto Mite. Both clans agree that the younger son, Waja, was childless; thus both apparently claim descent from Koju. At the same time, this ancestor apparently had at least two wives, since it was specifically from a junior wife, Ludu, that Béna people derive. The seniority of Wagha is also consistent with the claim that Koju (or Koju Waja), was born in Wagha, the village founded by Géto Mite.

the earlier instated arrangement between Wayu and Keo. This is commemorated in the compound designation Tana Ki, Watu Wayu (Land of Ki, Stones
of Wayu), a usage obviously inspired by Tana Keo, Watu Wayu (II: 4).[23]

Some time after the reconciliation with Wayu, Ki became involved in violent
conflict with their Béna neighbours. As a result, the Béna people fled to Boba,
in eastern Ngada, where they sought military assistance from Jélo, a clan resident in the village of Boba Olo. After a peace was concluded with Ki, the Béna
refugees were able to return to Béna village. In recognition of their support,
Jélo was granted an area of land within Béna's territory, and some members of
the Boba clan founded a hamlet named Bo'a Boba. This occupied the coastal
site that later became known as Ma'u Béna, after the Béna population abandoned their former village and joined a small group of Jélo people there around
1940. Only then did the settlement acquire its present name. What is more, this
was the first time residents of the coastal village erected a *peo*—a stone column
that effectively replaced the sacrificial *kesi* tree the Béna people left behind in
Old Béna. Not long afterwards, the Ki people, too, abandoned their village, also
settling on the south coast, at a site now usually known as Ki Baru ('Baru' is
the national language word for 'new').

Béna's connection with Wagha has evidently survived its now virtually
defunct—and, it would appear, never particularly well-founded—association
with Ki. Indeed, the relationship of Wagha and Béna is now closer than their
common agnatic origin alone would entail. Owing to the extinction of the
senior estate of Béna (Léba Ludu) and its replacement by the house that holds
the premier position in clan Wagha, the two clans have in effect become united
in a single family.[24] They also claim rights within Jélo's estate. As a result, a
single man currently holds the position of earth breaker in respect of both the
stone *peo* in Wagha and the identical sacrificial instrument in Ma'u Béna.
Although this man now lives in Ma'u Béna, he possesses an equal right to
reside in the village of Wagha. In fact, his father, who died in 1995, had begun
to construct a new house in Wagha just a year prior to his decease.

Perhaps also reflecting this particular instance of multiple clanship is the
formal name of Wagha: Ulu Nunu, Eko Jélo. Resembling the designation
employed by Liwo (Ulu Nunu, Eko Nage), the first of the paired phrases is
consistent with the Wagha people's earlier occupation of the present site of
Liwo. By contrast, Wagha villagers explained the second phrase, Eko Jélo, 'Tail

---

[23] As a further expression of this reciprocity, whenever buffalo are collectively slaughtered (*pébha nai ngapi*) in
Wayu's village (Wulu Wayu), Ki is invited to contribute one animal. The inverse presumably obtains at collective sacrifices in the village of Ki. As a result of the same reconciliation, Wayu and Suga—the clan of Pori Moni's accomplice,
Ua Leo—instituted reciprocal rights to one another's fruit-bearing trees in an agreement similar to the one obtaining
between Keo and Bolo. The latter agreement, it may be recalled, was instituted to reconcile these two groups after
violent conflict also caused by the perfidious actions of the crafty Suga ancestor (II: 4: i). Ua Leo is further described
as having had a hand in a dispute between the Pau Leka groups Pau Kolo Ndinga and Béngi (II: 3: iv), from which he
derived a profit of seven fields.

[24] This family was further described as the only group with a rightful claim to the patrimony of Wagha, since all
other surviving members of the clan are descendants of retainers or slaves.

that is Jélo', as reflecting clan Wagha's association with clan Jélo in Ma'u Béna, which, of course, lies seaward of Wagha. In this connection, it should be mentioned as well that several statements, some by men of Liwo, identified clan Jélo as people of Old Béna who moved to Ma'u Béna, and furthermore as a clan related as *ka'e ari* to clan Wagha. While this does not quite agree with other accounts, which represent Jélo and Béna as distinct groups, it does accord with Arndt's brief history of the Ngadha region of Boba (1954: 360, 361), from where Jélo derived. In particular, Arndt describes clan Jélo as hailing from Béna, which he specifies as located near Ma'u Kéli (the settlement just west of Ma'u Béna). He also states that, in their move from Béna, the Jélo people were accompanied by clan Wagha ('Vaya' in his transcription), who not only established themselves in Boba but even replaced one of the original owners of the land there. Although Arndt does not say where exactly Wagha originated, he does give as the cause of Jélo's departure a case of incest that led to armed conflict within Béna. Interestingly, this is all rather reminiscent of the war Keo describe as erupting between Béna and Ki, the cause of the Béna people's removal to Boba, where they encountered Jélo.

Whatever the specific details, Wagha provides yet another illustration of how a single group can participate in several dual combinations. Forming one half of an agnatic pair with Ma'u Béna (and, formerly, the original Béna), the village of Wagha is further linked with Liwo in the common designation 'Liwo Wagha'. Whether the latter combination is usefully described as a double settlement, formerly or at present, is difficult to determine. In view of the distance between them, the two villages compose a territorial unity to about the same extent as do Keo Bélo and Munde. In addition, in the past the village of Liwo was more palpably conjoined with the village of Wulu Wogo; in fact in respect of their separate *peo*, these two groups, now sharing a newer settlement called Liwo, still reveal a manifestly dualistic pattern of co-residence. While in different ways paired with two other villages, Wagha itself similarly comprises two clans each maintaining separate sacrificial instruments. In this regard, Wagha further recalls another regular possibility of Keo social order. As shown, clan Wagha and clan Yéwe (or Wagha Yéwe) both recognize an agnatic relationship (*ka'e ari*) with groups resident in other villages and possessing other *peo*. In the case of the two branches of Yéwe, moreover, local groups acknowledging a common agnatic derivation maintain territory within the ancestral domains of different Land Mothers.

CONCLUSION

It is by now abundantly clear how dualistic arrangements can be fully understood only as outcomes of particular histories. Dualism is not a static form or principle of order but is revealed as a continuous process of Keo society. In order to develop this observation further, it will be useful to review the several major forms their dualistic organization can assume.

A particularly visible instance is the double settlement. Of the thirty-five villages (*nua*) surveyed above, between fourteen and sixteen (including ambiguous cases) form one half of a double settlement, while another four or six are described as having done so in the past. An equally common type of local dualism are single villages comprising two groups usually specified as 'clans' (*suku*). Most of these result from a merging of the two parts of a former double settlement or a joining of two more separate village populations. (Some of these have of course subsequently formed further double settlements.) Of the dozen or so villages which do not now form part of a double settlement, about half represent amalgamations of former double settlements.[1] As exemplified by Liwo, one also encounters what appear to be incipient or incomplete transitions from a double to a single settlement, the remaining dualism being discernible mainly in the continuing possession by each of two parts of separate *peo*, erected in landward and seaward sections of a village, or simply in the designation of these sections of a single village also as *nua* (as in Pajo Réja and Sawu Obo). A further variant of dualistically composed villages are several instances of local quadripartition. As shown, these are accounted for as mergings of two formerly separate *nua*, each of which itself comprised a pair of clans.[2]

In addition to double settlements and dualistically composed single villages, Keo social organization reveals other instances of pairing operative within groupings, often conceived as single clans, which share a village with one or more other clans. Variants include the following:

(a) Single clans whose names comprise two parts designating formerly separate clans (for example, Bajo Léwa, Bindi Loga, and Sopi Sabe.). These in turn participate in more inclusive local groupings that are themselves binary amalgamations.

---

[1] Included in the other half are two villages, Bale Wolo and Dhawe Yoja, which have only ever contained just one clan; the remaining four are Suga Bhoja, Munde, Paga, and Loka Kayo.

[2] It may be worth mentioning that such double pairings cannot readily be construed as instances of what Mosko (1985) identifies as 'quadripartite structure'. The contrast of elder (or older) and younger distinguishing components of the more inclusive dualism is, indeed, replicated within each component pair. Yet it is not at all obvious that this entails an inversion specifying the younger member of the younger pair as the homologue of the elder member of the elder pair, as Mosko's model would in this case evidently require.

(b) An almost identical pattern wherein a pair of co-resident clans (for example Wulu and Dhaga, or Céla and Bajo, in Nua Nage) are named with a compound (Wulu Dhaga, Céla Bajo) and sometimes represent themselves as a unitary clan. By contrast to (a), the two groups continue to be distinguished as separate clans, largely by virtue of being related as Land Mother and Defender.

(c) A pattern partly inverting (b) wherein a unitary social entity identified by a single name is comprised of moieties distinguished with the spatial modifiers 'Upper' and 'Lower'. As exemplified by the groupings named Bolo, Bale, and Loka Poma, these moieties are usually spoken of as separate clans, a practice that accords with each pair having resulted from a combination of groups professing separate agnatic origins. In another instance— clan Keo, resident in Keo Bélo—a pair of moieties, also designated as 'clans', derives from full brothers, after whom the two groups (Meo Wale and Wawo Wale) are named.

(d) Local unities comprising a pair of clans tracing agnatic descent to a brother and sister. The two instances of this pattern are Liwo (comprising Liwo Aga Reti and Liwo Bhoko Reti) and Koyu Yéwe. Contrary to the usual implication of the cross-sibling relationship, the paired groups operate for the most part like segments of a single clan, and indeed may be spoken of as such.

Reminiscent of the foregoing arrangements is the frequent division of localized clans (or clan segments) into just two estates (*ngapi*; I: 3: ii). It should be recalled that some pairs of estates comprise components claiming separate agnatic and geographical origins (for example, the two *ngapi* of clans Kota and Réja), like most residentially conjoined clans. Two is, of course, the minimum number of estates, or houses (*sa'o*), required for a group—a village or clan—to erect and maintain an independent sacrificial instrument (*peo*). At the same time, clans can, indeed, comprise more than two estates, so that *ngapi* dualism is a limit rather than a structural requirement.

External to these arrangements, yet similarly dualistic, are a series of extralocal unities involving a binary relationship between villages, or component clans. An instructive instance is the grouping named Bolo Bale (II: 1, 2). Comprising Bolo and Bale, resident respectively in the villages of Bolo (or Muka) and Upper Pajo Mala (Kate Bale), this dual unity has its basis in a former residential association—a tradition of common geographical origins outside of western Keo. The pairing moreover entails an implicit subsumption of the junior group by the senior, a feature equally evident in dually composed villages, if not in double settlements (see Section 3 below). While otherwise quite different, a comparable extralocal dualism inheres in the relation of 'land siblingship' linking the territories of clans Keo (Keo Bélo) and Wayu, segments

of the ancestral domains of Géra Ga'e and Lape Ga'e. As shown, similar relationships link clans in the villages of Pajo Mala, Nua Muri, and Muka (Bolo).
In turn, these invite comparison with the special relation of 'house siblingship'
connecting, for example, the seniormost houses of clans Kate and Suga (in
Upper Pajo Mala and Bolo respectively), as well as sundry ritual partnerships
operative within villages.[3]

Highlighting the formal identity of these various arrangements may risk
confusing binary relationships, which necessarily exist in all societies, with
culturally specific forms of social dualism. Indeed, while 'land siblingship' and
'house siblingship' entail reciprocal obligations of particular kinds, clans,
villages, and intravillage moieties forming pairs spatially aligned as components of single or double settlements do not display any specific or exclusive
form of reciprocity. Most notably, villages composing a double settlement are
not consistently related in any distinctive way. Nor do they divide special tasks
that would render them complementary parts of a functional whole.

1. Binary Relations

Particular residential pairings, of course, often coincide with binary relationships of a completely general kind such as *moi mame* and *ana weta* (wife-giver
and wife-taker) and *ine tana* and *ana tuku* (Land Mother and Defender, or
'defending child'). In these two relationships, one might also discern a
common conceptual link with local dualities inasmuch as Keo sometimes
employ the 'mother' and 'child' terms (*ine* and *ana*) to distinguish earlier and
later components of both single villages and double settlements (I: 1: iii). Since
Keo affinal alliance consists of houses occupied by 'children of sisters' (*ana
weta*) linked in a maternal line of origin, all three dualistic forms thus appear
to be represented identically by reference to the mother–child bond. In the
same way, it can also be seen how even the component villages of double settlements might be understood as a unity constituted by an encompassment of a
younger by an older component, an issue I take up again below. Nevertheless,
the actual coincidence of local dualities with the relationship of Land Mother
and Defender, or with an original or perpetuated affinal alliance is extremely
variable. Hence neither relationship constitutes a single constant source of Keo
local dualism.

As mentioned in the Introduction, Arndt (1954) characterized Keo settlements as comprising exogamous moieties practising symmetric exchange. How
erroneous his interpretation was can now be fully appreciated. First, affinal
alliance is not a necessary feature of dualistically constituted settlements; nor,
indeed, does the marriage system operate with reference to residential groups
of any particular sort. Secondly, even where components of local dualities are

---

[3] Here I refer principally to the arrangements called *ulu (or téngu) geu, kage sabhe* (I: 4: i).

represented as parties to a long-standing alliance, as is quite common, such relationships are, of course, always asymmetric. Thirdly, Keo alliance strictly speaking connects not entire villages, clans or other groupings bound together in local dualities but rather component houses. Also worth recalling is genealogical and other local historical evidence indicating that co-residence by affinally related groups, in a dualistically constituted single village or double settlement, has sometimes preceded the contracting of marriages. Alliance thus does not always lead to local dualism; nor does this sort of dualism inevitably result in distinct affinal connection.

Local histories frequently describe the initiation of an affinal alliance as simultaneous with the inauguration of a relationship of Land Mother and Defender. Yet by no means is alliance always an accompaniment of the territorial bond; hence these two relations, too, can exist independently of one another. Similarly variable is the coincidence of the Land Mother–Defender relationship and residence in the same village or double settlement. Why this should be so is obvious. Conferring Defender status on a group involves granting rights to a separate territory in which it founds a new village and sacrificial instrument (*peo*). In contrast, single villages usually possess but a single *peo*. Thus the minority of villages in which Land Mother and Defender at present share a single sacrificial instrument are evidently a secondary development, as, indeed, their individual histories regularly attest.[4]

Double settlements present a somewhat different picture; for several of these (for example the settlement comprising Kota Pau and Guyu Wolo) appear to have conjoined local groups identifiable as Land Mother and Defender since their inception. Comparable in this regard are groups that have incorporated Defenders into their own village while allowing them to erect separate sacrificial instruments. Exemplified by Keo Ondo, Paga, Munde, and Wagha, all these villages were founded by primary, or senior, Defenders of one of the Ga'e siblings, the principal Land Mothers (*ine tana mére*), who later admitted second order Defenders into their villages. This pattern appears more characteristic of the smaller territories of the younger Ga'e siblings, as well as the Pau enclave (II: 3). In contrast, the present or original occupation by Land Mother and Defenders of quite separate and non-contiguous settlements, associated with central and peripheral parts of a single ancestral territory (I: 1: iii), is most marked in the domain of the seniormost Land Mother, Lape.

Only a portion of local dualities, therefore, reflect co-residence by clans related as Land Mother and Defender. Of the eight currently extant double settlements just five comprise villages containing clans related in this way. (The

---

[4] This is not to say that all of these are the result of particularly recent, let alone colonial era mergings. In fact, two villages, Suga Bhoja and Lundu, appear to have operated with an internal ceremonial pairing of Land Mother and Defender—in respect of the two *peo* functions—if not since their inception, then for as long as anyone can remember.

three which do not are Pau Lundu, the Upper and Lower villages of Pajo Mala, and Oja and Wajo.) Similarly, of nine former double settlements—abandoned within living memory, or merged to form single villages—four at the most entailed a residential conjunction of Land Mother and Defender, while five quite clearly did not.[5] Combining the two sets of figures, and deleting two doubtful instances, positive and negative cases are thus about equal. A very similar result is obtained for single villages (including villages which are further subsumed as part of a double settlement). Of twenty-nine villages, just fourteen, thus fewer than half, contain a Land Mother and one or more Defender clans. Included among the fifteen which do not are seven villages inhabited by a single clan, and eight that comprise two or more clans connected in another way.[6]

In so far as a village usually possesses a single sacrificial instrument, the incidence of Land Mothers and Defenders combining to form a single village is subject to further qualification. Although in this arrangement the two parties can be described as sharing a *peo*, only in six villages do a Land Mother and a Defender actually divide the statuses of earth breaker and excavator (*ta koe, ta kabhe*) or trunk and tip rider—the Mother then, of course, occupying the senior position. In four instances where the statuses are not so divided, the Land Mother effects the ceremonial dualism internally, by assigning the positions either to component estates (as in the case of clans Wayu and Guyu Wolo) or to moieties that are themselves usually classified as 'clans' (for example, Upper Bolo and Lower Bolo, or Right Side Pau and Left Side Pau in Lower Pau Lundu). At the same time, the converse arrangement is also encountered. For example, Pau and Leka, the two clans whose names are conjoined in the designation of the present village of Pau Leka, are not related as *ine tana* and *ana tuku* and yet divide the statuses of tip and trunk rider in respect of the single sacrificial instrument they currently share with Béngi, a Defender of Pau (II: 3: iv). Comparable arrangements obtain in several other villages where the ceremonial positions are assigned to clans similarly unrelated.[7] In these instances, the independence of local dualism from the relationship of Land Mother and Defender, as well as from binary categories entailed in affinal alliance and collective sacrificing, could hardly be more evident.

Apart from villages comprising just one clan, the ritual division of earth breaker and excavator is, of course, further operative within a single clan in the

---

[5] The former figure concerns two doubtful cases: Old Nua Muri coupled with the village of Se, where the existence of an *ine tana–ana tuku* relationship is contested, and Keo and Bélo, whose status as a double settlement is equivocal. Among the five negative instances I include the former Kate and Bale, since only in the looser sense can these be classified as 'mother' (Bale) and 'child' (Kate).

[6] There are three cases where the matter is uncertain, namely Nua Muri, for the reason indicated in the preceding note, and Ki and Béna, for which the information is unclear (II: 6: iv). The seven formally single clan villages are Bale Wolo, Keo (Keo Bélo), Nua Obo (within Dhawe Mére), Dhawe Yoja, Oja, Wajo, and Eko Nila.

[7] Examples include Wulu (in regard to clans Tongo and Pata) and the village of Lui (as regards clans Lui and Nua Muri). Comparable instances concern clans Pajo Wolo (sharing a single office with Bindi Wae) and Kayo in Lower Pajo Mala, and clans Bale and Kate in Upper Pajo Mala (Kate Bale).

three villages where each of a pair of clans, related as Land Mother and Defender, maintains a sacrificial instrument of its own (Paga, Munde, Wagha). At the same time, in one such village (Paga), the senior member of the pair appears as earth breaker in respect of the *peo* of the junior clan. Similar arrangements connect Land Mothers and Defenders in several double settlements (Kota Pau and Guyu Wolo, the Dhawe and Obo sections of Dhawe Mére, and Wulu and Eko Nila), while in Munde the part of earth breaker (*ta koe*) at both *peo* is taken by the primary Land Mother resident in the neighbouring village of Keo Bélo. These arrangements, then, extend the number of cases where the two ritual statuses and the territorial relationship of Land Mother and Defender not only coincide, but also link the two parts of dualistically constituted settlements in a ceremonial unity. Nevertheless, the general point is sustained: settlement dualism is not reducible to either binary relation.

The point draws especial support from the several instances mentioned above, where ceremonial dualism within single villages links clans not related as Land Mother and Defender. As their histories reveal, all of these reflect amalgamations of formerly separate villages (for example, Pau and Leka), and thus formerly separate sacrificial instruments. What is equally noteworthy is the way all combine within a single settlement representatives of two ancestral domains. The feature is most pronounced where earth breaker and excavator, or trunk rider and tip rider, are Defenders belonging to the domains of two separate Land Mothers (as, for example, in Wulu and Pau Leka). A spatial juxtaposition of groups associated with different Land Mothers also obtains in some double settlements, for example in Pau Lundu and, in a more complex way, in the two conjoined villages of Pajo Mala—incidentally, the two settlements that first spurred my interest in Keo local dualism. What these double settlements, especially, suggest is a tendency of Keo social structure, reflected in relatively long-term social processes, to conjoin in space units previously unrelated and, indeed, manifesting major social contrasts, thereby producing local combinations whose enduring independence of parts is almost as palpable as their spatial conjunction.

2. *The Spatial and Temporal Articulation of Local Dualities*

All instances of Keo local dualism exhibit two constant features. One is a principle of temporal precedence, whereby dyadic components of both double settlements and single villages are consistently distinguished as older and younger (see Section 6 below). The other is a completely regular disposition of components in terms of the spatial opposition of landward and seaward, or *réta* and *lau*.

The use of a landward–seaward (or upstream–downstream) contrast in orienting houses or settlements, as well as in expressing a principal axis of direction, is extremely widespread in Indonesia.[8] As regards directional applications, Adelaar (1997: 53) has recently described the opposition of 'towards the interior' and 'towards the sea', reconstructed for Proto-Austronesian as *Daya* and *laSud* (cf. Keo *lau*), as 'the fundamental axis of orientation in Austronesian societies', and furthermore as the 'starting point for development into other directional systems' (1997: 77). Although not quite so widely encountered as their use in expressing direction, also common is the application of the same dual coordinates in defining ethnic categories (as in the well known examples 'Dayak' and 'Toraja') and in articulating relations between groups participating in single social systems or cultural communities (see Geirnaert-Martin 1992: 2, 15, regarding western Sumba). As shown, in Keo settlements the distinction of landward and seaward coincides with the contrast of 'head' and 'tail' (*ulu* and *éko*), which define the two extremities, or relative sections, of a village. Similarly, in a number of instances, dual components of both single villages and double settlements are diametrically distinguished as *wawo* and *au*, or 'upper' and 'lower', a concomitant pair implicating the units so named as parts of a larger spatial or social whole. Among double settlements, examples include the Upper and Lower (Wawo and Au) villages of Pajo Mala (II: 2), and among single villages the two moieties, or paired clans, named Bolo Wawo and Bolo Au in Muka (II: 1: iv).

Interestingly, the landward (or up-river) direction is identically conceived as a 'head' in various other Indonesian societies, for example, among the Toraja (Waterson 1990: 94), the Timorese Mambai (Traube 1986: 28), and, with certain qualifications, the eastern Sumbanese (Forth 1981: 67). On Roti, also, the anatomical term is linked with the primary direction, which in this case is 'sunrise' or 'east' (Fox 1973; cf. Forth 1981.). In purely linguistic terms, the same connection is, of course, discernible in numerous words for 'up-river, upstream', or words denoting the source of a river or stream, which reflect the same protoform as Keo *ulu* (see, e.g. Malay, BI *ulu*, cf. Rotinese *dulu*, 'sunrise, east'). Also noteworthy are instances where landward and seaward parts of a territory are associated respectively with older and younger parts of a population (as in western Sumba, see Geirnaert-Martin 1992: 2, 15; Kruyt 1922), or with groups of higher and lower rank (as among the Bornean Olo Ngaju, Schärer 1963: 65). Among Keo, however, this sort of social correlation of the spatial coordinates is problematic, as is further discussed below.

---

[8] Houses are oriented in the landward direction, for example, among the Toraja of Sulawesi (Waterson 1990: 92), on Bali (Covarrubias 1937: 88–93), and in the Tana 'Ai region of east central Flores (Lewis 1988: 155), while on Tanimbar houses face in the opposite direction, towards the sea (McKinnon 1991: 86). As in Keo and Nage (Forth 1991*a*, 1991*b*), elsewhere one finds entire settlements rather than single buildings disposed along a landward–seaward axis, as, for example, in Sumba (Forth 1981). In addition to the places just mentioned, the same contrast appears as a major direction indicator in Timor (Traube 1986: 28), Borneo (see, for example, Schärer 1963: 65–6), Seram (Jensen 1948: 222), the Kei Islands (Barraud 1979: 50–9), South Halmahera (Teljeur 1990: 36–46), and Fiji (Toren 1990), to name just several geographically separated instances.

In regard to possible links with social dualism, it is worth mentioning Blust's linguistic interpretation of dual organization with spatial concomitants as a feature of an ancient society associated with Proto-Malayo-Polynesian (1980, 1981*b*). The landward–seaward contrast, however, does not clearly figure in this, since Blust conceives of the organization as operating in a space dually divided into two 'sides' (1980: 225–6; 1981*b*: 69).

Especially for Keo double settlements, the fundamental character of the landward–seaward opposition lies precisely in the fact that, were component villages (*nua*) not disposed in this way, a double settlement would scarcely be recognizable as such. Although recent changes have occasionally obscured the pattern, comprehensive divisions within single villages as well typically correspond to this spatial contrast—other, less inclusive distinctions (for example, between senior and junior estates, or houses) then being articulated by the complementary axis of *mena* and *rale*, distinguishing right and left sides. As demonstrated earlier, the importance of the landward–seaward opposition for Keo social space reflects the primacy of this axis in an inclusive system of orientation in which all terms are defined by reference to the Ebu Lobo volcano or another inland peak. In all settlements the extremity associated with this central point is defined as the 'head' (*ulu*), and the opposite end as the 'tail' (*éko*). Thus, the head—like the conceptual centre articulating the entire system—is always landward (*réta*), and the tail seaward (*lau*). When compounded and suitably qualified with proper names, in formal speech the two anatomical terms then serve to designate a settlement as a social whole (as in Ulu Céla, Eko Bolo, the formal name of Nua Nage). As shown, Keo apply such *ulu–éko* names to some double settlements as well, although in at least two instances (Pajo Mala, Pau Lundu) this unitary naming can be construed as symptomatic of a partial transformation into single villages. Component villages of double settlements, of course, possess separate *ulu–éko* names, albeit ones that sometimes overlap or are partly identical with those of their pairs.

Whether the two parts of a double settlement constitute an anatomically defined whole in the same way as do single villages is thus somewhat moot. Yet the fact remains that both residential formations consistently comprise units defined as older and younger, the two components then typically occupying landward and seaward sections of an apparent spatial whole. In view of this regular coincidence of temporal and spatial contrasts, it might seem significant that the Keo term for 'head' (*ulu*) further conveys the partly temporal sense of 'earlier, ahead of, preceding' (cf. BI *dulu*, *dahulu*). Since groups designated as 'mothers', including Land Mothers, are by definition the earliest arrivals in a particular territory, one might further expect to find a regular correspondence between residential seniority and occupation of the landward (or 'upper') part of a settlement. Yet as the village ethnographies make abundantly clear, there is absolutely no consistency in this regard. Among both present and former double settlements, the number of instances (six) where the older *nua* is located landward (*réta*) of the younger is exactly the same as the total of inverse instances. Similarly, the figure for twenty single villages is eleven and nine respectively.[9]

---

[9] Complications in some instances require the exercise of judgement. There are a further ten cases where, owing largely to recent changes including the removal of houses to roadside sites, the distinction is no longer clear. Four of these, moreover, are villages inhabited by just one clan. With other single-clan villages, such as Keo Bélo and Oja, it is possible to make the determination with respect to component 'estates'.

Order of temporal precedence thus does not determine the relative disposition of older and younger components of dualistically constituted settlements. Since in several settlements the seaward section belongs to a group whose ancestor came to western Keo by sea (for example, Réja, Sawu, Wagha, and perhaps initially clan Béle Jawa when resident in Tola, a former village seaward of Keo Bélo), direction of derivation could conceivably be more significant in this regard. Also, in several instances where a younger group resides immediately landward of an older partner, present location appears similarly to correspond with the relative direction of the group's former residence. Yet by no means are all occupants of relatively seaward or landward locations held to derive from these directions; and, indeed, Keo themselves do not articulate any general principle in this connection. Even in the few cases where spatial dualism corresponds to an agnatic division of elder and younger ancestors, descendants of the elder may occupy either the seaward or landward part of the settlement.[10]

Once again, then, we find that dual components of Keo settlements do not directly correspond to the terms of asymmetric category pairs. At the same time, the spatial contrast of *réta* and *lau*, like the opposition of senior and junior, differs from pairs such as wife-giver and wife-taker and Land Mother-Defender, since, unlike these manifestly social dyads, both the temporal and spatial oppositions appear to be necessary elements in Keo settlement constitution. That is, although the component terms of each do not regularly correspond with the terms of the other, the coincidence of the two dualistic principles in single social spaces is invariant. The two contrasts moreover correspond not only in regard to their obvious dualism and asymmetry but also by virtue of a principle of encompassment, whereby subordinate terms are regularly represented as subsumed parts of wholes identified with the superordinate term. This much, of course, they also share with the affinal opposition and the contrast of Land Mother and Defender. Encompassment may be less obvious an entailment of the *réta-lau* opposition than, say, the contrast of wife-giver and wife-taker. Nevertheless, it is discernible in the closer link between *réta* and the conceptual centre around which the entire system of direction and orientation revolves. What is more, it is specifically by virtue of a relation of encompassment rather, or more than, any complementarity of social functions that dualities are conceived and treated as unities. How this applies to groups—clans or more inclusive groupings—that compose single settlements can now be explored further.

---

[10] Meo Wale in Keo Bélo (II: 4: ii) and Loka Poma Au in Lundu (II: 1: vii) illustrate the former possibility, while the senior division of Oja (II: 5: v) exemplifies the latter.

3. *Encompassment, Hierarchy, and Precedence*

How far dualistically constituted Keo communities present themselves as unities obviously varies between single villages (*nua*), the majority of which possess a single sacrificial instrument, and double settlements, consisting of two *nua*, each possessing its own sacrificial instrument (*peo*). In general, Keo social unity appears to coexist with manifest duality only to the extent that one member of a pair is subsumed by another, or a senior component is conceived as identical to the social whole in a relation recalling Dumont's concept of hier-archical encompassment. Whether double settlements can be called unities in this sense is addressed later. First, we need to review symptoms of encompass-ment in single villages.

In settlements possessing a single *peo*, an identification of the group claim-ing sacrificial precedence with the community as a whole accords with a general recognition of this party as the oldest and as founder of the village.[11] In a specific sense, this party is moreover regarded as the 'owner' (*moi*) of the *peo*; and where a forked sacrificial post is in use, the leader is designated as the rider of the 'trunk' (*pu'u*, also 'origin', 'source'). Indirectly associating the oldest group, and the first to sacrifice, with the village as a whole, is the identity of the instrument with the settlement whose centre and ritual focus it defines. At the same time, all sacrificial instruments embody a duality, identified with the two extremities of a forked *peo*, or otherwise with the inaugural functions of break-ing and excavating the earth. Hence the first group can be seen to subsume the second, the two together representing the entirety of the sacrificial collectivity.

Identification of whole and part is, of course, most palpable where a village bears the same name as a component clan or pair of clans (for example, Kota Pau). Of thirty-four cases, these number sixteen and six respectively. If to these are added the further four villages named identically to a single resident clan, then about 70 per cent of western Keo villages conform to this pattern. What is more, among the minority of villages whose names differ from those of any component clan, a nominal encompassment of junior by senior groups is sometimes suggested in other, less direct ways—as, for example, in the prob-able derivation of the village name Pajo Mala from the name of the clan Pajo Wolo.[12]

Further attesting to encompassment is the usage whereby junior clans, or later arrivals, are in effect named after senior ones. Examples include Bolo

---

[11] As in Dhawe Mére and several other villages described above, even where the part of earth breaker is taken by a Land Mother (usually resident elsewhere), the right to slaughter first at a given sacrificial instrument is still held by the principal owner, the seniormost segment of the Defender clan (I: 2: vi).

[12] Although this is the most common way of naming villages in general, it is noteworthy that all village names which do not coincide with clan names refer to plants or topographical features associated with the site. In most instances, moreover, the site is relatively recently inhabited. It is therefore arguable that in these instances it is specif-ically the site that is designated, and that only with time does the name become further associated with a village, conceived as a residential group and thus as something not entirely distinguished from a clan (see Section 4 below).

Suga, Wagha Yéwe, Pajo Kayo, and Pau Ngodho. Significantly, in every instance the first term denotes not just the senior clan but the entire village, while the second specifies the junior clan as a variety, or special instance, of the first. Thus Bolo Suga, for example, is construable as 'Bolo people who are Suga'.

Where single villages are named identically to a pair of component clans, over half of the compound names (four of seven) designate former double settlements which have since become single settlements (for example, Kota Pau, Pau Leka). The remainder reflect other amalgamations of previously separate local groups whose names are now retained to designate component clans (as in the case of Wulu Wayu). It is important to note, however, that all settlements named in this way actually include more than two named clans, so that here one is actually dealing with a kind of dual synecdoche. Since clans whose names are thus compounded are nearly always the two oldest,[13] this form of village naming further involves a nominal subsumption of junior groups by the seniormost pair. Hence it does not differ significantly from the more common pattern whereby younger clans are incorporated into a village bearing the same name as the single, oldest clan.

Even so, it is perhaps curious that in the majority of compound designations it is the name of the junior clan that appears first. The physical form of the settlements obviously plays no part here, since, as noted, younger groups are not regularly located either landward or seaward of older groups. If the pattern is of any significance, it would appear to be linguistic rather than conceptual or sociological. A key may be found by comparing this usage with names like Wagha Yéwe, denoting a junior segment (Yéwe) of a local whole that is named identically to its senior clan (Wagha). Thus, by placing the name of the junior element first (as in Kota Pau, or Pau Leka) one implicitly identifies a pair, rather than a partial entity, or a subordinate segment of an encompassing whole.

While less evident in regard to double settlements, a tendency to identify a local pairing of this sort with the name of one component village is also evident, for example, in uses of the names Dhawe (Dhawe Mére) and Nua Nage, and to a lesser degree Guyu Wolo, although, as these instances attest, the name employed is not always that of the component which is unequivocally older. We might also recall that, while 'village' is the primary or focal sense of *nua*, Keo sometimes speak of a double settlement as a single *nua*. This practice appears to have been taken a step further in Pajo Mala, where the name of the seaward *nua* (the original Pajo Mala) has come to be applied as well to the landward village (originally, and still alternatively, named Kate Bale), the two then being distinguished only with the modifiers 'Lower' and 'Upper'. The present

---

[13] An apparent exception is Suga Bhoja. This, however, is an alternative name for the village called Koyu Yéwe, after the oldest pair of clans.

tendency to speak of both Pajo Mala and Pau Lundu, another double settlement, as single villages may also owe something to recent historical initiatives, neither quite completed, to merge the components of each in order 'to make a single village' (I: 2: iii). Worth noting as well is the formal identity of names like Pau Lundu—incorporating the individual *nua* names Pau and Lundu—with those of single villages whose names compound those of two component clans. Indeed, a transition from one to the other is observable in cases like Pau Leka, where, following a relatively recent move to a new site, a former double settlement (Pau and Leka) has, indeed, become a single village.

4. Further Thoughts on 'Village' and 'Clan'

Another aspect of Keo social organization affecting part–whole identities within single villages is the variable application of *suku* ('clan'), especially in relation to the co-ordinate category of *nua*. Although generally translatable as 'clan', a variety of ethnographic particulars shows *suku* to be a polysemous term applied to several levels of segmentation—from groups otherwise identified as 'estates' (*ngapi*; see, for example, the two estates of clan Réja), to groups comprised of 'upper' and 'lower' moieties (like both Bolo and Bale), to pairs of distinctly named clans (such as Céla and Bajo, and Wulu and Dhaga). Distinctions among the various forms of local dualism listed at the beginning of this chapter turn largely on contextually variable uses of *suku*. Depending on how the term is applied, one and the same village can thus be represented as comprising two *suku* or one (divided into two estates), four or two, three or two, and so on. In other words, the polysemy of *suku* facilitates the interpretation of various local arrangements alternatively as unities or dualities.[14]

As noted, Keo assert that all clans (*suku*) at one time occupied separate villages (*nua*). Apparently supporting this idea, village populations immediately to the east of the present study area consistently represent themselves as single *suku* divided into segments distinguished with names of ancestors. Within the study area as well, there are contexts in which *suku* is applied to the entire population of a single *nua*, regardless of the particulars of its internal constitution. For example, in matters of marriage and affinity, when village components need not be distinguished in terms of alliance status, then the entire localized group can be represented as a 'clan' (*suku*) as well as a 'village'.[15] In the case of the Wulu (II: 6: ii), there is a more general, or less contextual, tendency to speak of a *nua* as though it were a single, identically

---

[14] One is here reminded of Barnes's reference to the use of *suku* in another eastern Indonesian society, where he remarks that 'the very imprecision of the word may be just the clue that leads to a proper understanding of Kédang institutions' (1980: 82).

[15] As shown, where distinctions of wife-givers and wife-takers are relevant, these are in fact more often articulated with reference to 'houses' than to 'clans'. Also, when recounting genealogies, Keo frequently know the village but not the clan of an affinal group. Consistent with this, it was noted earlier how, in intervillage marriages, all groups within a village can contribute to marriage payments (I: 4: iii).

designated clan, even though the further division of Wulu into named clans is well known. Treating a village as a single clan is perhaps to be expected where outsiders are unfamiliar with the details of its internal divisions. Yet the fact that Keo regularly speak in this way, and moreover do so in spite of the general knowledge that villages typically comprise two or more clans, nevertheless affirms that *suku* and *nua* are not so distinct as might at first appear.

For many purposes it is reasonable, indeed analytically necessary, to distinguish 'village' and 'clan' as terms of a whole–part relation. Yet, at some level, the two appear as aspects of the same social reality. The fact that Keo clans and villages are mostly named in the same ways is obviously pertinent here. Not only are most villages named identically to a component clan or pair of clans but a large majority (at least 80 per cent) of clans now incorporated into distinctly named villages bear the name of a former village or, less often, another geographical place of origin.[16] This, of course, follows from the pervasive representation, copiously illustrated by particular historical narratives, of component clans—or other, larger groupings contextually classified as *suku*— as formerly independent villages. By virtue of this former (and now forfeited) independence, however, naming groups that have subsequently joined others after their settlements of origin is more than a mere synecdoche, linguistic relict, or verbal convenience. Senior groups nominally identified with an entire multi-clan village are deemed 'original' people who have subsumed others whose 'real' (or 'true, authentic', *tenge*) place is elsewhere (I: 3: iii). Indeed, in so far as 'village' and 'clan' are conceptually equated, the latter might even be seen as 'sub-clans' that have obtained rights to land, and sometimes a junior ceremonial position, within the territory of longer established 'clan' members. The formal similarity, if not substantial coincidence, of this part–whole relationship, or encompassment, with that of wife-takers and wife-givers, and Defenders and Land Mothers, should be immediately apparent.

Beyond naming practices and verbal representations, the conceptual unity of 'clan' and 'village' (*nua* and *suku*) is firmly grounded in sacrificial practice. If the minimal sacrificial unity is a clan comprising two estates (*ngapi*) functioning as earth breaker and excavator (or trunk rider and tip rider), then a village incorporating two or more clans, all sharing a single sacrificial instrument (*peo*), is structurally identical to a single clan exclusively occupying a single village. The former operates no differently from the latter; and additional units beyond the minimal two, be they distinctly named clans or component estates of the senior clan, participate in collective sacrificing, proceeding in a single order of precedence, in exactly the same way. Recalling that *ngapi* ('estate') refers primarily to a unit of sacrifice, one might also say that when sacrificing at a single *peo*, all individual sacrificial groups, whether members of

---

[16] Of a sample of 56 names of incorporated clans, just five are definitely not village names. Of these, four are names of ancestors (Meo Wale, Wawo Wale, Béle Jawa, Ebu Pae). In another five cases, the derivation of the name is not known. Subtracting these ten from 56 leaves 46, or over 82 per cent of the sample.

the same or different *suku*, act exactly like the estates of a single clan. It thus becomes clear how senior groups in multi-clan villages may either retain the two paramount sacrificial positions within the clan or assign the junior position to a younger clan. Between these two arrangements, as well, there is no structural difference.

Given the radical connection between *peo* sacrifice and rights to land, the foregoing suggests that *suku*, like *nua*, refers largely to a territorial concept. This does not contradict a conception of a 'clan' as a unity of blood (*ya*). As has been shown, common blood, ultimately derived from a wife-giver considered as a point of origin, is more often conceived as a property of less inclusive groupings called 'houses' (*sa'o*). Nevertheless, just as named *suku* are sometimes spoken of as units of enduring affinal alliances, so an entire clan can be represented as a 'house'. As also demonstrated, the notion of 'house' overlaps considerably with that of 'estate' (*ngapi*), a division defined mostly by territorial and, therefore, sacrificial rights (I: 3: ii). For Keo, then, 'village', 'clan', 'estate', and 'house' refer not so much to progressively exclusive units within a single segmentary order—though contextually they can be conceived in this way—as to different aspects of the same social reality, distinguished with respect to external relations with other groupings of the same sort.

A final observation is apposite at this point. The fact that Keo mostly represent dualistically constituted settlements (both double settlements and single villages) as the outcome of historical processes of combination does not mean that every local population that has fused with, or become incorporated in, another was originally unitary, or was not itself once dualistically composed. If this were so, then dual combination would imply a radical structural change, occurring at a particular point in the evolution of Keo society, rather than an entailment of a continuous diachronic tendency. More likely, in the process of an immigrant population becoming incorporated as part of another settlement, earlier distinctions of clanship are superseded and hence eventually forgotten, the immigrants then becoming designated simply with the name of their former, independent village, which thus becomes their clan (*suku*) name. A transition of this sort was glimpsed, for example, in the histories of Bajo Léwa (II: 1: vii), Kota (II: 3: i), and Réja (II: 5: i), each representing a fusion of two separate groups, but now conceived as single clans in relation to the others with whom they share their present villages. It hardly needs pointing out that unification through fusion is as much characteristic of Keo society as is dualistic combination. Indeed, these are mutual entailments of the same process.

5. *Dualism, Tripartition, and Other Combinations*

It is by now evident how the dualistic order of Keo society facilitates the incorporation of additional groups within established settlements, and the merging of pairs of villages, without altering the fundamental structure of local communities. The same consideration illuminates numerous instances in which a particular dualistic arrangement is alternatively construed as tripartite or multiple. To a quite remarkable degree, settlements described (usually at an earlier stage of investigation) as comprising two named groups were later revealed to contain a third. Yet in all instances, third or further components could be accounted for as units subsumed by one term of a binary pair. Expressed formulaically, the process involves treating x, y, n (where n denotes a third group) as $x + y$ where $y = y + n$. Where four groups are discernible, one can derive $x + y$ from x, y, n1, n2 by way of the equations $x = x + n1$ and $y = y + n2$, and so on.

As noted in the Introduction, the appearance of third groups in arrangements otherwise represented as dualistic recalls Lévi-Strauss's analysis (1956, 1963) of dual organization as an epiphenomenon of tripartite structure. We are now able to see how this approach has limited relevance to Keo. While dualistic unities in this society may often seem compromised by simple enumeration, such unities are definitely not ordered by any underlying triadic structure, nor indeed by any numerical principle other than a dualistic one. Even so, a question remains as to why Keo representations sometimes leave discernible third and higher groups entirely out of account. One solution might be to view dualism as a cognitive model or prototype (Lakoff 1987). Pertinent here is a tendency of purely dualistic images to predominate in more general or abstract accounts, the sort the ethnographer is likely to record first, or ones offered by outsiders resident in neighbouring settlements. Dualistic representation should not, however, be confused with an ideal type to which actual instances only more or less conform. As indicated both by insider accounts and by the discrimination of components in the context of specific practices, settlements that palpably comprise three or more groups are nevertheless construed as dualistically constituted in ways described above.

Keo dualism is thus rather more than a culturally elaborated cognitive device. By the same token, dualism entailing a subsumption of third and fourth groups by more senior groups should not be taken for a simple artefact of a penchant for binary classification—nor, indeed, should unity articulated by the same principle of encompassment. As demonstrated in a variety of instances, groups identified with whole settlements, either nominally or by exercising precedence in collective sacrificing and other *peo* rituals, are socially superior, both politically and in regard to religious standing. Indeed, by virtue of their identification with the whole, and the status this implies as first occupant of a territory, senior groups are in principle able to deny separate rights, or any kind of membership, to co-residents. In this respect, the structural invisibility of the Bélo people in the village of Keo (Keo Bélo, II: 4: ii) may be seen as but an extreme instance of subordination by encompassment also affecting second or additional clans in other villages which do maintain a subordinate territorial and sacrificial presence. The situation of formerly independent clans subsumed as estates (*ngapi*) of other clans would then appear to fall somewhere between these two possibilities.

While relations between groups composing dualistic wholes are typically hierarchical, involving a subsumption of subordinate by superordinate components, as has been shown, particular asymmetries are nevertheless contestable, or at any rate susceptible of varying interpretations. The possibility of contestation does not contradict hierarchy, since competing positions involved in contested instances are articulated by recourse to the same principles of order as are uncontested instances. Alternative determinations of precedence, whether resolved or unresolved at present, sometimes turn on the contrast of first occupation of a particular village site versus occupation of a wider territory (as, for example, in Lower Pau Lundu, with regard to claims made by clan Bo Bana; II: 3: iii). Yet disagreement of this sort does not controvert the value attaching to residential priority; it merely concerns the level at which the value should apply. Even where the terms of a particular hierarchy have become unambiguously inverted (as, again, in Lower Pau Lundu, where clan Pau Padhi Mena has replaced or usurped Ngodho, even to the extent that Pau, the primary name of the first group, has long been applied to the village as a whole), the temporal priority and former social precedence of older groups is still generally remembered by Keo and, to that extent, recognized. At the same time, one may assume that, eventually, recollection of earlier arrangements will disappear altogether, local histories then becoming fully adjusted to accord with new social realities. Perhaps the most telling indication of this process, although by no means the only one, is the waning of Céla, the clan of the seniormost Land Mother, whose very existence is now known only to a minority of western Keo (II: 1). Nevertheless, as various ethnographic particulars suggest, the achievement of greater wealth or worldly power does not lead immediately to the inversion of existing hierarchies. For Keo, therefore, precedence based on temporal priority evidently retains a value quite independent of economic or political fortunes.

6. *Do Dual Settlements Exist?*

It is appropriate to end this study where it began, with double settlements. Being designated with no distinctive term and manifesting no special form of reciprocity or ceremonial unity, double settlements appear as enigmatic phenomena largely definable in negative terms. A review of cases reveals that the local pairings never combine groups recognizing an agnatic connection, neither as agnatic descendants of male Ga'e siblings (Lape, Géra, Gewo, and Lobo) nor more recently separated segments of single clans. As demonstrated in Part 1 (I: 3: iii, see Fig. 3), agnation connects the majority of Keo villages, through their component clans, with one or more other villages. Yet, quite remarkably, no two villages linked in this way compose, or formerly composed, a double settlement. Implying a mutual exclusion between this form of local organization and lineal fission, this finding accords with the attested tendency of groups that separate from the main body of a clan to move relatively far away, instead of founding an independent patrimony in the immediate vicinity of their original residence. Conversely, new clans typically emerge as additional components of existing villages as a result of immigration rather than internal segmentation of existing groups.

Further consistent with their non-agnatic character, double settlements are always constituted by combination, never by division of a pre-existing whole. Accordingly, some instances juxtapose units of the most inclusive level of contrast, conjoining Defenders of different Land Mothers and thus transcending the most general partitions of Keo society. In these instances, double settlements recall dyadic relationships of 'land siblingship'—for example, the one connecting Keo and Wayu. At the same time, they differ from the latter, most notably in the absence of unity based on reciprocal sharing of territory. Although a number of single villages, too, combine groups of diverse origins, unlike double settlements villages are always united around a single *peo* or a pair of (usually adjacent) *peo*. But in spite of their mostly negative appearance, one should not conclude that these settlements possess no unitary aspect, or do not in any sense constitute empirical communities. Whatever the previous relation between the two parts, double settlements typically result from one group inviting another to join it and become its companion, the two then providing mutual assistance and support (though of no particular or distinctive kind). Accepting the arrangement, moreover, the invitee receives a parcel of land from the longer established group—a transaction reminiscent of, but not to be confused with, the territorial connection of Land Mothers and Defenders.

As mentioned earlier, in addition to the regular spatial disposition of their components along the landward–seaward axis, double settlements share another constant feature with other dualistically constituted local groupings. This is the consistent specification of one component village as the older member of the pair. In this regard, as well as by virtue of their being bound by an obligation to provide a diffuse reciprocal support, double settlements can thus be understood as a particular instance of the polysemous category *ka'e ari* ('elder–younger', 'senior–junior'; I: 4: i), though one that evidently excludes agnation, the category's arguable focus. Articulating a basic binary structure of which other dualisms can be viewed as partial realizations, *ka'e ari* indeed appears to inform all instances of Keo local dualism. In this way, it might further be construed as an encompassing dualism to which, following an approach to dual organization advocated by Terence Turner (1984: 337, 364; 1991: 17–18), other, more overt and exclusive dualisms are attributable as specific manifestations, or 'transformations'. Relevant here is Turner's suggestion that with dual organization, hierarchical encompassment pertains not so much to the relationship of the parts of an empirical whole, as to relations between different dualisms.

In this connection we should first recall that *ka'e ari* is at once a unitary and a dual category. Comprising terms referring to the asymmetric contrast of older and younger (or, more specifically, elder and younger sibling), the compound phrase nevertheless applies as well to a variety of relationships that are manifestly symmetrical, where neither of the component parties need be specified as junior or senior—as in the institutions of 'land siblingship', 'house siblingship', and various ritual partnerships. In view of the contractual nature of these latter instances, *ka'e ari* at the same time transcends the contrast of combination and division (especially as this operates within agnatic groups) as analytically distinguishable features of diachronic social process.

Ka'e ari also embraces relationships where encompassment, or identification of one part with the whole, is a salient feature, as well as relationships where encompassment is either not evident or ambiguously attested. As might be expected, encompassment is most evident where *ka'e ari* pertains to an asymmetric relationship (as, for example, that of same-sex siblings) conjoining two parties that are consistently distinguished as 'older' and 'younger'. Accordingly, it is least evident in symmetric instances, where the components are not thus differentiated. Viewed in this light, double settlements again seem enigmatic. On the one hand, component villages are indeed distinguished as older and younger; on the other, being ritually and politically independent and connected in no special way, they appear not to be related by encompassment. As in the purely synchronic approach advocated by Turner, however, what is ignored in this perspective is the diachronic tendency for conjoined villages to merge and become single settlements. In other words, encompassment can yet be discerned in a general process whereby, over time, villages composing double settlements attain a unity nominally and in other ways identified with one component, which, of course, is normally the older of the pair.[17]

Also noteworthy is the way encompassment appears as an entailment of certain symmetrical instances of *ka'e ari*. More particularly, 'land siblingship' and 'house siblingship' suggest forms of mutual encompassment, whereby in any given instantiation members of one of two groups act, or are treated as, a part of the other group (I: 4: i). As shown, land siblings characteristically occupy villages that do not compose double settlements. House siblings may respectively reside in two component parts of such a settlement (as in the case of groups resident in Upper and Lower Pajo Mala; II: 2: i, ii), but this is neither invariable nor required. Together with double settlements, these special forms of 'siblingship' represent distinct, though in some ways similar, instances of the polythetic class of *ka'e ari* relationships. In addition to agnatic

---

[17] A historical alternative is for the two villages to separate, or for one to move away from the other. Yet this seems to have occurred only in the case of Bolo Yoga (II: 1: iii), where the cause was violent conflict.

relations, they further exemplify the quite remarkable variety of ways in which Keo villages are connected through external links involving constituent clans and houses.

As purely morphological dyads composed of preformed elements whose unity consists almost entirely in their potential to amalgamate, double settlements can be described as the most external form of social dualism. In this respect, they are usefully compared with what may be called the most internal form. Providing another instance of *ka'e ari*, and furthermore one in which the two components are asymmetrically distinguished as *ka'e* and *ari*, this comprises the two major statuses, linked with two separate houses or estates, associated with a *peo*. Variously named as earth breaker and excavator (*ta koe* and *ta kabhe*) or trunk and tip rider (*saka pu'u* and *saka lobo*), these as noted figure as the minimal form of dualism required to constitute a village as a territorially and sacrificially independent community. In so far as the pair of statuses provides the necessary and sufficient condition of Keo social unity, it might also be considered the most basic, and in that sense original, of Keo social dyads. Whereas double settlements are always constituted by combination, moreover, the pair can be constituted either by combination or division, that is, assigned either to two separate clans or to agnatically related segments of a single clan.

Although the pair of internal statuses thus contrasts with double settlements in several obvious ways, in other respects the two forms of dualism reveal a significant structural continuity which accords with the regular historical connection between double and single settlements. As shown (I: 2: vi), when actualized in sacrifice and other ritual contexts, the two statuses do not clearly compose a functional whole. Not being distinguished in respect of spiritual and temporal values, nor symbolically contrasted as masculine and feminine, only in a formal sense—that is, by realizing a culturally necessary dyad—can they be called complementary. As the positions of earth breaker and excavator, especially, reveal, the tasks that define the statuses—two stages in digging a hole—are, indeed, barely distinguishable. Instead, their real contrast lies in the temporal order of their performance, a relation of precedence, replicated in a sacrificial sequence, that is formally identical to one of the two constant features defining double settlements.

Owing to the greater differentiation of their definitive ceremonial roles, the last point applies less readily to the dyad of trunk rider and tip rider, the other variety of internal dual leadership (I: 2: vi). At the same time, differences between the two dyads, inextricably linked with different sorts of sacrificial instruments (*peo*), further illuminate the variety of specific relationships subsumable under the rubric of *ka'e ari*. To that extent, these differences may also shed further light on both the structural and diachronic properties of double settlements. As noted, *pu'u* ('trunk', but also 'source, origin'), the term defining the senior member of the alternative status pair, identifies not only the older part of a plant, but also the botanical whole. It thus subsumes the *lobo* ('tip', but also 'derivative'), just as the senior (*ka'e*) half of the ceremonial pairing, associated with the trunk both nominally and by virtue of the ritual act of riding it, encompasses the junior (*ari*). Expressing a palpably asymmetric and at the same time more unitary representation of the dyad constituted by way of an encompassment, the pairing of trunk rider and tip rider thus contrasts with the intrinsically symmetrical duality of *ta koe* and *ta kabhe*. For in itself this latter dualism is not obviously suggestive of encompassment.

As noted earlier, Keo often apply the terms *saka pu'u* and *saka lobo* to the other pair of statuses as well. Conversely, while *koe* and *kabhe* denote the major ritual tasks involved in planting a 'living *peo*', or sacrificial tree, when a 'dead *peo*' (that is, a forked Cassia trunk) is erected, it is usually the trunk and tip riders who serve respectively as earth breaker and excavator. Hence the two status dyads are not so separate as the foregoing analysis might suggest. Nevertheless, it is the duality of *ta koe* and *ta kabhe* in particular—by far the more common form of ceremonial pairing in western Keo—that resonates in the relation of villages composing a double settlement. Worth recalling here is the way the pair can transcend single settlements, as when a Land Mother serves as earth breaker in respect of the *peo* of a Defender. By contrast, the dyad of trunk rider and tip rider is invariably internal to a single village (*nua*), which is to say, a group sharing a single forked *peo* whose principal owner (*moi*) is always the trunk rider (*saka pu'u*). Significantly, this transcendence of *ta koe* and *ta kabhe* is attested even in respect of one forked sacrificial post, that of clan Néso in Eko Nila (II: 6: ii; see also II: 3: iii).[18]

Consistent with the lack of substantial complementarity between their component positions, the internal village pairings of earth breaker and excavator and trunk rider and tip rider equally suggest a kind of dual metonymy. Not only do the pairs stand for a unity, a single sacrificial order of precedence that can in fact comprise any number of units; they further epitomize any sort of dual combination where binary form is underdetermined by, and so transcends, functional values and complementary opposition. In a reduced form, double settlements can be construed in much the same way, that is, as a particularly visible instance of local dualism which expresses the dualism characteristic and constitutive of the larger social whole and which, like any metaphor or symbol, highlights one or more features of a part–whole relation while disregarding others.

As should by now be apparent, the notion of a 'whole society' among Keo is not to be confused with empirical wholes such as single villages or double

---

[18] Here, it may be recalled, a man of Tongo, the Land Mother resident in the older village of Wulu (Déna), acts as earth breaker when a new post is erected, while Néso serves as excavator. Similarly, clan Ngodho in Lower Pau Lundu (II: 3: iii) appears as excavator when planting the *peo* of Dhoki Paya in the adjacent village of Lundu (Upper Pau Lundu). In both instances, the positions of trunk rider and tip rider are then filled by groups internal to the single village in question.

settlements. There is, of course, no dual division exactly replicated in all western Keo settlements. Keo dual organization thus differs, for example, from
moiety systems in which an entire cultural community, or 'tribe', is exhaus-
tively comprised of just two parts. As is equally obvious, Keo villages are not
completely independent unities, since numerous ties of kinship and affinity
typically connect villagers with other villages. Especially noteworthy is the
degree to which clans recognize agnatic links with groups, bearing the same or
different clan names, in other villages. In addition, as demonstrated in several
instances (II: 1: ii, v, II: 2: ii), even a group possessing a *peo* of its own may
remain ritually dependent on another group established in another village.

On the other hand, something approaching a dually constituted 'whole society' may be discerned at a more inclusive territorial level. The region I have
delimited as western Keo comprises ancestral domains severally associated
with full male siblings surnamed 'Ga'e', as well as other ancestral figures. In
addition, while each domain is specifically identified with a particular ancestor
(or ancestral couple), the territory as a whole, including even those parts
belonging to the domains of ancestors not clearly connected with the Ga'e
siblings, is nevertheless conceived as the Land of Lape, referring to Lape Ga'e,
the eldest of the sons of Mother Ga'e.[19] Once again, therefore, one encounters
an inclusive entity most closely associated with a senior party (*ka'e*) subsuming
parts identified with a series of juniors (*ari*). The representation further
provides an especially clear illustration of how unity based on encompassment
involves an identity of a part with a pre-existing whole—in this instance, the
initially undivided territorial whole bequeathed by the parents of the Ga'e
ancestors, and particularly by their mother, Ine Ga'e.

To claim that Keo social dualism consists essentially in a binary distinction between groups and territories associated with a senior ancestor and
ones associated with junior ancestors, however, would be at once to say too
little and too much. Wherever one encounters enduring unities in Keo—
whether these operate within individual villages or between the components
of double settlements, or, indeed, extend beyond both—not only are these
unities characteristically dualistic but they are also consistently represented
as instances of *ka'e ari*. If anything, it is this concept, itself construable either
as a unitary or dual category, which, in its variety of applications, constitutes
the whole of Keo society, subsuming all forms of 'kinship' and in fact any
sort of positive social relationship. In this light, double settlements might be
understood as a limiting case of dualism realized in actual social spaces. A
double settlement can thus be seen as a palpable unity of population reflecting the dualistic form of the abstract social whole, and potentially combining
the most inclusive of contrasts, or the most general of divisions, that inform

---

[19] In this connection especially, it would be interesting to know whether a relation between *ga'e* and *ka'e*—apparently a reflex of the Austronesian prototerm for elder brother or sister—could be supported on linguistic grounds.

Keo social thought and action, while depending on none of these nor fulfilling any of their functions.

Having demonstrated the fundamental importance of *ka'e ari*, I conclude on a comparative note. The same relational category pair—even the compound expression itself (see, for example, BI *kakak-adik*)—is extremely widespread in Indonesian and Austronesian-speaking societies (see Fox 1980*c*: 331). Keo society reveals a particular elaboration of the conceptual dyad that, at least as much as any other, permeates the social whole and, to that extent, accounts for its characteristic morphology. In this respect the paired terms suggest a way in which both social and cultural similarities and differences in this part of the world (or 'ethnological field of study', to reinvoke J. P. B. de Josselin de Jong's influential concept) might be analysed and ultimately explained.

APPENDIX 1

Western Keo Kin Terms
(Men's Terms of Reference)[1]

1. *nange*	PPPPP, CCCCC
2. *nusi*	PPPP, CCCC
3. *kajo*	PPP, CCC
4. *ebu*	PP, CC
5. *ema*	F, FB (FZH)[2]
ema ta ka'e	FeB
ema ta ari	FyB
ema polu	FB, FZH, MZH, ZHF
6. *bapa*	FZH, MZH[3]
7. *moi* (or *ame moi*)	MB, MBWB, WMB
8. *ine*	M, MZ, FBW
ine polu	MZ, FBW
9. *mame* (or *ine mame*)	FZ, FZHZ, MZ, MBW, MBWBW, ZHM, WMBW (FBW)
10. *tu'a*	WF, WM, WFB (WMB, WMBW), SW, DH[4]
11. *ka'e ari*	B, FBS, FZS, MZS (MBS, MBDH)
ka'e	eB (and other older relatives, both male and female, in ego's level)
ari	yB (and other younger relatives, both male and female, in ego's level)
12. *li ana*	MBS, MBD
13. *éja*	WB, ZH, ZHB, BWB, SWF, DHF[5]
14. *coghe* (or *soghe*)	WZH
15. *weta*	Z, FBD, FZD, MZD (ZHZ)
16. *fai*	W
17. *yaki* (or *'aki*)	H
18. *ipa*	WZ, WBW, BW, MBSW, ZHZ, SWM, DHM
19. *lime* (or *ipa lime*)	WBW
20. *ana*	C, BC, MBSC, MBDC, WBC (FZSC)
21. *ane*	ZC (FZDC)[6]

---

[1] Specifications in brackets are ones that appear uncommon or atypical but were reported in more than one village and so are neither clearly idiolectical nor erroneous.

[2] These specifications are sometimes given as *ame*, a variant of *ema* more common in parts of Nage.

[3] Both are occasionally designated as *bapa polu* (compare *ema polu*).

[4] SW and DH can be specified as *ana tu'a* (*ana*, 'child').

[5] SWF and DHF can be distinguished as *tua éja*, a juxtaposition of *tu'a* (term 10) and *éja*.

[6] These specifications are alternatively labelled as *ane ana* or *ana ane*.

APPENDIX 2

Formal ('head–tail') Names of Villages

Although the form of the phrases does not permit ready translation, 'Ulu X, Eko Y' might be glossed as 'Head that is X, Tail that is Y'. To avoid repetition, the following designations are simply translated in the form 'Head:X, Tail:Y'. The name given first in brackets is in each case the ordinary name of the village. These are listed in the order in which the villages are described in Part II (Chs. 1–6).

(Nua Nage)

    Ulu Céla, Eko Bolo   //   Head: Clan Céla, Tail: Clan Bolo

(Keo Ondo)

    Ulu Feo Bhaya, Eko Nunu Kono   //   Head: White Candlenut Tree, Tail: Enclosing Banyan Tree[1]

(Yoga, Kuyu Wulu)

    Ulu Piga Sina, Eko Nunu Toli   //   Head: Chinese Plate, Tail: Rebounding Banyan Tree

(Bolo, Muka)

    Ulu Bolo Wawo, Eko Watu Wada   //   Head: Clan Upper Bolo, Tail: Stone of Wada[2]

(Suga Bhoja, Koyu Yéwe)

    Ulu Bhoja, Eko Suga   //   Head: Clan Bhoja, Tail: Clan Suga

(Paga)

    Ulu Nunu Gase, Eko Pu'u Nage   //   Head: Planted Banyan Tree, Tail: Tamarind Trunk

(Lundu, Upper Pau Lundu)

    Ulu Nunu Léwa (or Yato), Eko Kota Papa   //   Head: Tall (or Benign) Banyan Tree, Tail: Dividing Stone Wall

(Lower Pajo Mala)

    Ulu Kota Papa, Eko Rita Léwa   //   Head: Dividing Stone Wall, Tail: Tall Alstonia Tree

(Upper Pajo Mala)

    Ulu Rala Oto, Eko Kota Papa   //   Head: Motor Road, Tail: Dividing Stone Wall

---

[1] *Kono*, 'to enter', refers to the place being enclosed by the aerial roots, or secondary trunks, of a huge banyan that once stood at the spot, so that one had to enter an enclosed space in order to approach the tree closely.

[2] Wada, a personal name, is explained as that of an enemy killed when trying to invade Bolo village from the seaward direction.

(Kate Bale, former double settlement)
    Ulu Kota, Eko Nunu Kawi   //   Head: Stone Wall,
                                            Tail: Banyan Tree of Kawi[3]

(Pajo Wolo, former village; possibly applicable also to the present Lower Pajo Mala)
    Ulu Kéli Belu, Eko Taya Mai   //   Head: Mount Belu,
                                            Tail: Mai Tree Branch[4]

(Bale Wolo)
    Ulu Nunu, Eko Rita   //   Head: Banyan Tree,
                                            Tail: Alstonia Tree

(Kota Pau)
    Ulu Nunu Wuwu, Eko Lina Olo   //   Head: Banyan Tree of Wuwu,
    (or simply: Ulu Nunu, Eko Lina)   Tail: Old Lina

(Guyu Wolo)
    Ulu Nunu Bera, Eko Loka Ra'u   //   Head: Itching Banyan Tree
                                              (overgrown with irritating plants),
                                            Tail: Place of the Ra'u Tree
                                            (unidentified)[5]

(Kota Pau and Guyu Wolo together)
    Ulu Guyu, Eko Lina   //   Head: Guyu (=Guyu Wolo),
                                            Tail: Lina (=Lina Olo)[6]

(Pau, Lower Pau Lundu)
    Ulu Kota Papa, Eko Watu Mutu   //   Head: Dividing Stone Wall,
                                            Tail: Cluster of Stones

(Pau and Lundu, or Upper and Lower Pau Lundu together)
    Ulu Nuna Léwa, Eko Watu Mutu   //   Head: Tall Banyan Tree,
                                            Tail: Cluster of Stones

(Former village of Bo Bana)
    Ulu Nio Ba'a, Eko Watu Mutu   //   Head: Inclining Coconut Tree,
                                            Tail: Cluster of Stones

(Former village of Loka Nunu)
    Ulu Watu Mutu, Eko Kota Papa   //   Head: Cluster of Stones,
                                            Tail: Dividing Stone Wall

(Pau Leka)
    Ulu Réta Leka, Eko Bindi Loga   //   Head: Clan Leka Landward,
                                            Tail: Clan Bindi Loga

---

[3] Kawi refers to the Kate ancestor, Kawi Léwa. Hence the designation may refer specifically to the old village of Kate.

[4] *Mai* may refer to a species of *Alstonia*.

[5] Alternative forms of the name are Ulu Nunu Bera, Eko Nunu Wuwu and Ulu Guyu, Eko Loka Ra'u. Nunu Wuwu is 'Banyan Tree of Wuwu'. Guyu refers to the leading clan, also named Guyu Wolo.

[6] Another version is Ulu Wolo Sabi, Eko Lau Lina, 'Head: Wolo Sabi Village, Tail: Lina Seaward'.

(Old village of Béngi)
    Ulu Kuku Gini, Eko Ebu Toyo   //   Head: Kuku Gini, Tail: Ebu Toyo.
    (The two proper names are those of
    Béngi ancestors.)

(Lui)
    Ulu Lui, Eko Nua Muri   //   Head: Clan Lui,
    Tail: Clan Nua Muri

(Keo Bélo)
    Ulu Bélo, Eko Tola   //   Head: Bélo Village,
    Tail: Tola Village

(Munde)
    Ulu Pau Bhaya, Eko Bélo   //   Head: Pale Mango (Hill),
    Tail: Bélo Village

(Wulu Wayu, Bo'a Ora)
    Ulu Wulu, Eko Wayu   //   Head: Clan Wulu,
    Tail: Clan Wayu

(Pajo Réja)
    Ulu Pajo, Eko Réja   //   Head: Clan Pajo, Tail: Clan Réja[7]

(Old Village of Réja)
    Ulu Ko'u, Eko Réja   //   Head: Ko'u, Tail: Réja[8]

(Nua Muri)
    Ulu Se, Eko Late   //   Head: Clan Se, Tail: Clan Late

(Sawu, Sawu Obo)
    Ulu Obo, Eko Sawu   //   Head: Clan Obo, Tail: Clan Sawu[9]

(Dhawe Mére)
    Ulu Sua Sina, Eko Watu Mite   //   Head: Chinese Iron (site name),
    Tail: Black Stone

(Dhawe Yoja)
    Ulu Ndegho, Eko Tuka Gala   //   Head: Dip in the Ground,
    Tail: Gala Snake's Belly[10]

(Oja)
    Ulu Oja Nunu, Eko Kesi Nengi   //   Head: Oja (and) Banyan Tree,
    Tail: Kesi (and) Nengi Tree[11]

---

[7] According to Pajo people, this name was formerly applied to the separate village of Pajo. In that context, Eko Réja referred to the fact that Réja's former village was located seaward of Pajo's.

[8] Ko'u is part of the name of the ancestor of one division of the Réja people, and also his village of derivation.

[9] An alternative name, Ulu Bélo, Eko Sawu, is discussed in the text (II: 5: iii).

[10] *Ndegho* means 'depression (in the ground)'. 'Gala Snake's Belly' (*gala* is *Dendrelaphis pictus*) denotes a kind of thick stone rampart or barricade, in this case built at the seaward end of the village.

[11] Oja may refer to a particular tree of the species *Toona sureni*, or simply replicate the entire village name. *Kesi* is possibly *Lannea* sp.; *nengi* denotes an unidentified tree.

(Wajo)

    Ulu Loka Nunu, Eko Watu Raba   //   Head: Site of the Banyan Tree,
                                              Eko: Calcereous Stone

(Liwo)

        Ulu Nunu, Eko Nage   //   Head: Banyan Tree,
                                            Tail: Tamarind Tree

(Wulu)

        Ulu Dulu, Eko Lika   //   Head: Dulu, Tail: Hearthstones[12]

(Wagha)

        Ulu Nunu, Eko Jélo   //   Head: Banyan Tree, Tail: Clan Jélo

(Béna)

    Ulu Siu Toyo, Eko Nage Rona   //   Head: Siu Toyo,
                                            Tail: Rona Banyan Tree[13]

(Ki)   Ulu Ki, Eko Béna   //   Head: Ki, Tail: Béna[14]

---

[12] *Dulu*, which more specifically names a rocky area beyond the 'head' of the village, is unanalysable. *Lika*, 'hearthstones', refers to three boulders, resembling hearthstones in their triangular disposition, located some distance below the 'tail' of the village. Another expression of this form, Ulu Watu Leke, Eko Watu Ti'i, specifies the part of Wulu territory owned by clan Pata.

[13] *Toyo* is 'red' but could also be a personal name; Siu is either a site or personal name. The meaning of *Rona* in this context is not known. In his Ngadha dictionary, Arndt (1961: 473) lists the word as 'to make, create' and 'to cause, bring about, induce'. Ulu Siu Toyo, Eko Nage Rona also denotes the territories of Wagha, Béna, and Ma'u Béna considered as a unity.

[14] Eko Béna refers to the location of Béna village just seaward of Ki. It is not certain whether the phrases ever applied to the entire double settlement of Ki Béna, as their form might suggest.

APPENDIX 3

Names of Clans and Villages

Under (1), '*Clan names*', I list names that are applied to extant clans (using this term in the broadest possible sense), and in many cases to villages. The majority of Keo clan names are, or once were, also village names. Under (2), '*Village names*', I list the names of villages which do not simultaneously designate clans. Provisional plant identifications rely largely on Verheijen (1984, 1990). 'N' indicates that a clan or village name is also used in western Keo as a personal name; 'm' and 'f' specify the gender of the name.

(1) *Clan names*

Bajo: An overseas place-name; also the name of a former village. Possibly related to 'Bajo, Bajau' as the name of Indo–Malaysian sea nomads. (N: f, m)

Bajo Léwa: Two group names conjoined. In this context Bajo (see above) is partly linked with the name of the ancestor, Lage Bajo. Léwa ('long, tall') is the name of a settlement (Léwa Ngera) to the east. (Léwa, N: m)

Bale: The name of two clans distinguished as Bale Yape Wawo and Bale Yape Au (referring to their occupation of upper and lower sections of the same village). *Bale* in this context is locally recognized as meaning 'to transform, change into, become' (II: 2: ii). (N: f)

Bawa: A variant of Mbawa (see Ma'u Mbawa), the place of origin of inhabitants of Dhawe Yoja. (N: f)

Béle Jawa: The name of the clan's first (male) ancestor to arrive in the Keo region.

Bélo: Meaning unknown. (N: m)

Béna: 'Flat, level' (with regard to an area of land; synonymous with *déna, ndéna*). (N: f)

Béngi: According to local speculation, the term may be a variant of *péngi* ('to look downwards'), referring to the elevated location of the clan's former village of the same name.

Bhoja: From the name of the village, Téya Bhoja, in central Keo, from where the group hails. *Bhoja* can otherwise mean 'to curse'. (Arndt, 1961, glosses the word in Ngadha as 'to reduce, lessen, diminish' and 'expend'.) (N: m, f)

Bindi: 'Starfruit', from Pu'u Bindi ('Starfruit tree', *Averrhoa carambola*), the name of the group's former settlement.

Bindi Loga: see Loga, below.

Bindi Wae: see Wae, below.

Bo Bana: 'Hot explosion' or 'explode hot(ly)'. Locally explained as a reference to the clan's reputation as fierce warriors. In this context, *bo bana* is coupled with the phrase *cenga cara*, which refers to striking a flint to produce fire (*cenga*, 'sound of striking metal'; *cara*, 'hot to the touch, for example of a burning coal; red hot').

Boa: (see the group named Boa Tébo; also Boa Bajo or Bo Boa): Kapok tree (*Bombax* sp.). A former village name in the Nage region, from where the group claims to derive. The alternative name for the group, Boa Bajo, appears to associate it with clan Bajo Léwa. The element 'Bo' in Bo Boa is conceivably a contraction of *bo'a*, 'hamlet'. (N: f)

Bolo: The name of two clans, Bolo Wawo and Bolo Au. The name is attributed to Ola Bolo, 'place of Bolo, Bolo village', the clan's place of derivation in eastern Ngadha. (N: f)

Céla (Séla): Meaning unknown. The name of a hill and a settlement where the clan ancestor once resided. (N: f)

Dhaga: The term means 'to hold out the hands (to receive or catch something)'. Significance as a clan name is unclear.

Dhawe: The name of a village in northeastern Nage from where the clan reputedly hails. (N: f)

Dhoki Paya: *Dhoki*, 'corner, nook'; *paya*, 'bare, barren (of an area of land)'. The former name of the clan's old village before it was changed to Lundu (that is, Lundu Olo, or Old Lundu).

Doya (Ndoya): The name of the group's former village. (N: f, m)

Ebu Néso: (see Néso). *Ebu* is 'ancestor, descendant'.

Ebu Pae: The name of an ancestor.

Ebu Pata: Reputedly named after an island called 'Pata' in Riung Bay, from where the ancestor came. (Pata, N: m)

Ebu Poma: Name deriving from the toponym Wolo Poma (*wolo*, 'hill', *poma*, 'pool, wallow' (cf. Loka Poma).

Ebu Tongo: Sometimes construed as a personal (ancestral) name; whether *tongo* has any separate meaning relevant to its use as a clan name is unclear. (N: m)

Guyu Wolo: Named after the clan's ancestral village of Guyu Wula (*guyu*, a kind of giant bamboo, *Gigantochloa* sp.; *wula*, 'moon', specifies a light-coloured variety of *guyu*). The name was changed from Guyu Wula to Guyu Wolo when the group moved to their present village, located atop a hill (*wolo*).

Jadho: Locally glossed as 'high place', apparently in reference to the clan's occupation of the highest part of the village of Liwo.

Je'a: Derivation of the name is unclear, although as a clan name it may be taken from that of a former settlement (adjacent to Guyu Wula; see Guyu Wolo, above). In other dialects the term denotes the tree *Pandanus tectorius*, but in western Keo this is called *re'a*. (N: m)

Jélo: Meaning unknown.

Joka: 'To sit leaning to one side'; also denotes arm rings of brass or copper formerly worn from the wrist to the elbow. An informant speculated that the Joka people, hailing from Ende, may originally have worn or traded in these.

Kate: 'Wild cucumber' (locally glossed as BI *mentimum*, 'cucumber'); possibly *Tetrastigma* sp. or *Cayratia Rourea minor*. The clan is so named after earlier places of residence called Kate, Kate Kela, and Wolo Kate ('Kate Hill'; *kela*, 'kind of giant reed, wild cane').

Kayo: 'Thorn, thorny plant' (general term). The name of a former village, inhabited by a clan originally from Kayo Wawo in eastern Ngadha. The Keo clan Kayo is also known as Pajo Kayo. Loka Kayo, 'place with thorny plants', is the name of another village and clan unaffiliated with clan Kayo/Pajo Kayo. (N: m)

Keo: Sense and derivation as a village and clan name is unclear. 'Clan' Keo (also called clan Géra, after its ancestor) comprises two clans named Meo Wale and Wawo Wale (see below). (N: f, m)

Ki: Sword grass (*Imperata cyclindrica*).

Kota: 'To clear, cut forest' (connected with a former village of this name which had occupied a previously heavily forested site); 'platform of piled up stones; a stone wall or rampart'; a plant, *Canna coccinea*. Also attributed to the personal name of the clan ancestor, Riti Kota. (N: m)

Koyu: 'to peel, strip off (leaves)', but it is unclear whether this sense is related to the proper name. Name of the former village of the group also known as Ana Koyu ('children, descendants, people of Koyu'), and of a male ancestor of this group, Koyu Yengo. (N: m)

Laka: Name of the clan's former village located atop Wolo Laka ('Laka Hill') and of territory ceded to the clan, called Tana Laka. The name possibly derives from *laka* as a reference to a type of brown or yellow (possibly sulphurous) soil.

Late: A kind of tree, possibly the Nettle tree, *Dendrocnide* sp., or *Laportea* sp. The name is that of the clan's village of origin in southwestern Nage. (N: m)

Leka: According to local speculation, the name may derive from Kaju Leka, the residence of a female ancestor of the clan. *Kaju* is 'wood', but what *leka* might mean in this context is unknown. (N: f)

Lina: 'Clear (of water or the sky)', the name of the clan's former village.

Liwo: Meaning unknown (cf. Ngadha *livo*, 'to envelop, wrap up; to bundle up an infant', Arndt 1961).

Loga: 'Free, free flowing, to let flow freely', also 'diarrhoea'. It is unclear whether any of these senses are relevant to the clan name, which appears to have been brought from the group's place of origin in Ngadha. (N: f)

Loka Kayo: (see under Kayo)

Loka Nunu: 'Place of, near a banyan tree (*Ficus* sp.)', describing the site where the group originally resided. (Nunu, N: f)

Loka Poma: 'Place of, near a pond, wallow', or 'place of (people of) Poma', the region to the northwest from where the group reputedly derives (cf. Ebu Poma).

Lui: A tree with peeling bark, *Fraxinus griffithi*; also the name of a skin disease (*Tinea imbricata*, Verheijen, 1984: 76). (N: f)

Meo Wale: The name of the group's male ancestor, the elder brother of Wawo Wale (see below).

Munde: A village name, sometimes applied to clan Béle Jawa (see (2), *Village names*, below).

Ndoi: Meaning unknown. (N: f)

Néso: Meaning unknown. Name of the site first occupied by this group within its present territory. (Equating it with dialectal *néco*, an informant glossed the word as 'to shift position' and suggested that it might refer to people who regularly changed residence.)

Ngodho: 'To reach, arrive at (a relatively high place)', and in this context perhaps 'point of arrival'. The name of the group's earlier settlement, where their ancestor 'arrived' after leaving his village of origin.

Nila: A kind of tree (*Grewia* sp.) which yields good fibre. (The group derives from the village of Bawa Nila, in the region of Ma'u Mbawa. Nila is also a clan and village name in the Nage region.) (N: f)

Nua Muri: 'New village', referring to the group's earlier, independent settlement (not to be confused with the village of Nua Muri above Pajo Réja).

Obo: No known local meaning, other than as a personal name, though informants suggested the word might be related to *yobo*, 'valley, dale' (see also Nage *obo*, 'a cluster of trees or shrubs, patch of scrub'; Ngadha *cobo*, 'tree-top', Arndt 1961). (N: f)

Oja: A kind of tree (*Toona sureni*); also the name of the village occupied by this group.

Pajo: 'Forked piece of wood suspended in the centre of a house, from which vessels, containers, and the like are hung for safekeeping.' Also a village name, in which context the term seems to refer to a site spatially or conceptually central in relation to other locations or prominent landscape features. The old village of Pajo (Pajo Olo), inhabited by the clan Pajo, is thus described as having been bounded by two streams, the Lowo (River) Sopi and Lowo Bela. (N: f)

Pajo Wolo (see Pajo above): *Wolo* is 'hill'. The name is that of the clan's original village.

Pau: 'Mango tree' (*Mangifera indica*). The name of several settlements associated with clans so named, including Pau (Pau Lundu Nua Au), Pau Leka, and Kota Pau. (N: f)

Réja: Locally analysed as a combination of *re* and *ja*, referring to two sorts of ocean waves (see II: 5: i). The name of the group's original village, located near the sea; also locally linked with the ancestors' arrival by sea. (N: m)

Sawu: The island of Savu, from where the clan ancestor came. (N: m)

Se: A kind of large tree (unidentified). (N: f)

Sina (see clans Sina, Sina Wolo) 'China, Chinese', also 'immigrant, newcomer, foreign' and (as applied to manufactured objects) 'of the highest quality'. The name probably comes from Piga Sina ('Chinese plate'), the clan's place of derivation. (N: m)

Sopi Sabe: A compound of parts of the names of two male ancestors, formerly associated with two separate clans and villages.

Suga: No recognized meaning other than as a clan name, but possibly connected with *suga*, 'to appear, emerge (from the ground)'.

Tola: An alternative name for clan Béle Jawa. Meaning unknown. (Verheijen, 1990, gives *tola* as the Lionese name for the plant *Luffa aegyptiaca*).

Tunga: The clan's place of origin in eastern Ngadha (Taka Tunga). (N: f)

Wae (see Bindi Wae, Watu Wae): A kind of tree, possibly *Pterospermum diversifolium*; the name of the group's village of derivation. (N: f)

Wagha: Meaning unknown (N: f).

Wajo: A kind of large tree with edible leaves (unidentified). Also the name of the village in which the group resides. (N: m)

Wani Wona: *Wona* is the Mustard tree (*Moringa pterygosperma*). The name is evidently related to former places of residence called Au Wani and Guyu Wani. (N (Wani): m, f; (Wona): m)

Watu Wae (see Wae): *Watu* is 'stone', but the original name is said to have been Katu (*katu*, a tree, *Albizia procera*), the name of a clan in Wae, the group's village of origin.

Wawo Wale: The name of the group's male ancestor, the younger brother of Meo Wale (see above).

Wayu: A kind of tree (dialectal *waru*, *Hibiscus tiliaceus*), originally a village name.

Welu: 'To release, discard'. Named after the clan's place of origin, to the east. (N: f)

Wio: Local name for the island of Sumba. (N: m)

Wolo Sabi: 'Ironwood hill' (*sabi*, Ironwood tree, *Schleichera oleosa*); name of the group's former village. (Sabi, N: f)

Wulu (see clans Wulu, Wulu Wogo): A kind of bamboo with long internodes, *Schizostachyum blumii*, used to manufacture blowpipes and flutes. First applied to the village from which clans named Wulu and Wulu Wogo derive. The name is, however, also described as that of an ancestress of the Wulu clan Tongo. (N: f)

Wulu Wogo (see Wulu): Wogo is the name of the clan's ancestor, who initially resided in the village of Wulu.

Wuwu: 'Hole, vent'. Said to refer to the clan's former settlement near to a vent which once led to the sea. Also a large tree, *Sterculia foetida*.

Yéwe (also, Ewe): Meaning unknown.

Yoga: 'Rocky ground, area', 'to shear (head hair)', 'person'.(N: f)

(2) *Village names* (i.e. names that designate only villages, not clans)

Bale Wolo: Locally glossed as 'becoming a hill' (see Bale above, to which this village name is unrelated). (Bale, N: f)

Bo'a Ora: 'Hamlet in the middle'. The site presently occupied by the village also known by its older name of Wulu Wayu (see Wayu, Wulu, above).

Déna (Ndéna): 'Flat, level' (of land). Name of the present (temporary) site of the village of Wulu.

Dhawe Yoja: A compound formed of the clan/village names Dhawe and Oja (=Yoja; see above), groups related affinally to the Dhawe Yoja people (also known as clan Bawa). (Yoja N: f)

Eko Nila (see Nila, above): *Eko* is 'tail, seaward extremity'.

Keo Bélo: Name employed to specify the village otherwise simply called 'Keo' (see Bélo, Keo, above).

Keo Ondo (see Keo, above): *Ondo* is a kind of wild edible tuber, *Dioscorea hispida*, eaten in times of food shortage; also the name of a kind of tree.

Kuyu Wulu: 'Pasture land of Wulu (a female ancestor married into clan Yoga)'. The village is also called Yoga and Bolo Yoga.

Lundu (Ludu): 'Place enclosed with foliage' (cf. Ngadha *ludu*, 'to bar, barricade, block up; shut up, out; to shut or lock out with tree branches and similar materials', 'to cover, wrap up, veil', Arndt 1961). (N: f)

Munde: 'Citrus tree'. More specifically named after the many *munde uta* (*Citrus* sp.), a small, especially thorny variety of citrus used in making a condiment, which formerly grew near the site. (N: f)

Muka: 'To begin, renew, make new'. Name of the village also called Bolo.

Nua Muri: 'New village'. Named independently of the clan of the same name resident in the village of Lui.

Nua Nage: 'Tamarind village' (*nage, Tamarindus indica*). (N: f; occasionally m)

Paga: A kind of wild plant (BI *peria*), the balsam pear (*Momordica charantia*). So named after the many plants of this sort that once grew at the site.

Pajo Mala: Probably named after Pajo Wolo (see above). *Mala* is 'plain; flat, relatively low-lying area' (the opposite of *wolo*, 'hill, highland').

APPENDIX 4

Examples of Sacrificial Orations
(*bhea, bhea sa, sa bhea*)[1]

I. Sacrificial Oration of G. Sawi, a man of clan Yoga in the village of Keo Ondo.

1. *Nga'o poro pu'u Guyu Wolo mena sa'o ko'o B.B. ne'e T.M.*
   I descend from the village of Guyu Wolo, from the house of B.B. and T.M.[2]

2. *Tu tonga pégo réle Bo Boa réle sa'o ko'o ema E.R.*
   Escorted and proceeding up to Bo Boa, to the house of E.R.[3]

3. *Tu dhu pégo réle Lundu réle sa'o ko'o ema M.T.*
   Taken as far up as the village of Lundu and the house of M.T.

4. *Dhudha wa'a réle Suga réle sa'o ko'o ema U.*
   Going on as far as clan Suga (in the village of Suga Bhoja) and up to the house of U.

5. *Tonga pégo réle Bhoja réle sa'o ko'o K.M.*
   Looking out and proceeding upwards to clan Bhoja (in the village of Suga Bhoja), to the house of K.M.

6. *Badha wa'a lau Dhaga lau sa'o ko'o meka P.*
   Reaching as far seaward as clan Dhaga (in the village of Nua Nage) and the house of P.

7. *Tu dhu nuka lau Wulu lau sa'o ko'o meka T. ndi'i la'e ko'o M.K.*
   Taken seaward to clan Wulu (in the village of Wulu Wayu), to the house of T., who occupies the place of M.K.

8. *Tu tuli nuka mena Lui mena sa'o ko'o U.T., ngai bhila fua nuka.*
   Stopping by in the village of Lui in the house of U.T., a spirit like a rising wasp.

---

[1] English translations are provisional and are intended only to convey the represenation of movement of female ancestors from one group to another in marriage. Since the direction terms *mena* and *rale* (I: 1: i) have no ready equivalents in English, I have left them untranslated, except in one place where *rale* refers to the 'lefthand' side of a village. The terms *réta* and *lau*, by contrast, are glossed, usually as 'landward' and 'seaward'. All these terms, as well as *réle* ('up, upwards'), refer to the direction of a location reckoned from the place previously mentioned—except in the first line of the first oration, where *mena* describes the direction of a house in Guyu Wolo relative to the speaker's (or ego's) present place of residence.

[2] Initials denote male individuals, either ancestors or present members of houses from which women have been derived in the speaker's maternal line of origin.

[3] 'Bo Boa' is an alternative name for the group otherwise known as Boa Tébo or Boa Bajo, in the village of Lundu (II: 1: vii).

9. *Tu walo pégo rale Bajo rale sa'o ko'o K.K., roga ta petu kegu pu'u pi ame jeka pebe ebu.*
    Proceeding again to Bajo (clan Bajo Léwa in the village of Lundu), to the house of K.K., people who kindle (the fire) and embrace from the time of fathers and the generations of grandfathers (ancestors).

10. *Tu tonda pégo réta Yoga réta sa'o ko'o L.P. ne'e R.B, yoga ta meku malo bhila ko'o kua ta remi rajo.*
    Escorted on horseback landward to Yoga (the speaker's own clan), to the house of L.P. and R.B., men who are flexible but strong like rotan that makes the boat firm.

II. Sacrificial Oration of G. Jago Uko, a man who claims membership of clans Pajo Wolo and Kate, respectively in the villages of Lower and Upper Pajo Mala.

1. *Nga'o poro pu'u Uda Ulu Wolo one loka ko'o ebu Dhuge Boa, latu ta mia lika ne'e ta yangi api bapa P.D.*
    I descend from the village of Uda Ulu Wolo, (from) inside the place of the ancestors of Dhuge Boa, where the hearth is now lit and the fire is fanned by P.D.[4]

2. *Ngodho nuka Bo'a Wolo, Bo'a Wolo pau toto lepa one sa'o ebu Dh. D., ta latu ebu L.L., tau wake ngai ebu F.B., yoga ta bana bholo bani tuga seru, ate rebu ko'o meku.*
    Arrived in the village of Bo'a Wolo, in Bo'a Wolo particularly inside the house of Dh.D., now occupied by L.L., the spirit held high by F.B., men who go boldly and full of voice, with livers entirely benevolent.

3. *Sésu nuka mena Légu one ngapi ebu T.A., latu bapa D.D. tau jaga nua.*
    Went directly to the village of Légu, entering the estate belonging to T.A., where D.D. now guards the village.

4. *Dhanda wali nuka nua Laja, Laja ne'e moi one sa'o ebu S.S., latu ne'e ebu M.U. tau mia lika ne'e ta bana ara.*
    Taken further to the village of Laja, in Laja to the interior of the house of S.S., where the hearth is now lit and the flame kept hot by M.U.

5. *Tu wali Kuyu Wulu one lolo ko'o ebu L.Dh. tau sipo sagho tana Céla Bajo, latu ne'e moi N.R. ta bana pau ara.*
    Escorted once more to the village of Kuyu Wulu, into the place of L.D. who surrounds and protects the land of Céla Bajo, where it is now N.R. who keeps the flame hot.

6. *Pale nuka padhi rale one sa'o ko'o ebu L.T., latu ne'e N.L. tau landu ko'o pu'u kamu.*
    Moved over to the 'lefthand' side (of Kuyu Wulu), into the house of L.T., where at present N.L. holds up the trunk and root.

---

[4] Dhuge Boa refers both to a double settlement and pair of clans established in western Nage. This maternal line of origin generally proceeds from a northerly location southwards, toward the coast, as it were entering Keo territory with the fifth passage.

7. *Tiko bapo wa'a Pajo Kayo one sa'o ténda ebu J.L., latu ne'e bapa D.L. tau nemo pu'u kamu.*

   Headed completely in the direction of clan Pajo Kayo (in the village of Pajo Mala), inside the house of J.L., where D.L. now makes firm the trunk and root.

8. *Dhodho nuka Pajo Wolo one la'e ko'o J.- G.; réta tolo penga bholo, rale tana mona apa, bholo lake jeka réta Kate tau ana ghawe.*

   Descended to clan Pajo Wolo (in the village of Lower Pajo Mala), into the place of J. and G.; inside the house it was simply empty, down on the ground there was nothing, so it was until clan Kate was provided with an adoptee.

REFERENCES

ADELAAR, K. A. (1997). An exploration of directional systems in West Indonesia and Madagascar. In G. Senft (ed.), *Referring to Space*, 53–81.

ALMAGOR, U. (1989*a*). Introduction: Dual Organization Reconsidered. In D. Maybury-Lewis and U. Almagor (eds.), *The Attraction of Opposites*, 19–32.

—— (1989*b*). The Dialectic of Generation Moieties in an East African Society. In D. Maybury-Lewis and U. Almagor (eds.), *The Attraction of Opposites*, 143–69.

ARNDT, P. (1944). Der Kult der Lionesen (Mittel-Flores). *Annali Lateranensi* 8: 155–82.

—— (1954). *Gesellschaftliche Verhältnisse der Ngadha*. Studia Instituti Anthropos 8. Wien–Mödling: Missionsdruckerei St. Gabriel.

—— (1961), *Wörterbuch der Ngadhasprache*. Studia Instituti Anthropos 15. Posieux, Fribourg, Suisse: Anthropos-Institut.

—— (1963). Wirtschaftlichen Verhältnisse der Ngadha. *Annali Lateranensi* 27: 13–189.

Atlas van Tropisch Nederland. (1938). Uitgegeven door het Koninklijk Aardrijkskundig-Genootschap in samenwerking met den Topografischen Dienst in Nederlandsch-Indië. 's-Gravenhage: Martinus Nijhoff.

BARNES, R. H. (1974). *Kédang: A Study of the Collective Thought of an Eastern Indonesian People*. Oxford: Clarendon Press.

—— (1980). Concordance, Structure, and Variation: Considerations of Alliance in Kédang. In J. J. Fox (ed.), *The Flow of Life: Essays on Eastern Indonesia*. Cambridge, Mass. and London: Harvard University Press, 68–97.

BARRAUD, C. (1979). *Tanebar-Evav: Une société des maisons tournée vers le large*. Cambridge: Cambridge University Press/Paris: Editions de la Maison des Sciences de l'Homme.

—— (1990). Wife-givers as Ancestors and Ultimate Values in the Kei Islands. *Bijdragen tot de Taal-, Land- en Volkenkunde*, 146(2–3): 193–225.

BEATTY, A. (1992). *Society and Exchange in Nias*. Oxford: Clarendon Press.

BEKER, G. (1913). Het oogst- en offerfeest bij den Nagehstam te Boa Wai (Midden-Flores). *Bijdragen tot de Taal-, Land- en Volkenkunde* 67: 623–7.

BLOCH, M. (1992). *Prey into Hunter: The Politics of Religious Experience*. Cambridge: Cambridge University Press.

BLUST, R. (1979). Proto-Western Malayo-Polynesian Vocatives. *Bijdragen tot de Taal-, Land- en Volkenkunde* 135(2–3): 205–51.

—— (1980). Notes on Proto-Malayo-Polynesian Phratry Dualism. *Bijdragen tot de Taal-, Land- en Volkenkunde* 136(2–3): 215–47.

—— (1981*a*). Linguistic Evidence for some early Austronesian Taboos. *American Anthropologist* 83(2): 285–319.

—— (1981*b*). Dual Division in Oceania: Innovation or Retention? *Oceania* 52: 66–79.

—— (1991). On the Limits of the 'Thunder Complex' in Australasia: A reply to Gregory Forth. *Anthropos* 86: 517–28.

BOSSELAAR, G. A. (1932). Memorie van Overgave van de afdeling Flores. (Unpublished manuscript, Algemeen Rijksarchief, The Hague.)

BOYER, P. (1993). Cognitive Aspects of Religious Symbolism. In P. Boyer (ed.), *Cognitive Aspects of Religious Symbolism*. Cambridge: Cambridge University Press, 4–47.

CARSTEN, J., and S. Hugh-Jones (eds.). (1995). *About the House: Lévi-Strauss and Beyond*. Cambridge: Cambridge University Press.

COVARRUBIAS, M. (1937). *Island of Bali*. New York: Alfred A. Knopf.

DA MATTA, R. (1979). The Apinayé Relationship System: Terminology and Ideology. In D. Maybury-Lewis (ed.), *Dialectical Societies: the Gê and Bororo of Central Brazil*. Cambridge, Mass. and London: Harvard University Press, 83–127.

DIETRICH, S. (1989). *Kolonialismus und Mission auf Flores (ca. 1900–1942)*. Hohenshäftlarn: Klaus Renner Verlag.

DUMONT, L. (1979). The Anthropological Community and Ideology. *Social Science Information* 18(6): 785–817.

—— (1980). *Homo hierarchicus: The Caste System and its Implications*. Rev. edn. Chicago and London: Chicago University Press.

—— (1986). *Essays on Individualism: Modern Ideology in Anthropological Perspective*. Chicago and London: Chicago University Press.

Encyclopaedie van Nederlandsch-Indië. (1917). 2nd edn., (ed.) J. Paulus. 's-Gravenhage: Martinus Nijhoff, Leiden: E. J. Brill.

ERB, M. (1987). When Rocks were Young and Earth was Soft: Ritual and Mythology in Northeastern Manggarai. Ph.D. dissertation, State University of New York at Stony Brook.

FONTIJNE, L. (1940). Grondvoogden in Kelimado (Ambtelijke nota van den Controleur ter Beschikking van den Resident van Timor en Onderhoorigheden. Unpublished typescript, Koninklijk Instituut voor Taal-, Land- en Volkenkunde, Leiden.

FORTES, M. (1949). *The Web of Kinship among the Tallensi*. London: Oxford University Press.

FORTH, G. (1981). *Rindi: An Ethnographic Study of a Traditional Domain in Eastern Sumba*. Koninklijk Instituut voor Taal-, Land- en Volkenkunde, Verhandelingen 93. The Hague: Martinus Nijhoff.

—— (1989a). The *Pa Sése* Festival of the Nage of Bo'a Wae (Central Flores). In C. Barraud and J. Platenkamp (eds.), *Ritual and Socio-cosmic Order in Eastern Indonesian Societies*. Bijdragen tot de Taal-, Land- en Volkenkunde (special issue) 145(4): 502–19.

—— (1989b). Animals, Witches and Wind: Eastern Indonesian Variations on the 'thunder complex'. *Anthropos* 84: 89–106.

—— (1991a). Nage Directions: An Eastern Indonesian System of Spatial Orientation. In O. Grøn, E. Engelstad, and I. Lindblom (eds.), *Social Space: Human Spatial Behaviour in Dwellings and Settlements*. Odense: Odense University Press, 138–48.

—— (1991b). *Space and Place in Eastern Indonesia*. Occasional Paper 16. Canterbury: Centre of South-East Asian Studies, University of Kent.

—— (1993a). Nage Kin Terms: A New Form of Eastern Indonesian Social Classification. *Bijdragen tot de Taal-, Land- en Volkenkunde* 149(1): 94–123.

—— (1993b). Ritual and Ideology in Nage Mortuary Culture. In Tong Chee Kiong and A. Schiller (eds.), *Social Constructions of Death in Southeast Asia. Southeast Asian Journal of Social Science* (special issue) 21(2): 37–61.

—— (1994a). Considerations of Keo as an Ethnographic Category. *Oceania* 64: 302–16.

—— (1994b). Keo Kin Terms. *Anthropos* 89: 95–109.

—— (1994c). Review of S. McKinnon, *From a Shattered Sun*. *American Ethnologist* 21(4): 1006–7.

—— (1995a). Ethnozoological Classification and Classificatory Language among the Nage of Eastern Indonesia. *Journal of Ethnobiology* 15(1): 45–69.

—— (1995b). Two Terminologies from Eastern Keo. *Sociologus* (45(2): 153–68.

—— (1996a). To Chat in Pairs: Lexical Pairing as a Pervasive Feature of Nage Mundane Speech. *Canberra Anthropology* 19(1): 31–51.

—— (1996b). A Comparative Analysis of Nage Kin Terms: Western and Eastern Variations. *Bijdragen tot de Taal-, Land- en Volkenkunde* 152(2): 204–35.

—— (1998). *Beneath the Volcano: Religion, Cosmology and Spirit Classification among the Nage of Eastern Indonesia*. Koninklijk Instituut voor Taal-, Land- en Volkenkunde, Verhandelingen 177. Leiden: KITLV Press.

—— (1999). How a Wooden Horse became a Flying Naga: Recovery or Invention of Tradition among the Nage of Eastern Indonesia. In L. Aragon and S. Russell (eds.), *Structuralism's Transformations: Order and Revision in Indonesian and Malaysian Societies*. Tempe, Arizona: Arizona State University, Program for Southeast Asian Studies, Monograph Series Press, 141–67.

FOX, J. J. (1971). Sister's Child as Plant: Metaphors in an Idiom of Consanguinity. In R. Needham (ed.), *Rethinking Kinship and Marriage*. London: Tavistock Publications, 219–52.

—— (1973). On Bad Death and the Left Hand: A Study of Rotinese Symbolic Inversions. In R. Needham (ed.), *Right and Left: Essays on Dual Symbolic Classification*. Chicago and London: Chicago University Press, 342–68.

—— (1980a). Introduction. In J. J. Fox (ed.), *The Flow of Life: Essays on Eastern Indonesia*. Cambridge, Mass. and London: Harvard University Press, 1–18.

—— (1980b). Obligation and Alliance: State Structure and Moiety Organization in Thie, Roti. In J. J. Fox (ed.), *The Flow of Life: Essays on Eastern Indonesia*. Cambridge, Mass. and London: Harvard University Press, 98–133.

—— (1980c). Models and Metaphors: Comparative Research in Eastern Indonesia. In J. J. Fox (ed.), *The Flow of Life: Essays on Eastern Indonesia*. Cambridge, Mass. and London: Harvard University Press), 327–33.

—— (1987). The House as a Type of Social Organisation on the Island of Roti. In C. Macdonald (ed.), *De la hutte au palais: sociétés 'à maison' en Asie du Sud-Est insulaire*, Paris: Editions du Centre National de la Recherche Scientifique, 171–8.

—— (1988). Origin, Descent and Precedence in the Study of Austronesian Societies. Public lecture in connection with De Wisselleerstoel Indonesische Studien given at the University of Leiden on 17 March 1988.

—— (1989). Category and Complement: Binary Ideologies and the Organization of Dualism in Eastern Indonesia. In D. Maybury-Lewis and U. Almagor (eds.), *The Attraction of Opposites*, 33–56.

—— (1994). Reflections on 'hierarchy' and 'precedence'. In M. Jolly and M.S. Mosko (eds.), *Transformations of Hierarchy: Structure, History and Horizon in the Austronesian World. History and Anthropology*, 7(1–4): 87–108.

—— (1996). Introduction. In J. J. Fox and C. Sather (eds.), *Origins, Ancestry, and*

Alliance: Explorations in Austronesian Ethnography. Canberra: Australian National University, 1–17.

FRAZER, J. G. (1910). *Totemism and Exogamy: A Treatise on certain early forms of Superstition and Society*, 4 vol. London: Macmillan.

FREEMAN, J. D. (1981). *Some Reflections on the Nature of Iban Society.* Occasional Paper, Department of Anthropology, Research School of Pacific Studies. Canberra: Australian National University.

FREIJSS, J. P. (1860). Reizen naar Mangarai en Lombok in 1854–1856. *Tijdschrift voor Indische Taal-, Land- en Volkenkunde* 9: 443–530.

GEIRNAERT-MARTIN, D. C. (1992). *The Woven Land of Laboya: Socio-cosmic Ideas and Values in West Sumba, Eastern Indonesia.* Leiden: Centre of Non-Western Studies.

HALLPIKE, C. R. (1979). *The Foundations of Primitive Thought.* Oxford: Clarendon Press.

HAMILTON, H.A.L. (1918). Inleiding van een verslag over het landschap Keo. (Unpublished manuscript, Algemeen Rijksarchief, The Hague.)

HEURNIUS, J. (1855). Schriftelijck rapport gedaen door den predicant Justus Heurnius, aengaende de gelegentheijt van 't eijlandt Ende, tot het voortplanten van de Christelijke religie, en van wegen de gelegentheijt van Bali 1638. *Bijdragen tot de Taal-, Land- en Volkenkunde* 3: 250–62.

HOCART, A. C. (1970[1936]). *Kings and Councillors: An Essay in the Comparative Anatomy of Human Society.* Chicago and London: University of Chicago Press.

HOLY, L. (1996). *Anthropological Perspectives on Kinship.* London and Chicago: Pluto Press.

HUBERT, H., and M. MAUSS (1964[1898]). *Sacrifice: Its Nature and Function.* Transl. from the French by W.D. Halls. London: Cohen and West.

JENSEN, A. E. (1948). *Die drei Ströme: Züge aus dem geistigen und religiösen Leben der Wemale, einem primitiv-volk in den Molukken.* Leipzig: Otto Harrassowitz).

KANA, N. (1983). *Dunia orang Sawu.* Seri Budi 2. Jakarta: Penerbit Sinar Harapan.

KARTHAUS, P. F. J. (1931). Memorie van Overgave van de residentie Timor. (Unpublished manuscript, Algemeen Rijksarchief, The Hague.)

KOSTER, P. (1938). Memorie van Overgave van den aftredend Controleur van Ngada. Unpublished manuscript, Algemeen Rijksarchief, The Hague..

KRUYT, A. C. (1922). De Soembaneezen. *Bijdragen tot de Taal-, Land- en Volkenkunde* 78: 466–608.

LAKOFF, G. (1987). *Women, Fire and Dangerous Things: What Categories reveal about the Mind.* Chicago and London: University of Chicago Press.

LAME URAN, L. (1987). *Sejarah perkembangan Misi Flores Dioses Agung Ende.* Ende, Flores: Percetakan Arnoldus.

LEACH, E. R. (1962). On Certain Unconsidered Aspects of Double Descent Systems. *Man* 62: 130–4.

LEHMANN, W. (1984). Paroki St. Petrus Martir di Lena akhir abad ke 16. (Unpublished typescript.)

—— (1987). Menjelajah jejak-jejak patar pater Dominikan di bagian selatan gunung Lambo. (Unpublished typescript.)

LÉVI-STRAUSS, C. (1956). Les organisations dualistes existent-elles? *Bijdragen tot de Taal-, Land- en Volkenkunde* 112: 99–128.

—— (1963[1958]). *Structural Anthropology.* Transl. from the French by C. Jacobson and B.G. Schoepf. New York and London: Basic Books.

—— (1969[1949]). *The Elementary Structures of Kinship*. Transl. from the French by J.H.Bell, J.R. von Sturmer, and R. Needham. Boston: Beacon Press.

—— (1982[1979]), *The way of the masks*. Transl. from the French by S. Modelski. Vancouver and Toronto: Douglas & McIntyre Ltd.

LEWIS, E. D. (1988). *People of the Source: The Social and Ceremonial Order of Tana Wai Brama on Flores*. Koninklijk Instituut voor Taal-, Land- en Volkenkunde, Verhandelingen 135. Dordrecht: Foris Publications.

MAYBURY-LEWIS, D. (1989*a*). Introduction: The Quest for Harmony. In D. Maybury-Lewis and U. Almagor (eds.), *The Attraction of Opposites*, 1–17.

—— (1989*b*). Social Theory and Social Practice: Binary Systems in Central Brazil. In D. Maybury-Lewis and U. Almagor (eds.), *The Attraction of Opposites*, 97–116.

MAYBURY-LEWIS, D., and U. ALMAGOR (eds.) (1989). *The Attraction of Opposites: Thought and Society in the Dualistic Mode*. Ann Arbor, Mich.: University of Michigan Press.

MCKINNON, S. (1991). *From a Shattered Sun: Hierarchy, Gender and Alliance in the Tanimbar Islands*. (Madison, Wisc.: University of Wisconsin Press.

MOLNAR, A. K. (forthcoming). *The Grandchildren of the Ga'e Ancestors: The Hoga Sara of Ngada in West Central Flores*. Leiden: KITLV Press.

MOSKO, M. (1985). *Quadripartite Structures: Categories, Relations, and Homologies in Bush Makeo culture*. Cambridge: Cambridge University Press.

—— (1994). Transformations of Dumont: The Hierarchical, the Sacred and the Profane in India and ancient Hawaii. In M. Jolly and M.S. Mosko (eds.), *Transformations of Hierarchy: Structure, History and Horizon in the Austronesian world. History and Anthropology* 7(1–4): 19–86.

NEEDHAM, R. (ed.) (1973). *Right and Left: Essays on Dual Symbolic Classification*. Chicago and London: Chicago University Press.

—— (1987). *Counterpoints*. Berkeley, Los Angeles, and London: University of California Press.

ONVLEE, L. (1973). *Cultuur als antwoord*. Koninklijk Instituut voor Taal-, Land- en Volkenkunde, Verhandelingen 66. 's-Gravenhage: Martinus Nijhoff.

PAUWELS, S. (1994). Sibling Relations and (In)temporality: Towards a Definition of the House (Eastern Indonesia). In L. E. Visser (ed.), *Halmahera and Beyond: Social Science Research in the Moluccas*, Koninklijk Instituut voor Taal-, Land- en Volkenkunde, Proceedings 1. Leiden: KITLV Press.

PETU, P. (Sareng Orin Bao). (1969). *Nusa nipa: nama pribumi nusa Flores*. Ende, Flores: Arnoldus/Nusa Indah.

REUTER, T. (1992). Precedence in Sumatra: An Analysis of the Construction of Status in Affinal Relations and Origin Groups. *Bijdragen tot de Taal-, Land- en Volkenkunde* 148(3–4): 489–520.

RIEDEL, J. G. F. (1886). The Island of Flores or Pulau Bunga: The Tribes between Sika and Mangaroai. *Revue Coloniale Internationale* 2: 66–71.

RIVERS, W. H. R. (1914). *The History of Melanesian Society*. 2 vols. Cambridge: Cambridge University Press.

—— (1924). *Social Organization*. London: Kegan Paul.

RIVIÈRE, P. (1993). The Amerindianization of Kinship. *L'Homme* 126–8, 33(2–4): 507–16.

ROSALDO, R. (1975). Where Precision Lies: The Hill People once lived on a Hill. In R.

Willis (ed.), *The Interpretation of Symbolism*. ASA Studies 3. London: Malaby Press, 1–22.

ROUFFAER, G. P. (1923–4). Naschrift over het oud-Portugeesche fort op Poeloe Ende; en de Dominikaner Solor–Flores-missie, 1561–1638 (second part). *Nederlandsch-Indië Oud en Nieuw* 8: 141–8.

SAHLINS, M. (1981) *Historical Metaphors and Mythical Realities: Structure in the Early History of the Sandwich Islands Kingdom*. Ann Arbor: University of Michigan Press.

SATHER, C. (1996). 'All Threads are White': Iban Egalitarianism Reconsidered. In J.J. Fox and C. Sather (eds.), *Origins, Ancestry and Alliance: Explorations in Austronesian Ethnography*. Canberra: Australian National University, 70–110.

SCHÄRER, H. (1963). *Ngaju Religion: The Conception of God among a South Borneo People*. Transl. from the German by R. Needham. Koninklijk Instituut voor Taal-, Land- en Volkenkunde Translation Series 6. The Hague: Martinus Nijhoff.

SCHEFOLD, R. (1994). Cultural Anthropology, Future Tasks for Bijdragen, and the Indonesian Field of Anthropological Study. *Bijdragen tot de Taal-, Land- en Volkenkunde*, 150(4): 805–25.

Schetskaart van de onderafdeling Ngada (eiland Flores). Schaal 1: 50,000. 1916. Ch. Le Roux, 1e Luitenant belast met het traceren, & Lalamentik, Inl. Verkenner, 3e kl. 1916.

Sejarah Gereja Katolik Indonesia. (1974). 4 vols. Ende, Flores: Percetakan Arnoldus.

SENFT, G. (ed.) (1997). *Referring to Space: Studies in Austronesian and Papuan Languages*. Oxford: Clarendon Press.

SINGARIMBUN, M. (1975). *Kinship, Descent and Alliance among the Karo Batak*. Berkeley, Los Angeles and London: University of California Press.

SPERBER, D. (1975). *Rethinking Symbolism*. Transl. from the French by A. Morton. Cambridge: Cambridge University Press.

SUCHTELEN, B. C. C. M. M. VAN (1921). *Endeh (Flores)*. Mededeelingen van het Bureau voor de Bestuurszaken der Buitengewesten, bewerkt door het Encyclopaedisch Bureau 26. Weltevreden: Papyrus.

SUGISHIMA, T. (1994). Double Descent, Alliance, and Botanical Metaphors among the Lionese of Central Flores. *Bijdragen tot de Taal-, Land- en Volkenkunde*. 150(1): 146–70.

TCHERKÉZOFF, S. (1987[1983]). *Dual Classification Reconsidered: Nyamwezi Sacred Kingship and Other Examples*. Transl. from the French by M. Thom. Paris: Maison des Sciences de l'Homme/Cambridge: Cambridge University Press.

TELJEUR, D. (1990). *The Symbolic System of the Giman of South Halmahera*. Koninklijk Instituut voor Taal-, Land- en Volkenkunde, Verhandelingen 142. Dordrecht: Foris Publications.

TOREN, C. (1990). *Making Sense of Hierarchy: Cognition as Social Process in Fiji*. London School of Economics Monographs on Social Anthropology 61. London and Atlantic Highlands, New Jersey: Athlone Press.

TRAUBE, E. G. (1986). *Cosmology and Social Life: Ritual Exchange among the Mambai of East Timor*. Chicago and London: University of Chicago Press.

—— (1989). Obligations to the Source: Complementarity and Hierarchy in an Eastern Indonesian Society. In D. Maybury-Lewis and U. Almagor (eds.), *The Attraction of Opposites*, 321–44.

TULE, P. [n.d.]. The Muslim minority group in Nusa Tenggara Timur province. (Unpublished typescript lent by the author.)

TURNER, T. (1984). Dual Opposition, Hierarchy and Value: Moiety Structure and Symbolic Polarity in Central Brazil and Elsewhere. In J.-C. Galey (ed.), *Différences, values, hiérarchie: textes offerts à Louis Dumont*. Paris: Editions de l'Ecole des Hautes Etudes en Sciences Sociales.

—— (1991). Review of D. Maybury-Lewis and U. Almagor (eds.), *The Attraction of Opposites*. *American Anthropologist* 93: 216–18.

VALERI, V. (1989). Reciprocal Centers: The Siwa-Lima System in the Central Moluccas. In D. Maybury-Lewis and U. Almagor (eds.), *The Attraction of Opposites*, 117–41.

—— (1994). Buying Women but Not Selling Them: Gift and Commodity Exchange in Huaulu Alliance. *Man* (n.s.) 29(1): 1–26.

VERHEIJEN, J. A. J. (1967). *Kamus Manggarai, I: Manggarai-Indonesia*. Diterbitkan oleh Koninklijk Instituut voor Taal-, Land- en Volkenkunde. 's-Gravenhage: Martinus Nijhoff.

—— (1984). *Plant Names in Austronesian Linguistics*. Linguistic studies of Indonesian and other Languages in Indonesia, Vol. 20. Jakarta: Badan Penyelenggara Seri NUSA, Universitas Katolik Atma Jaya.

—— (1990). *Dictionary of Plant Names in the Lesser Sunda Islands*. Pacific Linguistics Series D, 83. Canberra: Department of Linguistics, Research School of Pacific Studies.

WAGNER, R. (1975). *The Invention of Culture*. Englewood Cliffs, New Jersey: Prentice-Hall.

WATERSON, R. (1990). *The Living House: An Anthropology of Architecture in South-East Asia*. Singapore: Oxford University Press.

WEBER, M. (1890). Ethnographische Notizen über Flores und Celebes. Supplement zu Band III von *Internationales Archiv für Ethnographie*. Leiden: Verlag von P. W. M. Trap.

WILLIS, R. (1990). Introduction. In R. Willis (ed.), *Signifying Animals: Human Meaning in the Natural World*. London: Unwin Hyman, 1–24.

WOUDEN, F. A. E. van (1968[1935]). *Types of Social Structure in Eastern Indonesia*. Transl. from the Dutch by R. Needham. Koninklijk Instituut voor Taal-, Land- en Volkenkunde, Translation Series 11. The Hague: Martinus Nijhoff.

INDEX

Italic numbers denote references to illustrations